# LANDSCAPES OF RESISTANCE

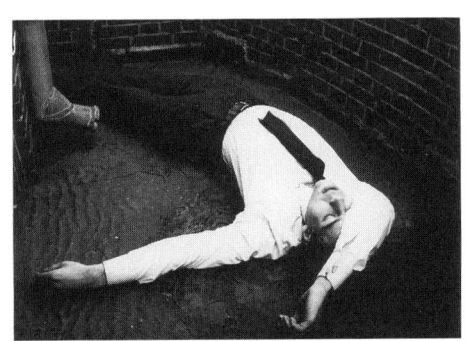

# LANDSCAPES OF RESISTANCE

The German Films of
Danièle Huillet and Jean-Marie Straub

Barton Byg

UNIVERSITY OF CALIFORNIA PRESS
BERKELEY / LOS ANGELES / LONDON

University of California Press
Berkeley and Los Angeles, California

University of California Press
London, England

Copyright © 1995 by The Regents of
the University of California

Library of Congress Cataloging-in-Publication Data

Byg, Barton, 1953–
    Landscapes of resistance : the German films of
Danièle Huillet and Jean-Marie Straub / Barton Byg.
       p.  cm.
    Includes bibliographical references and index.
    Filmography:
      ISBN 0-520-08908-1 (acid-free paper). —
    ISBN 0-520-08910-3 (pbk. : acid-free paper)
      1. Straub, Jean-Marie—Criticism and interpretation.
    2. Huillet, Danièle—Criticism and interpretation.
    3. Motion pictures—Germany.  I. Title.
    PN1998.3.S77B94   1995
    791.43′0233′092243—dc20                   95-7214

Printed in the United States of America

1  2  3  4  5  6  7  8  9

The paper used in this publication meets the minimum requirements of American National Standard for Information Sciences—Permanence of Paper for Printed Library Materials, ANSI Z39.48-1984 ∞

*In memory of Sigrid Maria Brauner*
*1950–1992*

"Look at this mountain, once it was fire."
Jean-Marie Straub/Danièle Huillet,
quoting Cézanne

# Contents

*Preface and Acknowledgments*   xi
*Introduction*   1

1  Straub/Huillet and the Cinema: Tradition and Avant-garde   7

2  Straub/Huillet, the New Left, and Germany   29

3  Traces of a Life: *Chronicle of Anna Magdalena Bach*   51

4  Formal and Political Radicalism in the Short Films of the 1960s   71

5  Time and Memory in Postwar Germany: *Not Reconciled*   95

6  *History Lessons* and Brecht's *The Business Affairs of Mr. Julius Caesar*   117

7  Musical Modernism and the Schoenberg Films   139

8  The Power to Narrate: *Class Relations* and Kafka's *Amerika*   164

9  Language in Exile: Hölderlin's *The Death of Empedocles*   178

10  Film as "Translation"   199

11 *Antigone*   215

12 Real History and the Nonexistent Spectator: Brecht, Adorno, and Straub/Huillet   233

*Notes*   249
*Selected Bibliography*   285
*Filmography*   293
*Index*   301

# Preface and Acknowledgments

*Not Reconciled* was the first Straub/Huillet film I ever saw, and I remember the shock vividly to this day. The breathtaking frustration the film provoked can only compare to my first reaction to Kafka's German: How can anything so simple be so incomprehensible, so threatening? How can anything so short seem so long? And, like Kafka, the film kept drawing me back with its ability to crystallize the burden of the past and the impulse to resist in just a few seconds of film time.

I want to thank Danièle Huillet and Jean-Marie Straub for their generosity and friendship, as well as for their films, which led me to look at the world and read German literature in a different way. I hope the following does a bit of the same, while it reveals their humor and compassion as well. For instance, Jean-Marie Straub noticed there were a lot of churches in St. Louis. They ought to like *Moses and Aaron* here, he said, since it is "a film about the man who invented God." And walking around my typically run-down urban midwestern neighborhood in South St. Louis, Danièle Huillet agreed that it is ugly, "but not only ugly." I realize that in my education and academic career I have partly been searching for some kind of cultural "authenticity," since my starting points were the midwestern assumption of cultural inferiority, especially in regard to Europe, and the intriguing way American mass culture has of affirming European high culture as a model, even while making fun of it. The connection between high culture and the culture industry, which Critical Theory seeks to understand, is also a connection I have to make on a very personal level: I teach German language, literature, and film to U.S. students, for whom European bourgeois culture is also distant and strange, yet its authority and influence remain. Having given up on the search for cultural authenticity, at least in the canon of European culture, I still have a strong wish to understand its power, especially in the context of the power of a united Germany as a state, which I feel more than ever must be distinguished from the values present in "German" culture. In this distinction lies a potential utopian space, for non-Germans looking at Germany and its history and art but even more crucially perhaps for the Germans themselves. Straub/Huillet films raise fascinating questions about "What is German" and what is not and about the artificiality of the divisions between "high" culture and "mass" culture.

Many, many people have helped me in large and small ways in the process of writing this book. Four chapters had their origins in my dissertation at Washington University in St. Louis, and I want to thank my committee for their help and encouragement then and since: Egon Schwarz, William H. Matheson, Thomas Elsaesser, Thomas Rimer, Michel Rybalka, Marcus Bullock, and Patricia Herminghouse. I would not have begun this work at all were it not for George Dolis, who introduced me to Straub/Huillet when he screened *Not Reconciled* for a group of graduate students in Ridgeley Hall at Washington University in the late 1970s on his old Graflex projector, and Richard Abel, who introduced me to the field of film studies at Drake University.

I have received an enormous amount of help in gaining access to Straub/Huillet films and other research materials. I want to thank the Department of Germanic Languages and Literatures at the University of Massachusetts, Amherst; Dean Lee R. Edwards; and former Dean Murray M. Schwartz. Jules Chametsky and the Institute for Advanced Study in the Humanities; Catherine Portuges and the Interdepartmental Program in Film Studies; Margaret Irwin-Brandon and the Arcadia Players; Deborah Linderman, Hans Vaget, and Dave Vikre at Smith College; and Lorna Peterson and the Five College Film Council all helped me bring Straub/Huillet films to the area for screenings and discussions. At the University Library, Edla Holm and the staff of the interlibrary loan division and John Stacey and the staff of the audiovisual division were extremely helpful. New Yorker Films provided access to films and photographs; thanks to Dan Talbot, John Montague, and Harris Due. Thanks also to Roberta Boehm of Photoreporters, Inc., and to Terry Geesken of the Museum of Modern Art Film Stills Archive. Others who generously provided material, information, help, and encouragement include James E. Cathey, Ramona Curry, John E. Davidson, Aris Fioretos, Patricia Galvis-Assmus, Joseph Gaubinger, Gerd Gemünden, Janine Heifner, Jeffrey High, Susan Jahoda, Elizabeth Keitel, Christine Kodis of the Goethe Institut Boston, Dave Korowski, Sara Lennox, David Levin, Mary Maynard, Charles Moran, Stephen Nissenbaum, Marcia Pauly, Andrew Reich, Karen Remmler, Christian Rogowski, Jonathan Rosenbaum, Eric Santner, Harry Seelig, Sunka Simon, Irene Starr, Harlan Sturm, Robert Sullivan, and especially Jan Whitaker, who helped me keep the project on track.

For a travel grant to Berlin, I want to thank Heidrun Suhr and the German Academic Exchange Service (DAAD). In Berlin, the amount of help I received was simply phenomenal, particularly from the staff at the Stiftung Deutsche Kinemathek and at the Deutsche Film- und Fernsehakademie Berlin: Ute Jensky, Peter Latta, Anne-Marie Lorenz-Tröstrum, Marian Martchewski, Christa Schabaz, Rolf Wentz, Renate Wilhelmi, Ria van der Zee, and Rosemarie van der Zee. Also in Berlin I received help from Bernd Koll and Edition Manfred Salzgeber, Frieda Behlen, Thomas Birkner, Michael Esser, Harun Farocki, Salomea Genin, Hans Hurch, Michael Klier, Friedrich Knilli, Stephen Laufer, Peter Nau, Astrid Ofner, Dieter and Silvia Schlenstedt, Ekko von Schwichow, Stephan Settele, and Lynn Whittemore.

Earlier versions of chapters 6 and 8 appeared in, respectively, *Essays on Brecht = Versuche über Brecht*, Brecht Yearbook, vol. 15, ed. Marc Silberman et al. (Madison: International Brecht Society, 1990), and *Gender and German Cinema: Feminist Interventions*, vol. 1 (Oxford: Berg Press, 1993). I am grateful to the editors of those publications, Marc Silberman, Sandy Frieden, Rick McCormick, Vibeke Petersen, and Melissa Vogelsang, for their helpful suggestions and for permission to republish here.

I am especially indebted to those who read and responded in detail to later stages of the manuscript: Thom Andersen, Susan Cocalis, Norman Cowie, Carol Donelan, John Gianvito, Michael Pauen, Catherine Portuges, Lawrence Ryan, Robert Stern, and Maureen Turim. Special thanks to John Gianvito for the title suggestion as well. Finally, thanks to those who guided the editing and production of this book for the University of California Press: Michelle Bonnice, Stephanie Emerson, and Sheila Berg; and to film editor Edward Dimendberg for his commitment to a book on Straub/Huillet and his kind support of this project.

That the name of my friend and co-worker Sigi Brauner appears in a memorial dedication and not just among these words of thanks is a source of deep sorrow. I hope these pages have at least a reflected spark of Sigi's passion for the beauty of the world and her defiant spirit.

Haydenville, Massachusetts<br>January 1995

# INTRODUCTION

There are more important things to write about than films. This alone is a good reason for writing about films by Jean-Marie Straub and Danièle Huillet. In their art they have taken to heart Kafka's advice: "In the battle between yourself and the world, second the world." In films that are simple in their visual construction, restrained in their camera movement, and precise in their editing, there are always brief points at which the reality of the world outside the film explodes with a violent, utopian force. In *Not Reconciled*, for instance, a tragic love affair is summed up in a single two-second shot of a young woman turning her head as she says, "They're going to kill you." An old woman shoots a Nazi sympathizer at the end of the same film, and another avenging woman shoots a gangster at the end of *The Bridegroom, the Comedienne, and the Pimp*, yet in each case the camera looks away. The "action" is always elsewhere, spilling out of the film. And in most Straub/Huillet films, sound separates itself from the image for the first time at the end of the final reel, impelling us out of the dream of the cinema and into the world again: Bach's organ music, the air horn of an Amtrak train, the thunder of an approaching storm, the Carabinieri's helicopter.

When one begins to think about a Straub/Huillet film, one inevitably confronts subjects outside the film itself—questions of reality and history, of the "look of the world" that has become so vulnerable. Since the political changes in Europe in the 1990s raise issues of the role of Germany as a world power and the future of a leftist cultural critique, the films of Straub/Huillet become all the more pertinent. Although most of their films are "German," Huillet and Straub are not. They moved to Germany from France at the end of the 1950s, then to Rome, where they have lived since 1969. Their vantage point as outsiders has allowed them to engage with German culture with a combination of critical distance and affection inaccessible to most German artists.[1]

This book has two primary goals. The first is to provide an English-language readership with access to the German cultural and literary context in which most of Straub/Huillet's rigorous and original work has been produced. The second is to investigate the relation of their work to both the "classical" cinema and to fundamental issues of film studies since the 1970s, especially feminist film theory, materialist film, and the avant-garde. Finally, the book attempts to reveal a side of Straub/Huillet that has so far been ignored—their strategy of rediscovering the fundamental visual pleasure of cinema through supreme concentration on its constituent elements, light, sound, and motion in the juxtaposition of landscape and poetic text.

One reason for the fact that the films point to worlds outside themselves is that none of them is a self-contained, original piece of fiction. Reminiscent of Walter Benjamin's project of composing a book from quotations alone, all are based on materials from other genres: novels, short stories, plays, poems, essays. They also often present historical documents and film footage. Each film respects the form of the text it presents, drawing it into sharp clarity by treating it not as a transparent technical element, as material for a story, but as a text, a material document. Furthermore, the films record their own confrontations with the text, the challenge made to the text by its setting, for instance, in a contemporary landscape. The films document the interaction between the original form and content of the text and the form of the film in which the text is cited or recited.

The method by which Straub/Huillet have turned works from German culture into the material for their films challenges both the notion of a literary "canon," the conventions of adaptation, and the question of national cinema. From their French and Italian vantage points, they undertake a deterritorialization of German cinema, appropriating German culture from the outside and "redeeming" repressed or marginalized authors, themes, or works of German history. German history and culture have produced both great beauty and great horror, and Straub/Huillet films constantly confront the two. In so doing, with their radical assertion that even the German language can be nomadic,[2] their films propose that German culture belongs to Europe and the world as much as it does to the Germans.

The German films Straub/Huillet have produced will be treated as follows: Chapter 3 explores the difficulties Straub/Huillet encountered in completing their first project (which became their third film): *Chronik der Anna Magdalena Bach* (*Chronicle of Anna Magdalena Bach*), 1967. Chapter 4 discusses the combination of radical politics and radical form in two short films: *Machorka-Muff,* 1962, based on Heinrich Böll's short story "Bonn Diary" ("Hauptstädtisches Journal"), and *Der Bräutigam, die Komödiantin, und der Zuhälter* (*The Bridegroom, the Comedienne, and the Pimp*), 1968, the last film completed by Straub/Huillet while they resided in the Federal Republic. The destruction and redemption of German history are explored in chapter 5 by way of the narrative structures of *Nicht versöhnt oder Es hilft nur Gewalt, wo Gewalt herrscht* (*Not Reconciled or, Only violence helps where violence rules*), 1964–1965, and the novel on which it was based, Böll's *Billiards at Half Past Nine*. Chapter 6 treats *Geschichtsunterricht* (*History Lessons*), 1972, the film based on Bertolt Brecht's novel fragment *Die Geschäfte des Herrn Julius Caesar*. Straub/Huillet's adaptations of Schoenberg are treated in chapter 7: *Moses und Aron* (*Moses and Aaron*), 1974–1975; and *Einleitung zu Arnold Schoenbergs "Begleitmusik zu einer Lichtspielscene"* (*Introduction to Arnold Schoenberg's "Accompaniment to a Cinematographic Scene"*), 1972. *Klassenverhältnisse* (*Class Relations*), 1983, based on Franz Kafka's unfinished America novel *Der Verschollene* (*Amerika*) is discussed in chapter 8, particularly in the context of feminist film theory on the position of the spectator in regard to film narrative. Chapters 9 and 11 treat the Friedrich Hölderlin films: *Der Tod des Empedokles oder: wenn dann der Erde Grün von neuem euch erglänzt* (*The Death of Empedocles or, When the green of the earth will gleam for you anew*), 1986, *Schwarze Sünde* (*Black Sin*), 1988, and *Die Antigone des Sophokles in der hölderlinschen Übertragung für die Bühne bearbeitet von Brecht 1948 (Suhrkamp Verlag)* (*Antigone*), 1991–1992. The theatrical staging of Hölderlin's texts against the landscape of Sicily presents a new challenge to conventional definitions of the cinema's relation to nature, myth, and history. The culmination of their work with Hölderlin, *Antigone*, also represented a return to Brecht by way of his 1946 translation.

A separate chapter (chap. 10) considers Straub/Huillet's approach to language and translation, drawing on the work of Walter Benjamin and Paul de Man. Their method of rehearsing with and directing actors treats each text as if it were a musical score, fixing in advance of the performance for the camera a deep connection between the actor's ability to remember (and think about) the text and that person's physical ability to recite it. Breathing, for instance, is rehearsed in connection with both the structure and meaning of the lines and the speaker's physical or personal qualities. It is also significant that Straub/Huillet often use actors who are not native speakers of German, or do not know the language at all. This makes for a remarkable deterritorialization of the language and opens up the possibilities of reception for German speakers and others. The concluding chapter reconsiders the relation of Straub/Huillet's film work to the connection of high modernism and mass culture in Critical Theory, by exploring the way the films juxtapose concerns of both Theodor W. Adorno and Brecht.

The importance of Straub/Huillet to discussions of film theory in the 1970s has generally overshadowed their connection to German cinema and culture in the U.S. reception of their work. This reception has also been quite limited between the early 1980s and 1995, partly due to the fact that subtitled prints of the films following *Empedocles* have not been available. Aside from numerous articles in the British journal *Screen* (mostly in the 1970s), there have been relatively few publications on Straub/Huillet in English. These include Richard Roud's book *Jean-Marie Straub* (1971) and Martin Walsh's chapters on their films in *The Brechtian Aspect of Radical Cinema* (1981). The retrospective of their work at the Public Cinema in New York in 1982 was accompanied by a program tabloid, edited by Jonathan Rosenbaum. Finally, they attended a conference at the Center for Twentieth-Century Studies that year on "German Avant-Garde Cinema: The Seventies," which may have solidified the impression that they belong to the extremes of the inaccessible avant-garde—an impression I hope to counter with this book.

Despite their relative obscurity in the United States, Straub/Huillet's work is at least as significant as that of European directors who are better known here. Straub/Huillet are among the major senior figures of the Young German Cinema of the 1960s, precursor of the New German Cinema. Along with Alexander Kluge, they are the foremost practitioners of a "Brechtian cinema" in German. Figuring prominently in the French and Anglo-American reception of this Brechtian strain of film theory since the 1970s, their work has been discussed in the contexts of "materialist cinema" and the "cineastes of the text" (e.g., Marguerite Duras and Hans Jürgen Syberberg).[3] Although Straub/Huillet's approach to film has been most closely connected to Godard and Kluge, important differences have become increasingly pronounced. Godard and Kluge have departed from the cinema somewhat in their recent work, combining techniques and media technologies of increasing complexity.[4] In so doing, their emphasis has been somewhat less on photography and on the "reality" of the subject before the camera lens than on investigating the manipulations available through the mechanical reproduction of moving images. As we will see, the radicality of Straub/Huillet lies in their continued exploration of the film medium through concentration and simplification. Rather than move toward computer graphics, video, and television, their works seek to approach the immediacy of early sound cinema or even the silent film.

Drawing heavily on the works of Adorno, Brecht, and Benjamin, this book attempts to demonstrate that Straub/Huillet's "redemptive" approach to history, particularly in the German context, avoids the pitfalls of "left-wing melancholy." Their consistently innovative modernism, although it shares much with avant-garde and postmodernist practice in the arts, will be seen to be distinct from both. In part, this emphasis is in polemical response to the tendency of criticism over the years to stamp Straub/Huillet as ascetic, minimalist, avant-garde, anti-illusionist, antinarrative, anticinematic, and static. Straub/Huillet have disputed all of these labels over the years, with increasing insistence. Helmut Färber published a thorough exposé of these errors as early as 1968, and the critical clichés have not changed in the intervening years.[5] Because of this narrowing of Straub/Huillet reception, I feel compelled to accent the opposite aspects of their work here: the playful, sensuous, cinematic, traditional (if not conventional), optimistic, future-oriented, and utopian aspects. As Straub has put it, "Film is the art of the moment; the art of 'Tarry yet, you are so beautiful.'" And Huillet, in response to a comment on the rigor of their method: "I hope not only that, I hope there is sensuality and pleasure [*Lust*] as well."

It is also a concern to distinguish between the intentions Huillet and Straub have in making their films and their critical, theoretical, and especially academic reception. One could easily ascribe importance to Straub/Huillet films based on their relation to the prevailing issues in film studies since the 1970s. Along with Godard, they stood as paradigms of a Brechtian political modernism that, via *Cahiers du cinéma* and *Screen*, stood at the foundation of much "countercinema" and critical film studies. Over the years they have earned the admiration of artists and intellectuals such as Karlheinz Stockhausen, Marguerite Duras, Alain Robbe-Grillet, Gilles Deleuze, Franco Fortini, and Peter Handke. Straub/Huillet are not content with academic recognition, however. Vincent Nordon has pointed out that any critic (in France at least) can now write about the "Straubian offscreen space," and there is even, in academic and theoretical film circles, what Nordon calls a "Straubian international." All this "doesn't interest me," Straub asserts,[6] and this is no doubt the reason for part of Straub/Huillet's intransigence when confronting both film professionals and film buffs: this is not their intended audience. Their intended audience is still "the people." Their attempt at a synthesis of high art and populism has its origins in the political and cultural hopes of the 1960s, which might be summed up by the comment of a group of Italian peasant schoolchildren from that time: "True culture, which no man has yet possessed, would be made up of two elements, belonging to the masses and mastery of the language."[7] The cinematic and artistic confrontation of the absence of this audience of "the people" will be a focal point of my examination of the films of Straub/Huillet. As Deleuze summed up the contradiction,

> Resnais and the Straubs are probably the greatest political film-makers in the West, in modern cinema. But, oddly, this is not through the presence of the people. On the contrary, it is because they know how to show how the people are what is missing, what is not there.... And the German people in the Straubs' *Unreconciled*: has there ever been a German people, in a country which has bungled its revolutions, and was constituted under Bismarck and Hitler, to be separated again?[8]

In the face of the critical and theoretical acclaim they do receive, then, Straub/Huillet persist in alienating their would-be friends with radical political polemics, on the one hand, and with appeals to simplicity and film tradition as opposed to radical innovation and experimentation, on the other. While examining Straub-Huillet's connection to theoretical and political debates, cinematic pleasure, and the connections between nature, myth, and history, I will concentrate on their "German" films. However, it is clear that these concerns—both in society and in the texts—could be found in other national or cultural contexts as well. Especially the relevance of their work to the successes and failures of the "New Left" extends from Germany to France, Italy, Great Britain, and the United States in one form or another.

The discussion of the "German" films of Straub/Huillet in this book will examine their unique "displacement" of German culture in the context of the postwar dilemma of finding a "usable" German past. While recent discussion of the postwar German cinema has rightly emphasized its melancholy self-obsession, Straub/Huillet stand apart from this phenomenon both aesthetically and politically. Their films provide a refreshing and stimulating counterpoint to those examined by Thomas Elsaesser, Anton Kaes, and Eric Santner in their recent books on German cinema and history.[9] We will begin, therefore, by examining the place of Straub/Huillet's work in political debates on film culture since the 1960s and then in the context of Germany and the New German Cinema.

# 1

# STRAUB/HUILLET AND THE CINEMA
Tradition and Avant-garde

In the only previous book in English devoted exclusively to the cinema of Danièle Huillet and Jean-Marie Straub, published in 1971, Richard Roud addressed the problem that their films were not well known in the United States. After almost twenty-five years, this task must be repeated. Despite considerable critical recognition and a solid place in discussions of New German Cinema, European cinema, and film theory, the films themselves are rarely seen here. I am also acutely aware of the contradiction in using an academic book to introduce an audience to films that simply demand to be seen—and more than once. This reservation is increased by the filmmakers' own skepticism of scholarly interpretation of film, especially of a biographical approach. For instance, in one of the outraged letters published in Straub's handwriting by the journal *Filmkritik*, he vehemently rejected Alexander Kluge's criticisms of the film *Fortini/Cani* in 1976 based on Straub/Huillet's position as authors.

> And now here come the Ph.D's! [*die Herren Doktoren*] . . . I would only like to let Schoenberg reply, for me as well: "In *Grove's Dictionary of Music* there is quite a good article that talks about *Moses and Aaron*. Partly nonsensical; namely, to bring the artist into it. That is the end of the nineteenth century, but not me. The material and its treatment are purely religious-philosophical."[1]

But some understanding of who Danièle Huillet and Jean-Marie Straub are is essential to an understanding of their unique collaboration as a couple and of two essential aspects of the way they work: their love of the cinema and their respect for every bit of labor that goes into a film production. The care they give to the smallest detail of film work extends from making sure that the meat of the animals slaughtered for sacrifice in *Moses and Aaron* was used by the local Italian butchers to Huillet's personally washing the window of an Amtrak railway car for the final shot of *Class Relations*.

This respect for all human endeavor extends to the film audience as well, meaning that Straub/Huillet are willing to argue with the audience rather than merely try to please them. Regarding the charge that their films are too inaccessible to reach a wide audience and have a political effect, their position echoes that of Bertolt Brecht, Hanns Eisler, and Theodor W. Adorno: An artist must try only to make the best art possible; to make things less well than one could so as to be popular leads nowhere, politically or aesthetically. This attitude seems more eccentric in the 1990s than it did in the 1960s, when young filmmakers energetically attacked mainstream cultural conventions. A precursor of *Filmkritik* quoted Walter Benjamin to connect the youth protest against the culture industry and the need to present an alternative to what people had been led to expect: "The public must always be proved wrong." As Hartmut Bitomsky has put it, "We are not used to so much respect; the almost complete absence of arbitrary manipulation is almost unbearable to experience. In the disturbing interconnections of things we begin to see our own impatience."[2]

Straub/Huillet share the view of Adorno and Eisler, two equally radical critics of the culture industry, that the interaction of audience and cinema contains revolutionary potential: "There is an ingredient of truth in what the public expects of the cinema: . . . [B]ehind the shell of conventionalized behavior patterns, resistance and spontaneity still survive."[3] And the resistance is to be found in part in the legacy of the early cinema.

> To the extent that the motion picture in its sensationalism is the heir of the popular horror story and dime novel and remains below the established standards of middle-class art, it is in a position to shatter those standards, precisely through the use of sensation, and to gain access to collective energies that are inaccessible to sophisticated literature and painting.[4]

Straub/Huillet films are an attempt to put together these two potentials: bourgeois high culture and popular film culture. Along with Brecht, Eisler, and Adorno, they reject the arrogance of experts who prevent modern works from reaching a wide audience because they presume to know in advance what the masses want and can understand.[5]

## Straub/Huillet's Authorship

The name Straub/Huillet, which applies only to both together, is both convenient and accurate as a shorthand term for two individuals working together with no concern for assigning credit. It does not erase the problematic fact that Jean-Marie Straub is still often regarded as the more significant, if not sole, auteur. Biographical material on Huillet and Straub is extremely limited. The few published biographical sketches were usually the result of direct demands from journalists and are thus "composed" and would require additional contextual support. The main "biographical sketch" has been repeated in various forms since it appeared in Roud's monograph and in *Herzog/Kluge/ Straub* (1976), the first major book in Germany to concentrate on their work.[6] The description of Straub is even read on camera by Huillet in a television portrait by Michael Klier.[7]

> Born "under Capricorn" (like the old lady in *Not Reconciled*) on the Sunday after Epiphany in the city that is the birthplace of Paul Verlaine ("Et si j'avais cent fils, ils auraient cent chevaux / Pour vite déserter le Sergent et l'Armée") and baptized under the name of one of the first draft evaders (Jean-Marie Vianney, priest of Ars) in the year Hitler came to power. . . . Until 1940 heard, learned, and spoke only French—at home and outside. And all at once I am only allowed to hear and speak German outside and have to learn it instantly in school (where as everywhere every word of French is forbidden). . . . After the liberation a pupil until the first diploma at the Jesuit Collège Saint-Clément (where I learned that disobedience is not only a poetic virtue) and then one year at the state Lycée, second diploma. Demonstration against the paltry programming of the film theaters in Metz; first contacts with the French police. From 1950–1955 leader of a film club in Metz, at the same time student in Strassbourg and Nancy. 1954 to Paris; project of a full-length film biography: *Chronicle of Anna Magdalena Bach*; Algerian Revolution; met Danièle Huillet . . .[8]

Richard Roud and Roy Armes have both written about the importance for Straub of the French filmmakers he admired or worked with in his youth, especially Jean Renoir, Robert Bresson, Alexandre Astruc, and Jean Grémillion.[9] In 1966, Straub was included in the journal *Filmkritik*'s "First Lexicon of the Young German Cinema," where his responses cite these early influences as well as indicate two themes that are still important today: an affinity with Hölderlin and a sense of a special relation to German culture as an outsider.

> "Jean-Marie Straub"
> [ . . . ] *Hospitation* with the following directors: Abel Gance (*La tour de Nesle*), Jean Renoir (*French Cancan, Eléna et les hommes*), Jacques Rivette (*Le coup de berger*), Robert Bresson (*Un condamné à mort s'ést échappé*), Alexandre Astruc (*Une vie*).
> 1958 flight from military conscription for Algeria.
> Since then in Germany, at first two years of traveling—on the trail of Bach.

*Filmkritik* broached the theme of nationality with the question, "What does it mean to you to make films as a Frenchman in Germany?" Straub's reply:

> That is, against the stupidity, the laziness of thought, the depravity that are demonstrated here, as B. B. [Brecht] says? Hyperion would answer: bleeding to

Jean-Marie Straub, 1960s (?). Courtesy Stiftung Deutsche Kinemathek.

death; I will add: for now not being able and permitted to reach the many to whom one would like to present one's films. This double answer applies also for Peter Nestler and some others. But it will change. That stimulates me—and also, to make films here as a Frenchman that no German would have been able to make—rather as no German could have made *Germania anno zero* and *La paura*, no American, *The Southerner* and *The Young One*—and no Italian would have been able to write *La Chartreuse de Parme*.[10]

At this early stage Straub mentions a number of projects that only much later would become films, attesting both to the struggle the filmmakers faced and to the consistency of their concerns. The projects mentioned in 1966 were *Moses und Aron* (based on Arnold Schoenberg's opera, in color), *Die Maßnahme* (based on Brecht's *The Measures Taken*), *Die Verfolgung und Ermordung Jean-Paul Marats* and *Die Ermittlung* (*The Investigation* by Peter Weiss), *Die Geschichte von Asaré* (based on a myth, reported by Claude Lévi-Strauss in *Le Cru et le Cuit*), a film about a cleaning woman in Munich, and "the comedy of the German film folk—based on original material."[11] Of these plans, only the Schoenberg project was realized, almost ten years later; Brecht remains central to Straub/Huillet, but the rights to *The Measures*

Danièle Huillet in the film *Über die Trägheit der Wahrnehmung* (*On the Lethargy of Perception*), directed by Klaus Feddermann and Helmut Herbst, 1981. Courtesy Stiftung Deutsche Kinemathek.

*Taken* could not be obtained, and *Pains of Youth* replaced it, on stage with Rainer Werner Fassbinder and the Action-Theater and in the film *Bridegroom* (1968). In 1992, Straub listed the following projects for the years up to 1997: a black-and-white film for television, something like Renoir's *Le Testament du docteur Cordelier*, with two months of rehearsal and eight days of shooting; a musical comedy (a wry reference to Schoenberg's *Von heute auf morgen*); *Conversations in Sicily*, based on the novel by Elio Vittorini, an Italian Communist intellectual.[12] Also for 1997, Italian television plans a video montage to be called *La magnifica ossessione* (*The Magnificent Obsession*).

Although Danièle Huillet is clearly one of the most important women working in the postwar European cinema, she remains almost totally ignored by film criticism. One reason for this is as scandalous as it is simple: Since all of Huillet's work has been in collaboration with Jean-Marie Straub and the two have refused to stylize themselves in any particular way as "artist personalities," the sexist assumption of the 1950s that Straub is the principal auteur of the two has remained unquestioned. Yet in an interview in *Frauen und Film*, published in 1982, Huillet removed all doubt that the works of Straub/Huillet are truly collaborative—and always have been.[13]

It is difficult to approach the reasons for Huillet's lack of recognition. She has not sought to call attention to her work on the films and has not identified herself as a feminist. Instead, for years she has stayed in the background, especially since she believes that interviews and discussions—in which Straub more readily engages—may do the films more harm than good.[14] Without presuming to impose consciousness-raising on Huillet, however, the Straub/Huillet division of labor and the perception of it certainly reflect sexism in the institutions of cinema. Critics even continue to falsely assume that Huillet and Straub are married and frequently include Huillet only by way of the term "the Straubs." Male critics have never felt it necessary to query Straub on this issue, and his greater visibility and volubility feed the assumption that he dominates in their teamwork. Furthermore, the single area in which Huillet does leave more of the decisions to Straub is the aspect of filmmaking that has been reified into the directorial "signature"—the set-up and framing of shots. The areas of more equal collaboration—e.g., script and mise-en-scène—and especially those areas in which Huillet may be more in charge—sound, editing, "scene design," and many producer's functions—all fit more readily the stereotype of women working behind the scenes.[15]

One could argue, on the one hand, that Huillet's toleration of this situation is in itself a result of sexism. On the other, any familiarity with the aesthetic project of Straub/Huillet films immediately puts such hierarchical thinking into question. From the very beginning, a principal aspect of their aesthetic has been to subvert the primacy of the visual in cinema by having the text, sound, duration, and editing clash with, rather than support, the image. For this reason, a feminist reception of Straub/Huillet might begin by cooperating with Huillet's concern for the films first and the gendering of authorship afterward. In her words, "What interests us are the products and not the names."[16]

Further study on the gender (and political) issues raised by Straub/Huillet's work methods and their reception would then certainly be warranted. This is not to say that Huillet has never stated a position on feminist issues. She did so in her 1982 interview, but always in the context of her work and the realities of history and everyday life. Even the radical cinema she and Straub have developed collaboratively she does not ascribe to their creative will alone: "Yes, but that came about also through our living" (Ja, das kam aber auch durch unser Leben).[17]

When questioned about her position on gender oppression and the presence or absence of women in Straub/Huillet films, Huillet gave a three-part answer. First, she pointed out the presence of women in the documentary aspects of the films, seen going about the work of everyday life. And if women's work is less visible on the streets and in the factories, that is part of the documentation the films provide. But Huillet objected to modifying the historical texts used in the films to include women after the fact: "To place a woman into the middle of Brecht where he had none would be false, also for the woman."[18] Her second answer was to point out that the film *Bridegroom*—although constructed from previously existing texts, like all their films—very clearly shows the oppression of women. This, too, arose from a documentary impulse: Huillet and Straub developed the idea for the film after walking by chance through the prostitutes' area of Munich, seen at the opening of the film. Third, Huillet stressed that she sees the liberation of women as more quickly attainable through general revolution—as in the resistance struggles of the third world.[19] And, consistent with the scrupulous respect for "reality" evidenced in Straub/Huillet films, Huillet categorically refuses to use film to fabricate a history for women using the methods of the "dream factory." "The dreams one has come only from reality and are only partly different from reality and are an attempt to escape from it," she says. "But always from reality and not from nothing."[20]

Furthermore, Huillet does not see her work as part of a countercinema that simply destroys the pleasures of the conventional narrative by reversing the system: "I don't believe that one can replace one oppression with another, and I also don't believe that one can fight one system with another, because then a thing becomes simply too rigid." To the suggestion that Straub/Huillet films, too, seem to be built on a strict system, based on renunciation, she replied, "I hope not *only* that. I hope that one can feel sensuality and pleasure [*Lust*] at the same time. Can sense the fragrance of things."[21]

What Huillet primarily distanced herself from in this interview is that aspect of feminist film that Gertrud Koch has traced from the *cinéma militant* through the theoretical emphasis on film language and identification.[22] Straub/Huillet films are instead more relevant to the reintroduction of Brecht and the Frankfurt school into the discussion of feminist theory, as proposed by Koch and Elin Diamond, for example. Diamond stresses the importance of Brechtian theory for feminism in theater because it allows space for "gestus" within the process of subverting the conventional means of representation.[23] Koch's article on Critical Theory, in contrast, suggests invoking phenomenology and existential psychoanalysis for film theory, examining the prelinguistic levels of the unconscious rather than the linguistic formations analyzed by Jacques Lacan. Koch's return to the fundamentals of perception and to the origins of film parallel Straub/Huillet's emphasis on a documentary attitude and a search for cinematic pleasure that is not predetermined by the culture industry and the "patriarchal orchestration of the look."[24] Thus Straub/Huillet move beyond the assumed renunciation of pleasure of what Teresa de Lauretis calls the "Brechtian-Godardian" program of the materialist avant-garde.[25]

Consistent with her position in the filmmaking couple, Huillet's biographical note of 1976 is briefer and dependent on Straub's, with a touch of wit added.

In a recent interview she describes her first childhood wish of becoming a peasant farmer, which her family laughed at, then a veterinarian. The 1976 note was the following:

> The most interesting thing about me is my date of birth; 1 May 1936. After the second diploma I went once to the Sorbonne and ran out again after a half hour, in hatred and terror. Then I prepared for the I.D.H.E.C.—and met Straub in the process. I wanted to make documentaries—ethnographic films. Also: I didn't like blond people with light skin at all; when I was small, I found nothing more beautiful than the girls at school in Paris (where I came only at age 13—before, I was in the country), who were dark. . . . But Straub simply was blond with very light skin, unfortunately! I had learned English and Spanish and then had to learn first German and finally Italian . . . quite dialectical.[26]

The biographical reticence of Straub/Huillet is partly the result of their modernist effort to efface the author in favor of the work: "What interests us are the products and not the names."[27] Biographical information about artists in general, Huillet has said, is "not very interesting." But their reticence about their own biographies is also connected to a position their work takes regarding authorship and subjectivity. Chapter 6 examines the one extensive interview Huillet has given regarding their work and seeks to explore a possible connection between Straub/Huillet's separation of the camera from the spectator and feminist theories on visual pleasure. Beyond this, there is much more work to be done regarding the gender aspect of Straub/Huillet's films and their manner of working together, which the domestic comedy of Schoenberg's opera *Von Heute auf Morgen* might stimulate when their film of that work is finished.

Although book and chapter titles of the 1970s refer only to Straub as the filmmaker, Huillet's presence has gradually, perhaps because of the women's movement, become more visible on the surface of the films and the criticism. For instance, in the early films she was not credited as co-director, although her *Frauen und Film* interview implies that the technical situation was not significantly different. Once her name began to appear more prominently in the credits, some critics at least began to speak of Straub/Huillet, Straub and Huillet, or at least "die Straubs" or "les Straub." A few even write of Huillet and Straub.

The fact that Huillet almost never gives interviews and seldom speaks in interviews with herself and Straub presents a problem for research, since most of the interview record of the filmmakers' intentions exists in Straub's words. In listing the origins of their projects, he says both "I" and "we"; she says only "we." Huillet is present at almost all the interviews, even if she never speaks. Often, however, she will correct or modify Straub's comments; sometimes she will make a contribution. Her comments also reveal her overriding concern for accuracy in descriptions of how their films were made; an example is her detailed commentary on Gregory Woods's "Work Journal" on the filming of *Moses and Aaron*.[28] Michael Klier's video concentrates on her active listening, which takes on the same weight of agency as the young man's silence at the end of *History Lessons*. Huillet has both stated and implied that Straub can answer for both of them[29] even though she fears that interviews do the films more harm than good, while Straub cannot resist entering into polemical exchanges. Straub, too, has regretted the rather vast interview record—mostly in his own words.[30]

The withdrawal of the "author" from the work is more consistent with Huillet's attitude, and Straub/Huillet have over the years carefully set up what they call the "rules of the game" for filming, which allow emotion or expression to come through only as a documentary effect and not as an authorial intention. In the context of the films, we shall see that this attitude toward authorship and subjectivity is a modernist, not a postmodernist, position. Although I suggest there are parallels between Straub/Huillet's film practice and feminist film theory, very few women have written about their work. The West German critic Frieda Grafe has followed their entire career, their work is included in a volume edited by Barbara Bronnen et al., and Maureen Turim has analyzed the shot structure of the Bach film by way of the concept of *écriture blanche* and contributed the chapter dealing with the importance of Brecht for their work in *New German Filmmakers* (1984); Gertrud Koch, whose work features prominently in chapters 7 and 8, has also written about *Moses and Aaron* in the context of visual representations of Jewishness. Koch places Straub/Huillet in the legacy of the Frankfurt school (Critical Theory) and argues that exploring these connections further would be productive for feminist film theory.[31]

One could speculate that Huillet's influence, which has at least become more visible over the years, has affected the increased reticence of the camera and the growing importance of sound and the voice. Although she may have initially given up her own plans to make ethnographic films to join Straub in his exile to Germany and the Bach project, an ethnographic approach has certainly resurfaced in their careful photographic studies of locations, landscapes, and the people in them. But again, it is difficult to separate what is new in this and what is Huillet and what is Straub; Straub, too, cited the documentarist Jean Rouch as an early influence in their work. Finally, Straub/Huillet have frequently referred to their career as the pursuit of two paths. The path from *Les Yeux ne veulent pas en tout temps se fermer ou Peut-être qu'un jour Rome se permettra de choisir à son tour* (*Othon*) of their earlier work, the film favored by Huillet—has led to *Moses and Aaron*, *Class Relations*, and *Antigone*. The path from *History Lessons*, a film preferred by Straub, has led to *Fortini/Cani*, *Zu früh, Zu spät* (*Too Early, Too Late*), and *Cézanne*. One could see in the alternation of these projects something of the love story that their career also represents, which is merely hinted at by the Marx quotation appended to the screenplay of *Chronicle*: that love involves contributing to another's self-realization through productive labor.[32]

I will not undertake a detailed analysis of the gender aspects of the relation of sound to image here, although a questioning of Straub/Huillet's teamwork along with the end product would be fascinating. Such a discussion might, for instance, invoke Kaja Silverman's work on the psychoanalytic aspects of sound, Martin Jay's study of the denigration of vision in twentieth-century French thought, or the volume *Modernity and the Hegemony of Vision*.[33] What I do hope to show in this book, however, is Straub/Huillet's resistance to the domination of nature in the cinema. They do this, on the one hand, by insisting, along with Siegfried Kracauer and André Bazin, on the power present in the "indexicality" of the photographic image, explicitly in rejection of the proposition, based on psychoanalysis and semiotics, that the cinema is a language. As Bazin wrote of Bresson (and, indirectly, Carl Dreyer), they, too, are concerned "not with the psychology but with the physiology of existence."[34] Their almost archaeological approach to location filming, for instance, records traces of the past that will vanish with time, yet "redeems" them as it records their passing. If special effects à la *Metropolis* are evidence of the male fantasy of creating life,[35] Straub/Huillet's scrupulous avoidance of such effects may bespeak an opposite fantasy.

"The grain of the voice," on the other hand, is also a consistent realm of exploration in Straub/Huillet's work, attempting to make sound—whether music or speech—become visible on the screen. Here, too, they have consistently worked against conventions of emotional, dramatic acting in a manner inspired by such antecedents as Brecht, Renoir, and Bresson. In this regard, Bazin's description of Bresson's *Diary of a Country Priest* applies: "The cast is not being asked to act out a text, not even to live it out, just to speak it."[36] But here again is a "redemption of physical reality."[37] As I attempt to show in regard to the later films, there is often what Straub refers to as a "spark" or "explosion" at the point where a speaker reveals the contradiction between a spoken text (the "inhuman" in language) and the living, breathing body necessary to produce the words.[38]

Straub/Huillet also question the notion of authorship by multiplying the form of their works, subverting the question of "originality." For instance, there are four "original" negatives for each of their Empedocles films and two each for *Antigone* and *Cézanne*. They are composed of the same shots in the same sequence but are of different lengths, since all the takes are distinct. A precursor of this was *Too Early, Too Late*, which had four separate voice tracks and no subtitles; there is only one visual "original" for all four, however, so the title of the film appears in all four languages at once. "Original" sound tracks in several languages exist for *Chronicle* as well, with Anna Magdalena Bach's narration in German, French, Italian, English, and Dutch. Also, several of their works were performed in other media: *Antigone* was performed on stage at the studio theater of the *Schaubühne* in Berlin before the filming (May 1991), as well as in the Greek amphitheater at Segesta for the local residents once the filming there had been completed. This is reminiscent of the performance of *Pains of Youth* by the Action-Theater in Munich which became the center segment of *Bridegroom*. The film of the opera *Moses and Aaron* was in part made possible by a concert agreement with Austrian Radio and resulted in a Philips recording as well as the film. Similarly, the sound track of *Black Sin* was broadcast in 1990 as a radio play in Berlin by RIAS and other stations, under the title "Empedokles auf Ätna." Most of the screenplays have also appeared in print, some of them embodying the only English translation of the texts involved, such as *Fortini/Cani* or Brecht's *The Business Affairs of Mr. Julius Caesar*. Finally, even their publications in response to the frequent requests from film journals tend to consist of quotations from other sources, often without citation. For instance, Straub's contribution to a special issue of *Cahiers du cinéma* dedicated to Wim Wenders consisted of a French translation of Kafka's short story "Jackals and Arabs," minus the title or author.

The problematization of "authorship" does not bring with it a complete deconstruction of the filmmaker as subject, however. On the contrary, although Straub has quipped that there is no such thing as "film history," in interviews Huillet and Straub consistently refer to figures of the "classical" cinema of the past, implying a belief in individual work within film tradition, especially because it is endangered. Their comments on the pitiful state of film distribution, exhibition, processing, sound recording, and so on, all reveal alarm at the debasement of "film culture" as an expression of life in industrial society. Here, as we will presently see, is the distinction between Straub/Huillet and both the "political modernism" with which they are in some ways allied and the postmodernism that their films in some ways resemble.

Since I am concentrating on the German films of Straub/Huillet, their considerable work in French and Italian needs to be introduced. Since their initial four "German" films made in the Federal Republic, Straub/Huillet's films fall into two categories, the "paths" of which they often speak, which include both German and non-German subjects. The paths are distinguished in part by the predominance of documentary or collage, on the one hand, and fictional narrative, on the other. The two strains of work extend from *History Lessons* to *Fortini/Cani* to *Too Early, Too Late* and from *Othon* to *Moses and Aaron* to *Class Relations*. With the exception of the documentary collage on Cézanne, the second strain has been the focus for all the Hölderlin films. The technique of setting a fictional story or drama in a landscape began with the French-language film *Les Yeux ne veulent pas en tout temps se fermer ou Peut-être qu'un jour Rome se permettra de choisir à son tour* (*Othon*) (1969), based on the Corneille play. It is acted in rapid-fire delivery, emphasizing the meter, by a cast of largely non-native speakers of French. The elements juxtaposed in the film create a dynamic and dense whole: the "difficult" seventeenth-century text, the ruins of the Palatine Hill in Rome, and striking compositions of the actors roaming these ruins above the twentieth-century streets of Rome. *History Lessons*, which also mixes modern and ancient Rome, differs from this in its virtual elimination of any "staging" of the Brecht text. As we shall see in chapter 6, narrative is produced in the Brecht film largely without acting on the part of the characters. This is the link to *Fortini/Cani* (1976), based on the book *I Cani del Sinai* by Franco Fortini. Rather than unfold a plot, Mark Nash and Steve Neal have sketched how the film investigates "the various conjunctures in the past and the present, and history as discourse, and the various forms that may take, as each relates to the individual subject (both Franco Fortini and the viewer)." The film raises the issue of time/duration while problematizing the position of the author quoting himself (as he reads a text written ten years earlier). The "layers of history" the film separates relate to the following modes of discourse, in Neal and Nash's observation.

Discourse of television and newspapers

Franco reading his book, *I Cani del Sinai*

Voice-over commentary

Visual discourse 'accompanying' the commentary

Handwritten discourse (identified in the script, but not in the film, as that of Fortini)[39]

In historical terms, the film's treatment of anti-Fascist struggles and the Arab-Israeli conflict links it to *Moses and Aaron* and *Introduction* in what has been called Straub/Huillet's "Jewish trilogy." In the juxtaposition of modes of discourse, cinematic means of structuring time, and the life of an author/composer, *Fortini/Cani* also connects to *Chronicle, Introduction to Schoenberg*, and *Cézanne*. *Dalla nube alla resistenza* (*From the Cloud to the Resistance*) (1978), based on two works by Cesare Pavese, falls into the category of *History Lessons* and *Too Early, Too Late* as well. It, too, has two parts—a twentieth-century text and a text regarding the myths of antiquity, each set in the appropriate landscape. Pavese's *The Moon and the Bonfires* looks back on the violent deaths of Italian anti-Fascist resistance fighters; *Dialogues with Leucò*[40] is a series of dialogues between heroes and gods, connecting myth and history and returning to an ambiguous stage in the creation of distinctions, such as that between animal and human, which are fundamental to grammar and language itself.[41] Such a juxtaposition of political engagement with profoundly contemplative issues such as myth, nature, and meaning points to the characters of Empedocles and Antigone in the Hölderlin films.

Three short films have been made in France: *Toute révolution est un coup de dés* (*Every Revolution Is a Throw of the Dice*) (1977), based on "Un Coup de dés jamais n'abolira le hasard," by Stéphane Mallarmé, and *En Râchâchant*

Danièle Huillet as the chorus in *Black Sin*. Courtesy Edition Manfred Salzgeber, Berlin.

(1982), based on a text by Marguerite Duras. The Mallarmé film would certainly deserve comparison with the works treated here, since it uses framing, duration, and the timbre of the voice to evoke the poem's experiments with typography. The invisible traces of history are also present, since the speakers are seated on the hillside where the Paris Communards were massacred in 1870. This placement of a character on transformed ground is echoed by Danièle Huillet's pose on the volcanic earth of Mount Etna in *Black Sin* (1988), in which she recites the lines of Hölderlin's chorus. *Too Early, Too Late* (1980–1981) is a special case, since English, French and German, and Italian versions were made using translations of the texts by Friedrich Engels and Mahmoud Hussein. This film points toward the importance of translation as a metaphor for Straub/Huillet's presentation of texts in the cinema, since the voice-over of this film necessarily is always at least 50 percent translated and read by a non-native speaker. *Cézanne: Dialogues with Gasquet* (1989) was commissioned by the Musée D'Orsay but was then rejected. The Cézanne film follows the impressionists in an attempt "to make it possible to sense the light" (Huillet). It contains excerpts from *Empedocles*, juxtaposed with ten Cézanne paintings, an excerpt from Renoir's *Madame Bovary*, and a voice-over containing texts of Cézanne's conversations with Joachim Gasquet.[42] *Lothringen! (Lorraine!)*, a film confronting the geography and history of Straub's place of origin, was released as this book was going to press.

## Straub/Huillet and Cinematic Tradition

Examination of Straub/Huillet's innovative work of over thirty years readily reveals their connection to film tradition. Their approach is the modernist one of reduction and simplification of form. As Hans Hurch put it, "The Straubs are no avant-gardists. They have only opened up a few old lines under the rubble of the cinema and carried them a bit further."[43] References to great artists of the classical cinema abound in their work as in their conversations. The first film, *Machorka-Muff*, is compared to a Western and to Fritz Lang's *M*; *Chronicle* and *Bridegroom* as well as *Too Early, Too Late* recall the early history of motion pictures; *Class Relations* sets a Keystone Kop chase on the streets of Hamburg. "Gangster" is a frequently recurring word in Straub's descriptions of both real and fictional villains. Writing of *Antigone*, Peter Handke finds Werner Rehm's Creon more imposing than Charlton Heston's Ben Hur and says that Astrid Ofner's Antigone is "one flesh with Liz Taylor's Cleopatra or the more physical, stubborn women and girls in Howard Hawks films."[44] Such comparisons are frequent in both the interviews and the criticism.

Straub/Huillet's wish to maintain explicit links to film history rather than break with it is evident in the films they have chosen to present along with their own work when asked to do so. In 1982 at the most recent U.S. retrospective of their films at the Public Theater in New York, they requested screenings of Glauber Rocha's *Antonio das mortes* (1969), Carl Dreyer's *Day of Wrath* (1943), Charlie Chaplin's *A King in New York* (1957), D. W. Griffith's *A Corner in Wheat* (1909), Luis Buñuel's *Land Without Bread* (1982), John Ford's *Civil War* (from *How the West Was Won*, 1962), Sergei Eisenstein's *Alexander Nevsky* (1938), Erich von Stroheim's *Blind Husbands* (1918), Jean Renoir's *This Land Is Mine* (1943), Kenji Mizoguchi's *The Story of the Last Chrysanthemums* (1939), and Luc Moulet's formal Western satire *A Girl Is a Gun* (1970).[45] Straub/Huillet refer to cinematic forerunners in regard to the two areas in which they are the most original, in the treatment of space and the treatment of sound. They have consistently stressed that each of their films begins with a place, a location, and is built from there. Straub has more than once cited Renoir as the source of this definition of "the filmic"—"a tiny dialectic between film, theater and life"[46]—but also varies it by replacing "film" with "the encounter with a place."[47] The Hölderlin films, in particular, have revived the connection to the Western. Handke writes that Straub/Huillet use "machinery and techniques not so different from Howard Hawks or Raoul Walsh."[48] And Laurence Giavarini finds the recourse to the Western associations of *Antigone* both radical and immediate, "thanks to the sun, the *éclat* of the sky and the space that is divided up by the shots."[49]

Dividing up space rather than manipulating it is fundamental to Straub/Huillet's attitude to the relation of art to the world. Echoing Bazin, Straub has divided artists into two "families," of which they would belong to the second, "who try to see the world and become a mirror that is as clean as possible (Cocteau said, 'The mirrors would do well to reflect better')." In the other group are those "who presume—sometimes with inspiration, sometimes with arrogance—to reshape the world." Straub then amended this description to include a third group making up 99 percent of the cinema: "the paratroopers." "Those are people who simply fall from the sky somewhere and boom, the camera is running already. They film something they have never even seen. They've never taken time to look at it. And to show something, one must have seen something. And to see something, one must have looked at it for years at a time."[50]

Straub/Huillet's treatment of space is thus as simple as it is difficult to achieve. In contradiction to Stephen Heath and much theoretical work on cinematic "language," space for them is not to be created by the camera but merely shown. Narrative is not necessary, since it is supplied by the text. For each scene, therefore, they experiment until they find the "strategic point." As Alain Bergala has explained,

> For Jean-Marie Straub [sic], the important thing is finding for each scene in the film—that is, for each shot, for each space—the single strategic point from which one can then film *all* the shots of the scene, changing only the axis and the focal length of the lens. "Directors of today," he says, "no longer take much trouble to restore the reality of a space. They jump from shot to shot, and so they compose frames that are not connected in relation to a space. It is much easier to make little corrections from one shot to the next than it is to find the single strategic point for the scene to be filmed."[51]

It takes much patience to find a single point where the camera can stand in order to record all the spatial relations without contradiction or interference from its own presence or the position of the "actors"—human or otherwise. There are no shots in Straub/Huillet films, for instance, where in "reality" one would see the camera that photographed another shot: such space "does not exist," Straub insists. I will describe Straub/Huillet's use of camera location in some detail, particularly in regard to a scene from *Empedocles*, but an evolution can be traced from their earliest films to the ultimate challenge of *Antigone*, filmed from a single vertical axis of view.

Regarding the mise-en-scène, a similar approach is taken to the use of language: Straub/Huillet attempt to simplify each shot to the point that it conveys one idea clearly; it becomes an empty frame, devoid of all expression. Only an "empty" frame can capture the invisible textures of the surface of the world that were the essence of cinema for Kracauer and a poetic salvation for Hölderlin. Straub refers often to Griffith's statement of 1947: "What the modern movie lacks is beauty—the beauty of moving wind in the trees, the little movement in a beautiful blowing on the blossoms in the trees. That they have forgotten entirely."[52] But Straub recalled another early context for the same observation in an interview regarding the Bach film, where he compared the motion of the musicians' fingers to the wind in the trees: the audience's delight at the films of the Lumières.[53] Kracauer makes a similar point in his *Theory of Film*.

> It rests on the assumption that film is essentially an extension of photography and therefore shares with this medium a marked affinity for the visible world around us. Now this reality includes many phenomena which would hardly be perceived were it not for the motion picture camera's ability to catch them on the wing. [ . . . ] Significantly, the contemporaries of Lumière praised his films—the first ever to be made—for showing "the ripple of the leaves stirred by the wind."[54]

This acceptance of photography as a baseline clearly distinguishes Straub/Huillet from the avant-garde and reveals the error of critics' tying them to the way "structuralist/materialist film-makers call attention to the material facts of film: the presence of sprocket holes, the grain and texture of the film; the movement of film through the gate of the projector; the factor of light in the registration of any image on film."[55] For Straub/Huillet, by contrast, "the greatness of film is the humbleness of being condemned to photography."[56] I believe this has been the most misleading effect of the reception of Straub/Huillet by way of the critique of film language, for instance, in Lacanian feminist theory. For example, although she is right in stressing Straub/Huillet's disruption of film conventions, Roswitha Mueller draws the conclusion from this that their films renounce access to the pleasure found in the imaginary: "Staying clear of the fantastic and pleasurable proximity to the imaginary, they insist on the materiality of the signifier by cleansing images and sound as much as possible of pre-established cinematic codes."[57] There are two sides to the process, however. Although Straub/Huillet call attention to the artificiality of cinematic codes, these codes, which exist on the level of the symbolic, are not the only source of pleasure. The access to the surface of things, as Bazin describes, is also an access to pleasure in the realm of the imaginary. As Rosalind Krauss has put it, "Whatever else its power, the photograph could be called sub- or pre-symbolic, ceding the language of art back to the imposition of things."[58] The "imposition of things" is precisely the source of the moments of joy to be found in Straub/Huillet films, as they evoke the photographic immediacy of the early cinema. Even more than for their treatment of visual and narrative structures, Straub/Huillet are constantly attacked—especially in Germany—for their use of sound and speech. With the sole exception of their first short film, Straub/Huillet have used live sound throughout their work, insisting on the direct connection between the sound and the image, the space, the air where it is recorded. They also prefer microphones that record more than just the actor's voice, rejecting radio microphones and lavalieres in favor of the traditional use of a hand-held microphone boom. Since the 1960s they have only worked with two sound directors, Jeti Grigioni and Louis Hochet. Hochet, whom Straub/Huillet refer to as the last great "Tonmeister" of the European cinema, has worked with Straub/Huillet from the Bach film to *Antigone*. Hochet had done the sound for Max Ophüls's *La Ronde*, and his older assistant, Lucien Moreau, had done direct optical sound on early Renoir films.[59]

To underscore their dedication to live sound and the beauty of texts recited by speakers who have difficulty with the language, both Huillet and Straub refer to the early sound films of Renoir. Here is one illustration of the consistency and harmony of their positions: twenty-five years after Straub had mentioned the foreign accents and the clumsy sound recording in these films in the context of the Bach film, Huillet remarked in 1993, "One of the things that makes me optimistic . . . is the beautiful speech of the woman in court at the end of Renoir's *La Chienne*."[60] The other precursor in their use of "unexpressive" treatment of sound is Robert Bresson, whose pronouncements on the speech of actors are nearly identical to their own. Here Bresson echoes Benjamin's concept of the use of a mechanism to reach a point free of all machinery.

> I maintain that a mechanical approach is the only proper one, as in playing the piano. In playing scales, playing as regularly and as mechanically as possible, one captures the emotion. And not when one adds the emotion, as virtuosos do. That's just it: actors are virtuosos. Instead of concentrating on the material, they give one their feelings in addition and say, "Look, that is how you must perceive the material."[61]

On the famous "neutral" diction of his performers, which is also shared by Straub/Huillet, Bresson speaks in terms similar to Kracauer's attitude toward photography. "For one thing, the diction is not neutral, it is true, I would say, right. The word 'right' is often not understood in the theater. Speaking must be automatic, like the gestures. From the automatism that makes up three-quarters of our lives comes the true, and not from what is thought and considered."[62]

Since the approach to sound, like the approach to the image, is a documentary one, the "unexpressive" delivery of the lines in Straub/Huillet films could be explained as arising simply from the requirements of their method: since they push all the structures of film to the limit and do not believe in manipulating the spontaneity of what appears *involuntarily*, that is, the truth, they control as much as possible what is produced voluntarily. And a line or speech must be delivered the same way several times for the requisite number of takes; and if an "expression" is included, it will not be done the same way every time, except perhaps by an experienced singer or professional actor. So an "inauthentic" way of speaking is introduced to achieve an "authentic" encounter between text and speaker. Otherwise, both the text as material and the act of speaking would be erased in favor of preconceived "meaning."

Despite the great amount of criticism locating the "Brechtianism" of Straub/Huillet in their violation of visual conventions,[63] the use of language and work with the actors is perhaps Brecht's most significant influence on them. In fact, consistent with the attitude toward photography described above, Straub has ridiculed the idea of approaching a film scene with any idea of "distanciating" it. However, even Renoir reported from personal experience that the originality of Brecht was in his work with the actors.[64] And Renoir's description of the actor's relation to the text also parallels that of Straub/Huillet: "The work only starts after absorbing the lines, after making the lines your own."[65] This influence is consistent in the work of Straub/Huillet but reaches a high point, no doubt, in the performances in *Antigone*. As chapter 11 illustrates, Straub/Huillet have adopted certain aspects of what Brecht referred to as a *Modell*, which he developed at the same time he was writing down some of his directorial methods in the "Little Organon for the Theater" (at Helene Weigel's insistence). Brecht put more and more energy into staging plays than writing them after his return to Germany, suggesting another similarity to Straub/Huillet. It cannot be stressed often enough that they never write the texts of their films but only "stage" them for the cinema.

The other crucial Brechtian influence on Straub/Huillet is his play *Die heilige Johanna der Schlachthöfe (Saint Joan of the Stockyards)*. It provided the second title for *Not Reconciled—or, Only violence helps where violence rules*—in 1965 and has been mentioned in interviews much later. A number of characteristics of Brecht's play can be found in Straub/Huillet's films and in their social and artistic positions. Formally most important is the concept of a "fan," or spectrum of diction, that distinguishes the characters. In Brecht's play, the grandiose and narcissistic verbiage of the capitalists mimics poetry of Schiller, Shakespeare, Goethe, and Hölderlin. The correspondence of diction to content carries over into the Caesar novel, with its "well written" and "badly written" segments. This experiment with form, as for Straub/Huillet, is not an exercise for its own sake but to show "the connection between certain ways of acting and their means of expression."[66]

Such a spectrum of diction is found in Straub/Huillet films, especially from *Class Relations* on, with professional polish juxtaposed with lay actors struggling with a foreign language. The typographical experiments of Mallarmé's *Throw of the Dice* also parallels this, with the timbre of voice, duration, and shot framing suggesting the poet's variations of type size.

*Saint Joan* also introduces the figure of a young woman whose revolutionary impulse is expressed in the demand, "I want to know." Like the young man's driving sequences in *History Lessons*, Johanna makes three "descents," reminiscent of popular allegorical morality plays, in order to learn how capital brings economic collapse and hunger via the meat-packing industry.[67] Because she finds the causes of the workers' miserable physical and moral condition in the powers above them, Saint Joan could also answer the criticisms Straub/

Huillet most often receive from well-meaning leftists. Some claim to admire the films personally but argue that the masses will never be able to appreciate them. Saint Joan, too, is told that the workers are debased, to which she replies, "If you show me, Mauler, the baseness of the poor, I will show you the poor's impoverishment."[68] If the "masses" are to change their situation, they have to know there is an alternative.

**Straub/Huillet and Political Modernism**

The relative marginality of Straub/Huillet in treatments of the New German Cinema, with its narrative, "art cinema" label, is based on the supposed "antinarrative" quality of their work as well as their outsider status. This judgment can be traced to the Anglo-American reception of their work since the 1970s, which relied mainly on the critical and theoretical interest in "political modernism." David Bordwell, for example, distinguishes between the narrative ambiguity of the art film and the "pedagogical" montage of what he calls the "interrogative strain in the historical-materialist mode of narration."[69] Elsaesser, too, relegates Straub/Huillet from the main investigation of New German Cinema to an "alternative approach" that connects it to the avant-garde, modernism, and a "postnarrative, 'deconstructive' cinema."[70] But Elsaesser sees the primary project of New German Cinema as a blend of art film, social cinema, and Hollywood variations that, even when transgressive, remains more conventionally committed to narrative than the alternative paradigms of Godard or Straub/Huillet.[71]

This identification of Straub/Huillet and Godard as "Brechtian" filmmakers is certainly important, but it has led to narrowing of the interpretive framework applied to their work.[72] Much recent theoretical writing has shown the virtues and limitations of the explosions of film theory in the 1970s of which the most intense treatment of Straub/Huillet was a part. D. N. Rodowick provides one history of the phenomenon in his book, *The Crisis of Political Modernism.* Rodowick traces the relevance in film theory of the "triangulation of Marxism, semiology, and psychoanalysis" and the theories of Louis Althusser and Lacan, especially as mediated in the journals *Tel Quel* and *Screen.*[73] Rodowick's description of a crisis implies that this theoretical approach in film culture eventually reached an impasse. And Colin MacCabe writes, "It was true that the independent sector had grown, it was true that many of the films made in the later seventies had been influenced by *Screen*, but it was also true that much of that influence had been catastrophic, linking a banal formalism to political didacticism in a formula which had nothing to recommend it—except to initiates."[74]

This pessimistic view, written at the beginning of the Reagan era, has a degree of merit, since what had been a vibrant and critical impulse in independent filmmaking had become elitist, self-absorbed, and overly concerned with formal questions. This situation may be mirrored by the academicization of film studies and film theory that also occurred in that period. These developments may not prove that the "Brechtian project" was a dead end, however, as much as they reflect a defensive and frustrated reaction to the failure (or defeat) of the cultural impulses of the 1960s. Therefore, getting beyond this impasse has been a major project of film theory since the 1980s, especially in feminist inquiries into the audience's pleasurable relations to the cinema.

Rodowick cites Peter Wollen's description of how feminist theory's application of both psychoanalysis and materialism can deal with this dilemma: "Wollen asserts that the lesson learned by Godard and Straub is that for Brecht there is neither a question of abandoning the realm of social reference outside of the play (or film) nor of equating antiillusionism with the suppression of any signified. . . . Wollen claims that Brecht's materialism reconciles antiillusionism and referentiality in his theory of distantiation (the *Verfremdungs-Effekt*) as an activity that encourages a fundamental dissymmetry in the film/viewer relation—the opening of a 'gap in space' between referent, representation, and spectator."[75] Although Straub/Huillet also do not believe in the existence of "film language," the process by which the elements are combined to make up their films indeed suggests parallels with analyses of literature and linguistics. In the final chapters, for instance, we will see connections between the "primitive" forms of Straub/Huillet films and the motion from temporal to spatial relations in Hölderlin's poetry. In the later films of Straub/Huillet, we see more and more the articulation of the elements Elsaesser's book has theorized in the context of early cinema, seeing "the generation of meaning in the film-text itself as a continuous process: one located in the tension between presentation and narration, rather than of formal patterning or a fixed semiotic system."[76]

By looking at the multiplicity of contexts in which Straub/Huillet films function, we shall see that they are not totally to be defined within the impasse reached by political modernism in Rodowick's critique. This impasse was based on a conviction that "theoretical practice" in the form of radical cinema could achieve some sort of political "break," couched in the context of binary oppositions such as "realism and modernism, modernism and semiology, ideological and theoretical practice."[77] Rodowick goes on to propose a way out of this impasse with terms that recall very much what Straub/Huillet's works most strongly encourage: "a practice of reading and . . . an intervention in the institutional formations of knowledge."[78] To the danger that such "reading formations" might return to the assumption of a unified subject, Rodowick contrasts the multiple subject positions posited in Foucault's *Archaeology of Knowledge*, which again are strongly suggestive of the decentering of space and narrative unity in Straub/Huillet films.

> Instead of referring back to *the* synthesis or *the* unifying function of *a* subject, the various enunciative modalities manifest his [sic] dispersion. To the various

statuses, the various sites, the various positions that he [sic] can occupy or be given when making a discourse. To the discontinuity of the planes from which he [sic] speaks. And if these planes are linked by a system of relations, this system is not established by the synthetic activity of a consciousness identical with itself ... but by the specificity of a discursive practice. ... Thus conceived, discourse is not the majestically unfolding manifestation of a thinking, knowing, speaking [reading] subject, but, on the contrary, a totality, in which the dispersion of the subject and his discontinuity with himself may be determined. It is a space of exteriority in which a network of distinct sites is deployed.[79]

This definition of the subject is appropriate to the explosion of the unity of the "author" in Straub/Huillet films, beginning with *Chronicle*, but especially clear in the Schoenberg short and *Fortini/Cani*.[80] The dispersed subject also corresponds to the "invisible audience" constantly suggested by Straub/Huillet films—a postulated subjectivity that necessarily is "exterior" to the text but is also its utopian future audience. At the conclusion of *Crisis of Political Modernism*, Rodowick turns to a "previously unrecognized and untheorized utopian dimension in the discourse of political modernism," the feminist aspect that a number of critics have explored. Rodowick cites Gertrud Koch in this regard.

The aesthetically most advanced films resist any facile reading, not only because they operate with complex aesthetic codes but also because they anticipate an expanded and radicalized notion of subjectivity. What is achieved in a number of these films is a type of subjectivity that transcends any abstract subject-object dichotomy; what is at stake is no longer the redemption of woman as subject over against the male conception of woman as object. What is at stake is less—and at the same time more—than the most general sense of the concept of subject: in the sense that Marx could speak of the working class as the subject of the revolution, in the sense that the women's movement could be the subject of the transformation of sexual politics. The most advanced aesthetic products represent a utopian anticipation of a yet to be fulfilled program of emancipated subjectivity: neither of a class nor of a movement or a collective, but as individuals, as concrete subjects [as] they attempt to insist on their authentic experience.[81]

Rodowick is bothered by the proposition that this "subjectivity" is to be found *in* the work of art and insists on critical and theoretical practice as its agent as well. The utopian aspect of it, however, as "yet to be achieved" must necessarily remain outside both art and theory, in the sum of the uses to which they are put: authentic experience. In the analysis of the individual films to follow, I explore the powerful aesthetic effects Straub/Huillet produce by attempting to reconcile the opposites in these debates, calling attention to the artificial devices by which film constructs meaning while at the same time invoking its immediate relations to the reality of the world. And beyond all this, they assert the connection between formal innovation and political practice in a historical context. In regard to the theoretical debates of the 1970s, this necessity has been observed by both Sylvia Harvey[82] and Colin MacCabe, who writes, "It cannot . . . be stressed too often that theory only and ever makes sense in relation to practice. The practices to which literary theory must always address itself are those that regulate our relation to a literary tradition which is both inheritance and oppression."[83] Straub/Huillet's sustained engagement with the traditions of music, theater, cinema, and literature seek a mediation between inheritance and oppression in the German context.

# 2

# STRAUB/HUILLET, THE NEW LEFT, AND GERMANY

### Straub/Huillet and the New Left

That the debates in film theory since the 1960s continue those among German leftist exiles in the 1930s only adds richness to the relevance of Straub/Huillet's work to the historical and contemporary context of German culture. The contemporary stakes are remarkably similar: the apparent separation of artists and intellectuals from the wishes of "the masses," the "failure of the student left to formulate a progressive aesthetics that had popular support,"[1] and the threatening rise of Fascist movements to fill the gap.

The decline in attention to Straub/Huillet films since the early 1980s, I argue, has to do with many factors unrelated to the films themselves, which have ventured into exciting uncharted film territory in this very period. Backlash against the 1960s and the cultural climate of Ronald Reagan, Margaret Thatcher, and Helmut Kohl brought a chill to leftist counterculture that has yet to subside in the aftermath of the cold war. Political and economic factors have made it more difficult to view *any* foreign films in the United States since the early 1980s, and the distribution of Straub/Huillet films has suffered from this. Finally, the resistance of German critics to the German films Straub/Huillet have made since 1984 has no doubt spilled over into other countries. The most positive reception— even to films as German as the Hölderlin works—has been in France.

Straub/Huillet refuse to accept limitations placed on the cinema by these conditions. Through the separation of the elements of its makeup, they reveal traces of layers of history going back to the beginnings of cinema and the beginning of the modern era; they place alongside each other gestures of political concreteness and utopian otherness; they point to the past with the future in mind. The profound optimism and militancy of even such a nihilistic film as *Antigone*, especially its continuity with their other work, places Straub/Huillet as a counterweight to the melancholy and immobility reached by both film theory and leftist politics since the 1980s.[2]

In film theory, we have seen that they have avoided the impasse of political modernism by not subscribing to the Althusserian conflation of theory and praxis but instead increasing the separation between aesthetic representations and political action. Despite what many have seen as a deconstruction of codes of film communication, they have also not moved in the direction of postmodernism's play of "infinite reversibility." By looking at their work as part of a larger formal and cultural/political continuity, one can perhaps step away from a melancholy theoretical impasse of postmodernism as well, of which Jean Narboni has observed, "Everything is leveled out in a sort of desperation that is a little melancholy. Obviously, the Straubs are everything but postmodern. In their work are themes, contents to which they hold hard as iron—political, cosmic, mystical contents."[3]

We have seen the affirmative function of melancholy in the context of postwar German history and the New German Cinema, and I argue that this melancholy has led to a certain complicity with anti-sixties backlash on the Left as well. Thus both Straub/Huillet and Godard are attacked for stubbornly refusing to adapt to the needs of the popular marketplace. This, rather than any specific discussion of their films, has been the main objection to Straub/Huillet's post-seventies work from both Wim Wenders and Alexander Kluge, for instance.[4]

The vehement rejection of Straub/Huillet films on the part of leftist or former leftist critics seems to be part of the phenomenon of wallowing in failure as a cultural unifier. The utopian gesture of connecting Hölderlin's Empedocles, for instance, with the "fête permanente" of the 1960s is felt to be unseemly by former student radicals, who, as Jürgen Habermas observed, have accommodated themselves with the "end of utopias" in the 1970s.[5] This revolt against utopia, which feeds an already pervasive animosity toward the sixties, has thwarted the former receptivity to aesthetic wishes to "have it all." A portion of Gilberto Perez's explanation for Godard's recent lack of an audience would apply at least as strongly to Straub/Huillet.

> If Godard is out of fashion nowadays, so, in many quarters, is beauty. Postmodernists mostly disown it. As a quality men see in women ("Beauty is pleasure regarded as the quality of a thing," said Santayana), feminists largely discountenance it. The Thatcherite aesthetician Roger Scruton thinks it too imprecise a notion for meaningful consideration; but an aesthetician who cannot talk about beauty had better find another line of work. On the left, beauty is suspected both of being elitist, the plaything of a privileged few, and of being a whore seductively selling the ideology of the ruling class. In the puritanism of today, a puritanism

on the right and on the left, beauty is to be approached with the protective crucifix of (right or left) political correctness.[6]

Martin Schaub, writing in 1976, takes the most extreme position against Straub/Huillet's claim to political relevance for their aesthetic method. "With *Othon* (1969) Straub and Huillet lost their footing in the base that sustained them. No matter how much they insist they have shown *Othon* in French factories and that it was the workers who best understood the revolutionary message of this film (in form and content), I have trouble believing it. And *Moses and Aaron* (1975) also seems to me to be more of a demonstration of method than a lever in the political struggle Straub still maintains he is waging."[7] After condemning Straub/Huillet films as "pedagogical" and "radically rationalistic," Schaub goes so far as a biting personal attack: "The development Straub has demonstrated in his life in past years is unsettling. I would term it 'loss of reality.' *Moses and Aaron* is dedicated to Holger Meins, and somehow I can compare Straub's [*sic*] development with that of the Red Army Faction. The Federal Republic, or even 'liberal' Europe, seems to compel such developments."[8]

The return to interrupted traditions in cinema, culture, and politics is required in order to break out of this paralysis. For this reason, Straub/Huillet deny that their films are non-narrative or anticinematic, as if the overthrow of traditional forms were their primary goal, as if radical aesthetics were their point of departure. This interpretation of the process is entirely backward and imputes to Straub/Huillet just the kind of formalistic pseudoradicalism with which the culture industry readily titillates itself. Walter Benjamin was perhaps not the first to note the ability of the culture industry to absorb criticism and turn it into just another disposable product.[9] Just as subsidized institutions of "high culture" allow privileged groups to cultivate the illusion that they do not participate in the culture industry, a destructive avant-garde serves to perpetuate the illusion of flexibility and freedom.[10] In a wasteful society, destructiveness is highly marketable as an aesthetic principle. Therefore, avant-garde art that merely negates the conventions and traditions of "high culture" still relies on this same artificial isolation of art, otherwise such taunts would be uninteresting. This kind of avant-garde is only apparently political. As Dana Polan puts it,

> This is why contemporary culture can accommodate formally subversive art: as long as such an art does not connect its formal subversion to an analysis of social situations, such art becomes little more than a further example of the disturbances that go on as we live through a day. And a work of art which defeats formal expectations does not lead to protest against a culture that deals continually in the defeating of expectations.[11]

In this regard, the statements of Straub/Huillet on their work have a rather conservative tone. They constantly stress how little is really new in the methods they use, how the traditions of cinema are indeed present in everything they do. Straub has expressed his aversion to the catchword "revolutionary" and insists, "we move forward only in very small steps."[12]

It is also backward to assume that Straub/Huillet came to their aesthetic innovations by intending to make political films. Political relevance is an effect of their work, not a cause. One need not have a political reason to depart from aesthetic norms. Such departure from the norm only develops political implications when it is understood that *adhering* to the norms is also a political act. As Straub puts it, echoing Godard, he does not try to make political films; he makes films politically.[13]

The moral claim Straub/Huillet make, then, is closer to André Bazin's description of neorealism than avant-garde experimentation or culinary "visual pleasure." Rolf Aurich cites Bazin: "To respect the real means in fact not to multiply its appearances; on the contrary it means to free it of all that is inessential in order to reach completeness in simplicity." Aurich then goes on, regarding *Too Early, Too Late* and *Empedocles*, "These are films that owe their richness precisely to their lack of ornament and their strict handwriting; these films reach that point where neorealism arrives at classical abstraction and universality (Bazin) and then extend it with substantial innovations. Huillet/Straub extend the neorealist film; they are therefore advanced moralists."[14]

One way out of the impasse of political modernism might be to examine what intellectuals to the East and South have made out of the same European heritage in the context of other political struggles over "realism" and the avant-garde. A lot of theoretical work in Eastern Europe and the German Democratic Republic (GDR), for instance, virtually unknown in the West, developed around the work of Bertolt Brecht, Georg Lukács, or the Russian formalists.[15] But, as Straub/Huillet imply with most of their films, true change can only come with the natural replacement of one generation with another. This perhaps will also bring a new reception of Straub/Huillet. An example would be the Parallel Cinema and *sinefantom* in Russia, just becoming known in the West. A new film journal in Hanover, *filmwärts*, has also self-consciously dedicated much space to a renewal of interest in Straub/Huillet in Germany. They have done so specifically in regard to the "negative" national identity we have located in the New German Cinema. For instance, a note on Reinhard Hauff's *Stammheim*, a film about the trial of the Baader-Meinhof terrorists, puts it in the context of "thoughts on Germany." The film's clichéd presentation of political violence is contrasted with Norbert Elias's "Thoughts on the Federal Republic,"[16] which accounts for the violence and radicalism of West German political culture via "the so-called economic miracle, fascism in Germany and above all the irreconcilability of the pre-war and post-war generations." Here the *filmwärts* editor sees a connection to Straub/Huillet's *Not Reconciled*, which is then recommended, along with Kluge's *Patriot*, as a correction to the *Stammheim* view of German history.[17]

In general, then, it is important to distinguish radical politics from radical aesthetics, not to use one as an alibi for the other or to assume that they are the same thing. Politics and aesthetics, like theory and practice, must be seen as concretely distinct but necessary to one another. The nature and development of the radicalism of Straub/Huillet must be traced carefully and concretely, since it consists, in the main, of a materialist approach to filmmaking.

Brecht, for instance, like Straub/Huillet, did not believe in innovation for its own sake but instead appealed constantly to classical traditions. He was highly distressed by the idea that his innovations might later be adopted for purely formalistic reasons, as indeed has often been the case.[18] As he wrote in his *Arbeitsjournal,*

> since i am an innovator in my field, some always scream that i am a formalist. they don't find the old forms in my works, and what is worse, they find new ones. then they think it is the forms which interest me. but i have found that i care rather little about form. at different times i have studied the old forms of poetry, short story, drama and theater and have only given them up when they stood in the way of what i wanted to say.[19]

The above could apply as well to Straub/Huillet as to Brecht with little modification. The phrase "what i wanted to say" illuminates the distinction made earlier regarding Straub/Huillet's opposition to film "language." Of course, this does not mean that the filmmakers withdraw from the film's impact entirely and leave the audience merely provoked and confused by an endlessly equivocal work of art. The renunciation of the conventions of film language is meant to avoid equivocation, while documenting the reality of contradiction. It is an alternative to the deception and manipulation of the viewer, which convey little "meaning" as far as the world outside the film is concerned. Indeed, such manipulation subtracts more from the viewers' experience than it adds. A similar opinion is reflected by Brecht's appeal for the simplicity and freedom of classicism.

> on abbreviation in the classical style: if i leave out enough on a page, i receive for the single word "night"—for instance in the phrase "as night came"—a full measure of imagination on the part of the reader. inflation is the death of every economy. it would be best for the words to dismiss their entourage entirely and meet each other with all the dignity they can generate from within themselves. it is quite wrong to say that the classicists forget the senses of the reader; on the contrary, they count on them.[20]

The classicism of Straub/Huillet films similarly consists of an exclusion of the unnecessary, the reproduction of feelings or pieces of information that the viewer already possesses. For this reason, it is wrong to say that Straub/Huillet films are non-narrative. They merely reduce narrative to its simplest form and refuse to subordinate visual narrative to that of a text. Conventional, commercial film is "pornographic," in Straub's opinion, and he describes the process of reducing the Brecht or Böll texts as that of removing all that is merely anecdotal. In regard to naturalism, Straub/Huillet also speak of "inflation." Like Brecht, they strive for realism, but their means are different from Brecht's. Straub commented in 1971, "I think that more and more the work we've got to do—though I have some reservations—is to make films which radically eliminate art, so that there is no equivocation. This may lose us some people, but it is essential to eliminate all the artistic, filmic surface to bring people face to face with the ideas in their naked state."[21]

Film language and film art are the "old forms" that stand in the way of ideas, of aesthetic confrontations with reality. The behavior of the artist, in stepping aside from industrialized production to rejoin an older history, is necessarily negative, reductive. The artist takes the revolutionary "tiger's leap" of history, as Benjamin called it, dialectics in practice. Arnold Schoenberg described his idea of rejoining artistic tradition in a similar way: "There is only one way to connect directly to the past and to tradition: to begin everything over again, as if all that had gone before were false; to grapple once again with the essence of the thing most exactly, instead of reducing oneself to developing the technique of a preexistent material."[22]

Here we arrive at a definition of artistic activity much closer to Adorno's than to Brecht's. But the relationship of the artist to history and to social change is a crucial issue for both of them, as well as for Straub/Huillet. If the artist can only produce authentic art by stepping outside of the reigning tradition, by reinventing language and form, then the bonds are severed which connect artist and audience. Rather than the language of a past culture, art now must speak the language of a culture that can only be imagined, a utopia. But the price for the freedom to create the new language is the surrender of the hope of transforming society by way of the old.

Thus Brecht and Adorno arrive by different routes at the same dilemma, with a similar hope. Both rejected a mimetic theory of art in favor of one projected toward the future. But this departure from mimesis leaves the future audience of art unimaginable, abstract, because any image of it would be a return to mimesis and an affirmation of the current order. Neither theorist was able to describe the prospect of a step beyond this contradiction, least of all in the medium of film. The films of Straub/Huillet, however, point toward this striven-for unity of theory and practice as well as the obstacles to it in contemporary Western society. The classicism of form and the simplicity of content remove from Straub/Huillet films the expectation of an image of society. Yet the historical materials, the aesthetic forms, and the contradictions between these and images from contemporary reality project a movement toward such a future society. Indeed, film only functions as a medium through its ability to suggest a world through a glimpse of a few fragments. The audience for such works is not the future society in which these contradictions will be resolved, however, but those who dare to imagine it now. Brecht claimed, "The alienation effect [*der V-Effekt*] is a social measure."[23] One might now conclude, materialist filmmaking does not replace social action; it requires it. The challenge is to find the audience of the future in the cultural marketplace of the present.

**Straub/Huillet and the New German Cinema**

Although Straub/Huillet have made a total of nine films based at least in part on German texts since *The Bridegroom, the Commedienne, and the Pimp* (1968), not one of them contains a depiction of postwar or contemporary Germany. The irony of this is driven home by the exceptions: In *Class Relations*, contemporary Hamburg is the setting for most of Kafka's *Amerika*, the land of promise that turns out to be just as corrupt as the old world. This underscores both their discontent with contemporary society and their search for German cultural traditions unscarred by fascism and war. Although I will argue that their taking German culture into exile in this way has been unique in the German cinema, the historical dilemma out of which it arises has been a central concern of the New German Cinema.

The critical literature on New German Cinema does not reflect this, however. Although they continued to make "German" films after 1969 and their work continued to receive attention in *Filmkritik* and the major German newspapers, Straub/Huillet became somewhat marginal to the phenomenon of the New German Cinema, as the major surveys of the movement confirm.[24] Despite their deep involvement with Germany since the 1960s, they are also not treated in the books of Santner or Kaes on German history, memory, and film. Even Elsaesser, despite his references to their relations to New German Cinema, does not write a section on "Straub/Huillet's Germany."[25] An important goal of this book is to demonstrate the significance of Straub/Huillet's work as a cinematic confrontation of German history and culture. Although they were not signatories of the Oberhausen Manifesto, which demanded public funding of film production by young directors, Straub/Huillet's film *Machorka-Muff* represents an early milestone of the Young German Cinema, precursor of the New German Cinema. Since these early years of attempts at revitalizing West German film production, the continuity of Straub/Huillet's involvement with the German cinema and German culture is matched by few, if any, other filmmakers.

Kaes, for instance, writes of Straub/Huillet's first two films as important beginnings for the New German Cinema's critical concern with German history, particularly the Nazi past. The significance of history to problems of German identity since 1945 and to the self-definition of the New German Cinema can hardly be overemphasized.[26] But not only were Straub/Huillet among the first to confront German history in innovative film work, their work offers a refreshing, militant, and optimistic contrast to the nostalgic and melancholy aspect of *Hitler, A Film from Germany*, *Heimat*, and *Germany in Autumn* and the New German Cinema's relation to the violent German past.

Along with their relevance to new approaches to German history in the 1960s, Straub/Huillet were also seen from the beginning as part of a movement to revolutionize film form and reform the film industry. In the 1960s this was seen more as a practical political phenomenon than as a theoretical project alone, part of the student movement in Europe, but it led to specific efforts for reform in film criticism and public film policy. In the decade preceding the student revolts of 1967–1968, much critical cultural activity in West Germany had challenged the continuities of the World War II generation on a variety of fronts. The beginning of film reform and the "Young German Cinema" is traced to the Oberhausen Manifesto (1962). Thomas Elsaesser, Eric Rentschler, and others have demonstrated the centrality of funding mechanisms to the emergence of the New German Cinema.[27] Straub/Huillet's search for funding for *Chronicle of Anna Magdalena Bach*, outlined in chapter 3, is exemplary of this development. The work Straub/Huillet did in West Germany, from *Machorka-Muff* to *Chronicle*, summarizes their connection to and distance from the Young German Cinema and the emerging New German Cinema. By the time New German Cinema was becoming recognized, they had left the Federal Republic for Rome.

Straub/Huillet were somewhat distinct from the Young German Cinema from the outset, since they already had a feature film project (Bach), had completed a short film, and were able to finance their second film, *Not Reconciled*, without the state subsidies that the Oberhausen group demanded. They thus do not belong, as James Franklin asserted, to "a post-Oberhausen second generation who were able to take advantage of the film environment created by the Oberhausen group."[28] It was only their third film, the Bach film, that received any support from the Kuratorium Junger Deutscher Film, and this was only late in the process and after a long struggle. That Straub/Huillet had begun their "revolution" in German cinema without the manifesto perhaps derives from their consistent assertion that they should have a place in the *commercial* film industry and their rejection of the "art film ghetto." This is more of the French than the German model, since the New Wave had been possible in the context of the commercial film industry, without going the German route of film schools and federal subsidy programs.[29] The German route had to be different, as Harun Farocki has observed, since there was virtually no functioning commercial industry there.[30] The industry was at such a low point that in 1961, for instance, no film could be found deserving of the Federal Film Prize.[31] Still, Straub/Huillet produced two films in the early 1960s before the Young German Cinema got on its feet. That they had done this, and that they were French, perhaps contributed to Straub's being quite celebrated among film rebels in West Germany.

The journal *Filmkritik* is a good barometer of this phenomenon. Its development parallels film reception, production, and theory in West Germany until both the journal and the New German Cinema "end" in the 1980s. *Filmkritik* began in 1957, and the main authors of its critical approach were Enno Patalas, Wilfried Berghahn, Ulrich Gregor, Theodor Kotulla, and Frieda Grafe. The eclecticism of its concerns is important to note, since it contrasts sharply with later developments in film theory and reflects a formative period in Straub/Huillet's development. In the early years, both before and after the Berlin Wall, *Filmkritik* had a cosmopolitan outlook on film, spanning from the socialist countries to the East (including the GDR) to the legacy of Italian neorealism and the French New Wave. *Filmkritik* was the main location of discussion of Godard, for instance. Even the slogan most often linked to the Oberhausen Manifesto, "Papa's cinema is dead," was a translation from French which had appeared in a report from Paris in the journal.[32] *Filmkritik* had developed out of that attempt at a film-theoretical journal, *Film 56*, and so on, which had marked the new reception of Brecht, Benjamin, and Adorno that began with the publication of their work in the late 1950s and early 1960s.[33]

*Filmkritik* enthusiastically marked each young filmmaker's success in the assault against the cinema of the old guard. Three such milestones were achieved by Straub/Huillet, Kluge, and Werner Herzog in the mid-1960s, which perhaps accounts for their being grouped together, for example, in the Hanser film volume *Herzog/Kluge/Straub* of 1976. By coincidence, both Herzog's *Signs of Life* and Straub/Huillet's *Chronicle of Anna Magdalena Bach* had been invited to the Cannes Week of the Critics in 1968,[34] perhaps the only thing these filmmakers ever had in common. Kluge had been hailed at Venice two years earlier for *Yesterday Girl*. This had been a political victory as well, since the film had been invited by the festival, not entered by the West German Filmreferent des Auswärtigen Amtes. This West German cultural functionary, Herr Rowas, had been the same one to protest the screening of Resnais's *Night and Fog* in 1957.[35]

Although at first skeptical of *Not Reconciled*, *Filmkritik* soon began to put this film, as well as *Chronicle*, at the top of its rating chart. The popular agitation that was necessary to get Kuratorium support for the Bach film was matched by audience enthusiasm for *Bridegroom*. When the jury of the Mannheim film festival refused to award the grand prize, the assembled audience at midnight discussions afterward successfully demanded that the mayor award the DM 10,000 prize to *Bridegroom*.[36] That Straub/Huillet's work belonged to a new era in West German film production was confirmed, like the later New German Cinema, by resonance outside Germany. After the 1965 London Film Festival, the Frankfurt newspaper cited the *London Times*' view that *Not Reconciled* was the most hopeful sign for the German film in twenty years.[37] French and U.S. responses were similarly positive. Richard Roud brought the film, the first of many by Straub/Huillet, to the New York Film Festival.[38]

As the New German Cinema began to receive notice in the late 1960s and early 1970s, Straub/Huillet were less central to the phenomenon compared to the impact of their films of the 1960s. They had certainly had an influence on the West German film scene—on critics such as Patalas and Grafe and on directors such as Kluge and Wenders. Fassbinder, who is seen with the Action-Theater in *Bridegroom*, said he learned to direct by observing Straub.[39] Wolfram Schütte, writing of Fassbinder's prodigious output in the early 1970s, called him the "newcomer awakened by Straub,"[40] and Franklin notes the influence of Straub/Huillet on his early work especially.[41]

The directors they had been closest to, however, did not become internationally recognized with the New German Cinema, such as those *Filmkritik* had called the "New Munich Group" in a feature of May 1966: Peter Nestler, Eckhart Schmidt, Rudolf Thome, Max Zihlmann, and Klaus Lemke.[42] Nestler, whom Straub once called the "best filmmaker in Germany"—and who appeared in Straub/Huillet's Schoenberg short—emigrated to Sweden. One reason these filmmakers may have been eclipsed by the New German Cinema is the fact that they were either documentarists or attempted a German version of the "cinephile" genre approach of the French cinema. The documentarists still receive little recognition in Germany or abroad, and the genre approach was overshadowed by the auteur approach of the Oberhausener.[43] One colleague from the Munich years who turned to feature films did become recognized, however: Wim Wenders. Perhaps as an homage to this connection, he includes a shot from Straub/Huillet's Bach film in his *Wrong Move*.

Straub/Huillet's work from the late sixties on, and their departure from Germany, separated them from both the emerging New German Cinema and what Elsaesser calls the "double impasse" reached by the Oberhausener. One side of the impasse had been the bureaucratization of film culture by the subsidy system. The other was the contradictory development of the Autorenfilm, which became the basis for the renown of the New German Cinema: the filmmaker's individual self-expression becomes a state-subsidized cultural commodity, "the author as aesthetic expert."[44] Despite its partial benefit from this same subsidy system, *Chronicle of Anna Magdalena Bach* was "an act of resistance" to it, as well as "a formulation and a critique of the *Autorenfilm* and its concept of the artist."[45]

Another ill effect of Oberhausen's wish to replace the film industry and subsidize the film artist was its often explicit contempt for the existing German public. Many critics identify Straub/Huillet with this attitude, to which they were in fact opposed.[46] Their formal rigor has been seen as ascetic and antipleasure, with such terms as "monklike," "saintfigure," "cult," "exercise," and "schoolmasterlike."[47]

Such a rigid view of Straub/Huillet's formal radicalism also obscures their important links to the New German Cinema. The shift toward an engagement with Hollywood norms and genres in the New German Cinema—the "search for an audience" Elsaesser describes—is partly a response to the Oberhausen dilemma. Straub/Huillet have consistently maintained a French tradition of engagement with the classical cinema, but they did not follow the path of either Kluge, who looked to statistical profiles of film audiences, or Fassbinder and Wenders, who explicitly adapted Hollywood role models.

## Straub/Huillet's Germany

Three concerns of the New German Cinema connect recent critical works on its relation to postwar German culture: its role in *Vergangenheitsbewältigung*, coming to terms with the past, and the quest for a "usable" past as the foundation for a German national identity; its attempt to define itself and its audience against or in relation to American cinema (Hollywood) and popular culture; and the Left project of the student movement to break with the domination present in both of the other two—the guilt of the World War II generation and the "colonization" by the American culture industry.

Mourning, melancholy, loss, and numerous related terms mark both the New German Cinema and the general relation to history in West Germany in recent years.[48] Santner and Kaes especially have connected this emphasis with the role of film as "mourning work." The purpose of the mourning process, as Santner puts it, is "the construction of a viable, empowering legacy."[49] Evocations of the past certainly predominate in the films Kaes and Santner focus on, and the challenge to a "viable legacy" posed by the Nazi past is seen by Elsaesser to be at the core of the "German identity" that has emerged in the period of the New German Cinema.

The nature of this empowerment and the definition of this subject or identity are problematic, however. Santner, Kaes, and Elsaesser all make clear that the mourning work going on in New German Cinema is not for the victims of Nazism but for the legitimacy of the German identity itself. The images and emotions that are evoked are thus connected to the experiences and memories of the Nazi era that have been tainted by guilt. The individual psychological metaphor of mourning work suggests that Germany needs to work through the damage to its collective ego caused by the exposure of the "evil" of Nazism and the removal of its object of identification—particularly the father figure Hitler. The goal of such a process for individuals, as Santner points out, is "empowerment" and the ability to live on without being debilitated by guilt.

The problem with the collective version of this process as seen in film is that it accepts the "biographical continuity" between Nazi Germany and "Germany" as such. It also accepts as right the identification of the collective emotions and ideologically charged images of Nazism with the collective memory of present-day Germany. In other words, it accepts the colonization of memory by Nazism. There is no other alternative.

Since this is not just memory, but mourning, the quality of loss is also necessary. But the "loss" of the carefree identification with Germany through Nazi images of it is an aesthetic one; the "loss" of the power associated with Nazi Germany has not taken place. Indeed, Germany is today more powerful than ever in its history. So to see a collective need for mourning in order to achieve some kind of "empowerment" can only exist in the realm of aesthetic identification with the state and not with the "power" of the state in itself. Straub/Huillet's approach to Germany is the inverse to this. Whereas there we see the problem as a cultural rupture in the face of political and economic continuities, Straub/Huillet propose cultural continuities as a form of resistance to political continuity. Whereas the New German Cinema's love of Germany is abstract and mediated by images, the love of Germany present in all of Straub/Huillet's German films is a concrete, experiential one.

In their interviews regarding Germany, they have always woven together these aspects of culture, memory, and everyday life. For instance, when questioned about the sources of their interest in German culture, they rejected the importance of early education (as Roud had stressed) in favor of their experience of living in West Germany for ten years. Before that, Straub's only relation to Germany had been the Nazi annexation of his hometown of Metz, which had engendered mostly resistance to the language and the conviction that the Bach film could only be shot in Germany. Beyond that, Huillet stresses, "The relations to Germany, they came mostly afterward, as we were living there."[50]

These relations to Germany, in contrast to the centrality of cultural images to other New German filmmakers, arose out of their particular practical and political struggles of living there.

> HUILLET: The relation to Germany is not a cultural one. But in Germany, because we lived there, and because the violence in Germany is perhaps greater or more open . . .
>
> STRAUB: . . . and we had to fight for ten years to get together the financing for the Bach film. Those are the relations we have to Germany! Much more than the so-called cultural ones.
>
> HUILLET: And to the class struggle. Germany is a good school for that.[51]

However, Huillet and Straub polemically refer to a continuity with German cinema and culture before the Nazis, partly as a foil to the Young German Cinema's claim to originality and the notorious break between the New German Cinema and German cultural role models. For instance, the following cat-and-mouse game between Straub/Huillet and an interviewer asking for opinions on contemporary filmmakers:

> JONATHAN ROSENBAUM: . . . Just which contemporary film makers do you admire?

>           *STRAUB:*  I don't know, Mizoguchi. No, I mean it, but he's dead.
>     *PETER GIDAL:*  Does that answer for both of you?
> *DANIÈLE HUILLET:*  Yes.
>           *STRAUB:*  Then at the other end of the ideological scale, it would be John Ford. Of course there is Renoir and lots of people, Fritz Lang.
> *JONATHAN ROSENBAUM:*  I was thinking more about film makers now.
>          *HUILLET:*  He means the living. Lang is still living, Renoir too.[52]

Straub goes on to speak of his continuing admiration of Godard, but the point of diverting the question from contemporary innovation to past models is telling. Similarly, he spoke of his polemical exchange with Alexander Kluge in the context of the Young German Cinema and Kluge's "caricature of Brecht":

> Kluge always goes on about the film which is created in the minds of the spectators; I don't believe it. Then I react like Rivette and state that film—let's not quibble over the words—is only based on fascination, and that it only touches people, and touches them deeply, when it is based on fascination, i.e., the opposite of distance or participation or some such thing, that the traditional attitudes of people . . . one never invents very much, Renoir said, not like Kluge, with whom I quarreled in Mannheim. He climbed onto the stage and said, well, what we are doing is new. We make films which are going to be created in the minds of the spectators. That is completely new and nobody has done it before. My films are like—and then he saw me down in the audience—my films are like those of Straub, for instance—then I was furious and stood up and said, the things I do are not new at all, they are traditional.[53]

We will look at the different Brechtianism of Kluge later on, but for the moment, the central aspect here is Straub/Huillet's respect for the institution of cinema *against* that of politics and its mystification of history. It was in the same interview that Straub asserted, citing the end of *Fort Apache*, that "John Ford is the most Brechtian of all filmmakers, because he shows things that make people think, damn it, is that true or not."[54] This contrasts sharply with the Young German Cinema's contempt for the audience that had been lost by the collapse of the German film industry, an audience that Fritz Lang had still addressed in the 1950s. For the lived experience of this audience, Straub has not contempt but great warmth and sympathy.

> *Der Tiger von Eschnapur* and *Das indische Grabmal* are the only films that are superproductions without being superproducts, which are made with all the

money that he had at his disposal without creating a smokescreen. And which nevertheless are not made *against* money; because now, that's easier to do: Godard, in his evolution, has discovered that it is necessary to make oppositional films. But for a man of Fritz Lang's generation, this wasn't possible, an idea like that. And yet he succeeded in making these two films, where he really gave something to the Germans who had been dying of hunger for so many years—since '33 and even before '33, up to the Currency Reform for which the leftist intellectuals had so much contempt, until the moment when the people would begin again to be able to know a little what it meant to live: this is what has been called the German economic miracle. For a good many people, this was the first time that they finally revived, that they were eating normally—of course there was the speculation and all the rest, okay. (The arrival of the consumer society, that's the negative aspect of it.) But Fritz Lang, at this moment, made something for the people which was a gift, let's say, of gold. . . . The producer was really eager to make a golden calf. Fritz Lang made a film.[55]

This attitude to the audience separates Straub/Huillet from the avant-garde more than anything else, since they expect the audience to understand their films without the mediation of specialists.

### Kluge, Reitz, and Syberberg

Despite their similarities, one must therefore distinguish the "Brechtianism" of Straub/Huillet and Alexander Kluge. Many of their techniques are similar, to the extent that Kaes's descriptions of them are almost interchangeable.[56] But the author's relation to the film's materials is quite different. One similarity Kaes notes is the presence of printed texts in both Kluge and Straub/Huillet. But the gesture of inserting title cards to break up the narrative calls attention to the director's subjectivity. Like Kluge's voice-over, the cards are another intrusion of the author's voice, consistent with the "tone that hovers between elegy and irony." Although apparently inviting the spectator to take apart the work as well, the author's position is clearly superior, if not condescending.[57]

Straub/Huillet make no such pretense at not being in control of what is on the screen—"[the filmmaker] is still an author"[58]—but the attitude of this author is different in the two methods. When Straub/Huillet include printed or handwritten texts in their films, they may punctuate the narrative as in silent cinema, but they are never title cards authored by the filmmakers. Instead, all the texts revealed in their films have other authors, and the gesture of including them leans the film from narrative in the direction of documentary. This is the effect in both *Chronicle* and *Machorka-Muff*. More extreme cases are the less narrative forms of the Schoenberg short and *Fortini/Cani*. Here Straub/Huillet present printed documents in a series along with other types of documentation and do not call special attention to the author's gesture. They do, however, call attention to the presence of a cinematic author, as the camera tilts to allow the spectator to read. This does not put emphasis on the author but on the technology; the viewer becomes aware that the duration of reading needs to be coordinated with the impersonal duration of the camera movement and that someone had to do this.

Another partial similarity is the contemporary fictional character in search of history, as found in *History Lessons* (Kaes cites only the Brecht novel)[59] and in the person of Gabi Teichert, the history teacher in Kluge's *The Patriot*. In both cases, a fictional character is placed in a "documentary" setting, creating a tension around the blurring of distinctions. The tension is not the result of blurring the distinction in *History Lessons*, since it is only in the spectator's memory that the young man driving through Rome is a "character." In the driving shots, on the cinematic level, he is only a person driving through Rome—no more or less fictional than the people on the streets around him. The case of Gabi Teichert is quite different, however. This fictional character actually goes to a Social Democratic Party Congress and poses questions to actual politicians who are expected to answer. Thome, one of Straub/Huillet's Munich colleagues from the 1960s, found this objectionable. "If a filmmaker pokes fun at the people in front of the camera at their expense, that's the worst thing for me," Thome writes of the scene of Teichert and the politicians. "I had to leave, I could not bear to watch it, seeing people filmed like that."[60] The levels of reality—the camera, the "author," the fictional character, the actor, and the "real world"—are collapsed here, while Straub/Huillet keep them carefully separate.

The ambiguous yet authoritative presence of the author in constructing this confrontation of fiction and reality puts in doubt the Brechtian quality of Kluge's work entirely. As Elsaesser writes, "Kluge's protagonists are invariably the appendages of a discourse that is rarely, if ever, capable of questioning its own authority and, instead, by letting voice-over dominate the image, subjects the characters to the tyranny of the commentary." Kluge's superior attitude to the characters and the audience, Elsaesser notes, has also been criticized by Handke and Wenders. Handke's reaction to Kluge's 1968 film, *Artists under the Big Top: Disoriented*, might also apply to his more recent collage work for television: "One constantly recognizes things: names, faces, people, personalities, dramaturgical clichés, phrases, but above all attitudes [Einstellungen]; attitudes of the film towards the things and the people it shows. . . . Due to the fact that the words are formulated, formulaic, unambiguous and not playfully quoted . . . they make the pictures into picture-puzzles instead of leaving them as images."[61]

It is the ambiguity of the author's intervention that is the problem here. Straub/Huillet, partly at Huillet's insistence, have progressively tried to let the materials determine the articulation rather than an author's gesture, calling attention as much to itself as to them. At issue for Straub/Huillet, for instance, was the inclusion of an expressionist painting by Georges Rouault in *Chronicle*. It was Straub's attempt at connecting the sufferings of Bach to another artist's work and, by extension, to the filmmaker's hand. Huillet found this self-indulgent, and their work has shown no such interventions since.

When Kluge makes a collage out of the fragments of war and suffering in German history, it is not clear whether the memory and suffering he is evoking is or is not his own: authorship is evident, but it evades responsibility for its position in the construction (as in the fictional interviews). Where Straub/Huillet use memory to refer to an absent German subjectivity, Kluge uses memory to evoke the suffering body. But even when the protagonist is a dead soldier's knee, as in *Die Patriotin* (*The Female Patriot*, 1979), the impact of the film's fragmentations is to awaken memories of some unified "German" subjectivity. And as Kaes points out, to speak of *German* suffering in such a one-sided way reveals "a highly ambivalent political agenda covertly at work in the film."[62]

A similar problem is even more evident in the films of Edgar Reitz and Hans Jürgen Syberberg. Santner sees a necessary and positive value in their work.

> Reitz and Syberberg, in their films *Heimat* and *Our Hitler*, respectively, produced the two most ambitious attempts by recent German artists to create works of national elegiac art: works that make use of the procedures and resources of mourning to constitute something like a German self-identity in the wake of the catastrophic turns of recent German history. In each case the task of mourning involves the labor of recollecting the stranded objects of a cultural inheritance fragmented and poisoned by an unspeakable horror.[63]

Although Brechtian theater has been a major influence on Syberberg's theatricalization of the cinema, both he and Reitz show a good deal more affinity for Wagner in the grand scale of their works and the development of leitmotifs of reminiscence over long periods of film time. Syberberg's *Our Hitler* (*Hitler, ein Film aus Deutschland*, 1977), spans seven hours, while Reitz's *Heimat* (1984) consists of eleven parts for a total over fifteen hours. The sequel, *Die zweite Heimat*, is some twenty-six hours long.

The difference between Straub/Huillet and these filmmakers is their relation to memory, and this is a major one, given the recent past in Germany. Straub/Huillet's Bach film was once criticized for being a sort of family album, composed of Anna Magdalena's memories of her husband. As we shall see, the poignancy of this aspect lies, in Straub/Huillet's work, in the unbridgeable distance the film carefully inscribes between the documents of Bach's life and the memory they might evoke in the living. *Heimat*, by contrast, literally employs the metaphor of the family album and unselfconsciously invites the viewer to be part of the family remembering the past in a German village.

Syberberg's films differ from those of Straub/Huillet most strikingly in his use of highly artificial studio staging. While Straub/Huillet's cinematic simplicity evokes the early cinema of F. W. Murnau, Stroheim, Griffith, and ultimately the Lumières, Syberberg conjures up the specters of the great artists of the Golden Age of cinema in a magic act more reminiscent of the other early film inventor, Georges Méliès.

Syberberg's collage technique, a veritable séance in the Hitler film, has led critics to link him to postmodernism. His works are at their most effective in juxtaposing anachronistic fragments from all periods of German cultural history and a multitude of genres and media, from the Punch and Judy show to Wehrmacht radio broadcasts. But Syberberg is not a postmodernist because he actually longs for the past he is mourning, as is clearly revealed by the rather consistent authorial voice in his films and his conservative, idiosyncratic (if not outright reactionary) essays.

This elegiac quality in Reitz and Syberberg, which I would call nostalgia, is not to be found in Straub/Huillet. The process of mourning, which supposedly is to overcome melancholia, is a constituent part of the aesthetic of Reitz's and Syberberg's work. In Straub/Huillet's films there is no mourning, no melancholy: they simply show the fragments of the world that is lost. The distance to the past is inviolable.

The result is an apolitical quietism in *Heimat* and *Our Hitler*, compared to the resistance to authority found in Bach, Antigone, or even Schoenberg and Brecht and Böll, with all their shortcomings. Certainly there is more of a cultural inheritance to be found in exile than in the soliloquies of Syberberg's narrators about the banality of Americanized German culture or Reitz's accusation that the Americans, with the television film *Holocaust*, had "stolen our history." Both Reitz's and Syberberg's work reveal the postwar mistrust of returned exiles that is thematized in *Not Reconciled*. They have such a nostalgia for the past that it obscures their view of Germany "as it is." Straub/Huillet films, however, show the love of country expressed by going into exile, as seen in *Not Reconciled* and *Empedocles* and in Antigone's speech on Heimat (by Brecht, the returning exile):

> Falsch ist's. Erde ist Mühsal. Heimat ist nicht nur
> Erde, noch Haus nur. Nicht, wo einer Schweiß vergoß
> Nicht das Haus, das hilflos dem Feuer entgegensieht
> Nicht, wo er den Nacken gebeugt, nicht das heißt er Heimat.[64]

The project of recollecting the fragments of a German identity is necessarily asymmetrical, since it is not possible to bring back to life the many human victims of fascism, but it is quite possible to revive the forces that murdered them. Indeed, it is the continuity of some of these political and institutional forces with which the world is still confronted.

In his discussion of the films of Reitz and Syberberg, Santner seeks an alternative in postmodern "playful nomadism" and in the necessary mortification of language found in Benjamin and de Man. I argue, however, that the force of the films of Reitz and Syberberg and perhaps even Kluge is not playful and nomadic but deadly serious. It tends toward the ideology of a unified Germany with a history restored to continuity. Straub/Huillet's historical continuity, in contrast, is that of opposition—a history of the victims who happen also to have resisted and survived. These traces are in the physical bodies and landscapes or cultural artifacts they photograph, as well as in the implied historical memory that can understand monuments without legends attached. No one would disagree with Reitz's assertion that we (we Germans) must work on our memories. But he presumes to illustrate in his Heimat films what those memories are to look like and who the rememberers are. The frequent appearance of monuments in Straub/Huillet films merely records an absence that looks outside the film for an explanation.[65] Far preferable is the erection of monuments that do not "represent" twentieth-century Germany at all yet suggest an audience remember the beauty and destructiveness they commemorate, while being the prisoners of neither.

The confrontations between present and past, between language and film form, are as important in *Antigone* as they were in *Machorka-Muff* or *Bridegroom*. For instance, Martin Walsh has linked the plot of *Bridegroom*, the film's visual form, and German history with a concept of freedom that may apply in all three contexts.

> But Lilith is not the only prostitute to be freed. The other is art, specifically film art, which, in the course of these 23 minutes, has evolved through its principal historical stages, until reaching its liberation in the materialist presentation that is Straub's own. The killing of the pimp is, metaphorically, the killing of Germany's decadent cultural heritage—the specifically German implication being raised in the graffiti that opened the film: "Stupid old Germany, I hate it over here, I hope I can go soon . . ." If Straub has laid "stupid old Germany" to rest, the cinema has been liberated from its stifling conventions, and the film's movement from the sordid opening to the celebratory close cements the significance of this new beginning.[66]

## An Alternative Cultural Identity

In his institutional study of the project that unites the disparate artists of the New German Cinema, Elsaesser writes of their search for Germany and a German audience. In a period when German unification raises yet again the question of German national and cultural identity, the contradiction between economic and military power and cultural feelings of inferiority, racial versus civil definitions of identity and otherness—all this makes the project of Straub/Huillet, from the very beginning of *Machorka-Muff*, as relevant today as it ever was. This, more than the incidental "theoretical" interest of their work and even more than its place in a hypothetical "film history," is the place they would claim for their films—a contribution to the cultural shaping of a new, non-nationalistic and nonmilitarist Europe. As they wrote in the introduction to *Antigone*,

> So, one year before the Year of Europe, 1992, we want to attempt the most European of all films: a great Greek dramatist, two German poets, German actors from West and East Berlin (*Schaubühne*, Gorki Theater), French technicians (Camera: William Lubtchansky, with whom we shot the Kafka film in Hamburg in 1983), the Sicilian landscape and a director with three fatherlands: Germany, Italy, France. Is there a better celebration of the true Europe?[67]

The post-1968 leftist identity, the problematic identity of New German Cinema, and the German identity in general are all typified by melancholy; the films of Straub/Huillet are not. Instead they are touchingly positive about Germany as perhaps only foreigners who know its dangers but also its beauties can be. But their "love of Germany" manifests itself not by representing the country but only the displacements of its language and cultural artifacts.

The difference between the allusions to Hollywood cinema in Wenders and Fassbinder, on the one hand, and in Straub/Huillet, on the other, also relates to the context of a German subjectivity or national identity. For the New German Cinema, as Elsaesser and Timothy Corrigan have written, dependence on Hollywood was both a problem and a source of identification.[68] Thus it became a project of the New German Cinema to reproduce aspects of Hollywood in their films and even in the personae of the directors. Wenders and Fassbinder rework genres from Hollywood and include characters who mimic characters from Hollywood movies, and both these tactics refer to the situation of the West German cinema and to their own situation as derivative. Clearly Fassbinder and Wenders have been able to do "original" work with this derivative material as an aspect of its composition, often taking the physical form of excerpts from films or songs and the presence of the film apparatus itself within the narrative framework of the film. Examples would be *Kings of the Road*, *In a Year of 13 Moons*, and *The State of Things*. The world of the cinema becomes part of the texture of the psychological world in which their films operate. As Wenders's character in *Kings of the Road* puts it, "The Yanks have colonized our subconscious."

While these allusions to Hollywood are thus opaque and identifiable as such, allusions to Hollywood and early cinema in Straub/Huillet films are transparent. Indeed, in most cases they claim they are subconscious and only become visible—even to the filmmakers—after the film is finished. The nature of this connection to past cinema is thus technical and formal and not thematic or narrative. The shooting or projection of a film is never present in a Straub/Huillet film. The utopian Germany they evoke through the cinema is a Germany without the cinema.

But the evocations of American cinema in Fassbinder and Wenders also block the way for Straub/Huillet films, they assert, since these products function as a substitute for a confrontation with the real thing. The complacency that results—they term it ignorance and arrogance—allows people to consume a "nostalgia for the American cinema, when the audience has seen nothing of Chaplin, Griffith, or John Ford." By projecting their dreams of the cinema into their films, Wenders and Fassbinder collaborate in the narrowing of audience demand and distribution that has gradually excluded even Godard from general distribution. There is no resistance or solidarity to be found on the basis of such films that accept the terms of Hollywood marketing. For, as Huillet has put it, "Cinephilia is also a lack of ambition."[69]

Another method of re-creating a film culture that Elsaesser observes in the New German Cinema is the "author as intertext," the interconnection between films due to the recognizability of their actors. Elsaesser gives as examples Fassbinder's ensemble, Rüdiger Vogler in Wenders's films (and Von Trotta's *Marianne and Juliane*), and numerous others.[70] Like the choice of interconnected film titles, this is in part a marketing device that also adds to the reality effect of the "film world" as a counterpart to the real world and German society.

Where Straub/Huillet's work enters this intertextuality, however, it applies it self-consciously as part of a spectrum of acting styles that spill out of the cinema fiction into documentary and lived experience. The past roles and skills of the professional actors they use thus join a collage of messages that includes other manifestations of language, literature, and the biographies of individuals. For example, the theatrical fulminations of Mario Adorf, Alfred Edel, and Werner Rehm reveal aspects of their own professional lives, the role they are playing, and the construction of cinema simultaneously. The choice of the equally professional Libgart Schwarz for the most extreme expression of suffering and pathos subtly distances the audience from those emotions as well. The casting of the controversial journalist and author Erich Kuby as General Machorka-Muff, or Howard Vernon as Hermocrates/Manes in the Empedocles films doubly alludes to each man's other roles and their political context.[71] Protagonists in Straub/Huillet films, however, are almost always played by (usually young) lay actors who bring experiences to their performance of the texts that come from outside the cinema or theater. Gustav Leonhardt as Bach or the gentle and earnest German teacher and amateur violinist Andreas von Rauch as the hero Empedocles are examples. Perhaps the most powerful acting of all is delivered by Gottfried Bold as the banker in *History Lessons*. Bold was editor of a trade union newspaper in Cologne, who had been fired from an earlier job for refusing to write GDR (the official name of East Germany) in quotation marks as the right-wing press always did. The experience of acting in a Straub/Huillet film is also historicized by the fact that Vladimir Baratta, Howard Vernon, and Andreas von Rauch repeated their roles from *Empedocles*

Vladimir Baratta as Pausanias and Andreas von Rauch as Empedocles in *The Death of Empedocles* (1986). Courtesy Edition Manfred Salzgeber, Berlin.

Andreas von Rauch as Empedocles and Vladimir Baratta as Pausanias in *Black Sin* (1988). Courtesy Edition Manfred Salzgeber, Berlin.

in the later version, *Black Sin*. The second film thus documents their physical aging in a temporal world separate from the texts.

Finally, we will look briefly at the evocation of German history and the German landscape as an aspect of mourning work or the search for Heimat. Elsaesser stresses that the search for Heimat after Germany's shame and fragmentation stands behind much of New German Cinema production. Even the exotic faraway lands sought out by Herzog, he asserts, are expressions of this German longing. The confrontation with the Other, either in Herzog's romantic exoticism or in Ulrike Ottinger's more ethnographic variety, finds its counterpart in the mournfully nostalgic investigation of German lands in Reitz and Wenders. These images of Germany and the world evoke a sense of distance and loss as the basis of the damaged German identity of which so much has been written. The impossibility of living in these spaces, their unreachable artificiality, is underscored by Wenders's juxtaposition of German landscapes with the imaginary American Southwest. These are not images of the world but of the postwar West German mental landscape.[72]

As they do not attempt to represent the German public, Straub/Huillet also do not parallel this attempt to represent the world as a counterpart to a German identity. The landscapes they photograph, which Elsaesser links to Herzog's exotic locations as signs of abstract "otherness," are instead sites bearing visible signs of human history. Although Straub/Huillet do not show contemporary Germany, they attempt to make of the German language itself a home. As Straub has put it, "Language is the house one is born in or works in or suffers in or enjoys in. And if one has no connection to language, no relationship with language, then there are no structures anymore; there's nothing there anymore."[73] As later chapters will investigate, Straub/Huillet's presentation of nature and language, in contrast to or in harmony with a narrative/narration, traces "the history of barbarism" that Benjamin spoke of and records the signs of resistance. Straub used a more graphic metaphor in describing the price paid for progress that is behind the appearance of the world: "Every step one takes is, without knowing it, into a puddle of blood."[74] Rather than a melancholy fixation on Germany and its guilt, however, Straub/Huillet seek the seeds of resistance in the exile of language. This displacement, Europeanization, and humanization of German culture can only be welcomed given the legacy of this century.

# 3

# TRACES OF A LIFE

*Chronicle of Anna Magdalena Bach*

*Chronicle of Anna Magdalena Bach* will be treated first, because it was the first project Straub undertook even though it was only realized as the third Straub/Huillet film. It is also the film that brought Straub and Huillet together and brought them their widest international recognition.[1] The story of their struggle to get the film produced spans their entire ten-year residence in West Germany (1959–1969). Straub/Huillet's filmmaking practices, their long-term confrontation with German culture, and their other projects of the time all developed out of the Bach film.

*Chronicle* is composed of images of documents from Johann Sebastian Bach's life, musical performances in historic locations, and a few fictionalized scenes—all held together by a voice-over narration by his second wife, Anna Magdalena Bach. The film begins with Bach's tenure as *Capellmeister* at the court of Anhalt-Cöthen, where he and Anna Magdalena met, and ends with her description of his final illness and death. The role of Bach is played by the Dutch harpsichordist Gustav Leonhardt, and Anna Magdalena is played by Christiane Lang-Drewanz.[2] The film marks a transition in Straub/Huillet's work in that it initially had a script that was written by the filmmakers rather than excerpted from other texts as in all subsequent films. But whereas Roy Armes writes that *Chronicle* is the only Straub/Huillet film without a literary source, this is not accurate.[3] Most of the language of the film is taken from documents: letters, texts of cantatas, the necrology.[4] Although Straub claimed only the title came from Esther Meynell's book, *The Little Chronicle of Anna Magdalena Bach*, the narrational gesture and the chronological sequence of music and events parallel its structure.[5] The method of letting musical structures suggest the form of the film rather than being subordinate to it is, however, a consistent aspect

*51*

of Straub/Huillet's treatment of all the material they select for their films. Research on the documents concerning Bach's life also brought the filmmakers into contact with Heinrich Böll, whose work forms the basis for their first two finished films. And finally, the struggle to make the film, involving as it did the rallying of colleagues from various countries, reveals the political nature of filmmaking in Europe in the late 1960s. In this period, the formal difficulty of the film was taken as an aspect of its revolutionary value, something that became less and less possible from the 1970s onward. Straub traces his own beginnings as a film director to the Bach project. He at first suggested that Bresson make it but was told he should make it himself, since it was his project. Thus Straub began his path toward directing his own films "as one falls into a trap."[6]

The saga of Straub/Huillet's struggle to get the film produced in Germany is as complex and compelling as a film plot.[7] In an interview with *Cahiers du cinéma*, Straub listed the reasons the film had been turned down. "One pretext: it's a fiction film. Another pretext: it's a documentary. A third: it can't be an audience success. What is piquant is that this last pretext comes from the North-Rhine Westfalian 'Kultusministerium' [Ministry of Culture] which subsidizes precisely films on music."[8] The idea for the Bach film originated in 1954,[9] and the screenplay was written and researched between 1954 and 1959. The film could have been made as early as 1959, when the producer Hubert Schonger offered financing for it if Straub/Huillet could raise the remaining DM 100,000. But the search for financing delayed the film another eight years, with two films intervening.[10] Straub/Huillet had tried every possible avenue from the smallest distributor to Bavarian Television, UFA, and DEFA, the state-owned studio of East Germany. A representative of the Pallas film company in Frankfurt who had been ready to support the film met with a car accident.[11] Grants were repeatedly denied by the Federal Film Subsidy Board in Bonn and by the Culture Ministry in Düsseldorf.[12] These efforts were not in vain, however, since the contacts made in the long struggle to get funding for the Bach film led to both the material and the financing for the two Böll films as well as to the stage production at the center of *Bridegroom*.

Straub said that he had met Böll in Paris when he had been looking for someone to consult about the language in the Bach screenplay. Böll's advice had been to leave the antiquated German exactly as it was except for a few minor changes such as the more comprehensible phrase "to appeal" in place of "vozieret."[13] After meeting Böll, Straub/Huillet became interested in making a film based on his work. Because of the availability of funding, two such films preceded the completion of the Bach project: *Machorka-Muff* (1962), based on Böll's political satire "Bonn Diary"; and *Not Reconciled* (1964–1965), based on the novel *Billiards at Half Past Nine*. The struggle for funding of all three films is treated at greater length in the next chapter.

Between the premiere of *Not Reconciled* in 1965 and the summer of 1967, Straub/Huillet were able to get partial funding for the Bach film, primarily through the co-producers Franz Seitz in Germany and Gianvittorio Baldi in Italy. The months before the actual shooting began in August 1967 were a battle of nerves. The Kuratorium at first rejected the application for production support, prompting supporters of the project to create the Verein Filmkunstfonds e.V to raise money through "shares" of at first DM 1,000 and later DM 500. The fundraising effort, coordinated through the journal *Filmkritik*, listed among its supporters Alexander Kluge, Volker Schlöndorff, Enno Patalas, François Truffaut, Enrique Raab, and Artur Brauner.[14] Only in July 1967, a month before shooting, did the Kuratorium approve DM 150,000, about half of what less distinguished films received. By that time, however, Straub had already filmed the Leipzig Town Hall with the DEFA cameraman, since all arrangements had been made. Film stock was purchased, with additional footage ordered in reserve, and contracts were signed with Music House Film- und Fernseh-GmbH, which carried musicians' expenses and Straub's salary while the additional financing was still uncertain. Despite the film's artistic success and its invitation to festivals such as those at Berlin and Cannes, the West German film bureaucracy was unmoved. In the summer of 1968, the Filmbewertungsstelle Wiesbaden refused to assign any tax-reducing quality rating to the film—neither "besonders wertvoll" (excellent) nor simply "wertvoll" (good).

When asked about his strategy for making a film about such a major German cultural icon, Straub has claimed that he had been initially unaware that Bach was viewed as such and had begun his work with a blithe lack of prejudice, with the naïveté of a child.[15] That Bach was indeed a German cultural icon became clear as Straub encountered resistance to the production, sometimes disguised in nonsensical technical reservations, such as the claim that there was no place to put a camera in an organ loft. Finally Straub had come to the conclusion that people "consciously wanted to obstruct the film, to prevent Bach's music from getting into the movie theaters. This music had to stay in the concert halls."[16] This resistance to the film, especially by businesspeople and cultural functionaries, led Straub to more provocative statements. For instance, he noted that Bach was relatively unknown in Germany and connected the Bach project to the political struggles around the Böll films by calling it "yet another film about the unresolved German past."[17] The reference to the anti-Fascist impulses of *Not Reconciled* is of course not merely a result of the reaction to the film but has always been close to the inspiration for Straub's generation to approach European cultural icons.[18] Confronted with a "bunch of suits" (*Filmfritzen*) or "Gesetzeshüter"—

Bach's employers on the Town Council (Ernst Castelli, Paolo Carlini, Hans-Peter Boye). Courtesy New Yorker Films.

Kafka's guardians of the Law—Straub raised the polemical stakes, saying the film was dedicated to the Viet Cong, with whose struggles against overwhelming opposition he could identify.[19]

Aside from the provocative statements vis-à-vis administrators of culture, Straub/Huillet's work on the Bach film was guided in the main by carefully thought out principles, combined with long years of research and experimentation. Straub had left France for Germany in 1958 rather than be inducted into the army for the Algerian War and had traveled with very little money through both West Germany and the GDR in search of locations and documents for the Bach film. Of this period, Straub reported, "Danièle accompanied me now and then and in between went to Paris to get some money." In the GDR, they visited Eisenach, Arnstadt, Erfurt, Weimar, Dresden, Leipzig, and Mühlhausen and found that most of the actual locations of Bach's work were unusable because of nineteenth-century alterations. "The Thomas school, where Bach lived for thirty years, was torn down around 1900. The Thomaskirche in Leipzig was altered by an organ in a horrible neo-Gothic style."[20] In the old Prussian State Library in East Berlin and in the State Archives in Marburg and Tübingen, Straub/Huillet microfilmed ten times the number of documents that finally appeared in the film. The search for the authentic locations of Bach's life to shoot the film indicates a practice that Straub/Huillet have never abandoned. The choice of location is never arbitrary and has indeed preceded the screenplays in some instances. The films then explore the physical traces of history that human activity leaves behind and confront these spaces with texts or musical pieces.

Another primary goal, from a musical point of view, was to get away from "romantic performance practice."[21] To this end, Straub/Huillet dedicated much time and travel to finding performers who could use the original baroque instruments, a practice that was not at all common at the time. For instance, they were told that it was out of the question that anyone would ever play a natural trumpet again. But as Straub noted with some pride in 1968, "In the meantime they've managed it, not without some impetus from my film project, which could almost have been realized in 1959."[22] It was also not easy to find a chorus that would take the risk of dedicating only three boys to each part, that is, a choir of twelve. The live recording of uninterrupted performances also goes against industry practice. Straub saw this as an attempt to restore integrity to the musical structures that are so often totally shattered by the power of the cinema to reconstruct them.

> We know that nowadays musical recordings are made of a thousand pieces. One simply edits a musical movement, which after all should be a whole, and always was in concert up until the invention and development of sound recording technology; a movement begins and is played to the end. It has a tension from A to Z. . . . Music always consists of following a thought to its conclusion, and that applies to its reproduction as well. So something had to be done to counter the violent habits of current recording techniques, and I hope with this film I have done something in that regard.[23]

The actual application of this approach is contradictory, of course, since Straub/Huillet are making films that are not mere documentations of performances. They do not make arbitrary cuts in the musical pieces they use in their films but rather seek to make cuts that are cinematically motivated and musically defensible.[24] Presenting excerpts of the Bach pieces, with none played in its entirety, stresses the autonomy yet interdependence of the elements of the film, which is part of its theme in other respects.[25]

In her article on *Chronicle*, Maureen Turim has investigated the arrangement of Straub/Huillet's "cinematic materials" in terms of shot length and composition, rhythm and montage. Distinguishing the film from works of minimalism, despite apparent similarities, Turim describes Straub/Huillet's relation to previous cinematic codes in terms of "écriture blanche," a concept developed by Christian Metz and related to Barthes's idea of "zero-degree writing."

[*Écriture blanche*] is the refusal of certain codes (cinematic and narrative) in preference of others which do not yet appear to be fixed codes. It is the refusal to be "recognizable as cinema." Because it simultaneously deconstructs the codes of the classic narrative cinema, disturbing the plenitude of the earlier cinematic text, and presents new codes which startle and thus call attention to themselves, *écriture blanche* is not only marked by its instrumentality to an intellectual purpose, but is marked by its emphasis on the process of its own construction.[26]

My only quarrel with Turim's assessment is the degree of emphasis placed on intellectual and ideological motivations for deconstructing what she calls the "style of the bourgeois writer-craftsman."[27] We have seen that Straub/Huillet's modernism professes great respect for the work of earlier "craftsmen" in the cinema. Furthermore, although Turim does relate her formal analysis to questions of narrative and cinematic space, there is more to be said in regard to history, memory, and German culture on this basis, as we will also see in later chapters. Finally, the emphasis on the intellect seems to obscure the powerful emotions that can be evoked by Straub/Huillet films, not to mention their emphasis on "play."

Two sequences of shots Turim analyzes can help clarify this distinction. Her description of shots 45, 46, and 47 is productive for an appreciation of the relation of composition to editing in all Straub/Huillet films.[28] The sequence begins with Bach reading a letter he has supposedly just written, then Anna Magdalena Bach in close-up leaning against a wooden panel listening, and finally both of them in a medium shot, which reveals that she is actually much closer to him than the previous shots had suggested, that is, against the same desk at which Bach is sitting. Turim compares the shock of this realization of Anna Magdalena Bach's placement in space to the total lack of spatial orientation for the first image of her in the film, shot 2, an explosively short diagonal close-up with no solid connection to the spaces preceding and following it. The powerful effect Turim describes here is the revelation that there is more continuity in the physical space than the cinematic form had implied.

She contrasts this with the later scene in which Bach forcibly replaces the leader of the boys' choir in the middle of a performance (shots 63–67). This is one of the very few scenes actually acted out in the film. It is also the longest sustained dramatic sequence, since it begins with Bach's entreaty of the governing superintendent of the Thomasschule to take his side in a dispute with the Rector over who is to be in charge of instruction (shot 62) and extends to the two shots of Bach supervising the choirboys at a meal in the refectory, where it becomes clear the boys have had to obey the Rector and Bach has been defeated (shot 67).

In contrast to the scene of Anna Magdalena and Sebastian above, Turim emphasizes that the cinematic codes here imply a greater spatial and temporal continuity than is visible in the shots. The Rector's return to confront Bach in shot 65 seems to follow his exit in shot 64 immediately. The stairway on which the first confrontation takes place (a favorite location since German expressionism) seems to be contiguous with the doorway to which the Rector returns, and the musical performance seems to have just ended, yet the viewer realizes with a shock that the time of the events must be appreciably later.

The accompaniment of this drama by the Kyrie is indeed a juxtaposition of the sacred with the profane. Because the music is performed with such seriousness and without interruption over the dispute, the sincerity of the religious expression and the artistic passion are not doubted. But at the same time, the film insists on stressing the material basis on which such work rested: As Bach's position is being threatened, we hear the only composition in the film by another composer, Leone Leoni. Turim also sees this scene as central to Straub/Huillet's reinvention of cinematic conventions, since the replacement of the choir leader is for her "the most potentially conventional segment of the film." "Instead," she goes on, "the perturbation of time and space through the destruction of the montage codes of continuity (working against them both by implying a greater discontinuity than exists within the narrative and then a greater continuity than exists) maintains the *écriture blanche* code destruction of the film."[29]

One can carry this analysis further, however, to examine the context of the sequences where the codes are contradicted in this way. In the first instance, the shocking revelation that Anna and Sebastian have been much closer in space than the cinematic devices had shown produces a shock of intimacy that is all the greater because it stresses the distance between the physical presence of the actors, the characters they represent, and the text being read. This distance is emphasized by the placement of the movement in the two-shot (shot 48), where Anna Magdalena crosses from the right of the desk, behind Sebastian, and to the window at the left—a compositional element with profound significance at the end of this and other Straub/Huillet films (*Not Reconciled*, *Bridegroom*, *Class Relations*). The discontinuity persists, as Turim observes, because her motion does not begin before the cut. However, the motion is anticipated by the fact that she looks up halfway through the shot, toward the window we see in the next shot. But greater continuity of motion from shot to shot would not only mitigate the shock of intimacy, the motion itself would lose some of its meaning, since it would partly be subordinated to the cinematic narration. This intimacy is underscored by the way in which Anna Magdalena lightly strokes her hand across her husband's back as she walks past him. She continues to look out the window, as we only now realize this was the object of her gaze, and walks in a graceful arc around Sebastian and turns toward him again as she sits on the window seat. The indication of a physical bond is thus couched within her simple motion across the frame, as her gaze has moved from inward

Johann Sebastian Bach (Gustav Leonhardt) and Anna Magdalena Bach (Christiane Lang-Drewanz). Courtesy New Yorker Films.

to outward to inward again, from toward the camera's line of view to perpendicular to it to away from it. Since they do not touch in any other shot of the film, this juxtaposition of physical closeness and visual discontinuity is a striking gesture in the film.

The significance gained by gesture and other movement within shots is thus a result of their separateness and autonomy. This, in the realm of mise-en-scène, corresponds to the "counterpoint" Turim describes between shots.[30] "Counterpoint" and "variation" are apt terms to describe the broad repertoire of autonomous cinematic effects the film employs. Camera movement, for instance, which critics have sometimes insisted is not even there, creates a striking pattern. All but two of the pans and tilts are over two-dimensional graphic images: the letters, music, and pictures by Bach's contemporaries of the towns mentioned. The two pans thus become significant in themselves: the first pans from Gustav Leonhardt's hands on a double keyboard up to his face as he reads the music; the second pans along the ceiling from one side of the Apollosaal in the Berlin Opera to the other. One could argue that the pans and tilts on the "documents" correspond to the viewer's act of reading, which at some times corresponds to the "reading" by the narrator or by the musical performers. The rarity of a pan across a three-dimensional space challenges the transparency of the device and suggests that it is also to be "read" as if it were a two-dimensional document.

Counterbalancing the pans, tilts, and rhythmic cuts between what Turim calls the "graphic inserts" in the film are the long diagonal shots of the musical performances, sometimes containing a track in or out at a carefully selected moment. If the pans and tilts call attention to the kind of reading one does in a film, the tracking shots investigate the camera's and the viewer's relation to space. As Turim puts it, some of these shots could be seen as a dissertation on the effect of camera movement itself.[31] This kind of formal variety must not be underestimated. The range of sound includes complex music, the voice (on-screen, offscreen, or voice-over), and silence. The visual spectrum is similarly broad: the two-dimensional flatness of manuscripts and engravings, intricate and rich images of baroque organ lofts, performers' wigs and instruments; punctuating images of trees against a sky with clouds, waves striking against a stony shore, an expressionist sunrise by Rouault, or simply black film.

As we shall see in regard to the formal analysis of *History Lessons*, there is a narrative context that forms part of the counterpoint as well. Rhythm and temporality are pleasurably explored in cinematic terms, but in the process, issues of memory, emotion, and cultural meaning are raised as well. An example of this intersection between narrative and form exists in a sequence from the film that corresponds to an anecdote in Meynell's *Little Chronicle*. Meynell recounts the story of a cask of wine received as a gift from Bach's cousin, who lived too far away to visit regularly in person. The incident has a humorous cast, since the frugal Bach was required to pay a good deal in shipping expenses to accept the cask, which turned out to be almost half-empty. Calculating the cost of the wine on this basis, Bach wrote to the cousin asking not to receive any more such gifts. The humor in the narrative arises, however, not from the documentary record but from the narrative gesture of Meynell's fictional Anna Magdalena, whose words these are. The film, however, does away with the humorous gesture and instead breaks the incident down into several components. First, Bach is greeted on the stairway of his home by an enthusiastic six-year-old daughter who gleefully announces that the gift of the cask has arrived. Then Anna Magdalena narrates the situation with the cousin, recounting facts that are found in the letter. At the same time, Bach's letter is itself shown on the screen in three successive shots. It concludes with the verbose and formal postscript enumerating the expenses involved, which is the documentary source of the humor.

The tensions in this short scene are extreme: The narration in voice-over by Anna Magdalena acts almost as the *basso continuo* throughout the entire film and functions here as a link to the wider narrative context of remembering Bach's life. The scene starts with the greeting by the little girl, a reenactment of domestic joy that is simple and brief enough to be entirely convincing. At the opposite extreme from this contemporary example of film fiction is the other cheerful aspect of the sequence, the humorous postscript requesting to be spared such expensive gifts. This, however, is not fictionalized in any way but is merely presented to the viewer in visual, documentary terms. Most viewers will certainly not even be able to read it on the first viewing of the film, and the narration does not call attention to it. Yet here is the narrative counterpart to the performance of the musical pieces that have also been pictured in the film. We see the letter as the physical evidence that the events occurred and are given three avenues of access to the facts: the film narrative, which "imagines" the activity in the Bach household; the process of remembering by way of Anna Magdalena's voice; and finally, the viewer's reading of the letter. This act of reading is emphasized by the tilts from top to bottom, and the fictionalization is documented as Anna's narration repeats sentences taken from Bach's own text on-screen. Throughout, the film shows no writing of either music or text, only "performances" based on reading.

This connects the film's narrative to the performance by the musicians, which is also an act of reading and recitation from documents that have been interpreted. The music thus produced has an emotional effect, touching both secular and spiritual issues, and this effect is preserved by way of the tensions Turim has described and the counterpoint or layering of their narrative contexts. Music critics writing about *Chronicle*, however, have tended to see the emotional content as intrinsic to each piece of music alone.

Two critics writing in 1968 made detailed comments on the effect of cutting and arranging the selections. Both Friedrich Hommel and Joachim Kaiser recognize the uniqueness of the film's respect for the music and its performance. Kaiser concedes that Straub "succeeded, in pursuing his conception, in achieving musical photography of a restraint and appropriateness hardly seen before. The camera is not transmusically motivated and does not distract with pseudo-virtuosity and optical tricks from the musical material."[32] Hommel also finds that the fact that only complete musical movements are presented "attests to the care with which the musical exhibits are treated here."[33] Both object, however, to what they see as the inconsistency of the film's attitude to the music. The opening chorus of the St. Matthew Passion or the cadenza of the Fifth Brandenburg Concerto are allowed to have their effect, as Kaiser puts it, but he finds their juxtaposition with the andante from the Italian Concerto played by Johann Elias Bach "totally superfluous."[34] Despite the respect the film shows to the structure of the pieces, Kaiser criticizes the filmmakers for using some passages as "background music," and even more so for shifting abruptly in attitude from the quotidian to the sacred.[35]

Both Kaiser and Hommel also criticize the abrupt editing between contrasting pieces. Hommel sees this as an intentional denial of a "breathing space" for the audience: "Emotions, such as those that are released through the applause of a concert audience, are undesirable. The screen is to remain pure.''[36] Kaiser objects to the fact that the music, which on the one hand is given so much weight in the film, is forced into ''a goosestep order (as if all pieces were as similar as geese) on the other.'' The result, as Kaiser sees it, is the evocation of a vague and undifferentiated sensation of baroque piety and joie de vivre as the culture industry would present it.[37] Although he also would not go so far as to insist on the romantic large-orchestra presentation of Bach's work, Hommel sees the film as being unnecessarily limited by small-scale ensembles and the ''stiff and one-dimensional performance style'' of Leonhardt as Bach.[38] The effect of the film seems to be, then, that the music is presented in a convincingly authentic style but is irritatingly contextualized rather than being allowed to stand on its own.

The emotional frustration noted by both critics deserves investigation, since it cannot be possible that emotions are simply forbidden. Instead, there is a definite evocation of emotion in the narrative and in the characters of Johann Sebastian and Anna Magdalena Bach. Neither writer has taken the narration of Anna Magdalena Bach very seriously, despite the attention called to it by the film's title. For instance, the mistakes in the singing of the ''Trauer-Musik'' aria are lamented, without considering that the woman playing Anna Magdalena, not a professional soprano, is singing on camera. The relation of the musical texts to the narrative is also largely ignored, and the English subtitles do not include them at all. For instance, following an image of Anna Magdalena severely ill in bed and the commentary relating how Bach was summoned home, the film reel ends with a peaceful image of clouds between the tips of two trees. The sound is from the cantata ''Wachet auf, ruft uns die Stimme'' (BWV 140), with the text

> *Soul:* When com'st thou, my Savior?
> *Jesus:* I'm coming, thy share.
> *Soul:* I'm waiting with my burning oil.[39]

Hommel connects the domestic narrative to his criticism of the small-scale ensembles. ''Where Bach's life's work is narrowed down to the perspective of the silently suffering Anna Magdalena, it is ultimately unavoidable that the film takes on the pattern of a family album, in which homey and small-format music-making is recorded as the foundation of all music for posterity.''[40] Kaiser is even more sarcastic about Anna Magdalena's ''housewifely tone'' and believes the music's domination of the film keeps its narrative from being convincing. ''If the numerous musical insertions are only to prove that music dominated in Bach's life, the proof is derived from arbitrary material such as could be appropriated from any artist's biography.''[41] Hommel sees a contradiction in the filmmakers' attempt to avoid ''illustrating any image of Bach constructed by historians.'' Instead the film withdraws to an arrangement, where the facts are to speak for themselves. But [Straub] seems to overlook one thing: without interpretation, facts indeed only speak for themselves, or for anyone: Bach's wig would fit a Handel just as well, and no one prevents us in this carefully reconstructed milieu from replacing one Leipzig cantor with another one. Similarly, in even such a faithfully reconstructed interior with house musicians fiddling on old instruments, nothing would stand against playing Telemann music rather than Bach music on the sound track.[42]

What Hommel has missed here is the tension between meaning and lack of meaning that Turim is able to describe using semiotic terms.

We are left with a lack of an easily determined signified, which in effect throws us back to the materiality of the signifier. Signification is achieved not directly (signifier X representing signifieds Y, Z, etc.) but on a bias, through addition, comparison, contemplation of the signifiers, their unintelligibility, their refusal to make sense. We need more than one engraving of a town to build the concept of engravings being a form of representation minimally legible to our modern perception, more than one close-up of music to develop the concept of music as a written code, highly formalized, but legible only to musicians. . . . Thus in this segment the montage of these elements emphasizes that this film is as much about the attempt to recover the past through its records as it is about the life of one man, Bach. It is about antique maps of cities which have since changed, about a script style which is nearly illegible to modern eyes. It is also about the role codes play in communication, about the relationship of musical notation to sounds heard as music. The narrative does not explain these illusive signifiers. . . . The disjunction instead frustrates our attention, the narration with its own terrorization of the text, its lack of immediate comprehensibility is part of its challenge and meaning.[43]

The lack of an obvious relation between the records of Bach's life and his canonization in German culture is thus quite intentional. There is no attempt to make Leonhardt look or sound the way Bach might have, as the film studiously avoids "reenactments" of character or historical events. The images of the documents, the reconstructed (or rather, the rediscovered) spaces where Bach worked, and even the music itself do not bear any incontestable relation to Bach's life as an individual. Instead, to use Grafe's words, documents "function as evidence, as proof; they are not absorbed by the story. In another story they could testify to something else."[44] The central question posed by the film—and I assert that it is the question that lends aesthetic power to it, rather than a proposed answer—is how the music of Bach (as a cultural treasure, religious expression, or simply pleasing music) can at all be connected to the physical life of a historical individual. This is not just a question for interpretation of historical artifacts but rather has a connection to all the dramas of contemporary life: how can anyone, artist or not, know what will be remembered as essential to one's character or as valuable to the lives of others (contemporaries or posterity)? To borrow a phrase from Christa Wolf, one concern of the film is "Was bleibt"—what remains. And what remains of Anna Magdalena's life consists mainly of a few lines written in a Bible and the music she copied for her husband.

Here, the juxtaposition of musical performances with the invented narrative of Anna Magdalena, the domestic concerns as well as the professional struggles, alternatively puts the emphasis on both. Some of the irony of this narration may be lost to some viewers, since the German texts that are sung are not subtitled, such as the cantata text, "How merrily will I laugh" when the world is falling apart.[45] Reference to Bach's identity as an employee also recalls the device Godard uses to expose the material basis for filmmaking, the series of checks signed in close-up at the beginning of the film *Tout va bien*. But in the case of the Straub/Huillet film, it is the lives of Bach and his loved ones that are expended. The emotional cost of this expenditure is not acted out in the film, nor is the emotion evoked by the acting. The words alone are to convey the professional conflicts and the personal memories, while it is left up to the music and the editing to evoke emotions. The film does not explain what it was about Bach's life that made it possible for him to become a cultural monument. Instead we are confronted with the possibility that, for Bach, perhaps the small pieces composed for Anna Magdalena were just as important as the works for his churches or patrons. In the film, the large public works were no more important to her.

Straub thus would not have been exaggerating when he described the film as a love story. The displacement and concentration of emotions in many aspects of the work are consistent with this description. In this respect, Hommel's complaint that the work resembles a "family album" may not be that far from the filmmakers' intention. Straub did speak of a scene in one draft of the screenplay where he imagined the Bach family on a picnic, a scene that is included in Meynell's *Little Chronicle*.[46]

In addition to the narrative stress placed on domestic situations, the absence of an audience for the performances in the film functions to intensify the viewers' emotional concentration. Hommel is correct that the usual channeling of the listeners' emotions through applause is impossible due to the relentless pace of the film editing. In addition to the absence of listeners in the film with whom viewers could identify, spatial relations also emphasize the work of performing and inhibit identification with an imagined concert audience. The camera is most often positioned at an oblique angle to the space toward which the musicians seem to be directing their performance. Camera motion underscores this effect, beginning with the Brandenburg Concerto that opens the film: After Leonhardt's solo cadenza, the camera tracks back to reveal the ensemble that finishes the piece with him. The precision of this motion was only possible with the big

64   Traces of a Life: *Chronicle of Anna Magdalena Bach*

Christiane Lang-Drewanz as Anna Magdalena Bach. Courtesy New Yorker Films.

Mitchell camera on tracks, a sharp contrast to the much looser use of zooms by other filmmakers since the 1960s.[47] An even more striking example is the cantata (BWV 42) in shot 48. At first, with voice-over by Anna Magdalena and then Bach, the camera frames Leonhardt conducting the "Sinfonia" from the organ. Then it tracks back to reveal the musicians and the tenor, who is seen waiting patiently for his entrance. To begin singing, however, the tenor turns shockingly toward a space that was not "real" to the scene up to that point.[48]

The result is a sensation of distance, which also is explicitly intended by the filmmakers. As in all of their work, the "separation of elements" is a fundamental principle in *Chronicle*. Straub speaks of the three kinds of "reality" that are accessible where Bach is concerned: "the music, the manuscripts or original texts, and the letters, along with the necrology." To make of this something more than a documentary film, Straub goes on, one has to introduce human beings—that is, the musicians—into the equation. The reality of the traces of Bach's having lived is therefore in tension with the image of Gustav Leonhardt playing the role of Bach.

> We won't necessarily say to the spectator, "that is Bach." I would say, the film will instead be a film about this Mr. Leonhardt. Even in the "points" from Bach's life one will respect the performer of Bach as Mr. Leonhardt. The film, the play

consists in bringing him together with these three realities: "writings," "texts" and "music." Only when the ignition between these four elements functions will something come out of it.[49]

In describing what interests him in the work of a performer producing this spark, Straub speaks of layers. He praises the work of Leonhardt because he did not erase all traces of his previous approaches to each scene in developing new ones. Straub's criticism of professional actors is that when they alter their approach, they completely forget what was there before. Nonprofessionals, apparently because their "natural" actions are more essential to the performance, do not erase these impulses but only suppress them.[50]

The supposed asceticism and rigor of Straub/Huillet's method thus seeks to increase the film's impact, not frustrate the audience. The use of original instruments is not chosen out of a desire for aesthetic "purity," for example, but, as Straub has said, because "the music of Bach can reach people of today with the greatest force when it is performed with the means that Bach had at his disposal, because these means are actually new to modern people."[51] The "newness" of the instruments and the distance provided by the costumes are complemented by the concentration on the act of performance itself. Despite the recurring complaints of critics about the "uncinematic" lack of motion in the film—including the absurdly revealing phrase "unless one can call making music motion"[52]—the action of performance and the risk of accident present in any sustained shot of a demanding performance are precisely what Straub finds as exciting as the early motion pictures.

> [The quality of chance] exists in every fraction of a second of the film, if only because every musician could make a mistake in every fraction of a second, and there are many of them before the camera. The duration multiplies the quality of chance even more. It's a joke when some say it's a static shot, the camera doesn't move, nothing happens. There is more happening than in a pan, a car chase, or a pursuit. Every finger is moving, and one even senses the air, and besides, that is the essence of the cinematographer: They say when people saw *Le déjeuner de bébé* or *L'arroseur arrosé* by Lumière, they didn't cry out: Oh! bébé is moving, or l'arroseur is moving. They said, the leaves are moving in the trees. The bébé who moved they had already seen in the magic lantern. What was new for them was precisely that the leaves were moving. The "leaves" in the Bach film are the fingers and hands of the musicians and the unbelievable gestures of Leonhardt, which are not at all monotonous.[53]

One part of the equation in the Bach film is the "documentary quality" of the performances—the spark that is to be ignited between the types of reality. Straub has gone so far as to maintain that the reduction of the nondocumentary aspects actually increases the "novelistic" quality. He contrasted the Bach film with *Machorka-Muff*, in which the inclusion of "reality" was meant to make the film more "realistic." Here, he maintains, with even more "real" elements, "in spite of everything the whole becomes almost only a novel."[54] Huillet, too, speaks of this layering of separate elements as an important aspect of their films. Her term is "archaeology." "Fiction is important for us, because, when it is mixed with documentary images or a documentary situation, a contradiction is created, and a spark can flash up. Fiction is very important, in spite of everything, to somehow ignite a fire. (Straub: I think what interests us is to show layers . . .) Huillet: not to eradicate traces, but to build on them."[55]

The "fiction" of the Bach film is carefully defined as that aspect of the film that arises almost in a shock effect by the confrontation between documentary and fiction. The music and the manuscripts presented to the camera and the documentation of the present performance confront the fiction of Anna Magdalena Bach's remembering these images as her husband. The historical memory evoked in the audience by a film about a major cultural figure is juxtaposed in the fiction with the private memory of his wife. This memory, in turn, resonates with the tension and use of memory involved in any performance. The musicians and actors are also acting out a memory, both in performing a past composition in the present and in reciting a memorized text. Suspense is generated because something could go wrong, be lost or forgotten. The fictional confrontation with documentary reality traces the border between present and past, between life and living memory and death.

A number of critics have noted this presence of death as a major theme of the film, and this was also an aspect of the Meynell book from which it takes its title. Meynell's Anna Magdalena says, for instance, "All Sebastian's noblest music was evoked by the thought of death—that used to frighten me a little, now I understand better what was in his heart."[56] In the film, the texts of both the music and the narration of Anna Magdalena make the theme of death quite explicit. Klaus Eder notes that the shot of informal playing of excerpts from Anna Magdalena Bach's "Notenbüchlein" with a small child playing at her feet "is surprising first in its beauty, but also proves an intensive relationship to music in the Bach family; one senses that music belongs to everyday activity." But the large number of children Bach fathered was often reduced by the intervention of death, and this fact is also juxtaposed with the music. As Eder goes on,

> The actor of Anna Magdalena reports this in sober, completely unemotional words as if it didn't touch her at all (which is true: an actress is speaking the text); Danièle Huillet's editing follows this information with a cantata ("Christ lag in Todesbanden") that wrests peace and beauty out of inescapable death. Straub shows that Bach's music is an answer to his own life, to the good or mostly difficult situations in it; it is the continuation of life by other means.[57]

Jörg Peter Feurich stresses, however, that the music does not directly illustrate the narrative.

> Thus the musical incidents are not only not integrated into the biographical moment—one perceives a leap of phenomena just where they seem to stand in causal continuity or proximity. For instance, when the report of the deaths of two children accompanies the image of Anna at the keyboard with her child playing at her feet, or when the suicide of the Co-Rector seems to correspond to a Memorial cantata.[58]

Hommel sees in this evocation of death yet another trivial effect.

> In Bach's music [Straub] senses everywhere the nearness of death of a cultural late phenomenon, even perhaps something like the Golgotha of occidental music. And only for this reason does *Chronicle* seem to be photographed so without optical ambition: because he sees incarnations of Bach's music arising everywhere, almost mystically, wherever historical facticity enters the picture. Perhaps it has escaped him as he mulled over his mystical theme, that with this drift toward death that he uncovers everywhere in the life and music of Bach, he is only varying the popular sentimental theme.[59]

These two comments reveal how the film presents Bach's music both as an accompaniment to his own mortality and that of those close to him and as a commentary on his historical period.

The force of the film, however, has to lie in the present. If we are to take Straub's comment seriously, that this is a love story, what does it tell us about the possibilities and limitations of such love and its representation in film? As Eder observed, part of the so-called Brechtian method applied by Straub/Huillet (which may have more to do with Renoir) is the practice of keeping emotion out of the performance, so that the structures and meanings themselves can allow an emotional reaction to develop in the viewer. This emotional reaction, I argue, is the result of the unbridgeable juxtaposition of present and past tense in the film, which is also an evocation of mortality and the struggle against it—through both art and memory.

Feurich has noted, for instance, that a major fictional premise of the film is established in the simple statement of Anna Magdalena at the beginning of the film, "He was . . ." From this point on, we are made aware that Bach is dead, that she has survived him, and that these are the memories that she has constructed to remind herself of him. But the viewer's relation to this depiction of the past becomes ambivalent through this doubling of the distance. In Feurich's words,

> The past tense, which at first registers her distance from the years in Cöthen, soon becomes ambivalent. It also describes the distance from the dead person whom she has outlived and from herself while he was alive: a distance that approaches

our own, but by such a small degree that we only clearly become aware of the distance from both. When Anna speaks in the past tense, then she ultimately speaks for us too, in constant ambivalence, because she is only present in a "monotone" voice, quoting, reporting. "Capellmeister, Director . . ." are now only facts that do not pretend to contain anymore the past life from which they are left over.[60]

That these are memories and not depictions is underscored by the presence of documents but also by the fact that scenes are enacted in a documentary style, as if they were indeed images in a family album. Schütte notes that the filtering of the image of Bach through Anna Magdalena's memory is consistent with the fact that there is no attempt to represent aging in the presentation of Gustav Leonhardt. This is part of the attempt to preserve the "foreignness" of the past as represented in the film; therefore, as Schütte notes, Bach is not shown composing "but playing music, 'in practice'; no dialogic tension; if there are dialogues, they are treated as blocks placed next to each other."[61] All this gives the film a structure that is not subordinated to a "unified, unbroken line and motion" but rather is a "chain of different types of punctual intensities of the material."[62] Similarly, Feurich notes that "the levels of music, scene, insert, dialogue, and voice-over chronicle stand independently next to and after each other; they not only do not displace or limit each other, but also the manifest contrasts are only appearances: it is a world of simultaneous realities."[63]

Along with the isolation of scenes as locations of memory, there is the arrangement of text into blocks. This, according to Straub, was an evolutionary process of excluding the exchanges between Bach and Anna Magdelena that would have given the illusion of their living in the present. Instead, all the words of the film refer to him in the past, from the standpoint of those—both Anna Magdalena and the audience/filmmakers—who survive him.

Tension between present and past exists in any block of text, as it does in the performance of music. The distance between the words, their meaning, their origins, their recitation, and the audience is an absolute reality. Most cinematic practice, however, attempts to hide this reality, whereas Straub/Huillet call attention to it. The variation between professional actors and lay performers will be discussed elsewhere, but regarding these texts, Straub has stressed both the attraction of accents and the difficulty some actors have in pronouncing German. For instance, in the French version of the Bach film, the on-camera texts are subtitled, but the voice-over narration is spoken in French by the same actress as in the original. Straub said, "I was glad that I could do that. . . . I love accents in film very much. The language is more alive, when it is spoken by someone who has difficulty with it. Then there are hindrances, which produce a greater veracity. . . . This is not new, since the films of Renoir that encountered the most resistance were also those in which characters spoke with an accent."[64]

The film unites two types of resistance: the resistance of the documents against their appropriation (partly conveyed by the difficulty of performance) and the resistance against death represented by both the life and work of Bach and the act of memory in the fiction of Anna Magdalena. Straub speaks of the difficulty of "holding the two ends of the chain together: that it is to be my tale about Bach and still not for a moment improbable as the tale of Anna Magdalena Bach."[65] Huillet had noted already in typing the screenplay that "this was a film about death," and this awareness—building on such fictional sentences as "A few weeks before Sebastian's death . . ."—gave Straub and Huillet a sense of vertigo that at times awakened the urge to end the project altogether. The final crisis was presented in the editing of the last reel.

> Then we cut the last reel, where the vertigo started again, as if it were a film in itself. Then it fit together and we noticed that we had won a victory. . . . That is also one of the novelistic aspects of the film, that it tells of a life that burns like a candle. I think a novel recounts a life; the novels of the nineteenth century, the novels of Dostoyevsky and Balzac recounted a destiny. And here one has, perhaps for the first time, a destiny on the screen. . . . The last reel of the film is the proof, that death is the most unnatural thing—I mean that literally—in the world. The last reel gets faster and faster: it is a race, a wager against time. And suddenly it is completed, burned up.[66]

The material nature of life being expended through work, which produces the "love story" of *Chronicle*, is touched on by a quotation from Karl Marx that forms the frontispiece of the published screenplay. In the quotation Marx writes of human production as being an avenue both to essential self-expression and to love: ". . . to have been for you the mediator between you and the species, and thus to be known and perceived by you as a completion of your own essence and as a necessary part of yourself, and to know myself confirmed in both your thinking and in your love. . . . Our productions would be as many mirrors from which our essence would shine unto itself."[67] Bach's labor may have been alienated by the constrained conditions under which it occurred, but the memory of his productivity is a free, human act of love that resists that alienation. Bach's artistic resistance against death and the constraints of his working conditions complements the resistance of both Anna Magdalena and the authors of the fiction against forgetting. Here, despite his naïve disclaimers, Straub makes quite explicit political claims for the role of the film within a leftist understanding of the role of the artist.

> And it is good that someone who "represents" Bach should have had nothing to do with what happened in Germany from 1933 on, either directly or indirectly. [ . . . ] On the other hand, I discovered in Mr. Leonhardt someone who was much more than an intellectual, who had a great sense of childhood and of provocation. These two traits were very important for Bach. He was and is by far the best

Gustav Leonhardt as Johann Sebastian Bach. Courtesy New Yorker Films.

interpreter of Bach music. And he took on this musical experiment, a risk, without calculating as most intellectuals do before they will even cross the street: "Oh, what a risk, can I run such a risk?" This is also the reason there are no politics in Germany, because one always pursues the politics of "No experiments."[68]

This film is a bit troublesome. The viewer is in the situation of the Leipzig town councilors, who could not have known that they were dealing with the great Bach. Perhaps it did not interest them. Works of art were not yet sanctified and recognized. But the viewer is also in the position of a twentieth-century person, who knows that this music has been mummified and that it has rightly become a Work of Art.[69]

# 4

# FORMAL AND POLITICAL RADICALISM IN THE SHORT FILMS OF THE 1960S

The two short films *Machorka-Muff* (1962) and *The Bridegroom, the Comedienne, and the Pimp* (1968) unite in concentrated form the political and formal radicalism for which Straub/Huillet became internationally known by the late 1960s. *Machorka-Muff* is closely connected to *Not Reconciled* (1964–1965), which is treated in the next chapter, since both films are based on works by Heinrich Böll. Both Böll films confront the violence of German history and the difficulty of "coming to terms with the past" (*Vergangenheitsbewältigung*), combining rage at the continuities with the militaristic and Nazi past, affectionate sorrow at the shame Germany thus brings on itself, and a silent memorial to the victims. *Bridegroom* couches political rebellion in a concentrated reinvention of film convention and genre that has retained its modernist ability to shock for over twenty-five years. Since it features performances by Rainer Werner Fassbinder and the Action-Theater of Munich, *Bridegroom* marks the point of intersection between Straub/Huillet and the radical origins of what became the New German Cinema.

## *Machorka-Muff*

In *Machorka-Muff*, a former Nazi officer enters the West German capital in triumph to lay the cornerstone for the Academy of Military Memories and is welcomed by the political, religious, and aristocratic elites. In interviews, Straub has referred to *Machorka-Muff* as the story of a rape—the rape of Germany by the military—whereas *Not Reconciled* is the story of the frustration of violence, since a German rebellion against twentieth-century militarism and Nazism never occurred. Also, he has somewhat facetiously described both of them as "Westerns"—*Machorka-Muff* a Western in the present tense, *Not Reconciled* a Western in the past tense.[1] The sheriff in *Machorka-Muff*, however, never rides into town to deal with the gangsters on the screen; "the avenger is in the audience."[2]

The remilitarization of West Germany in the 1950s was Straub's "first political rage," a sign that the country would be prevented from finding its own way out of the wilderness of World War II. For decades he has spoken with compassion for the Germans of the 1950s who were just beginning to have enough to eat after the horrors of the war and were then forced or led to remilitarize. Similarly, Straub is not at all arrogant in regard to the undernourished German film culture of the 1950s and praises the Fritz Lang films produced in West Germany by Artur Brauner.[3] As we have seen, Straub/Huillet thus distance themselves from the contemptuous attitude toward the German public exhibited by the Young German Cinema arising out of the Oberhausen Manifesto, portions of the leftist intelligentsia, and the student movement. As Huillet said regarding student reactions to the Bach film in 1968, "If they laugh when they hear talk of God, they will never make a revolution."[4]

The ability of Straub/Huillet films to provoke both the cultural establishment and rebels in politics and film is indicated by the long and arduous production history of *Machorka-Muff* and *Not Reconciled*, begun only after Straub/Huillet were forced to put the Bach project on hold. After meeting Böll to consult him on Bach's language, Straub read *Billiards at Half Past Nine* and immediately wanted to make a film out of it. This script was also turned down by both Bonn and North Rhine–Westphalia and finally submitted to Rob Houwer, who would have produced the film if Straub had not stubbornly insisted on original sound.[5] Similarly, a producer named Hans Eckelkamp at Atlas-Film, to whom Böll had sent the script for *Not Reconciled*, might have made the Bach film had Straub accepted Herbert von Karajan as the lead.[6] When *Not Reconciled*, too, failed to get immediate support, Straub/Huillet developed a scenario based on "Bonn Diary." The association with Schonger, who had been interested in the Bach film as well, failed because of the producer's reservations about the directness of the satire: He was convinced it would simply be banned and his money wasted.[7] Straub went to Eckelkamp at Atlas-Film. While the producer was expressing his reservations about the commercial viability of *Not Reconciled*, a visitor in his office looked over the scenario for *Machorka-Muff*, which Straub had also brought along. This visitor, Heiner Braun, eventually played the role of Nettlinger in *Not Reconciled*. At this meeting, he said he found the scenario amusing and persuaded Eckelkamp to guarantee DM 12,000 for the production of *Machorka-Muff*. After work began, the producers were persuaded to provide DM 20,000, and the filmmakers raised the remaining DM 11,000 themselves. Since the publisher, Witsch, had not yet acquired the rights to the story, Böll simply gave Straub/Huillet permission to use it for the film.[8]

The difficulties of *Machorka-Muff* did not end with the financing, however. The producers attempted to interfere with the editing, and the distributor, Atlas-Film, disowned the film after it had been turned down by the Oberhausen Festival. It only got a semiofficial screening after Straub distributed a provocative leaflet at the festival announcing an underground screening.[9] Critics praised the film and condemned its exclusion, but it was only released a year later. Atlas-Film did not pair it with a Western or even with a promising art film like *The Silence*, as the filmmakers would have preferred, but with a number of less promising titles.[10] Marketing of the film was further hampered by the rating given it by the Filmbewertungsstelle. Since it was rated only "Wertvoll" and not "Besonders Wertvoll," exhibitors received less of a tax credit for showing it than the films with the higher rating. The film was also not approved for holidays or viewers under eighteen years of age. All of this was, of course, intended to hinder the film without appearing to actually censor it. In France, as Straub remarked, it would simply have been banned.[11]

Despite the film's difficult beginnings, *Machorka-Muff* won Straub/Huillet some renown, including a congratulatory letter from Karlheinz Stockhausen.[12] Buoyed by this, they became even more dedicated to the longer Böll project and decided to produce *Not Reconciled* themselves. Huillet calculated that they could make two-thirds of the film for DM 50,000, which they would raise themselves in the confidence that the remaining sum could be won on the basis of the finished portion.[13] Godard, Nestler, Huillet's mother, and other friends and relatives helped Straub/Huillet raise the DM 50,000, and the production was furthered by a credit from Walter Kirchner of Neue Filmkunst in Munich, even though it was later withdrawn. The cinematographer from *Machorka-Muff*, Wendelin Sachtler, had been successful enough to offer to work for free and to lend the blimped Arriflex camera for the film. He later asked for and received his payment of DM 10,000.

After showing the rough cut to Böll, who was less than pleased but indicated they should go ahead and finish, Straub/Huillet took another four months to raise another DM 22,000 and finish the film. Still lacking a distributor, they went with the film to the Berlin Film Festival in July 1965. The film was rejected by the regular festival, but perhaps wishing to avoid the absurd situation of *Machorka-Muff* at Oberhausen, Enno Patalas of *Filmkritik* organized a special screening. Announced only by posters saying, "New Narrative Forms in Cinema, *Not Reconciled*," the screening became the *succès du scandale* of the year.

Most of the scandal came from Böll's publisher, Witsch, who had ordered Straub/Huillet to stop work on the film and who now demanded that it be destroyed. Straub/Huillet quickly took the film with them to Switzerland, perhaps to evade this threat, but also—as Straub has insisted was the real reason—to work on the subtitles while staying with a friend.

After much anguished and often bitter debate with Witsch, with Böll uncomfortably caught in the middle, Straub/Huillet won approval to have the film distributed but not to show it on television. Böll, who wanted to avoid all this conflict and concentrate on his work, was eventually worn down by the filmmakers' indignant appeals to his solidarity and his earlier verbal commitment to the project. He finally gave them permission for full distribution but begged in conclusion, "Please don't write me any more such letters!"[14]

The political atmosphere surrounding *Machorka-Muff* was thus much different from that only a few years later with *Bridegroom* or *Chronicle*. The film seems now to be a biting political satire, with strong surrealist elements, and is considered a breakthrough for the German cinema. At the time, however, it seemed too radical to be comprehensible. Straub and Huillet had not been signatories of the Oberhausen Manifesto, and the explanation Straub cites for the film's exclusion from the festival is that they were told, "If we show this film in competition, we will make ourselves look ridiculous—as intellectuals of the Left." "Who? Never heard of them . . ." was Straub's caustic reply.[15]

Another criticism of the film from the Left was that it does not show a "militarist"—in other words, the political satire is not specific enough. This criticism perhaps foreshadows much of the political objection to Straub/Huillet films up to the present day. They are utopian but not specifically connected to current politics and therefore challenging to their friends as well as their foes. Form and politics are important to the seventeen-minute film in roughly equal proportions, perhaps accounting for its continued impact. Reinhold Rauh has chosen it for the subject of two recently published studies, maintaining, "More than in many other films, the few minutes of *Machorka-Muff* concentrate together film history and film policy/politics."[16] Rauh also considers *Machorka-Muff* a lone, early precursor of the New German Cinema and, in the period of the Oberhausen Manifesto, "the very first film to seriously propose a new conception of film in the Federal Republic."[17]

The analogy to the Western is useful in considering both the politics and the form of *Machorka-Muff*. The Böll short story "Bonn Diary" was first published on 15 September 1957, the day of the election that "consecrated" the remilitarization of West Germany.[18] Böll's satire is bitingly antimilitarist, with scathing depictions of army officers whose fame rises with the number of casualties their own forces suffer. Largely avoiding reference to fascism in this dynamic, Böll concentrates on the smooth collusion of aristocracy, church, and military to succeed—"And in a democracy too." "A democracy in which we have the majority of Parliament on our side is a great deal better than a dictatorship."[19]

As in a Western, Machorka-Muff is an evil gunslinger who comes into town and easily takes over because of his villainous reputation. The film does not "act out" this takeover but shows only the confirmation and celebration of the victory. The plot of Böll's "Bonn Diary" follows the events of four days recorded in diary entries by Erich von Machorka-Muff, a former major in the Nazi Wehrmacht who is to be rehabilitated and promoted to general. Mostly concentrated on the Tuesday after he arrives in the capital on Monday night, the story consists of a number of commemorations of milestones for Machorka-Muff. As the film review by Helmut Färber noted, all of these have been more or less foregone conclusions, and the story thus has both a dreamy quality and an unreal tempo. The events are not occurring as we are told of them, only their public recognition. The ritualistic nature of the scenes depicted implies that, through behind-the-scenes manipulation, history is repeating itself—or continuity is being restored. The film underscores this, beginning with the words on-screen after the title: "No story; a visual, abstract dream."

Peter Nau has also observed that the diary element of the film in the form of the voice-over adds a level of temporal distance to the narration of the Böll text.[20] In the latter, all the action is narrated from the point of view of the author of the diary, looking back in time. In the film, the action is narrated in present tense, while the voice-over, representing a later temporal point of view, comments on it. These comments, Nau asserts, are not blended with the "reality" of the film but are set among the other temporal and dramatic levels of the film in a montage. This he describes, citing Brecht, as a "literarization of film."[21] The film is therefore not an illustration of a text but a construction of cinematic materials. In Nau's words,

> The literary text by Böll, the newspaper articles, the music ("A musical Offering" by Bach, the "Transmutations" by François Louis, as well as the song "Once I Had a Comrade," played by a brass choir at the dedication ceremony), the bodies of the actors, their individual manner of speaking, the sound of their voices—these elements go into the film as raw materials and permit, separate from one another, not blended together, the insight into its construction.[22]

The central event described in Böll's text is Machorka-Muff's triumphal entry into Bonn, the capital city of the Federal Republic of Germany, for the laying of the cornerstone of the Academy of Military Memories, the creation of which had been a dream of his youth. Another victory consists in the major's formal recommissioning at the rank of general. Before the cornerstone ceremony, he is visited by a government minister, who greets him as "General" and presents him matter-of-factly with the documents of his commission. A third event in the story is the grotesque revisionist rehabilitation of General Hurlanger-Hiss, after whom the academy is to be named. Legitimized by unpublicized research by Machorka-Muff's fiancée, Inn, this event is enacted by way of Machorka-Muff's reading of the speech containing the new information on war casualties. Finally, the denouement of the story consists of two steps, each conveyed in a very short diary entry for Wednesday and Thursday. On Wednesday, possibly carried away by the emotions of his military success,

Machorka-Muff becomes engaged to Inn (Inniga von Zaster-Pehnuntz: All the cronies of Machorka-Muff bear absurd, usually alliterated aristocratic-sounding German names). The Church, in the person of a priest, immediately sanctions this union of military and aristocracy by annulling Inn's previous seven marriages (as civil ceremonies).[23] On Thursday, Machorka-Muff mentions an "annoying interlude"—the intrusion of political discord into his dream of success. The opposition has complained about the academy project, and Machorka-Muff responds in astonishment, "Opposition? What's that?" The response of the military man reveals that politics is anathema to him and disrupts his project of reconstructing historical memory: "Opposition—a strange word, I don't like it at all; it is such a grim reminder of times that I thought were over and done with."[24] This resistance to the intrusion of conflict and memory that is uncomfortable for Machorka-Muff is actually a last reference to a theme that occurs throughout the "Bonn Diary" and in *Billiards at Half Past Nine* as well. Machorka-Muff's project in creating his academy is repeatedly couched in terms of reconstructing memory and history, and the language of the story calls attention to this: In addition to the name and purpose of the academy, there is also the Latin inscription Machorka-Muff proposes, MEMORIA DEXTERA EST, and the title of his first lecture, given on the last day of the diary, "Reminiscence as a Historical Duty." The type of memory that Machorka-Muff supports is that which leads to the construction of institutions of state power. Military memoirs are less important than the stone building where they are to be written—in Böll's words, "through conversations with old comrades and cooperation with the Ministry's Department of Military History." The political power this represents is more important than the building: "My own feeling is that a six-week course should suffice, but Parliament was willing to subsidize a three-month course."[25]

The element of class is also included in the role that memory plays. For the powerful, memory is a justification for building monuments to their power, but for the less powerful, it merely signifies sentimentality and comradeship. This is made clear by the contrast between the reminiscences of Machorka-Muff's first visitor in Bonn, his former adjutant, Heffling, and Machorka-Muff's mental observations while he is speaking. The diary does not report the reminiscences the two men of unequal rank share, apart from the introductory words, "Remember the time at Schwichi-Schwaloche, the ninth . . . ?" (Which are implied to come from Heffling and in the film explicitly do so.) It does contain, however, Machorka-Muff's distracted comment, "It is heartwarming to observe how powerless the vagaries of fashion are to corrode the wholesome spirit of the people: the homespun virtues, the hearty male laugh, and the never-failing readiness to share a good dirty story are still to be found. While Heffling was telling me some variations on the familiar subject, I noticed Murcks-Maloche had entered the lobby."[26] Since an important comrade in the plans for the academy has arrived, Machorka-Muff merely glances at his watch

Machorka-Muff (Erich Kuby) in civilian clothes. Courtesy New Yorker Films.

and "with the sound instincts of the simple man he [Heffling] understood immediately that he had to leave."[27] Time is in the control of the powerful, as is memory. The only activity, along with the brief dialogue, in this scene is the ordering of drinks, and this, too, is a marker of status. For his subordinate, Machorka-Muff orders a double schnapps; for Murcks-Maloche and himself, he orders two Henneseys.

The film's adaptation of these actions is one of three departures from the temporal content of the story, and, in each case, the effect is consistent with the domination of time that Machorka-Muff is in the process of enacting. The insignificance of the subordinate's reminiscences and Machorka-Muff's class superiority are conveyed by the camera. It does not remain with the conversation but instead follows the major's order for the double schnapps, waiting over fifty seconds for the drink to be poured and brought. It is the power of the military man's order that "acts." When the schnapps is brought, the conversation is begun and concluded in a matter of seconds. The second conversation, with a powerful comrade, does take place while the drinks are brought and concludes with a close-up of the cognac glasses raised in a toast.

The power to control time and memory is thus inscribed in the film sequences that follow the effects of Machorka-Muff's whims: the securing of a drink, the idle browsing in a newspaper (which actually provides a concentrated survey of the advancing remilitarization of Germany with Christian Democrat support), and an idle walk through the city. The time in each case may be irritatingly empty to the audience, since it is not accompanied by narratively introduced memories, but in each case, they provide evidence of the time and memories that this character proposes to possess.

Machorka-Muff's domination over time is contrasted in the story with a number of terms that make him seem dreamy and swept away with emotions in response to the magnitude of his successes. The word *ergriffen* (moved, deeply stirred) is one of the most frequent in the story, and other phrases invoke Machorka-Muff's physical and emotional swooning at what is transpiring: "abandoning myself wholly," "resigned myself with a sigh," "I was too moved to undertake any serious business that morning," "melancholy overtook me," "I got out of bed, followed her in a kind of daze," "I must have swayed for a moment and suppressed a few tears."[28] This dreamy attitude corresponds to the reminders present in the story that there is no suspense here, that all that is happening is a restoration of a past order. When Murcks-Maloche tells him of the success of the plan for the academy, which of course he already knew, he turns it into a kind of military ceremony: "I felt constrained to stand up; I was filled with solemn pride; historic moments have always moved me deeply."[29] In the film, this scene ends with the ceremonious clink of the brandy glasses.

An ironic counterpart to this swoon over a consummation that is nothing new comes after his decision to marry Inn. Both are in a gay mood, as Machorka-Muff observes, "Inna was elated, I had never seen her quite like that. 'I always feel like this,' she said, 'when I am a bride.' " Machorka-Muff's emotions are stimulated by the sensation of power, and his enjoyment of power is never far removed from a sensation of lust. For instance, his engagement to Inn (whose family was only ennobled two days before the kaiser abdicated) is stimulated by "military memories," and his proposal is even couched in terms of his own military rank: "I felt encouraged when she whispered (in church) that she recognized a colonel as her second husband, a lieutenant-colonel as her fifth, and a captain as her sixth. 'And your eighth,' I whispered in her ear, 'will be a general.' " Machorka-Muff's daydreams about the Academy of Military Memories are also punctuated by sexual fantasies. While preparing for a "rendezvous with Inn," he muses that she would be the right wife for him, despite their differing religious backgrounds. Böll does not describe their rendezvous and copulation but rather Machorka-Muff's musings, which connect war and sex: "all the same, the numbers link us together symbolically: she has been divorced seven times, I have been wounded seven times. Inna!! I still can't get used to being kissed on the street. . . . Inna woke me at 617 hours." The sexual intercourse that occurs in the space of Böll's ellipsis is referred to twice in Machorka-Muff's memories in the next few minutes, as his attention goes back and forth between her and the Hurlanger-Hiss files she has prepared for his speech. "Lost in daydreams of her gift of love, I heard the band music: melancholy overtook me, for, like all the other experiences of this day, to listen to this music in civilian clothes was truly an ordeal." And one of the events was sexual intercourse. The arrival of the minister of defense, to which he also responds dreamily, is also scintillating because it occurs near "the rumpled bed in all its delightful disarray of love."[30]

The nearness of power and sex in Machorka-Muff's consciousness becomes even clearer in his two references to the pleasure or diversion that military officers can get from working-class women. The first instance occurs when his subordinate Heffling invites Machorka-Muff to come and visit sometime, saying, "My wife would be delighted." Machorka-Muff's commentary: "And I promised Heffling I would come and see him. Perhaps an opportunity would offer for a little adventure with his wife; every now and again I feel the urge to partake of the husky eroticism of the lower classes, and one never knows what arrows Cupid may be holding in store in his quiver."[31] The second such reference to sexual exploitation has an even more explicit relation to violence and "military memories." It is an unrealized part of his plan for the academy: "I was also thinking of having a few healthy working-class girls housed in a special wing, to sweeten the evening leisure hours of the comrades who are plagued with memories."[32] Obviously, these memories will not be of the sort to be included in the memoirs the officers are to institutionalize. The film includes in voice-over the first of these comments but excludes the second and the inscriptions Machorka-Muff plans for the portals of the academy: MEMORIA DEXTERA EST; BALNEUM ET AMOR MARTIS DECOR.

The sexual aspect of Machorka-Muff's conquest of the capital city is still implied in Straub's description of the story as a rape. The cultural form that this rape of Germany takes is to be that of monuments and institutions. Here, both the story and the film introduce a theme that is significant to all Straub/Huillet films, the difference between monument and memory. Again, Machorka-Muff provides a useful contrast to *Not Reconciled*, which is about the destruction of monuments in order to reawaken memory. Here, the laying of a cornerstone, dedicated to "military memories," is celebrated. It is to be a place where military officers from the rank of major up can gather to write their memoirs.

The treatment of history that will be introduced here becomes obvious in the dedication speech by Machorka-Muff: He "corrects" the supposedly shameful record of Field Marshal Emil von Hurlanger-Hiss, who had reportedly lost only 8,500 men in the retreat from Schwichi-Schwaloche, when, "according to the calculations of [Hitler's] specialists in retreat . . . his army should, with the proper fighting spirit, have had a loss of 12,300 men." Machorka-Muff reveals with satisfaction that the losses can now be established at 14,700 dead.[33]

This scene, which Nau terms the "satirical high point of the film," is given a special status by its striking cinematic construction. The general's speech

Machorka-Muff (Erich Kuby) back in uniform. Courtesy New Yorker Films.

dedicating the Academy of Military Memories is filmed from above so that emphasis is placed on the cornerstone, his gloved hands holding the papers, the lapels of his uniform, and his cap. From this high angle, the camera tracks in, so that first the papers, then the decorated visor of the uniform cap grow larger. In the process, the eyes recede and eventually disappear except for the suggestion of a fold of skin. The nose and moving mouth—he is a "mouthpiece" after all—become the only signs of his bodily presence. Because of the dramatic effect of this tracking shot, critics misinterpreted it as a series of close-ups, isolating individual aspects. But the continuity of the shot increases the shock of the close-up that does conclude the speech. As the "honorable" figure of 14,700 casualties is named, the camera drops to a low-angle close-up of the fully "exposed" face of the officer, who then steps away leaving the camera to dwell on the empty gray sky. After the brass band plays, the high-angle shot is repeated, showing the mason laying the cover on the cornerstone and Machorka-Muff ceremoniously tapping it down with a hammer.

This visual isolation of Machorka-Muff from his surroundings exaggerates his identification with his role at that moment, as indicated by the gloves, the uniform, and the pages of his speech. It also reduces and concentrates the visual image as his speech becomes most grotesque: He measures heroism by senseless loss of life, evokes continuity of Hitler (with the cozy familiarity of the nickname Tapir) as an authority, and bemoans the ludicrous "disgrace" that

Laying the cornerstone of the Academy for Military Memories in *Machorka-Muff*. Courtesy New Yorker Films.

Hurlanger-Hiss suffered—punitive transfer to Biarritz where he died of food poisoning after eating lobster.

The surprising angle of the shot, the point of view that is only that of the camera, not of any possible character or theatrical audience, also concentrates the cinematic nature of such shots. Nau sums up the production of meaning through this separation of elements.

> The speech is reproduced intact, but the speaker is captured from various, fragmentary and unusual perspectives. Therefore no reality effect is produced, resting on image and sound doubling each other so as to produce an illusion of reality. Instead of giving the appearance of the film reflecting a reality outside itself, the sequence of the dedication ceremony is only to be seen as a specifically *filmic* reality, so that *in each moment* it conveys the explicit expression of the film.[34]

Eric Rentschler places this concentration of filmic reality into historical context in his discussion of the song "I Once Had a Comrade," New German Cinema, and U.S. president Ronald Reagan's controversial visit to the Bitburg military cemetery in 1985. Rentschler notes that the music begins over a shot of the "empty" sky after the speech and the laying of the cornerstone: "We become able to see the music, to read its importance in this setting, to reflect on the meaning of this song and the tradition it implies, a tradition the Academy for Military Memories means to restore, a legacy that Straub/Huillet every bit as forcefully want to undermine."[35] The cinematic form thus allows "sound to have space to step into the image"[36] and "involves the spectator in the construction, providing space to see through the historical fiction presented here."[37]

Three types of narration are used in the film to convey Böll's satire. Nau pointed out the contrasting moods of two of them: the voice-over narration of the diary and the abrupt intrusions of the dramatized passages. A third, the documentary, will be examined presently.

The narration provided by the diary entries is at times illustrated or acted out by the film. The contrast between the film images and the ironic, short commentary of Machorka-Muff is, if anything, more effective than the story's form. Rather than being embedded in his musings, the comments conclude and set off the meaning of visual sequences. For instance, his dream on his first night in the capital is seen in the film. In the story, he reports seeing hundreds of pedestals with shrouded statues on them, which reveal countless images of himself in uniform bowing in acknowledgment as the shrouds are removed. He touches the pedestal that bears his own name. In the film, we see Machorka-Muff asleep and then the dream images, reduced to three shrouded figures arranged at an angle rising to the right, accompanied by organ music (Bach). The three figures bow when the shroud is removed, and he touches his own name on the pedestal. But it is only in the next shot, when he is shaving, that we hear the self-satisfied commentary of the diary: "Such dreams one only has in the capital." Such a comment resonates with other points in the diaries, where Machorka-Muff says things like "Only in uniform can one . . ." and each of these illustrates the relish with which he enjoys his rediscovered power.

The film departs from the text in its depiction of the walk Machorka-Muff takes through the city because he is too restless and "ergriffen" to undertake anything serious. The film excludes his comment, "Although I was in civilians, I had the impression of a sword dangling at my side; there are some sensations which are really only appropriate when one is in uniform."[38] The film does connect the uniform with erotic thrills as it is revealed to Machorka-Muff, however, with wildly rapid close-ups alternating between the uniform, Inn's face, and his leering expression. The film replaces this sensuous relish of walking through the city, armed and in uniform, with several shots following Machorka-Muff after the voice-over simply states, "After Murcks had driven to the ministry, I wandered through the city." The relation of the Western gunslinger to the town he is taking over is suggested by the shots that follow. Böll's text stresses the physical side of Machorka-Muff's feelings as he walks, and Nau has noted how the film undertakes a Brechtian "literarization" of film by placing the temporal and physical elements of narration next to each other so that their narrative structure is revealed after they have been presented, rather than implied beforehand and then fulfilled.[39]

The meaning of the walk through the city emerges only after it has taken place. Since Straub gave the film the "formula" M = M and connected it to other gangster films, Fritz Lang's *M* is suggested when the murderer sees images in shop windows reflecting his own psychological obsessions. First, Machorka-Muff is shown crossing streets and plazas. He looks at the shop window of a pharmacy with the picture of a very old man next to a mechanical figure that does gymnastics on a bar. In the lower left of the window is the slogan "To grow old—to remain young, that is the wish of us all." He then picks up a visiting card on the steps of a Chinese restaurant. The card, addressed to "Chérie," appears to be an invitation to a sexual encounter, with a meeting at a club called the Queen of Spades, in the Nymphenburger Strasse. Another possible reference to *M* is the cry of a young girl, "Mummy, the lights are going on!" as the major walks along the streets. A second shop window shows women's fashions in the military style of the Hussars.

Finally, the camera makes a 180-degree pan over the Rhine and the suburbs behind it, ultimately stopping with a bridge in the background and Machorka-Muff in profile filling the left side of the screen. At this point, he shifts from his anticipation of his fiancée to memories of his old general. The voice-over accompanying this panorama is, "Uplifted by the certainty that my plan had become reality—once again I had every reason to recall one of Schnomm's expressions: 'Macho, Macho,' he used to say, 'you've always got your head in the clouds.' He had said it when there were only thirteen men left in my regiment and I had four of those men shot for mutiny."[40]

The sexual anticipation that Böll's text juxtaposes with the military memories and the anticipation of the later military ceremony is merely suggested in the film. At this point, the memory leads Machorka-Muff to marvel at the militarization of Germany that "these Christians" had been able to achieve and wonders what his old general would have to say about it. Here is where the documentary aspect of the film is introduced in the form of newspaper clippings. Straub describes the method as the opposite of the Bach film: "In Machorka-Muff I made use of reality, so that the fiction, let's say the satire, should become more realistic." But he stresses that most of the film is fiction, whereas the newspaper sequences make up only one and one-half minutes of the seventeen-and-one-half-minute film.[41]

While he kills time in the city, Machorka-Muff idly looks through the newspapers. The newspaper clippings are shown full screen, at first alternating at angles, then horizontally, so there is no longer a suggestion that these particular articles are in the paper Machorka-Muff is reading. Instead, they form yet another surrealistic intrusion into the film, much like the dream sequence, and are also accompanied by organ music (a dissonant improvisation by

François Louis). The newspaper articles document the preparation for German rearmament on a number of fronts:

> Religious/philosophical: "Is a Christian permitted to kill?" [Christ did not insist that soldiers give up their profession.] "The most perfect Christian will be the most useful soldier."
> Economic: "Armament industry in free competition."
> Political: "Defense is the citizen's duty."
> Adenauer: "Neutralization would be acquiescence."

Strangely enough, Färber criticized the film for not being radical enough in 1964, since the devices "still available" to the cinema, particularly the strategy of ellipsis and the exclusion of a more penetrating intellectual content, reveal its impotence.[42] The critique brought a quick response from Straub, which is typical of his comments on the films over the years. In a letter to *Filmkritik*, he defends the militancy of his work against those who misinterpret it: "I have forged out of the Böll satire a naked weapon for those who are neither 'militaristic' nor 'antimilitaristic' (antimilitarism is, like laughter, a narcotic for the privileged).... Even supposed leftist intellectuals react to *Machorka-Muff* as if they had expected pornography and were shown a marble venus."[43] Straub asserts that the quality of the weapon is not dependent on a "message"—which would fall into the category of pornography—but on the film's aesthetic integrity. It is a weapon, but "for those who have eyes and ears for what my old master Robert Bresson calls 'matière cinématographique.'" This double gesture of political radicality and loyalty to *artistic* tradition is then repeated with Straub's double dedication of the film "to the author of *The Resistible Rise of Arturo Ui* [i.e., Brecht] and to that of *The Rise and Fall of Legs Diamond*" (i.e., Budd Boetticher, who directed the film at Warner Brothers in 1960) and his conclusion that it is "built on the equation $M = M$."[44]

This stance in regard to a leftist response to Straub/Huillet's first film is characteristic of Straub's political and aesthetic polemics. Most often, the explicit gestures placing the works into contemporary political contexts are in the form of a dedication, mentioned either in the film or separately by Straub. *Moses and Aaron*, for instance, had difficulty being cleared for television broadcast because of a handwritten dedication to Holger Meins in the opening credits (Meins died in a hunger strike in prison as a suspected Red Army Faction terrorist);[45] the Bach film was "dedicated" in conversation to the Viet Cong;[46] *Antigone*, in Straub's comments immediately following the stage production in May 1991, to the one hundred thousand Iraqi victims of George Bush's New World Order.[47]

In his letter on *Machorka-Muff*, Straub connects his political radicality to a respectable aesthetic tradition with the references to Bresson, Brecht, and Lang and to a leftist tradition of political art (regarding capital and violence, with the reference to Brecht's *Arturo Ui*). But in all the debates over Straub/Huillet films, Straub has denied that they are incompatible with the "popular cinema." Hence the reference, along with Brecht, to a contemporary product of the Hollywood studio system, *The Rise and Fall of Legs Diamond*. All of these gestures against the categories of film culture still play a role in *Antigone* in 1992. Here, as early as 1964, is a sign of resistance to the "art cinema ghetto" that some perceive as the bane of New German Cinema in its confrontation with Hollywood's world domination.[48]

Straub's cinematic utopia envisions high art films such as those by Straub/Huillet coexisting with mainstream forms. This is not an acceptance of the impoverishment of the mainstream cinema, but too often Straub/Huillet's distance from the mainstream obscures their longing for a popular film industry that would include their films. This is another sign of their "respect for the audience," that they do not wish to address an elite. After all, Straub's letter says Machorka-Muff is for "lovers of the Western," and he would have liked the short film to have preceded Westerns in theatrical bookings.[49]

Despite the public anticipation of what fruits the Oberhausen Manifesto of 1962 would bring, the selection committee did not choose Machorka-Muff for the 1963 festival. Although the influence of the old guard had certainly not been dismantled by the manifesto, even "leftists" opposed the film, according to Straub. Even Böll refused to defend Straub/Huillet's film of his work, which Straub ascribed to fear of the unpredictable mass film audience as opposed to the readers of his literary work. The novelist here perhaps merely reflects the separation between film and literature that was greater in West Germany than in France, for example. If filmmakers thought of themselves as *Autoren*, the inverse was generally not the case.[50] But if Böll thought the film satires of the 1960s too explicit, he did not successfully avoid political controversy. By the 1970s, Böll was accused of being an "intellectual father" of left-wing terrorism and a terrorist "sympathizer." Hence the irony he contributed to *Germany in Autumn*: by 1977, even Sophocles' *Antigone* is too controversial for German mass media distribution.[51]

### *The Bridegroom, the Comedienne, and the Pimp*

It is perhaps testimony to the uniqueness of the period of the "student movement" around 1968 that the political significance of *Bridegroom* was widely appreciated. In this film, the relation to contemporary politics is not nearly as clear as in *Machorka-Muff*, and the modernist separation of elements reaches a high point. Yet the film received the award of the Mannheim Film Festival in 1968, not because of a jury decision, but because of the popular demands of the youthful crowd discussing the films after the festival was over.[52]

The revolutionary political impulse of the film remains even more general than the reference to "resistance" in the Bach and Böll films. As in the earlier work, artistic forms are the means chosen to express this liberation, and the connection to Germany, or any other political entity, remains metaphorical. Aside from the language and locations, the only reference to Germany in the film is in the graffiti of the opening shot, behind the titles, with the words, scrawled in English among other barely legible names and dates on a wall of the telegraph department of the Munich Post Office, "Stupid/old Germany/I hate it over here/I hope I can go soon//Patricia/1.3.68."[53]

As in a musical structure, this time more in the sense of heterogeneous variations on a theme rather than a fugue, a motif is established: a female prisoner who desires to escape. The static, fifty-second shot of the graffiti is followed by a tracking shot along the Landsberger Strasse in Munich. The shot is photographed from a vehicle proceeding with varying but almost constant speed, so that the sidewalk and the businesses facing the street are observed from right to left. Anticipating the driving shots in *History Lessons*, this tracking shot derives its pacing and "action" from the appearance and disappearance of identifiable elements before the neutral, urban-industrial background—the people who work at night on this street, the prostitutes, walking, standing, talking to each other or to men who pull up in their cars. Aside from these women's ephemeral presence, pace and variety are lent to the shot by the dramatic appearances of billboards and industrial signage out of the darkness—signs generally for steel plants and oil companies, accompanied by several gas stations, the only other location of human activity. To the theme of female imprisonment is thus added the motif of economic production and exchange: heavy industry, energy, and women's sexuality, all presented in parallel fashion to the camera as commodities.

At the same time as these motifs are being presented to the viewer without interpretation, the dilemma of cinematic form is also raised. The camera still has not isolated an image or an action, since its tracking from right to left is constant. Almost two minutes at the beginning of the shot are silent, adding to the evocation of the origins of cinema. Here the question of the "birth of the movies" is proposed: When does one cut the film? While posing this question of the birth of the movies, with all the elements present—human labor, industrial infrastructure, market exchange, light, motion, and commodified desire—the shot avoids the issue by fleeing the cinema temporarily to another source of aesthetic structure, the music of Johann Sebastian Bach. The music begins in the middle of the shot and is itself an excerpt from the Ascension Oratorio, also with a text praying for deliverance: "Thou day, when wilt thou be / In which we greet the savior / In which we kiss the savior / Come, make thyself appear!"[54] Once the music begins, however, it provides to the film a reference to time that gives logic to the cut at the end of the shot, simultaneous with its conclusion. This method of calling attention to the artificial connection between real time and cinematic narrative time is echoed at the conclusion of Fassbinder's *The Marriage of Maria Braun* (1978) as well. The conclusion of the explicitly timed "seven minutes" of soccer action on the sound track determines the end of the film's narrative with the explosion of Maria's house.

The Bach music supplies a stark contrast to the mundane scene before us. The spirituality of the religious text and the choral singing shockingly elevate the commodity exchange implied by the visual image. The most striking effect, however, is the transformation performed on the visual image by the presence of sound, especially this beautiful and lofty music. First, a dimension of meaning is added, another evocation of the longing for escape; and second, a sense of temporal structure or rhythm is added to the visual track, so that an expectation arises that its eventual cutting will have a meaning. Indeed, the music supplies both to this shot and to the end of the film one very practical requirement: an expectation in the audience that there is a reason to cut the film at the place where it cuts because the musical passage has come to its ending. This, of course, is perceived as the reverse of the actual procedure, since the end of the music is matched to the chosen final image or the end of the film roll. Then the music is laid over the shot from the end to the beginning. The crucial decision is thus not the ending of the visual track, which is the sensation aroused in the viewer, but the *beginning* of the sound track (a technique similar to that of *Introduction to Schoenberg's "Accompaniment to a Cinematographic Scene"*).

The use of the sound track to give structure to the film also relates to Straub/Huillet's use of texts for the same purpose. Since the filmmakers separate to a great extent the narrative structure from the cinematic form of their films, the narrative of the texts—or the simple duration of their delivery—provides one method of determining beginnings and endings of shots. The connection to early cinema is made by calling attention to the difference between the two logics, that of cinema and that of narrative. *Bridegroom* thus functions as a precursor to Straub/Huillet films that juxtapose text and landscape, such as *History Lessons*, *Fortini/Cani*, and *Too Early, Too Late*. It also recalls the centrality of editing to the filmmaking of Straub/Huillet, and Huillet's role is perhaps the greater here. As Handke put it, "Editing is the essence of film." And after giving directing students hands-on experience with editing *Empedocles*, Straub/Huillet wondered why the students still wanted to study directing at all.[55]

The motif of Bach's Ascension Oratorio returns at the end of the film as the poetry spoken by Lilith concludes with the words "eternal father of lights." Rather than the conclusion of the choral passage from the film's first shot, we now hear its beginning, signaling an element of rebellion against the constraints of the world as we see it before us. Again, the end of the musical passage dictates the end of the visual track, and the theme of deliverance is repeated. Lilith, another prostitute, has liberated herself from her pimp at the end of the film and, in a gesture repeated in other Straub/Huillet films, turns toward the light of a window.

After the initial driving shot ends, following the cues of the music, another "movement" begins which does not initially appear to take up any of these themes. Rather than the shock of beginning and remaining in the visual space before a moving camera, the next shot returns the camera to the interior, a static camera, and the world of the theater. If the initial shot corresponded to the early cinematic tradition of Lumière, with its documentary emphasis, the second might logically connect with the other early film tradition, Méliès's studio-bound work (minus the magic). Historically, however, the world we see before us is an anachronistic one: The shot consists of the entire performance of the play *Pains of Youth* (1926) by Ferdinand Bruckner, as adapted and directed by Straub at Munich's Action-Theater in July 1967.[56] Straub had initially wanted to direct Brecht's *The Measures Taken*, but the Brecht family would not grant the rights. Instead, the group offered Straub the Bruckner piece, which he initially resisted until he had reduced it to a mere eleven minutes. It was performed on the same program as Fassbinder's first play with the Action-Theater, *Katzelmacher*. The antinaturalism of the performance is obvious, which at least in an abstract sense could connect to the cinema of Méliès. But even more pertinent is the source of the play—the expressionist theater contemporary with the "Golden Age" of German cinema in the 1920s. This—again without the magic—is the cinema of *Dr. Caligari*.

It would seem that the reduction of a full-length, three-act play to eleven minutes would destroy the original aesthetic impact, but, given the expressionism of the original work, this is not entirely the case. In the filmed performance, the actors walk through their roles, taking positions in relation to each other as they recite machine gun-like the lines that reveal the action taking place. Straub has indicated that it may be impossible to understand all of the content of what is taking place but that this is not a disadvantage, since what one does perceive is a series of constellations. This is not at all inconsistent with expressionism or the Chamber Theater that developed parallel to it in 1920s theater and film: The characters are significant not as naturalistic representations of individuals but as types in dramatic situations or hierarchies. Even in Straub's reduced version of Bruckner, these constellations are clear: the aristocrat, the devil-may-care medical student, the arrogant pimp, the innocent maid from the country. The cynicism of the postwar 1920s and the 1960s in regard to bourgeois culture and power structures is evident in both versions. The threat of the pimp to force any woman he chooses into prostitution (or marriage), the ridicule of German classical culture (Goethe) as a mere trapping for empty vanity, and the close connection between sex and death (murder or suicide) are striking similarities between both the early 1920s and the late 1960s: "You long for it as for the knife," as the character Freder (played by Fassbinder) says. Only a cryptic fragment of a Mao quotation provides a link to politics of the 1960s in this shot. Most of the slogan is obstructed by backdrop, but as with the drastically cut play, the sense is clear: "Only when the arch-reactionaries are —— will it be possible to ——." Similarly, Straub called the film "the last judgment of Mao and of the Third World on our world."[57]

Again by way of contrast, this shot develops the theme of temporality initiated by the traveling shot, but in an entirely different direction. In the shot on the street, a sense of rhythm only arises from the random comings and goings of the women and cars, in interaction with the constant motion of the camera itself. Once the music begins, a rhythm is added to the shot from outside that gives it an aesthetic structure without altering its content. In the stage shot, the rhythm arises only from the delivery of the lines and the motion of the actors. At first viewing, most people have assumed that the performance of the film is entirely expressionless, but this is far from the case. Since the delivery of the lines lacks expression, this actually serves to exaggerate two aspects: meaning and time.

Because so few cues are given as to the identity of these people and their projects, we are all the more intent on figuring them out and are all the more shocked by their lack of affect in the face of conflict, violence, and death. Rather than attend to their histrionic *demonstration* of these experiences, we are able to ignore the necessary walking about in order to strike the poses that reveal the constellations where they take place. Since the attention to the acting is reduced and the concentration on the language is increased, the temporal element is also exaggerated, this time by the speed of the actors' line delivery, the placement and length of their pauses, and the pauses introduced by physical movement from one constellation to another. Far from being monotonous, this rhythmic arrangement of sound and silence is quite musical and dramatic.

Their collaboration in the political theater of this period was also the source of Straub/Huillet's influence on Fassbinder. Most critics limit their influence to the latter's early films, such as *Katzelmacher* (1969), which in the stage version was performed together with *Pains of Youth*. In the Fassbinder film, the actors are also arranged in almost two-dimensional constellations against rather static backgrounds, which are then broken by abrupt entrances and exits from the sides. Contrasted with these scenes are tracking shots of alternating pairs of characters who walk toward the camera as it moves backward through a narrow apartment courtyard.

Fassbinder had also dedicated his film *Love Is Colder than Death* (1969) to Claude Chabrol, Jean-Marie Straub, and Eric Rohmer,[58] and the arrangement of characters to show "attitudes," as was done in the Bruckner play, persists throughout Fassbinder's work. Wilfried Wiegand connects *Effi Briest* (1972–1974), for instance, back to the "Dreyer-Bresson-Straub tradition."[59] Also, Fassbinder's avoidance of exterior or landscape shots, except to show how inaccessible they are, seems to connect to Stockhausen's description of the camera as "sheet lightning" in *Machorka-Muff*.

That Fassbinder "learned to direct" from Straub and the evidence for this in Fassbinder's early work confirms the "Brechtian" aspect of cinema they share in regard to work with the actors. Fassbinder's irritation with Huillet as the more "rigid" of the two indicates that she and Straub rehearsed the Action-Theater actors together. In a 1974 interview, Fassbinder confirms this aspect of Straub/Huillet's influence.

> *Q:* Has Straub influenced you?
> 
> *RWF:* Straub has been more like an important figure for me.
> 
> *Q:* But weren't you inspired by him to use a slow narrative rhythm, and a principle of real time in which occurrences on the screen last exactly as long as they do in reality?
> 
> *RWF:* What was more significant for me was that Straub directed a play, *Krankheit der Jugend* (Ferdinand Bruckner) with the Action-Theater, and even though his version was only ten minutes long, we rehearsed it for all of four months, over and over again, for only two hours a day, I admit, it was still really crazy. This experience I had with Straub, who approached his work and the other people with such an air of comic solemnity, fascinated me. He would let us play a scene and then would say to us, "How did they feel at this point?" This was really quite right in this case, because we ourselves had to develop an attitude about what we were doing, so that when we were acting, we developed the technique of looking at ourselves, and the result was that there was a distance between the role and the actor, instead of total identity. The films he's made that I think are very beautiful are the early ones, *Machorka-Muff* and *Not Reconciled*, up to and including *Chronicle of Anna Magdalena Bach*, though *Othon* and other films since then have proved to me that what is most important to him is not what interests me in his work.[60]

The third portion of *Bridegroom* leaves the theater and enters the realms of ritual, love story, and the gangster genre. This section is composed of nine shots, and for the first time, camera motion is coordinated with the movement of a character and with cinematic suspense in the form of a car chase. As with the static shot of the power constellations in the Bruckner play, here we also have only a suggestion of the characters (even less): The woman bids her lover good-bye, urging him to be careful. The man's motion to the elevator produces the powerful expectation that it will follow him when he reaches the entrance of the building, but instead the next camera placement is from behind the man lurking in wait in a car outside. So the doubling of point of view—our initial identification with the character named James and the second identification with a malevolent pursuer's view of him—creates in a single edit the sense of a gangster film or film noir. The absurdity of the reduction is an added aspect of distance from the drama: A VW Beetle pursues James's BMW. He leaves the car at the end of a reservoir and runs up an embankment (the only energetic movement in the entire film). His pursuer enters the shot from the right, scrambling up an embankment after him, but seems to be daunted enough by James's kicks to slide back down out of the frame as James continues to struggle upward.

With this sequence, crystallizing the drama of a car chase into three shots, we have left the world of Méliès's early cinema to reach perhaps Buster Keaton, for whom the position in the frame and motion into and out of it have existential power. The narrative space of these three shots is abstract but is defined totally by the sense of danger and a chase: James leaves home, descends, enters the street and the public realm (the car), is pursued out of the city into nature (with the sound of falling water). The sequence begins and ends with static shots, but in the intervening shots the camera pans left, right, and left. To escape, he ascends again into an unknown space, but in any case out of frame and in a direction where no camera movement has followed.

The next shot confirms that he has escaped, since it depicts the marriage ceremony between James and Lilith, the woman he had left before being chased. Their vows, conducted in an austerely modern chapel and photographed in a single shot, constitute a different kind of ritualized performance than the theatrical shot. Here there is no dramatic variation of rhythm but only the repetition of the expected ritual, also in the real time it takes to recite them. The only drama engendered by the shot is that of its composition in relation to the camera and a real or implied audience. Here it is quite dissimilar from the Bruckner play, which had been photographed from an angle only slightly to the left of center, and instead related to the performance spaces of the Bach film. The angle of the shot reveals the couple to be married on the right, spaced carefully so that the priest and his attendant are visible on the left. The open space of the composition, however, is toward the front of the church (the left) rather than toward the back where the congregation would be. There is no reason to believe that there would be a crowd, but the ritual does refer to witnesses of the wedding who also commit themselves to support the married couple in the future.

This is reminiscent of the exclusion, but implied presence, of an audience in the Bach film. The composition shifts the weight away from an actual congregation of witnesses, but the text invokes one. Thus the audience is presented with the possibility of taking the place of the witnesses. But the angle of the shot makes it a conscious tension rather than a "natural" identification with the space of the audience as in the theater segment.

The shot of the wedding is followed by a more dramatic mise-en-scène as we see the car of the wedding couple emerge from the distance and arrive, followed by the panning camera, at a new suburban house. As they disembark, James recites poetry to Lilith, lines from St. John of the Cross, beginning, "The time at last came / For the old order to be revoked, / To rescue the young Bride / Serving under the hard yoke."[61]

Peter Jansen has observed that the film follows an alternating structure of exterior/interior/exterior (although this is not strictly true, since the third section includes both interior and exterior shots).[62] His observation of the use of empty space is of interest, however, although it also assumes a schematic consistency that goes beyond what Straub/Huillet actually construct. Jansen asserts that a space is *always* shown (regarding interiors) before the people enter them and in the long shots (such as, in *Not Reconciled*, Schrella crossing the housing blocks that are his childhood home or Johanna's long walk to get the gardener's gun): "The imagination of the viewer has each time already penetrated the scene, is present in it and at home, before the figures of the film join in."[63]

The effect of this seems to be somewhat different from what Jansen implies, however, especially in the shots of approaching cars in *Bridegroom*. There is the element of almost satirical suspense, since each long shot of an approaching auto could be seen as part of the car chase. It is not entirely true, however, that the spectator is at home in these shots. The suspense created by the car's long approach is perhaps exaggerated by the fact that the spectator's quizzical imagination is already "at home" in the shot, but the approach of the car also disrupts that familiarity. In the first car chase, the loudness of the sound and the fragmentation of the cars as they break the bounds of the frame once they reach close-up are disturbing. The comfortable space set up in the long shot is spilled over by the violent vehicles, and the viewer becomes aware of space outside the frame that had been inviolable for the seconds previous.

The arrival of the car in the final sequence of *Bridegroom* is another matter. This time the frame is not broken, but instead the camera pans to the left to follow the car and to reveal a house—another narrative space—that had not been visible before. This again builds suspense and disrupts the "at home" feeling that Jansen describes. The result is a dramatic interaction between space, mise-en-scène, and camera movement—which all work on audience perception separately to create an effect.

The shock of the cut reveals Fassbinder, the pimp from the Bruckner segment, already inside and holding a gun. This also goes against the pattern Jansen describes, since the camera retroactively takes on the dual function of narrating and lying in wait, as it had done in shot 2 of the film noir sequence.

The final shot of *The Bridegroom, the Comedienne, and the Pimp* (Lilith Ungerer). Courtesy New Yorker Films.

But here, the narrative structure is carried by forces independent of the threat of the pimp to resubjugate Lilith.

The camera moves quite wildly in this scene, starting with a nearly full shot of Fassbinder threatening, "One doesn't flee our family so simply, Lilith," echoing Inn's claim at the end of *Machorka-Muff* that no one has successfully opposed her family either. After the pimp has spoken, the camera pans and tilts right to show Lilith and James, then pans straight across to the left, following Lilith in an uninterrupted movement to the window. There she delivers her final speech from St. John of the Cross about the passion of her "heart of clay" that burns with flames that quench thirst and would rise "up to the high peaks / of that eternal Father of Lights." The shock of this second pan, however, is that its smooth, level motion records the "melodramatic" act of Lilith's taking up Fassbinder's gun and shooting him as she walks past him toward the window. Only Lilith and the gun are framed in the briskly moving shot; Fassbinder is not visible even though the pan crosses above the space where he was initially seen. Neither the motion of the camera nor the pattern of the poetic exchange between Lilith and James has been interrupted.

The effect of this camera movement, as one can see in related shots in *Not Reconciled* and *Class Relations*, is for the character's liberation to be inscribed across a camera movement that is not dependent on "narration" but that has a telos of its own. After the camera has come to rest and Lilith recites her last verses, it then slowly tracks in to place her more literally on the edge of the window frame. Outside, the leaves blowing in the wind become even more vivid as the Bach music is repeated to the close. Much like the pans to windows at the end of *Not Reconciled* and *Chronicle of Anna Magdalena Bach*, the evocation of the cinema's essence in light and framing, independent of the character's lot, intimates an avenue of liberation.

# 5

# TIME AND MEMORY IN POSTWAR GERMANY

*Not Reconciled*

*Not Reconciled or, Only violence helps where violence rules* and the novel on which it was based, Heinrich Böll's *Billiards at Half Past Nine*, concentrate a vigorous critique of German fascism and militarism, a memorial to the victims, and fragments of German history and domestic life over decades as viewed through the kaleidoscope of a single day. The relation of history, time, and memory in *Not Reconciled* anticipates the dichotomy between word and image in *Moses and Aaron*: memory is invoked here by the lack of an image, by absence and paralyzed time. *Not Reconciled* traces the recovery of denied memories in three generations of a family of Cologne architects. The men have repeatedly subordinated their architectural skill to military purposes, at great human cost, and the grandmother, Johanna, commits a "terrorist" act to force a confrontation with this legacy.

Although *Not Reconciled* depicts an anonymous war memorial in its opening shot, the film as a whole suggests the Holocaust "countermonuments" of which James E. Young has written.[1] The countermonument does not seek the permanence of stone but instead documents its own fragility and disappearance. The memorialization of history through the work of delegated "specialists" such as archivists or artists may be a way of replacing memory itself: "In effect, the initial impulse to memorialize events like the Holocaust may actually spring from an opposite and equal desire to forget them."[2]

For the same reason that countermonuments by contemporary sculptors seek to perpetuate memory by negating their own survival, Straub/Huillet's film opposes active remembering to a memorialization of German history. To do so, they seek to empty the photographic image of narrative information, since, as John Berger puts it, photography threatens to replace memory. Thus, as

Elsaesser notes, *Not Reconciled* exhibits a "refusal to make the image signify and represent what in fact can only be grasped as bodily loss and absence."[3] The relationships they set up between narrative fragments, cinematic space, and time undermine the oppressive permanence of physical monuments of German culture. Through the gaps they construct in the fabric of memory, they leave room for human action to enter into history again. Like much of Straub/Huillet's work, these memories condemn Nazism for the sake of constructing out of this history a better Germany. As Handke put it, *Not Reconciled* "threw open the door to another Germany behind the usual one."[4]

### Böll's *Billiards at Half Past Nine*

Böll's novel *Billiards at Half Past Nine* is almost entirely constructed of memory, since it tells the story of three generations of a Cologne family from the point of view of a single day, the eightieth birthday of the respected architect Heinrich Faehmel. The events of the day culminate in a single point as well, a gunshot fired by Heinrich's wife, Johanna Faehmel. The transformation of this temporal structure into film will be the focus of a comparison of *Not Reconciled* with the novel, after we examine the novel's treatment of German history, fascism, memory, and resistance.

Heinrich Faehmel's reputation was established when, as the first step of his career in the city, his design for the Abbey of St. Anthony was accepted over the proposals of powerful local firms. Heinrich's son, Robert, also trained in architecture, spends his well-regulated days in nearly complete seclusion. He has an office for "architectural estimates" (statics) and plays billiards each day at half past nine, while talking to the hotel boy, Hugo. Robert has one secret from his family: As a demolition expert in the war, he quite efficiently destroyed his father's abbey to give the retreating German army the "field of fire" demanded by a deranged general. Representing the third generation, Robert's son, Joseph, is also an architectural student. Having discovered the secret that his father had destroyed the abbey, Joseph decides to abandon his studies rather than help rebuild it.

Among Robert's contemporaries, three figures are prominent. His wife, Edith, was killed by bombing in the war. Partly in response to this loss and the death of a son in World War I, Robert's mother, Johanna, had gone to the railroad yards, demanding to be sent away with the Jews. She has been in a sanatorium for sixteen years, for her own protection. Schrella and Nettlinger are both school classmates of Robert's. Schrella returns from exile on this day, only to be arrested for his implication in a prewar plot to kill the Fascist Vacano, the school gym instructor who has since become chief of police. Nettlinger, who as a schoolboy was part of Vacano's Fascist "auxiliary police," now has the authority to get Schrella out of jail. Schrella had been forced into exile because he was a "Lamb" resisting the "Buffaloes," the terms Böll uses for the political polarization of the Weimar Republic. Böll's criticism falls most heavily on the Buffaloes, who are not Nazis as such but conservative nationalists who propped up the Nazi party after its electoral setbacks in 1932. That is why both the novel and film place so much emphasis on the patriotic militarism associated with World War I, the kaiser, and Hindenburg.[5]

In the novel's structure, Robert stands on the side of stasis, while Johanna moves the novel toward activity. Johanna's husband, Heinrich, stands between the two.[6] Robert's central role is suggested by the title, since he is the character who plays billiards every day at 9:30 A.M. The first line of the novel announces a threat to his routine in the form of the unexpected, *das Unvorhergesehene*, the unprecedented: "This morning, for the first time ever . . ."[7] Nettlinger's threatened intrusion into the billiard game at this moment is a present-tense action that contrasts with the frozen time of Robert's routine.

Unlike his mother's reaction to trauma, Robert's withdrawal from time has its roots in the *postwar* period's gradual frustration of the goal of his demolition: to erect a "monument" of rubble to the victims of fascism and war.[8] In the form of St. Severin's Cathedral (the counterpart of the Cologne cathedral), the frozen structures of the past provide the restrictive framework within which Robert Faehmel must live. But his interactions with Hugo, Schrella, and Johanna bring time back to life again.

When Nettlinger attempts to interrupt Robert's billiard game, Robert has been telling Hugo stories about his youth. This act, too, is presented by Böll as a sudden exception to the routine, introduced without transition (as it is in the film as well): "Stories? What stories, boy?"[9] Both the stories and the location of the billiard room relate to St. Severin's as a central motif. For instance, Robert equates his asking Schrella why he was persecuted, a question that would lead to their resistance activity and exile, with "saying good-bye to St. Severin's dark tower."[10] Robert also uses the church to illustrate the principle of "field of fire." First he seizes it as a handy example, an obstacle between the billiard room and the bridge that might be a military target. But Robert also hints at the fact that during the war St. Severin's was his enemy, and perhaps it still is: "And believe me, Hugo," he says, "I'd have blown St. Severin's to smithereens."[11]

Robert recalls his use of delaying tactics in rounders games (a sport resembling baseball and cricket) to protect Schrella from the malicious attacks of the Fascists. Böll's description of the memory begins "and he saw himself" to describe Robert's own habitual motion as he would hit a ball with a bat, and the verb tense does not change as the narration shifts to the historical past and the events of a certain day, Saturday, 14 July 1935. As other players in the ball game begin to shout to him, they receive identity—Vacano, Nettlinger, Schrella. The time is then more precisely given—"three minutes and three seconds to the final whistle, thirteen seconds too many"—too long to prevent Nettlinger and the others from injuring Shrella.[12] But despite Robert's habit of

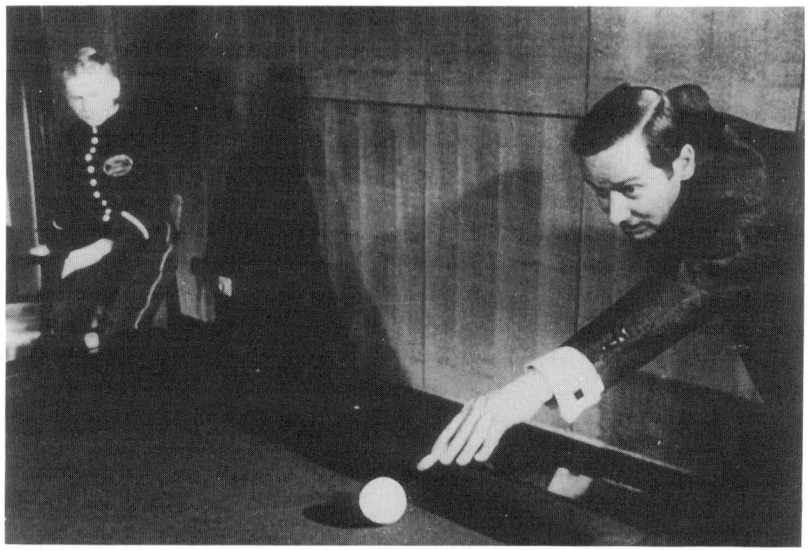

Georg Zander as Hugo and Henning Harmssen as Robert Faehmel in *Not Reconciled*. Courtesy Museum of Modern Art.

using the strict forms of games to escape history, he eventually reveals that he did participate in the anti-Fascist struggle. This participation is initially described in the abstract terms of a mere gesture (as are many acts with political consequences in the gamelike configurations of the novel), such as Robert asking Schrella the question "Why?" or Edith's smile or Ferdi Progulske's voice on the telephone, asking, "Are you coming, or aren't you?"[13] After the ineffectual bombing attempt planned at the meeting Ferdi refers to here, Ferdi is executed by the Nazis and Robert and Schrella flee for their lives into exile.

Because Robert is now telling this story to the hotel boy, Hugo, the ritualized retreat from memory begins to melt into a salvaging of the lessons of the past for the present. At the end of the chapter, the knowledge of history Hugo has gained provides a basis for action in the present. Robert asks Hugo's advice about admitting Nettlinger, and Hugo says he should not do so, thus linking the experience of the two generations.

In contrast to the function of narrative between Robert and Hugo, the more conventionally "novelistic" question "Who destroyed the abbey?" does not generate the plot. The secret that the builder, destroyer, and rebuilder of the abbey are three generations of the same family is ironically shown to be irrelevant. The family's "reconciliation," to the extent it occurs at all, is not a revelation but a foregone conclusion. The three characters involved never even speak of it aloud. Instead, only the resultant possibilities of reconciliation are hinted at by the breakdown of the novel's fissureless facade. Anything can happen now that the rituals of isolation and withdrawal have broken down.[14]

The novel, therefore, has pointed the way that Heinrich and Robert would have to go to stop playing the games of respectability, but it also shows that they do not go this way. They do not make public their satisfaction that the abbey was destroyed and remain unreconciled to the incompleteness of the destruction that was to be a monument to Edith and all the others. And this task cannot be completed by Robert adopting Hugo, who reminds him of Edith's smile, or by the sudden cancellation of their daily rituals such as the old man's breakfast at Kroner's or the billiard game. These actions resolve the novel's plot, but its historical themes remain unresolved.

The neatness of the billiard game structure of the novel and the apparent reconciliation of the other characters are literally exploded by Johanna Faehmel at the novel's conclusion. Only Johanna is able to get time moving again because her withdrawal from time is literal (due to her "insanity") whereas that of the others is metaphorical. She recounts the past as a litany rather than as a narrative; for instance, she forces Robert and Heinrich to walk the "stations" of memory.[15] The past is present to her, allowing her to comment more radically on both the past and the present. Her recollection of the 1942 view of the "German future" is a strong reminder that conformity to the present implies a commitment to its view of the future. Here we see the "present" of the novel as it was projected in the wishes of 1942:

> "The twenty-one-year-old Sgt. Morgner has become the thirty-six-year-old Farmer Morgner. He stands on the bank of the Volga. Work done, he smokes a well-earned pipe, one of his blond children in his arms, lost in contemplation of his wife milking the last cow. German milk on the banks of the Volga. . . ."You don't want to hear any more: Good, then leave me alone with the future. I don't want to know how it is in the present. Aren't they standing on the banks of the Volga?[16]

It is through the character of Johanna that the withdrawal from time ceases to be a private game and achieves a public, historical dimension. Johanna's return into the flow of time is also the most literal. In the sanatorium, there is no past, present, or future: "hier ist immer *heute*" (Time is always *today*). "Here we don't think of time as an indefinite continuous concept but rather as separate units which must not be related and become history."[17] This might sum up the major thrust of the novel: time *should* become history.

Johanna's departure from the realm of arrested time is a graphically physical one. The novel actually describes how time begins to move forward for her again. She calls the number for the time of day on the telephone and listens to the times change until she hears "a harsh gong stroke." "Time flows into her face" as she departs from the "eternal today."[18] Johanna is also characterized in the novel by her laughter, and it is this Nietzschean laugh that she also brings back into the world from the sanatorium: "Still, my laughter may be small but powerful energies are hidden in it, more than in Robert's dynamite."[19]

As we shall see in the discussion of the film, Johanna gets time moving again by journeying to get a pistol and firing it at a politician pandering to the ex-Nazis for votes. Johanna's gunshot unites the members of the family on their way to Heinrich's birthday party as each of them (except Hugo) reacts to the sound. Each thread of the narrative stops for this moment, as if it were the point where they all intersect. As an event that is present to all of them, it unites them, becomes a part of their history, and signals the beginning of their physical motion toward each other. The sound of the shot is described in similar terms all three times it is heard: Unlike the gong striking the hour, it is a "short, brittle sound, not especially loud." But significantly, it is still new, unusual, and noticeable, something very foreign. Yet after identifying the sound as a shot, Robert merely says, "I believe we ought to go upstairs now."[20]

The act that gets time going again for the Faehmel family is also the only clearly political act in the novel. But although it is understood to be a reaction to the murderous hypocrisy of the politicians—"they'll kill you all for less than a gesture"[21]—it is unlikely to have political consequences, since it was committed by a woman assumed to be insane. But more important than its possible political effect, Johanna's gesture inscribes an arc between past and future. First she intends to shoot old Vacano as he rides in a military parade; then she considers his successor, Nettlinger; but finally she decides on the more abstract target—"respectability" and the politician of the future, whose crimes are much more subtle than those of the past. The political act, here, is to understand the connection. Hence Georg Lukács's praise: "The 'senseless' shot fired by an insane woman, with which *Billiards at Half Past Nine* ends, is one of the few humanly genuine ways of coming to terms with Germany's Fascist past, precisely because it encompasses what came before and after Hitler as well."[22] In this gesture, then, time ceases to be composed of unrelated units and becomes history.

## *Not Reconciled*

The opening shots of Straub/Huillet's film provide a number of contexts not present in the novel. First of all, the title has been changed to *Not Reconciled or, Only violence helps where violence rules*, which resonates in several directions. In addition to evoking the unreconciled past that Robert and Heinrich Faehmel have attempted to escape, it suggests that the film will depict a violent society, which it does. Yet the violence that reigns is never shown in practice, only in its results, for instance, in the case of Schrella putting on his shirt or Robert being bandaged after beatings. "Only violence helps where violence rules" is a quotation from Brecht's *Saint Joan of the Stockyards*, a literary precedent from 1929–1930 that juxtaposes the visionary charisma of Joan of Arc with the brutal exploitation of the poor practiced by Chicago meatpackers. Like Johanna Faehmel, Brecht's Johanna Dark traces the origins of violence to those who exercise power and not to their victims. The film's depiction is thus distinct from most violence in film and television, which exhibits a problematic fascination with violence itself and therefore "slips onto the side of the police."[23]

A second Brecht quotation is appended to the credits which calls attention to the film's approach to representation: "'Instead of wanting to create the impression that he is improvising, the actor should rather show what the truth is: he is quoting.'—Bertolt Brecht."[24] The "truth" of the film is thus neither the plot nor the characters but the *documentation* of the actors' performances. Following the credits, two monuments in Cologne are shown while the first eleven measures of Bartók's *Sonata for Two Pianos and Percussion* are heard. The first is a monument in memory of five victims of the Gestapo, with the walls of the Klingelpütz town prison in the background. No fictional time or place is being established here, since the music is simply added to silent film. The Bartók sonata, which itself dates from the period of rising fascism in Hungary before Bartók's emigration, is quoted later in the film as documentary footage of World War I is included. In both cases, the music helps to separate the "present" of the filmmakers and historical reality from the fictional "present" of the film. Similarly, the intentionally prolonged titles, the shots of the monuments, and the Brecht quotation emphasize the filmmakers' intervention. Yet the Klingelpütz prison will later become the location for a fictional event, just as the execution of young people is to become an element of Böll's fiction. The second monument is in memory of the Second World War dead of Cologne: *The Mourning Woman* by Gerhard Marcks. This is also significant for Böll's characters, since Johanna Faehmel is one such mourning mother.

The image of a monument without information about what it commemorates, like a countermonument, places the emphasis on the act of remembering. A monument is not a bearer of information but instead an aspect of one of two processes. First, a monument states publicly for a group of people that some consensus exists as to the importance of the person or event commemorated. This strengthens the community's sense of cohesiveness, identity, and history. The destruction and defacement of monuments usually accompany threats to such consensus. The second process takes place once the consensus or the community itself has ceased to exist. Monuments of past societies record the differences between past and present values and demand explanation. Their lack of meaning, their failure to function as monuments in the original sense, attests to the fact that time has passed, that historical development has taken place. Monuments that reflect no consensus left in contemporary society can become a focus and a weapon of struggle, an obstacle to or a goal of a new consensus. The recent debates over Holocaust memorials and museums (in the United States and elsewhere) and the debate over the German memorial to the "victims of war" in Berlin illustrate this.[25]

Straub has indicated his conviction that no such consensus exists and that the films are intended to reveal this fact and to divide the audience: "I think the value of our films, if they have a value, consists in the fact that the audience (there is no such thing as an audience, because it is made up of classes) is divided by them."[26] The film can do this by bringing before a large audience (Straub was speaking here of television broadcasts) monuments about which a consensus does not exist. The absence of an automatic identification of what is commemorated reveals also the absence of "the audience" that would commemorate it.

One link between the monuments at the beginning of *Not Reconciled* and *Billiards at Half Past Nine* is their commemoration of people such as Ferdi and Edith whom Robert wishes to memorialize with his dynamiting: victims of the Gestapo, victims of the war. Yet such monuments do *not* exist in the novel, so introducing the film with them seems contradictory. A productive explanation for this contradiction may come from considering the film itself as a monument to their loss.

The novel's narrative does not follow the theme of a "monument" to a positive conclusion. If the destroyed abbey is a monument to the dead, then it is such only to Robert, and thus it is not a true monument in the public sense. Robert's further urge to destroy merely falters, so that no monument to Ferdi and Edith is ever achieved. Similarly, Robert's father does not go very far in the novel to destroy his own function as a public monument. In many ways he and his son represent respectability before the community up to the very end. The only contemporary and outwardly public (political) rebellion is taken by Johanna. Since this, too, is an act limited to the context of the novel for resonance, the suggestion was made that the novel itself was the only thrust made from the circularity of its own structure into the realm of history and politics. If the reconciliation of past and present is to take place, it must take place outside the novel, for the structures of the novel allow only a limited sign of rebellion. An indication of the failure of rebellion on the part of Robert and Heinrich has already been noted in the fact that their signs of rebellion all lie entirely in the past. This is the aspect of the novel that the film stresses to the point of using it as a structural principle, following from the title *Not Reconciled*.

The shift of structural attention from the novel to the film, then, the shift to a structure based on elements "not reconciled," is above all a shift in the treatment of time. The film does not develop the opposition between time that has stopped and time that moves in the texts that are spoken. There is no author's voice in the film to say "Time glared at Hugo"[27] or "Time flowed into her face and blanched it deathly white [mit tödlicher weiße]."[28] Yet the same opposition is present in the film, in the way of concretely presenting the novel's characters so that their position regarding time becomes visible in the form of the film.

The film's narrative begins with the scene between Robert and Hugo in the billiard room discussed earlier. By eliminating the authorial commentary and restricting the length of the film shots in accordance with the laconic speech of the novel, the film makes it shockingly clear that the past is tremendously more important for Robert than the present. Instead of informing us, as does the novel, that Robert repeatedly tells such "stories," the film sets up a contradiction of narrative space.[29] The establishing shot of Robert playing billiards and saying to Hugo, "Erzählen, Junge, was?" (Stories? What stories, boy?) (shot 3), lasting only three seconds, is so compressed that it establishes no narrative space. The audience has no time and no combination of shots to feel comfortable with the space of this billiard room. The style of this shocking cut from the sound of the billiard balls after Robert's single sentence is also parallel to the abrupt contrast between the curt lines of direct dialogue and the commentary in the novel.

Instead of being told that Robert's memory consists of lines and formulas, not feelings, the audience only sees the lines and images that Robert remembers. The abruptness of the cut to the rounders game in shot 4 is also parallel to the absence of a change in verb tense in the novel as the narrative switches setting.[30] The superiority of the past over the present is established by the fact that the narrative begins here, in the past, with the voice-over of Robert, literally narrating the action. So for Robert, at least, *Erzählen*, or narrative, necessarily takes place in the past, but this is not true for the audience. Narrative space is still not developed in the flashback sequence: the audience is given no point of view with which to identify. The long shot of the rounders game *documents* the action Robert narrates, but it does not narrate it cinematically: we hear Vacano's whistle, but we do not see who he is; we hear in the voice-over that Schrella is being abused, but we do not see this happen. Instead, the action documented in the shot of the game runs counter to this narration: we see Robert hit the ball, follow it with his eyes, break his bat; this is the formula of his memory. Later as Robert asks Schrella the question "Are you Jewish?" (shot 7), this, too, is only pictured as following the game in time. A spatial or logical connection is not strongly provided, so the question most strongly functions to remind the audience that Nazism is the background here. The key to all this is the presence of the voice-over of Robert, which gives a narrative sense to these shots which the audience cannot discover merely by looking. The result is that narrative space *for the audience*, rather than developing in the longer flashback sequences, is retroactively placed in the three-second shot of the billiard room. By means of the auditory link between the voice saying "Stories? What stories, boy?" and the voice-over actually providing this narrative, the audience has remained in the billiard room; it is the location for the present tense and spatial presence of the story.

This location for the narrative is again confirmed by the contrasting use here of cause-and-effect editing: Robert asks for a cognac, Hugo leaves the room, we see him at the bar. The contrast to Robert's story is striking. There is a clear sense of location, visual narrative progression, no voice-over. With Hugo, we are in the present. Hugo's way of fitting into the film's structure, as opposed to the thematic structure of the novel, is by contrast rather than by similarity. He does not tell of his own past as a victim of persecution but instead provides a contrast to Robert's story by acting out his thoroughly vacuous role in the contemporary setting. There is the "ugly" old woman with whom he must play cards and the leader of the sheep cult who wants him to be the "Holy Lamb" in her new religion (shots 9–14). Straub/Huillet have rightly removed the arbitrary justification for Hugo's appeal as a Lamb and have delayed the comparison of his smile to Edith's. But we do see his innocent face and follow his structural role as a witness to the contradictory narratives.

The narration of the flashback to Robert's past then continues as in the novel until the interruption by Nettlinger. Again a strikingly short shot without any time for the audience to comfortably locate it places an action and a person in Robert's memory: in another shot lasting three seconds, we see Edith for the last time in the film, as she says to Robert "They'll kill you" (shot 26). As the novel says, memory does not become feeling, remains formula; but the shock of brevity amplifies the audience's sense of loss as other characters refer to her.

Nettlinger's arrival at the hotel subtly continues the narrative space developed in Hugo's sequence. Here we have the same clues for assuming present tense and continuous time, and even the setting of the hotel can be easily assumed based on this continuity and the rhythmic link to Hugo's scene: each of Hugo's and Nettlinger's present-tense actions (both near one minute in length) follows Robert's flashback scenes after periods of just over two and one-half and three minutes, respectively. As in the novel, Nettlinger is the outside element that forces the confrontation of past and present. We have already noted the synthesis that takes place in this regard in the novel as the relevance of Robert's stories becomes clear to Hugo and the latter advises Robert to avoid Nettlinger. The film achieves a more complex synthesis. So far two segments of visually present narrative have alternated with two segments in the past, narrated in voice-over. A synthesis is then added in which Robert is actually seen explaining the past in the billiard room while Hugo is seen listening; Robert is seen acting in the present. The realm of Robert's action, however, is much more limited than that of the present-tense characters Hugo and Nettlinger. The billiard room is very simple, and all its elements are called into play. The function of the billiard game is obvious; in the segment in question (shots 34–39), the past spoken of by Robert is visually present only in the form of St. Severin's steeple, barely visible outside the window. Its lack of prominence in the shot through the window places greater emphasis on the act of looking in that direction, by Hugo, by Robert, and by the audience (the camera pans to the view with Hugo's look on a signal from Robert). This is the first time the film audience is forcefully given such a clear sense of *looking*. Such an action to bring about strong identification with the characters is generally carefully avoided. The compositional weight of the curtains and the window itself also become relevant later in the film as present and past are again confronted. Here the shot of Hugo looking concludes with the assertion, "I would have blown St. Severin's sky high" (shot 36). But Robert's implied gesture toward and through the window is contradicted two shots later by his only other action involving the space of the room. First Hugo disappears behind a door to learn that Nettlinger wishes to be admitted and returns to stand before the door as he speaks his line (shot 38). Then Robert asks his question of Hugo from the opposite door, hears the answer, and leaves (shot 39). In terms of Robert's actions, then, a synthesis of present and past has been achieved by his telling the story at the window and with reference to his real goal, the destruction of St. Severin's.

But the fact that this past is not reconciled in the practice of the present is made evident by the simple drama of the doors. Robert has still had no contact with the narrative space shared by Nettlinger and Hugo; the freedom of action the window suggests has at this point only a fleeting existence. The use of doors to suggest a double narrative space within a simple mise-en-scène is common in Straub/Huillet. Doors punctuate the Bruckner drama in *Bridegroom*, we see Karl Rossmann pulled through the stoker's door in the Kafka film, and Bach's confrontation with his rival takes place at the door to a choir loft. In *Not Reconciled*, Heinrich's proposal to Johanna involves the opening of a door, and the door to Johanna's room in the sanitorium, where Robert and Heinrich meet as they pass through, separates her time from that of their world outside.

The suspense surrounding the reason for Robert's obsessive routine and the threat posed by Nettlinger, which begins the novel, is replaced by the unresolved tension between past and present in the segments just described. The theme "not reconciled" gives form to the film.

The novel's presentation of the ways in which Robert, Heinrich, and Johanna take refuge in the past has been discussed. It is only Johanna who, in the context of the novel, is able to break out of her routine and perform a political, public act (albeit with dubious effect). Robert's and Heinrich's change of routine—the destabilization of the structure of motif and metaphor in the novel—has been seen to remain within the confines of private life. The fact that Heinrich and Robert are still unable to confront the present with the past, made evident by the "not reconciled" passages in the novel,[31] becomes the central structural contrast in the film. In the novel, Robert and Heinrich imagine refusing to attend the rededication of the abbey because they are "not reconciled" to the inverted values it represents. Yet they do accept the invitation, despite their thoughts, and the past does not become a public issue. This is the fact the film stresses, since we are not aware of their thoughts and this is another sense of their being "not reconciled": no action has yet linked past and present.

The two Faehmels accept the abbot's characterization of the "blind zeal" that destroyed the abbey and agree to attend the ceremony, which is to be conducted in a spirit of reconciliation. The analysis of the novel here has made it clear that the rebellion of Robert and Heinrich belongs to the past. The use of voice-over as the old man tells his story reminds us that this past is very much the present for Heinrich. This contradiction is strengthened in the film by the absence of his few feeble gestures of rebellion—destroying medals, canceling breakfast, and so on. We only hear him say that he "would have given all the Crucifixions down the centuries to see Edith's smile again" (shot 118). His rebellion is an attitude, not an act.

The scene in which Robert and Heinrich fail to make their true feelings known to the abbot follows two sequences in which other characters attempt and fail to link present and past. In the first Joseph describes to his fiancée, Marianne, his father's rebelliousness and strength of principle but is unable to explain why he (Joseph) has suddenly lost interest in building (shot 123). The dilemma here is the same as in the novel: what role can the younger generation play if its progenitors already stand for both terrorism and respectability? The film does not, as does the novel, follow this to the point of suggesting the self-destructiveness of the young represented by Joseph's daredevil driving. Instead, as in the case of Hugo, their environment is simply revealed to be very restricted in its possibilities. Whereas Hugo's hotel environment is corrupt and vain, the space in which all other young characters move is virtually empty. As Joseph gives his inconclusive description of his father, the camera tracks backward to keep Joseph and Marianne in a close shot as they walk toward the camera along empty railroad tracks and power lines, a setting that could even suggest death, as Straub has noted.

After having followed Joseph and Marianne's inconclusive movement for almost two full minutes, the next sequence stresses Schrella's movement as he returns to his childhood home and also fails to connect past and present. In shot 125, he denies recognizing the sister of Ferdi Progulske, the childhood friend who was executed. Schrella is then seen crossing a large open field, walking away from the stationary camera, toward the workers' apartments in the background of the long shot. Conventional narrative would be likely to use editing or camera movement to trace Schrella's progress toward his former home, but this uncut shot (126) stresses the distance in time and space by forcing the character to do all the work and the audience to work with him. It is not an easy task: he walks slowly, and at the end of the long fourteen seconds of the shot, the field is still empty and the apartments still far away. The next shot extends this feeling of distance and difficult movement by contrasting means. Schrella is not seen arriving at his door, but instead a 300-degree pan slowly takes in the look of the street, with no sign of familiarity. Just as the foreignness and difficulty were stressed in shot 126 by the camera's not following the character (not helping him and the audience to make progress and feel at home), shot 127 stresses foreignness also by the absence of cutting. A cut to a shot of Schrella at the door would have implied that the circular pan had been from his point of view, but instead, at the end of the pan, the camera discovers Schrella and the little girl at the door, and no point of view for Schrella is established. He is a foreigner here, in strictly cinematic terms. His foreignness in time is stressed by the abbreviated dialogue—which leaves out his emotional suspense described in the novel. He asks, "Yes, the Schrellas, don't they live here anymore?" and the girl replies with certainty, "No, they never lived here." In the novel, the child suggests that someone else may know the Schrellas, but the film lets the word "never" from the mouth of a small child resonate in all its ironic finality.

These three shots of Schrella (125–127) and the one in which Schrella reflects on his failure to confront the past (130) bracket the shots with the abbot, which document a similar failure on the part of Robert and Heinrich (yet in the novel, Schrella's lines are adjacent to the dialogue with the child). This series of shots, 125 to 130, therefore, represents a climax of the film as a monument to the failure of these characters to do anything in the present that restores any life to their past.

A turning point in the narrative exists in the brief moments of communication between fathers and sons. The novel includes two such instances, where fathers ask their sons for advice. The initial instance between Robert and Hugo, whom Robert intends to adopt, is in both the novel and the film. In the final scene of the novel, a parallel exchange takes place between Robert and Heinrich. Heinrich refuses to receive a visitor by the name of Gretz, who had denounced his own mother to the Nazis, with the aside, "Or do you consider this the time and place, Robert, to receive a certain Mr. Gretz?"[32] This exchange is replaced by a conversation in which Heinrich finally reveals to Robert his acceptance of the destruction of the abbey he designed (shots 115–122), a parallel to Robert telling Hugo, "I would have blown St. Severin's sky high" (shot 36). The unity brought about by this conversation is conveyed by the simple use of conventional reverse angle editing: For a few minutes the audience is allowed to see the speaker (almost) from the listener's point of view, and as Heinrich begins to say "I would have given all the Crucifixions down the centuries . . . ," the shot is cut to a reverse angle of Robert listening. In a conventional film, this kind of cut would be transparent, merely the narrative device expected by the audience to link speaker and listener. But in the context of this film, the rare use of a conventional cut also succeeds in *meaning* that communication is, for once, taking place between these two people. It happens at no other time in the film. Earlier they have only met on the way to and from their visits to Johanna, passing each other between two doors—another sign of the limits of their action.

A third conversation completes the pattern of Robert's recollection of the past in the present: again he speaks in the billiard room, this time to Schrella. Here again, Robert is confined. Because of a high camera angle we do not even see the window anymore. Robert leans against the white door and speaks with Schrella about how so many people from their past have either died, disappeared, or been rendered harmless. Their reaction to the present is one of passive cynicism—the "opposition" is no different from the governing party, even "the list of stereotypes has dwindled" (shot 150). The only action to be spoken of here is that of going to Heinrich's party and of adopting Hugo, but there is no visible motion outside the realm of the family and the past. Since Hugo will be joining the family, he is sent off to pack at the end of the sequence, but even his exit is heard and not seen.

Since paralysis has been a central motif of both novel and film, the increased motion of the characters is striking as they come together at the conclusion. This begins with Schrella's visit to his childhood home and Robert and Heinrich's conversation with the abbot, after which they meet Joseph and Marianna and get into a car to return to the city. Schrella is moving, too, and he speaks in the very next shot but for the only time in the film in voice-over. Like Robert and Heinrich, he, too, has denied the past and cannot act in the present, although the past would seem to demand it. Thus his voice-over, isolated in this single shot after the Faehmel family gathers, becomes a comment on their failure (shots 128–129) as well as on his own (shots 125–127). His words immediately follow the family's departure from the abbey: "I have sinned, have greatly sinned: I did not want to see any recognition light up in Erika Progulske's eyes, or hear Ferdi's name from her mouth." Shot 130 is linked to shot 129 through sound and camera movement as well: there is no dialogue in either shot, and the action is merely observed; Schrella's voice-over is not simultaneous with the shot of his walking toward the city but draws attention to the preceding shots.

The rare camera movement, which first appeared in shot 127, also links shots 129 and 130. As the Faehmel family leaves the abbey, the camera pans to follow their car for the full time it takes for it to leave the camera's field of vision. This occurs at the point where the door of the abbey enters the frame, so the camera tilts up and rests on the spire of the abbey. The symbol of the cultural continuity that Robert and Heinrich had wished to see destroyed triumphs once again. Shot 130 resonates with this motion by way of a similar pan from left to right that finds Schrella in a position similar to that of Robert's first memory in the film—on a bridge over the Rhine ("a pagan river," as Straub has called it).[33] By contrast, instead of explaining his persecution by the others (shot 7), he is now confessing his sin. The pan also follows Schrella as he begins his return to the city, ending with a view toward the spire of the cathedral (St.

Severin's). This is both a parallel to the abbey in the previous shot and an indication of the destination of all the characters. The action converges in the hotel, facing the cathedral.

Just as all the other characters in the novel are separated from Johanna by their varying relationships to time and the past, these shots separate the others from Johanna by way of the voice-over commentary and the return from a failed pilgrimage. Johanna's manner of existing in the film is unique, and her motion is the only one that has consequences. Of the three characters who narrate the past—Robert, Heinrich, Johanna—Johanna is the only one whose stories are not related through voice-over and who speaks both of the link between past and present and of taking action to free her dead son (fallen in World War I) from the bad influences that survived him. Robert does not tell Hugo that Nettlinger has become a government minister. The audience must make this connection. But Johanna does make this connection with Vacano: "I shall be the Lord's instrument: I have patience, time doesn't press me. One shouldn't use powder and wadding but powder and lead; crackers do not kill, my boy. You should have asked me: now he has become Chief of Police" (shot 109). For Robert and Heinrich, there is a gap between past and present—signified by the detached flashback shots and the voice-over—that does not exist for Johanna. The correspondence to the stream-of-consciousness narration in the novel's chapter 5 is very strong here. For this narration on the basis of thoughts, all time merges into a psychological present. The film stresses Johanna's uniqueness in this respect by not using voice-over for her reminiscences, although Robert speaks in voice-over even in the short time he leaves her room to "talk" to his dead brother Otto. For Johanna there is only the present, in which past and future are linked. Therefore, even though she speaks of the same past to which Heinrich and Robert have referred in their flashback sequences, she always speaks on camera as if she were narrating events that are taking place now.

As all the other characters move together toward the city in the spirit of failure just described, Johanna begins to move as well. The filming of her departure from the sanatorium is similar only to Schrella's pilgrimage in the film, but, unlike him, she does achieve her goal. First the distance and the time she must cross to reenter reality are revealed in two long shots, 138 and 139. The first shows the door of the sanatorium, then Johanna walking out the door and around the building to the garden. The stationary camera and slow pace (the shot lasts 33 seconds) heighten the significance of Johanna's simple short walk. The next shot (39 seconds long) does the same, as Johanna is shown walking away from the camera through a long greenhouse, but this time she does not leave the frame. Unlike Robert and Heinrich, who are associated with closed doors and restricted motion, Johanna opens the greenhouse door and shockingly transforms the right half of what was a very two-dimensional composition into extreme depth of field. There is also an open window in the

Martha Ständner as Johanna Faehmel in *Not Reconciled*. Courtesy Straub/Huillet.

upper left of the composition, a black square in the gray building beyond the greenhouse. Finally, as her goal is achieved (she gets the gardener's pistol from his worktable), she is seen in a close shot and the camera now follows her in a pan as she leaves: the resistance has been overcome, but even this third shot lasts 35 seconds, bringing the total to 107 seconds for this single act. In cinematic terms, Johanna's action began when her black gloves were seen in the mirror as she prepared to leave (shot 137). Straub went to great pains to keep this image because it is reminiscent of Cocteau's *Orphée*.[34] Through this mirror, Johanna is reentering life.

After the long process of liberation contained in her journey to get the gun, her journey to the hotel need not be shown. Instead, we see her telephone the hotel to reserve room 212 "with balcony," and as we see and hear the porter on the other end say the word "balcony," the setting shifts to the hotel and remains there. The next shot (145) is of a window opening onto the balcony adjacent to the one on which Johanna will next be seen. Thus her motion, so slowly and painfully begun, exerts influence on the narrative of the next several scenes: she calls the hotel, which becomes the scene of action until she fires the pistol; only then does the setting shift again. This points out Straub/Huillet's technique of establishing location by way of its relevance to structure rather than through the omniscient storytelling convention of establishing shots. We

Martha Ständner as Johanna Faehmel in *Not Reconciled*. Courtesy Museum of Modern Art.

are never shown the Prince Heinrich Hotel from outside, and it is in reality a composite of several locations. Instead we come to know it by way of its relevant elements: Hugo, the desk clerk, the billiard room, the windows, balconies, and draperies, and the proximity to St. Severin's.

Inside the hotel, the power plotting of the politicians visually and narratively balances the cynical passivity of Robert and Schrella, and the two sequences are bracketed by Johanna's action, which opposes them both. She is the character whose confrontation with the present ends neither in compromising resignation nor in the refuge of the family. Her return to the hotel by way of a telephone call also places her opposite the powers behind Mr. M., an unidentified politician, who also conclude their business by telephone. This makes it all the more logical that she next appear opposite him on the corresponding balcony. As Straub has noted, Johanna and M. are linked by the word "balcony" as well, with which both their scenes end (145, 148).[35]

The confinement in the sequence between Robert and Schrella is contrasted with Johanna's ultimate freedom in shot 159 as she fires her pistol. This shot stands alone in the film both as the climax of its action and as a structural keystone. In Straub's view, the sense of freedom in this shot rests on its being uncut.[36] The only motion within the shot is that of Heinrich, who walks into the frame from the side, speaks to Johanna, then leaves the frame by walking toward and past the camera. The camera begins in medium shot, tracks in to record the exchange between the two characters, then tracks out again as Heinrich leaves, to frame Johanna in the window as she raises her arm to shoot.

Like the similarly structured shot of Karl and Therese discussed in regard to the film *Class Relations* (chap. 8), this shot stands against and comments on the rest of the film in many ways. It records the unity of character, location, and time, since all other such units in the film contain at least two shots. For instance, freedom has often been suggested by the windows in the film—in the billiard room, in Johanna's room, or as the avenue of communication for the young Johanna and Heinrich. Here, finally, Johanna stands outside the window on the balcony. Having left the barely suggested hotel behind her, she is virtually suspended in space. This departure is amplified by the fact that St. Severin's—referred to as a potential target earlier in the film—now virtually fills the screen with its dark weight. Johanna's manner of uniting past and present is again unique. It has already been noted how in this moment Johanna unites past and future in choosing which villain to shoot at. In cinematic terms, however, it is important that these targets not be visible: the cause-and-effect thrill of the shooting is irrelevant to its purpose in the film. Instead the image of the woman with her arm raised to fire, suspended outside the hotel room opposite the cathedral facade, culminates the intersection of the history of her family with German history. As the novel states, the target is not merely a person (Mr. M.) but respectability; the film shows, therefore, the cathedral and not the minister as the "target."

Thus Johanna's shot contrasts her not only with her invisible target, M., but also with her husband (who advises but does not stand with her), her passive son, and all the other partial and contingent acts in the film. Her act alone is visually balanced and framed, sovereign, self-contained, and complete—except for the extension of the pistol hand into offscreen space.

The concluding five shots of the film alter the narrative resolutions of the novel. In the novel, the gunshot serves as a way of bringing together the entire family at one point in time, but the film records no simultaneous reaction to the gunshot. Instead, it concentrates on action outside the hotel *after* the shooting. As in the novel, Joseph, Marianne, and Leonore (Robert's secretary) are visiting the Roman Children's Graves under the city when the shot is fired, but the sound is omitted (shot 162). In addition to recalling Robert's passion for demolition (and the discovery of an "older" past), these shots return the film to the more normal pace and content of everyday life. Yet the dialogue unites past, present, and future for the characters, which happens only at isolated instances in the film. In addition, these characters are the only ones in the film who move from place to place in the town center: they are seen arriving at the Cafe Kroner to be told the old man's party has been canceled. The young people apprehend what has happened and move in accordance with it. The final shot, as a commemoration of Johanna's act, also culminates its significance.

Camera movement again reveals relationships by sweeping across the family sitting around a huge birthday cake in the architects' studio. But this time the pan begins with the characters instead of ending with them. First it records the united family and the twofold expectation for the future: personally, that Johanna will return, and politically, that "the look of astonishment will not disappear from his [M.'s] face." After documenting the presence of all the characters together for the only time in the film, the pan quickly continues—against the direction of their gazes—to the window, again the avenue of freedom. Outside is the Rhine, with all its ambivalent associations for Straub, but as the screen fades to white to the accompaniment of the music of Bach, the image becomes the visual opposite and fulfillment of Johanna's pose to fire the pistol from the balcony. All traces of the constraints of history and cultural monuments are removed; the cathedral is gone. Only the music suggests a link between liberation and continuity. It is the same Bach suite Johanna had disrupted in an earlier flashback to World War I by muttering the litany "the fool of a kaiser." But here the overture is played, a new beginning.[37] This liberation becomes all the more convincing when one compares the camera movement to the window with the final scene of the novel: The united family there witnesses Heinrich's destruction of the abbey in cake form, the cathedral's substitute. The film manages to do away with the real thing.

The placement of the fictional narrative of the novel within a context of documentary elements and the freedom created by the filmmakers' formal decisions are important aspects of *Not Reconciled* as well as of the films to be examined in following chapters. For Straub/Huillet, documentary is fundamental to all film art.[38] Even the fictional drama contained In *Not Reconciled* is documentary on one level: a documentary of its (re)enactment, its quotation from the novel. Just as the words of the novel do not openly express emotion, neither does the style with which Straub/Huillet present them. The texts are offered as documents, facts—placed in a context but not interpreted.

The documentary nature of the film's setting is a separate element and provides a fruitful sense of context for the words, acts, and characters of the novel. For instance, the monument to the young people executed by the Gestapo is the *real* basis for the fiction of the novel. The Cologne cathedral in the film is at once St. Severin's and itself. Cologne is both the real, contemporary city and the setting of the novel's fiction. The film is able to surpass the novel in this ambivalence most effectively in the merging of Heinrich Faehmel's past and German history. When documentary footage from World War I is introduced (shots 79–88), Heinrich is no longer the narrator telling his personal story; Straub/Huillet's camera is no longer even the one doing the filming. The viewer is forced to place Heinrich's story in both a historical and an aesthetic context that has a reality prior to and independent of the film. A similar effect is achieved by the documentary photos projected behind the abbot to depict the destruction of the abbey and other religious/cultural treasures (shots 66–76).

Here the split between fiction and documentary is synchronous. The newsreel segments are embedded in Straub/Huillet's fictional narrative, while the back projections make the viewer aware that two cameras, that of Straub/Huillet and that of a historical documentarist, have recorded two temporally separate realities. The subjects, then, are also brought into contrast. The abbey was "needlessly" blown up by Robert, while Monte Cassino—the real monument in the photo—was destroyed in a costly battle justified by the rationality of war. While stressing the artificiality of the cinematic image, Straub/Huillet also stress historical facts that must be addressed.

Rather than negating feeling, I argue that the film's formal structure actually increases the audience's freedom to respond emotionally as well as intellectually. For instance, since Robert's achievement has been to keep memory from becoming feeling, Johanna's act provides a great release of pure feeling in the film. In the long shots that follow her—each over thirty seconds—stasis becomes motion, darkness becomes light. The audience's freedom of response is preserved in the climax of the film as well, where Johanna fires the pistol from the balcony (shot 159). Straub stresses that the old woman is truly free because the shot contains no cuts. The audience, however, is free for the same reason. The distance provided by the form leaves the motivation up to the character: she sees the targets, she has the mission to fulfill (i.e., the liberation of her character), and she decides to lift the pistol to fire. For the first time in the film, her husband gives her advice. This communication between them, not found in the novel, furthers the impression of the uniqueness of her act. The audience is allowed to contemplate this act from outside and as a whole but is not distracted by dramatic tension created by cuts to the politician or the military parade on the street. Instead, they are allowed to feel the significance of the drama: The camera moves, Heinrich moves, the decision is made, the action occurs all in real time and space. The full fifty-six seconds allow the event to register in full significance as opposed to the abbreviated actions of much of the rest of the film. The freedom of imagination and emotion granted the audience by this treatment of time has also been present in the scenes of Schrella's walk across the open field or Johanna's journey to get the gun. The time required for these emotionally significant events in the present contrasts with the brevity of the treatment of the victims, stressing their absence: Edith is seen in memory for fourteen seconds; Ferdi Progulske (the boy executed in 1935) is seen for eleven; the word "Jew" is spoken exactly once.

Composition, editing, camera movement, and motion within the shots all have an effect on the narrative and the emotions it can stimulate. Critics have often noted Straub/Huillet's preference for diagonals, for instance, but have underestimated the aesthetic and thematic significance of the contrast with more symmetrical composition.[39] Scenes in *Not Reconciled* involving the characters' inability to reconcile past and present are most often shot in diagonals. In addition to making a simple set "vibrate with life,"[40] Straub/Huillet's diagonal shots keep the viewer from relaxing at the point of a perspective triangle in relation to the screen. In this way they are able to vary the sense of narrative space inherent in all three-dimensional pictorial representations. Not only is the viewer not at rest as the subject for whom the composition is created but the composition itself, devoid of a vanishing point or balanced perspective focus, contains lines of visual interest that come back into the frame rather than seek to escape to another triangular point opposite the viewer on the other side. The restlessness thus created makes it possible for the viewer to feel a new sensation when, for a good thematic reason, balanced perspective returns. The profound peacefulness of the shots regarding Johanna are examples, as is the reverse angle technique (the conventionally transparent device for linking people together in film space) as Robert and Heinrich speak to each other.

Another aspect of the freedom to feel allowed by such a strict style involves the emotional response to a type of acting that does not attempt to manipulate an emotional response. Just as the visual forms and rhythms are potential stimuli for emotion rather than transmitters, so, too, are the actors. Straub cherishes the example of old Heinrich in the film, on whom the text he recited over and over again begins to make a visible, personal impression: "The old man becomes simply human."[41] It is the shot in which Heinrich is speaking to Robert (who is offscreen) at the train station (shot 117).

> It is very clear right in the middle of the shot when, without my having given him any direction, at the moment he says, "I had thought I loved and understood your mother, but only then did I understand her and love her," he spontaneously lowers his eyes behind the brim of his hat, and it is only when he continues, "and understand you all too, and love you," that he raises his eyes. It is obvious that is only possible because the text has become a part of him. At this moment he is truly a kind of "incarnate word," and even though at the beginning the text was strange to him, in spite of that, and actually because of that, he coincides with this "word" at its point of arrival.[42]

The strict form, precisely because it does not prescribe a certain emotional impact in advance, becomes a mechanism of creation and discovery for both filmmaker and audience. And such discoveries are documented, not manufactured, by the film.

The documentary character of the film as compared to the novel's fiction is paralleled by the film's "musical" structure, which both reflects and surpasses the patterns in the novel. To the structural variations of the cinematic devices noted above, one can add subtler considerations: the change in locations, the decline in the amount of time spent in each location as the film progresses, the increasing motion of the camera, the increasing motion of the characters within a single shot. Even the formal connection between words, sounds, or visual elements ties the film together musically: the sound of the billiard balls, the gunshot, and the champagne cork (shots 3, 145, 159); the sight of names in print: Heinrich Faehmel (shot 56), Robert Faehmel (shot 30), Ferdinand Progulske (shot 17); or the sound of the word "lamb" applied in various contexts to the young Schrella (shot 7), Hugo (shot 12), Marianne (shot 123), and Edith (shot 112).

As freedom of action in a historical context is more strongly suggested in the film than in the novel, so is the critical aspect of that potential: nothing has yet been done. The novel strained unsuccessfully to resolve itself through a vague hope that the Faehmel family will offset the evils around them. But the structure of the film draws attention away from this narrative, anecdotal conclusion. The critique of the present in the film has been directed at both its lack of action and its lack of a clear connection with the past, but this critique in the film is leveled as much at Schrella and Robert as at Nettlinger. None of them visibly reveals what he was in the past, but only Schrella and Robert deny their past identities. Whereas the novel is at a loss to describe what has happened to make someone like Robert retreat, the documentary look of the film is somewhat able to compensate for this. There is no need to build up the suspense of Robert's obsessive routine to hide from his past. The film merely reminds the viewer that any contemporary could have a past such as Nettlinger's, Robert's, or Erika Progulske's. Robert is a kind of war criminal, as Straub points out.[43] The film places them in real settings in contemporary Germany. While the novel stopped at 1958 and looked back at 1945, the look of the film remains contemporary: telephones, hotels, billiard tables, and teacups have not changed; a Mercedes is still a Mercedes. And one must ask what it takes to preserve the smooth appearance of such continuity.

# 6

# HISTORY LESSONS AND BRECHT'S THE BUSINESS AFFAIRS OF MR. JULIUS CAESAR

Proceeding logically enough from the title, most critics have considered Julius Caesar to be the unifying structural device in Brecht's novel fragment *The Business Affairs of Mr. Julius Caesar* (*Die Geschäfte des Herrn Julius Caesar*), written between 1937 and 1939.[1] Despite its strategies of demystification and Marxist analysis, the novel is still seen primarily as a narrative of a segment of Caesar's career. Although the historical novel's conventions of identification are challenged, it is still assumed that the reader can identify with Brecht's authorial voice as a basis for subjectively unifying the novel.

It is equally plausible, however, to consider the novel as the narrative of the young biographer's frustrated investigation of the "real" Caesar. The narrator who sets out to write a biography of Caesar some forty years after his death represents a consciousness to which all the contradictory evidence about Caesar's life is presented, with varying degrees of mediation by Brecht's other characters. As the myth of Caesar as hero gradually crumbles amid these contradictions, the effect on the narrator—and on the contemporary reader—logically becomes a central question.

In *History Lessons*, their 1972 film based on Brecht's Caesar novel,[2] Danièle Huillet and Jean-Marie Straub emphasize the problem of the narrator's position by making him into a contemporary protagonist. The young man in modern dress interviews four contemporaries of Caesar, all in costumes of antiquity: a banker, a jurist, a poet, and a peasant legionnaire. These interviews are separated by three long shots of the young man driving through contemporary Rome, with the camera in a fixed position directed over his shoulder from the back seat of a small car.

*117*

Although Straub/Huillet have removed nearly all of the novel's limited narrative material, *History Lessons* is not non-narrative as a result. Instead, the film can be seen as following through radically on what Herbert Claas has termed the coincidence of the narrator's point of view with a filmic one.[3] Rather than "violating the fiction built by Brecht,"[4] Straub and Huillet's film provides a basis for moving beyond the "Brechtianisms" of 1970s film theory as Sylvia Harvey has enumerated them: "distanciation, anti-illusionism, deconstruction, the critique of identification processes and the dismantling of 'classical' narrative."[5]

*History Lessons* is perhaps the film most responsible for bringing Straub/Huillet into the discussions of antinarrative and political modernism. Its production and reception coincided with the burgeoning of film theory in the 1970s, a search for a theoretical praxis forged out of psychoanalysis, Marxism, and feminism. Straub/Huillet's radical approach to film and politics led critics to misinterpret their commitment to narrative and "modernist" notions of form and beauty. In order to praise them as true practitioners of the political avant-garde, Martin Walsh tended to exaggerate their rejection of narrative,[6] whereas Peter Gidal attacked them for presenting "equivalents" of Brecht's texts.[7] Careful analysis of the rather unformed driving shots as well as the formalistic composition of the interview sequences has been undertaken by Christopher Roos, Gilberto Perez, Maureen Turim, and Martin Walsh.[8] Their discussions demonstrate that Straub/Huillet's Brechtian approach, although having traits in common with avant-garde film, is more productively thought of in terms of a modernist juxtaposition of formal elements.

Building on their analyses of the film's form, my comparison with Brecht's novel here explores the importance of narrative to Straub/Huillet, who do not share the avant-garde's claim that all narrative is oppressive. The young man in the film is not a ready-made equivalent of Brecht's narrator but rather a device to reveal how a liberating narrative could be constructed. The context of German history and the political dilemmas of post-1968 Europe are also much more significant than interpretations of "antinarrative" would imply. By comparing the narrative structures of film and novel, we can explore the persistence of the contemporary obstacles to the type of historical understanding Brecht sought. Finally, I will propose that the film's structure as a quest by a contemporary "narrator" does not ignore but rather problematizes what Harvey calls a "concern with a subjectivity conceived of in collective and class terms that has been largely absent from the psychoanalytic tradition in film studies."[9] In both form and content, the film proposes a historical consciousness that does not remain trapped in inherited forms.

### *The Business Affairs of Mr. Julius Caesar*

The "demythologization of Caesar" should not be seen as the primary goal of Brecht's novel but as a means to an end.[10] The overturning of the popular image of the "great personality" as the moving force of history was a radical undertaking in the years 1938–1939. Adolf Hitler was being taken more and more seriously as a world leader. The Caesar fragment attacks the Fascist strategy in two ways: first, by erasing the grandeur of the great personality as the form-giving element in history, and second, by formally subverting the narrative form given to history that supports such a view. The importance of the cult of a fatherlike leader to Fascist movements is quite clear. But it must also be understood that the creation of such an image for consumption by large numbers of people is an aesthetic undertaking. There is a great deal of accuracy in Syberberg's metaphor of Hitler, Goebbels et al. as artists—filmmakers "staging" World War II as a background for the role they continue to play as cultural commodities.[11] Brecht sought to undermine this strategy of transmitting the great personality through the form of his novel. He did not seek merely to tarnish Caesar's image but to expose the process of creating such an image.

Brecht's approach to Caesar was for this very reason as political in form as in content. Pessimism and isolation made the work more difficult and ultimately led to its abandonment. Harro Müller sees the pessimism as the logical consequence of Brecht's rigorous Marxist analysis, while Herbert Claas sees a contemporary connection to Brecht's dilemma in the persisting depoliticization of the working class.[12] Here, too, we see the dilemma of post-1968 Europe resonate with Brecht's situation. Clearly, the novel was written for an audience—German workers conscious of their own interests—that did not exist or could not be reached. Only after Books I through III of the novel had been shown to some German workers was Brecht encouraged enough to go on. "They understood everything, even the details."[13] The audience easiest to reach was not sympathetic. Ten months earlier Brecht had noted, "Benjamin and Sternberg, very highly qualified intellectuals, didn't understand it and urgently suggested including more human interest, more of the old novel!"[14] To follow this advice would have meant a return to psychology and a single narrative line, which gives the impression of inevitability. For Brecht, the opposite was most important, as he noted: "Writing 'Caesar,' I have just now discovered that I must not believe for a moment that it had to turn out as it did."[15]

To "portray" Caesar without making history seem to follow an inevitable course is thus as much a formal problem as a question of content. "More of the old novel" would mean a return to mimesis, which implies just such an inevitability. In Müller's words, "Mimetic theory therefore means an end to the dialectical relationship of consciousness and its object, thus negating consciousness as a determining factor in reality."[16] Brecht's formal experiment in the novel is aimed at maintaining the dialectical interplay of consciousness and its object. To this end, he splits the points of view of the narrative, giving none of them a privileged position where the "truth of Caesar" as a personality is concerned.

Klaus-Detlef Müller places the structure of the Caesar fragment in the context of a general strategy of historicization and historical critique. In this view, the novel passes through three stages of consciousness. First is the assumption of the narrator at the outset that history is the work of individuals and that a biography of Caesar is thus an adequate approach. The second step is for this assumption to be placed in doubt by the facts. The information and opinions obtained by the narrator from people he interviews or from the diary of Caesar's secretary, Rarus, do not add up to a unified, heroic view of Caesar's personality. Even the "progress" Caesar represents is invisible in much of this testimony. The third step, then, is the application of a materialist critique to this confusing information, suggesting that economic processes, not personalities, determine the laws of history.[17] Müller is certainly right in asserting that these steps are present in the novel, but he assumes too great a degree of homogenization in their formal presentation. Part of the problem is also the fact that Brecht's experiment was never completed, and one must at least speculate on the internal and external reasons for this.

The central experiment in the Caesar novel, and perhaps also a barrier to its completion, is that the most naïve and conventional narrative is that of the framing story. This narrative, along with the narrator's assumptions, cannot remain a "framing" structure, because the novel's strategy as a whole destroys it. To phrase it in accordance with Müller's scheme, the narrator embodies the first and second steps of consciousness, but he is not capable of moving on to the third. To have him "see the light" after his assumptions have been disputed by fact would be to return to a conventional mimetic narrative. His enlightenment would have to be somehow present in potential from the beginning, perhaps by virtue of his inquisitive nature. Brecht's narrator, however, does not wish to have his assumptions challenged, and throughout the novel these challenges remain external to him and external to his narrative as well. Here lies both the genius and the failure of Brecht's experiment.

The novel is divided into four books, with the following titles: I. Career of a refined young man; II. Our Mr. C.; III. Classical administration of a province; IV. The three-headed monster. All the framing narrative in the novel is contained in Books I and III. Books II and IV consist entirely of Rarus's diaries. The purchase of the diaries from the banker is the impetus for the framing story. They of course also contain various narratives from Rarus's point of view, describing the poverty in Rome, Caesar's daily financial troubles, Rarus's troubles with his lover, and the latter's unemployment due to the influx of skilled slaves.

Book I relates the first visits of the would-be biographer to Caesar's banker, Mummlius Spicer, to negotiate for a look at the diaries. What the narrator must unwillingly accept in the bargain is the commentary of Spicer. The first section, Caesar's "career," contains the most directly personal of Spicer's comments, which the narrator already finds heretical. He concludes at the end of Book I,

> What little he had to say about the founder of the empire, one of the greatest men in the history of the world, was quite obviously meant to portray him as an

especially depraved offspring of an old family.... I was out of patience. Had I not been determined to obtain the priceless papers, I would have stood up to go long before. I wanted to wait only long enough to get the papers, then leave with them to finally learn something about the real Caesar.[18]

The narration is marked by a similar tone throughout the first book: the biographer expresses his disinterest in both the economic and cynical personal reports of Spicer and the political generalizations of Spicer's visitor, the jurist Afranius Carbo. Carbo sees democracy and trade as intertwined principles, and after his assertion that Caesar's founding of the empire was only a continuation of the ideas of the Gracci, the narrator complains, "As far as these two gentlemen were concerned, my book was already written,"[19] and Brecht uses the opportunity to provide more ironic details regarding Spicer's estate.

Aside from the diaries of Rarus, there is only one witness from whom the narrator hopes to learn something of the "real" Caesar: the old legionnaire. But his account of the peasants' personal suffering as a result of economic change also fails to recognize Caesar's greatness, and the narrator leaves the interview disgusted and perplexed.

The novel reveals no similar reaction against the diaries of Rarus. However, the narrator is somewhat depressed by the violence and confusion of the Rome described in the diaries and is relieved to be on Spicer's peaceful estate, three decades after the events. He no longer complains bitterly about Spicer's long lectures but merely reiterates his skepticism about their relevance.[20] At the end, he reports only being lost in thought as he leaves with the last of the diaries. Brecht concludes the narrative by returning to the ambience of Spicer's estate: a runaway slave, sought earlier in the day, has not been found. The singing of the slaves, which had begun the book, has also ceased. The slave quarters are silent.[21]

The narrator thus never reaches the third step in Müller's scheme; he never becomes critical of his own undertaking. At most, the reader can deduce that he is no longer so self-assured. He indeed notes in his narrative how times have and have not changed between Caesar's day and his own. The confusion that conflicting representations of the past has created has not led him to a new analysis but rather to silence. As a more neutral narrator, he becomes merely Brecht's tool of montage, devoid of identity. He records the political exploitation of the threat of uprisings, described by Spicer's last guest, the poet Vastius Alder. The corruption of democracy within Rome is placed beside the "peaceful" subjugation and administration of the provinces of the empire, described by Spicer. The narrator reaches no synthesis; he even ceases to think about Caesar.

What synthesis is possible in the novel is therefore independent of the narrative. The narrator, by virtue of his misguided quest, is incapable of changing enough to incorporate a synthesis. Ironically, the characters who do not undergo a process of narrative evolution are those who *do* have a critical view of both Caesar and the investigation at hand. Spicer, for instance, makes numerous ironic comments critical of the motives and practice of historiography.[22] He also has no use for building a legend around Caesar, since the facts alone, impersonal as they are, are the material basis for his wealth and status. He has merely recognized and pursued his interest, and Caesar is simply an aspect of this beneficial development.

The poet Vastius Alder has a similar point of view regarding Caesar and even expresses it in terms that apply to the novel itself as well as to the listeners in the narrative. As Spicer is able to separate historical legend from his own interests, so the poet separates political instrumentality from the stuff of art. His attitude places any "representation" of Caesar in doubt, because to him the "great man" had no character at all, was pure instrumentality. Caesar was but a great man of the generic type.

> This kind of people is copied from one book to another, down through the centuries. A few strokes of water color are enough. I doubt whether a poet—you will excuse me, Spicer—inclined to write about him could come up with more than two lines. Not everything which has a surface develops patina, and art is patina, is it not? . . . For poetry, the man of whom we speak is something into which Brutus stuck his sword. You can repeat a thousand times, "The founder of the Empire, a formula of world scale!" It doesn't develop patina, this formula. Of course, why worry about art? I'm afraid I'm partisan.[23]

Both the language and the intention of the poet virtually banish from the novel Caesar as a personality. He is no longer even named but referred to only as "the man we are speaking of," "something into which Brutus stuck his sword," "our formula," and "your employee." Significantly, the narrator neither protests, as he would have done earlier, nor reflects or comments, as he might if he had understood and undergone a change in his character. But the remark he does make, having forgotten Caesar, almost hints at a link between the economic and political context into which the various speakers have placed Caesar by this point and the mundane details that are all the narrator is capable of perceiving.

> The difference between the banker and his guest was extraordinary, almost indescribable. Both were of humble origins: Spicer was the son of a freedman; Vastius was even a freedman himself. Both had played as children in the alleys of the capital; as men both sat in Caesar's Senate. But the banker still smacked his lips at meals, and the poet and soldier was almost at the point of going back to smacking his.[24]

The narrator has succeeded in making a connection between Caesar and the interests of class, but it is merely incidental and not part of any new perspective he has achieved. Since narrative is ineffective, the hand of the author becomes visible.

In some passages, then, the novel succeeds brilliantly in demythologizing Caesar by subjecting the "personality" to multiple perspectives.[25] The problem remains, however, who is able to take advantage of these multiple perspectives. The banker and his guests are given magnificent texts to speak which "possess for long stretches the analytical sharpness of Marx and the satirical linguistic wit of Karl Kraus."[26] Although their perspective is the broadest, they have nothing to gain by exchanging their views on Caesar. As we have seen, however, the narrator is even less able to take advantage of the multiple perspective offered him, and the structure of the novel makes it clear that he has no self-interest that compels him to do so.

All that remains is the effort of the reader to apply the multiple perspective to matters of his or her own historical interest, but this is a synthesis that the novel cannot concretely bring about. To the extent that it does so, it calls itself into question as a novel. Part of its story, its usefulness as a whole to someone, simply cannot be told. The independence of the diary segments is an example. There is no narration of the act of reading them. The reader's confrontation with them is not mediated by that of the narrator. Instead, the two "readings" become one. The result is simply not there in the novel; the reader must process this raw material alone.

Ironically, the same principle applies to the speeches of Spicer and his guests. Since they, too, occur in long blocks of prose, they take on a certain independence. To the extent that they do speak directly to the reader, as someone who can make use of the analysis and information, they render the narrator superfluous. Indeed, many of his comments that punctuate the long passages appear to be simply novelistically inept. The narrative is a nuisance.

These contradictions go to the center of Brecht's creative activity at the time. The lack of a "protagonist" or a synthesis is more than merely a formal dead end; it reflects Brecht's isolation and his lack of an audience. The "difficulty of finding heroes" reflects some historical pessimism as well.[27] The refusal to offer a synthesized, homogenized retrospective view of Caesar in the novel is based on the impossibility of such a view of Hitler. The formal principle was a result of Brecht's refusal to delude himself in questions of political reality.[28] Therefore, Werner Mittenzwei tends to oversimplify Brecht's relationship to tradition as a unified aesthetic strategy. He shows little concern for Brecht's confusion and despair when he could not hope to have a German audience and could not be sure that he ever would again. Mittenzwei misses the point when he concludes, "Yet he was not able to achieve the new type of novel he sought. The link to the novelistic tradition of the eighteenth century had long been broken. Brecht's attempt must be regarded as a failure."[29] Yet the tradition referred to was indeed broken off, by concrete historical processes, both in the years of exile and after Brecht's return to Berlin. Brecht is no more (or less) responsible for the failure of his experiment in the novel than he is for the failure of German culture in the face of fascism. Klaus Völker seems insensitive to the situation faced by artists in this historical position. The irony seems a bit cruel in his comment, "A not insignificant source of Brecht's incredible productivity in the years 1938–1941 is the realization that his opinions on art and politics were hardly in demand anymore."[30] Brecht recognized that his aesthetic limitations were reflections of the political defeats of his time and that he could not write for a liberated Germany when the agents of that liberation were nowhere to be seen. Although his journal entries seldom contain a plaintive tone, the effect of this situation on the Caesar novel is movingly expressed in the following entry, of 25 July 1938:

> the whole c-concept is inhumane. on the other hand, inhumanity can't be represented without the presence of an image of humanity. the social system cannot be represented unless one sees an alternative. and i can't just write from the point of view of the present, i must be able to see the alternative path as a possible one for that time as well. a cold world, a cold work. and still i see, between the writing and during the writing, how degraded we have been in our humanity.[31]

To see the other path as possible was a profound challenge in the years of the rise of fascism in Germany, one it was probably impossible to confront fully. Völker reports, regarding the work on *Puntila* in 1940, "The practice of literature proved to be far removed 'from the centers of all-governing events.' The playwright had to admit to himself: 'Puntila has almost nothing to do with me; the war, everything. I can write almost everything about Puntila; about the war, nothing.'"[32]

This is the modern artist's intolerable situation, which became most extreme under fascism but which persists as long as consciousness is under occupation by the culture industry. The artist must be hopeful that society will survive and that social change will restore a sense of the values preserved in art. And this hope must also compel the artist to push artistic tradition forward, even though its social basis is in question. This is why Brecht's dilemma resonates with that of the political avant-garde in film and film theory after 1968. In an essay published in the British journal *Screen*, Franco Fortini describes Brecht in these roles during the period under discussion.

> The fact is that in reality Brecht lived both functions: on the one hand the passer-on of a message that had to go "under the sweat-stained shirt . . . through the police cordons," the role, that is, of the scribe to whom tumultuous artisans assign the task of putting down their truth on paper; and on the other the mission of the man whose words to himself are: "Know that you do it for yourself, so do it properly." In the poem of 1939 from which I have quoted above, the situation of the "outlaw," with all its problems of double citizenship and double identity, is expressed as literally intolerable.[33]

Fortini continues that many writers had felt integrated into the Communist party as a "society within a society" and as a "concrete anticipation of socialist society." But after the victory of Nazism and the Hitler-Stalin Pact, even this identity was no longer possible. Fortini concludes, "On the eve of the Second World War a number of writers finally discovered what the working class should have known for at least a hundred years: that they had no home-land."[34]

### Brecht's Caesar Novel and *History Lessons*: A Common Formal Dilemma

Colin MacCabe has criticized the Straub/Huillet film by asserting that "it is impossible to understand for what audience *History Lessons* was made."[35] This should stand as a first indication of the strong correspondence between the dilemma of Brecht's novel and the post-1968 dilemma of the film. Deprived of a homeland, deprived of "tumultuous artisans" charging him with "the task of putting down their truth on paper," Brecht offers views of history that neither support an aesthetic form nor point toward a productive reception in existing society. The narrator becomes as silent in the face of Caesar as the German working class becomes in the face of Hitler. Straub/Huillet leave the dilemmas of the novel intact with regard to its own time, but they also reveal its contemporary resonance. The "slave quarters" are still silent today, but the artist persists in imagining that history could have been different, that change is possible.

Much of the text of the Caesar novel is missing from the film *History Lessons*. Yet if one sees the novel as a formal confrontation of the powerlessness of art in the face of history, it is all there, perhaps with fewer aesthetic self-contradictions. The film does indeed contain all the major characters in Brecht's framing story and in approximately faithful proportions. Only the anecdotal details are removed—the personal stories of Spicer's estate and of the narrator's journey. The character of the narrator and the diaries of Rarus are the most obvious deletions, yet the structure of the film replaces and transforms these elements.

Let us begin with the narrator and the narrative in general. In contrast to the analytical overview provided by the banker and his guests, the clowning pretentiousness of the narrator is irritating (but does not produce "distancation," a *Verfremdungs-Effekt*) and allows no room for development of consciousness. The film eliminates this personal tic of the narrator but thereby restores his function as a vehicle of narrative continuity and even progress. The young man is situated between the extremes of the film: he is somehow between the Rome of 1972 through which he drives and the world of the costumed characters to whom he listens; he is also between the audience and these two aspects of the film, in a visual sense, in the driving sequences and, figuratively, as a narrative link in the interviews. The "narrator" of the film is not merely identified with a heroic view of Caesar, and his experience is therefore not exhausted by having such a view challenged. His attitude is only slightly similar to that of the novel's narrator in that he asks questions and is contradicted. He, too, is receiving information that he did not seek at the outset, but this experience enriches and confirms his presence in the film, *as* the bearer of the narrative.

The positioning of the young man as a bearer of the narrative is independent of both Brecht's text and conventional film action. This independence of the film's form from its text derives largely from the use of preexisting material, the basis for all Straub/Huillet screenplays. Texts become part of the documentation of history to be confronted by the formal fiction of the film. Straub/Huillet stress that the audience should be aware that everything seen on film is fiction, and the separation of their own work from the production of literary texts serves to emphasize this. The historical events presented in the texts are separated from the audience both temporally and aesthetically; nothing is portrayed as happening "now," and past events remain in the past; the literary form of the historical materials is separate from the film form that accompanies them. Not to stress these distinctions would amount to deception on the part of the filmmaker. In an interview from 1972, the year of *History Lessons* and *Introduction*, Straub/Huillet described this "deception" and its avoidance by way of "preformed materials" as follows:

> STRAUB: ... I think the deception comes about when one gives people the impression that something is happening in the moment the film is running, something they call "action." It isn't true; when a film is running which doesn't rest on deception, nothing is happening, absolutely nothing. That can only happen in the spectator, whatever happens. And that can only come about through the combination of the images and sounds ...
>
> HUILLET: That is, of forms ...
>
> STRAUB: ... of forms that go through the ears and the eyes and through the minds of the spectator and into his [*sic*] reflections.[36]

To illustrate the importance of film form in preserving the audience's freedom to reflect, we will look at the way in which Straub/Huillet construct the narrative around the young man. His importance is not established by a role in a preconceived narrative but by the fact that he serves as a unifying element to suggest narrative possibilities.

The question of a unifying element is appropriate because there is no element of the film that is present in every shot. No narrative structure is given from the outset to provide unity to the film, which is divided between the "interviews" with the four eyewitnesses and the shots of the young man driving through Rome that punctuate them. However, certain elements do link the large sections together. For instance, the first several shots are only concretely linked to what follows by the sound of the streets of Rome. The film does not explain that these maps of the shrinking Roman empire (and the statue of Caesar that follows) are products of the Fascists and that they are actually on the street.

Yet the street noise and the abrupt cutting are sufficient to give the feeling of instability. The noises link these shots to the shot of the statue, which almost equals their combined length. The name *Caesar* is present only in the subtitle; the maps and the statue are conveyors of questions, not of information. Their lack of "content" links them to the long shot from the back seat of an automobile being driven through the streets of Rome, but their abruptness is in contrast to the "constant" shape of the driving shot.

Here the only other linking element besides the street sounds of Rome is introduced—the figure of the young man driving the automobile. Later, as men in "antique" costumes speak, it is the presence of the young man in contemporary dress, listening, that links these shots to the rest of the film, although the sound and background, too, are those of Rome in 1972.

Surprisingly, however, these links, elementary as they are, do not persist through the whole of the film. In shots 42, 43, and 44, the "interview" with the poet Vastius Alder, neither the young man nor the sounds of Rome is present.[37] Yet these three shots are not foreign to the film. A unified tissue has been established by this time, which even the radical shift to shot 42 is incapable of breaking. By shot 42, we perceive that the young man is the character whose journey shapes the film. Most of the shots of the film, aside from the sounds of Rome in the first three, have him as a constant element. He is included by way of a narrative structure of reverse angle cutting, to a certain extent, implying dialogue even when he is only listening to the text. In the sequence mentioned, the young man does not appear, but his presence and his point of view are assumed by the viewer.

The film includes a wide range of depictions of the human figure. The most stylized are at the beginning—the heroic statue of Caesar—and at the end—a woman's face carved in stone, an ancient fountain. In between we are witness to a wide range of human activities as we follow the young man on his journey, a journey both physical and mental, that spans most of the film. First the viewer sees the young man driving through the streets of Rome. No indication is given of a destination, and the camera remains stationary through the driving shots (from now on to be referred to as *Spaziergänge*—"strolls"—Straub's name for them; they correspond to favorite walks Huillet and Straub would take from their home). The first of the three such shots lasts eight minutes, forty seconds.

The camera is stationary all this time, but the car in which it is placed is not. Therefore, the Spaziergänge are at the same time tracking shots of working-class, residential Rome, through which the car passes, and stationary shots of the young man, seen from the back, driving. Driving is one of the young man's most vigorous actions in the film. Yet the Spaziergänge, if one refuses to dismiss them as boring and devoid of content, require more analysis even to describe briefly how they are composed. We cannot consider here the succession of individual images that appear and disappear as the car moves. Each viewer will have a different perception of the people, vehicles, and buildings,

The young man (Benedikt Zulauf) in *History Lessons*. Courtesy New Yorker Films.

qualities of light, sky, and foliage, and the rich sound. Beyond this, however, there are constants to observe. Walsh has pointed out the fragmentation of the film frame itself, which is achieved by the simultaneous motion and motionlessness of the camera.[38] One might even at this juncture become concretely aware of the absolute artificiality of any "stillness" in motion pictures. Part of the image appears to move, part does not. But since the car is in motion, the apparent stillness of its interior is an illusion caused by the camera's motion with it.

The segments of the frame that contain motion into and out of the camera's view are in turn divided into smaller frames, similar to shots of a film-within-a-film. As the car moves, the windshield, the two side windows, and the sunroof produce four tracking shots. A fifth shot of an intermediate nature (another frame in any case) is present in the mirror, which constantly shows part of the young man's face. We see the activity of the young man, looking, waiting, driving, and this is distinct from the motion we see this bring into view—in the moving pictures in the various frames and in the changing light and color in the car itself. There are even images and changes of light in the reflections in the dashboard instrument lenses and the glare in the windshield. And finally, all this interacts with motion that is independent of the motion of the car, outside on the street.

Up to this point, none of these observations has depended on an external introduction of the young man as a character. No narrative framework is given at the outset to explain his identity or actions. But while this breaks up a conventional narrative flow, it does not negate it. The young man eventually takes on the function of a narrative protagonist as a result of strategies of composition and the material connection between shots. As we will see later, the fact that the young man is the visual link from scene to scene and that he is seeing and hearing what the audience sees and hears is enough to make him into a narrative protagonist, even though the meaning of his "quest," "journey," or criminal investigation is unclear. The tradition of bildungsroman, picaresque novel, crime thriller, and road movie all conspire to make this narrative assumption irresistible for the audience, despite the lack of many contextual clues.

The sounds of Rome and the very presence of the young man have already been seen as links between the diverse segments of the film. One last link lies, of course, in the Brecht text, which we hear on the sound track as we see it being either spoken or listened to. There is no voice-over in the film. As with the identity and destination of the young man, the *content* of the text is not essential to its role. Like the young man himself, the text's presence in the structure of the film helps the action become one action, almost in an Aristotelian sense, making the film, at the end, the story of the young man's investigation.

If we examine the text in its presence in the film as sound, related through composition to the images of the speakers and listeners, we discover patterns that lend great weight to a very few shots. For instance, the young man speaks very little in the film, and all but one of his utterances could be classified as short questions that pursue the investigation. Only the schoolboylike recitation of the story of Caesar and the "pirates" is not directed at receiving a direct response, but even it provokes a lengthy correction by the banker. It is distinguished by its great length (ca. 3 minutes) and the fact that it alone shows the young man walking as he speaks, in a grassy, relatively open area. The relation between text and composition also goes against conventional narrative: The young man is offscreen in more than half the instances in which he speaks. In only four shots of the film's fifty-six does he speak alone on camera. This increases the impact of these short, interrogative shots as it distinguishes the young man from the other characters, most of whom speak alone on camera for long passages.

Straub/Huillet thus construct a progression in the young man's position in relation to the other characters, his environment, and Brecht's text, which does not depend on any external narrative or identification. The motif of movement for the young man is three times asserted by the automobile shots, once by his only long speech concerning the "pirates" and at another crucial point that will later be contrasted with the role of the banker. His main use of language, however, is to ask questions, and as he does so, entirely in the early part of the film, his visual presence is much inferior to that of others. All the other characters are seen and speak *before* a question comes from the young man. He speaks only to the banker and the peasant. He is visible but silent while the jurist speaks; while the writer speaks, he is no longer even visible.

The progression described here occurs entirely between the first and the third Spaziergänge, only to be dramatically reversed after it. The young man has progressed from a polite interrogator to a silent listener to an invisible yet suggested "protagonist." This is the crucial significance of the consistent "presence" of the young man in each shot of the film, which spills over into the sequence where he is not seen (shots 42–44). That the young man is indeed a narrative protagonist has only emerged through the variations in his bearing as the film progresses. The final stage in this development is the last section of the film, following the third Spaziergänge. Now the young man is totally silent but seen alone on-screen for long periods, alternately with the banker, intently listening to the latter's long speeches. He is no longer asking questions or moving, but he occupies the full screen, no longer turned away from the camera but toward it. Looking and listening, two of his major activities throughout the film, now reach their most powerful and richest presence.

In his article on *History Lessons,* Martin Walsh described the formal strategies of the film, including the formal bracketing of scenes and the young man's role. But, perhaps because of his deductive approach, Walsh stresses the arbitrary nature of film form to an extent that is not justified by the film itself. Regarding the young man, he writes, "For Straub/Huillet's formal decisions (particularly with respect to camera placement) are designed to ensure that the undercutting of the 'young man's vision of history' is maintained in *History Lessons*: and this they achieve by refusing to place the audience in a situation of identification with the young man, by only rarely making our point of view that of the young man."[39] Here Walsh is contrasting the narrative form of *History Lessons* with conventional illusionist films (he mentions *Citizen Kane*) that systematically place the camera in such a way as to *force* the spectator to identify but in such a way that, as a result of the evolution of film "language," the identification seems automatic. Walsh is right that such techniques of editing and camera placement are avoided in favor of the patterns that he terms "arbitrary." Yet the analysis above suggests that the spectator will indeed identify with the young man and will follow the progress of the character as it develops through the formal variations of the shots. Therefore, the form is by no means arbitrary. But instead of identification being the result of passive reception on the part of the viewer, it, like the rest of the ways of reading the film Walsh mentions, is the active production of meaning on the part of the spectator.

The absence of conventional means of producing identification or narrative does not mean that narrative and identification are not intended or desirable. On the contrary, the very nature of photography, which Straub/Huillet do not radically subvert, implies identification and narrative. The formal justifications for visual representation in Straub/Huillet films simplify the narrative structure as much as possible in conventional terms, so that the use made of it by the viewer can be as complex as possible. As Brecht put it, the convention is not wrong in itself—it just has got in the way.⁴⁰ The identification with the young man in *History Lessons* is not constantly sustained, but it is clearly likely to occur anyway, for entirely conventional reasons. For instance, after each of the Spaziergänge, the next shot contains the young man, whom even Walsh calls the "narrator" in this context. The film does not insist that this be perceived as his having arrived at a destination, but the likelihood is there. Also, each of the "dialogues," with one exception, begins with a two-shot, placing the young man as the constant character whom the spectator is "following" through the film.

Again it must be stressed that the content of the text and the "identity" of the young man are not necessary for the recognition of these functions. The next step is to make it clear that this structure, although built according to its own internal logic, does not exist in a vacuum. The film form does not exist separately from the text by Brecht, nor are the forms of the shots irrelevant to each other. This is the second instance in which Walsh attempts to put the film into formal categories that do not fit it. In this case he begins with a concept of Brechtian aesthetics, drawing from Roland Barthes the idea that in epic theater the most important unit is the scene, not the whole play: "There is no development, no maturation.... [T]here is no final meaning, nothing but a series of segmentations, each of which possesses a sufficient demonstrative power."⁴¹ Walsh goes on to apply this Brechtian generalization to the text in *History Lessons* as follows: "Straub/Huillet respect Brecht's segmentation of the text, and support it primarily through their editing strategies, which deny any sense of narrative development or interpretation of the verbal text; rather each sequence is closed in on itself, defines its boundaries, its fundamental separation from the rest of the film, in accordance with Brecht's episodic theories."⁴² Later he again stresses that Straub/Huillet's editing strategies "in no sense themselves support the *content* of the segments. There is no homogenization of the filmic elements to make possible a transparent reading of the verbal text."⁴³

These assertions must indeed arouse our curiosity. It should be obvious that the supposed lack of narrative development is clearly contradicted by the abstract form of the film as I have described it. Of course, we readily agree that there is no homogenized final meaning here, and no transparent reading of the text. But to sever the relationship between the film form and the text, to see no "sense of narrative development," is to impoverish both the film and the text. This conclusion is quite the opposite from that of Martin Walsh and Stephen Heath, whom Walsh cites in his article. Their deductions proceed according to the logic of formal structures but ignore their narrative significance. Heath writes, "Brecht declares his own point of view to lie in the montage, that is in the undercutting of the young man's vision of history as the will of great men, by a multiple focus on the economic and political determinations operative in Caesar's rise." Walsh goes on to assert that "it is the

The banker (Gottfried Bold) in *History Lessons*. Courtesy New Yorker Films.

formal, structural aspect that is crucial; only in (through) that can we specify Brecht's stance. This common formal emphasis marks a decisive point of intersection between Brecht and Straub/Huillet."[44]

This interpretation glosses over the structural problems of the novel. Indeed, the montage is important, but it is addressed to a consciousness beyond the narrator's place in the novel and perhaps to a nonexistent audience. The undercutting of the young man's vision of history is indeed achieved by the presentation of "economic and political determinations," but this, in itself, does not require montage. On the one hand, one might agree with Walsh and assert that Brecht's stance is most closely allied with the attitudes of Spicer and his guests. The montage of the novel, however, points toward the impossibility of achieving "a stance" under such conditions and even questions the helpfulness of Spicer's explanations. But when Brecht wrote that what interested him was the montage, he was indeed dealing with this latter dilemma. It is therefore anything but a purely formal consideration. Writing of the contrast between the "Rarus sections" of the novel and the "Spicer sections," Brecht describes the former as "badly written" and the latter as "well written," where style is concerned. Aside from a few episodes in which Rarus is moved to stylistic power, the diaries' beauty, Brecht notes, remains on the architectural level. Spicer's part, however, "permits better reflections and the satire becomes more direct, but thereby the architectural element is weakened."[45] The montage, therefore, is not merely interesting to Brecht as a way of undercutting a false view of Caesar but as an investigation of the difficulty of achieving a stage of reflection and control over the processes of history.

Walsh quite aptly cites Walter Benjamin's "Theses on the Philosophy of History" in this context, but his application of them to *History Lessons* remains too general except when applied to the Spaziergänge. Three of Benjamin's concepts that apply to the film are the idea of wresting tradition from conformism, from becoming a tool of the ruling classes;[46] the view of the task of historical materialism as that of constructing moments of stasis out of the flow of events; and the conviction that "historicism gives the 'eternal' image of the past [and] historical materialism supplies a unique experience with the past."[47] By separating form and content for both Brecht and Straub/Huillet and by isolating the structural elements of *History Lessons*, Walsh has failed to see how historical materialism applies to the entire montage and to the interaction of form and content.

Regarding the Spaziergänge, the audience is invited to try to make some historical or narrative sense out of the unformed view of Rome, to create moments of stasis. Walsh rightly stresses that this world is kept "outside" the space of the narrative and that the audience also is not allowed to feel located in this space. The crucial aspect, apart from the inside/outside dichotomy, is the process of motion and stasis. The pictures are always moving, even when they stand still, and the motion of the world outside, the car and the driver, and the camera itself are all aspects of the historical flow that must be arrested. This assertion makes sense because the contrast of motion and stasis is not just crucial for the Spaziergänge but for the film as a whole. Each of the Spaziergänge, for instance, begins with the car in motion. Although the material of the shot is largely unformed, the composition and the beginning and end imply a previous, intelligent act of choosing an excerpt, as we saw in the case of *Bridegroom*. In a parallel way, the confrontation with the men in historical costume also begins after the "motion" has begun, referring to a narrative beginning that the choice of the filmmakers has intentionally and recognizably excluded. The first words of the Brecht text, for instance, clearly call attention to the exclusion of exposition: "At the time he no longer, as far as I know, did anything at all." The shot establishes the banker talking to the young man, who is barely visible in the frame, and the phrase "at that time" makes it evident that previous speech has been cut.

The cuts in the text and the cuts in the film serve the same structural purpose as the interruptions of Brecht's narrator. Therefore, it is a mistake for Walsh to ascribe to them purely formal significance.[48] The formal structure of the film is the filmmakers' tool to expose the dialectical interchange of motion and stasis in history. The film's formal construction also provides a pattern of reality through which the figure of the young man can move without being consumed by it. The filmmakers' formal thought at work here does not depict or delimit the character of the young man but liberates it. The moments of stasis in the film, the construction necessary to the conquering of history, do not have the young man as their subject. Instead, the moments of stillness remain outside him, allied to the structure of the film *through* which, not merely *within* which, he moves.

This freedom of the young man to digest the historical moments of stasis, to confront the stasis of the text and move beyond it, is also the freedom of the viewer. (It should be noted that all the texts used by Straub/Huillet in their film represent, materially, such static moments of history. The relevance of translation to this context will be examined in chapter 8.) The young man's motion through the film is the only element that unites the film's various formal elements while pointing beyond them. This freedom is most clearly a function of camera movement. As noted before, the young man moves through Rome in his car, with the camera behind him. While reciting the "textbook version" of Caesar's encounter with the "pirates," he moves toward the camera, which tracks to follow him. Although this is the only version the young man has of the story, he does not act as if he identifies with it, as does Brecht's narrator. The conflicting versions are therefore not based on characters or beliefs but produce a formal contrast, one of the moments of stasis in the film. At the end of shot 16, the young man keeps walking for about thirty-eight seconds, further emphasizing his independence from what he has said. At the beginning of the next shot, the banker's contrasting answer is also delayed. Thus the moment, the space, between two versions of a story achieves a visual, material weight that is enhanced by the contrast between the field and the bench.

Of paramount significance to our analysis is the textless beginning of shot 17, which shows both characters, the banker and the young man, in motion for the only time in the film. The quality of their motion confirms the dissimilarity of their roles. The speech begins after the banker enters from right of the camera and sits down, on the left end of the bench seen at the beginning of the film. As he sits, he begins speaking, and "conventional composition" would put the listener offscreen right, on the empty side of the bench. But the shot has begun, as shot 16 had ended, with the young man walking, still with his coat over his shoulder, now from offscreen right to offscreen left, and very near the camera, so that only his head and shoulders are seen. The banker walks in and stays there, implying a convention. The young man's motion into and out of the frame explodes the space in a manner reminiscent of Griffith or Renoir.[49] The banker is a captive of both the shot and the text; the young man is free.

Another contrast is the static point where the banker, at the end of his speech in shot 26, looks straight ahead without blinking for about fifty-two seconds. This view has all the pastness and flatness of a "wanted" poster, in contrast to the later shots of the young man's active, yet silent, listening. The assertion Walsh makes that formal choices, such as that "enclosing" the banker, are arbitrary, therefore misses the most important effect of these choices. The fact

The banker (Gottfried Bold) near the end of *History Lessons*. Courtesy New Yorker Films.

that the filmmakers' intelligence is seen at work, that their design is visible, has a liberating effect on both the narrator and the viewer. Walsh notes that "no one language dominates any other" in the film, but he sees this as merely a way of forcing viewers to construct their own readings, "to work at a plurality of possible readings." MacCabe may have a point here in asserting that such a defense of the film smacks of a kind of "work ethic."[50] What is lacking here is the sense of play in the filmmakers' art and the joy implicit in the discovery of the free interplay between aesthetic beauty and harmony and "meaning."

By contrast, Walsh minimizes the narrative aspect of the increased distance between the banker and the young man at the end of the film. Yet, as has already been seen, this fact does far more than "express" the young man's mounting rage. (I must assert that although rage may be present, even in the actor at the time of filming, this rage is not "expressed" at all. At most it can be sensed in the increased speed of the third car ride, in the fact that his sleeves have been rolled up, or in the seriousness of the young man's face, listening. But these are already readings supplied by the viewer.) This wider background of the last shots allows the audience to enjoy the beauty of the garden. The young man now has as much visual weight as the banker speaking, and the greater space around the young man as he listens underlines the freedom described in his crossing of the screen in shot 17. The film's form has been our tool to render

The young man (Benedikt Zulauf) near the end of *History Lessons*. Courtesy New Yorker Films.

historical moments, historical "treatises," subject to examination. Yet we have not been drawn into this structure; it presents the narrative, it presents the text, but through the implications of its formal development, its motion, its strategy of making excerpts, it constantly reminds us that there is more: there is a world outside this film. And we are in this world outside.

The Spaziergänge can thus be seen as analogous to Brecht's Rarus diaries. The audience confronts them directly, without their being given a form that integrates them into the experience of the film. Walsh stresses their otherness and the viewer's separation from them. But the viewer is separated from them only as a viewer of this film, and the film's reluctance to pretend to "show the world outside" is manifest in the cinematic variables that these shots expose. Just this reluctance to show "the world" allows the viewer to feel, like the young man, free to move with the film's structures and in the end, to go beyond them. The film may or may not help viewers to new insights. In any case, the usefulness of such insights, like the acting-out of the young man's freedom, resides not in the film but in the world it cannot show.

The young man's freedom is thus conveyed only by the simultaneity of his identification with the film's formal motion and his separateness from it. His progress is coincident with his motion in the film and with his growing weight as an element of composition, in opposition to other visual elements and to the spoken text. His presence has also been a structural prerequisite for the narrative space of the entire film, a unifying motif. His liberation from this tie to cinematic form is ultimately achieved, however, when the form continues to assume the presence of his consciousness (and that of the viewer) without requiring his visual presence, as either object or agent of film fiction.

This leap is achieved through the use of the only two zooms in the film, the first ever used by Straub/Huillet. The first, as we have seen, is at the beginning of the "problem sequence," shots 42, 43, and 44. The zoom approaches the villa of the writer from the rocking boat in the water, yet it never arrives at a point of rest. Just as the logic of the film implies the presence of the unseen traveler and listener in this sequence, so does it identify this zoom with his motion. Yet the zoom is the only camera movement in the film that cannot be that of a human being as well, and this is no doubt the reason Straub/Huillet usually avoid it. The impulse to identify with it is a cinematic contradiction; in this use it separates the motion of the cinematic form from that of the narrator or the viewer's identification. The leap of freedom comes when, at the conclusion of the text, the young man again becomes invisible and his journey is completed instead only in the closure of the cinematic form. As the banker speaks his last line, he is again imprisoned, this time in the closest shot of the film. The extreme shortness of the shot is also shocking after a series of shots one and a half to three minutes in length. The banker's head is seen from the side, as if he intends to move, but the shot and his head are immediately cut. Here one could indeed read "rage," but the young man is not seen acting it out. The rage is formal, and any connection to the young man, as in the earlier instance of the widening space, is a mental process on the part of the viewer. Then, in the final shot, the zoom toward the fountain completes the motion begun earlier in the film. This time the zoom does come to rest on the female face in stone (vomiting in rage, as Straub has put it)[51] while the excerpt from the Saint Matthew Passion is heard, expressing "the people's" rage at Judas's betrayal of Christ. But at the end of the zoom, marking the opening of the text to include music and words not by Brecht, as well as a separate reference to a "people" who do not have an interest to put forward, the camera and the film remain at peace. The monument of Caesar has been replaced by the anonymous face of a woman; the text is extinguished; the young man and the audience leave to carry these memories with them into the world outside.

The significance of form in *History Lessons* implies that it is an oversimplification to see the film (or Brecht's novel) either as a demystification of Caesar or as a demystification of (film or novelistic) form. The formal discussion of the novel indicates that the form itself challenges the dominant view of history. The form of both novel and film does not replace a false view of Caesar with a "correct," Marxist one. Instead, the form forces a shift of attention away from Caesar and onto the processes of history and the inadequate tools available to understand them. Walsh's conclusion that "Caesar is the prototype of the modern capitalist"[52] therefore points in the wrong direction. Although it supplies some Brechtian "entertainment" through its humor, there is little to be gained by depicting Caesar or "The Capitalist" now as heroes, now as villains.

The depiction of Caesar is not the goal of either work, it is the erosion of such "depictions." In this regard the film is able to go further than the novel, with added contemporary relevance. In the novel, a unified, heroic view of Caesar is dissolved, but so too is the narrator's character, to whom it was significant. Furthermore, the diaries persist in assuming the importance of Caesar as a personality on one level, and this fragmented view of Caesar is not superseded. Ironically, the Marxian/Brechtian point of view that might do so is also imprisoned among the fragments of the narrative, in the long speeches of Spicer, Alder, and Carbo. The film, however, is able to dissolve the image of Caesar (or of any narrative "personality") as a mover of history, while at the same time it provides a framework from which to view this process. But both Brecht and the filmmakers are careful not to assert that such a work can therefore expose or explain the true movers of history, whether they are emperors, capitalists, anonymous social processes, or even "the people." Brecht indeed saw the temptation to flee from the horror of the irrationality around him into the haven of rational analysis. This explains his decision to imprison the banker's analysis, which sounds so much like Brecht's own voice, in a heterogeneous framework. The analysis can be made *in* the work of art, but Brecht refused to erase the contradiction between a historical agent in motion and a consciousness at rest that can make such analyses. *History Lessons* also stresses that knowledge is trapped in the various fragments and that no homogenizing scheme could encompass it and finally contain the truth. Instead, the film invites the viewer to move through this pattern of fragments, using the tools of perception to become less susceptible to the manipulative power of either historical stories or analyses and to make use of them while leaving them behind. Here the film points forward to Straub/Huillet's treatment of the character of Empedocles.

The irony of Brecht's lack of an audience is related to the gap between Straub/Huillet and expectations of either representation or instruction in film. Films will not materially contribute to social change by describing capitalism as the enemy or by teaching that it functions according to the demands of economic or social and political forces. Social change can only come about if someone makes use of this knowledge, and the work of art cannot presume to prescribe how this is to come about. The contradictions between the "inscribed reader" and the "social subject" open a space for liberation.[53] But since knowledge is not a replacement for action, the narrator's action (reaction) falls outside the film and can only be suggested by the interplay of purely aesthetic forms.

# 7

# MUSICAL MODERNISM AND THE SCHOENBERG FILMS

It is both logical and fantastic that the biblical injunction against idol worship should have led to the abstraction of modern art. Yet modernism still concerns us as we are caught between the culture industry's ceaseless flood of images and meanings and the challenge the horrors of the Nazi extermination camps have posed to the possibility of artistic expression at all. As Theodor W. Adorno put it, "To write poetry after Auschwitz is barbaric."[1]

It is appropriate that the life and art of Arnold Schoenberg have become part of Straub/Huillet's treatment of the contemporary dilemmas of culture and politics in the films *Moses and Aaron* (1974–1975) and *Introduction to Arnold Schoenberg's "Accompaniment to a Cinematographic Scene"* (1972). The difficulty of reconciling modernist artistic form with politics is an explicit problem of Schoenberg's opera *Moses and Aaron*, and Straub/Huillet demonstrate the issue's continued relevance with both films.

The name of Schoenberg is almost synonymous with modern music, or "the new music" as Adorno called it in German.[2] *Moses and Aaron*, considered one of Schoenberg's masterworks, was never completed. He composed the first two acts in 1930–1933, that is, just before he reconverted to Judaism and left Germany in the face of Nazi persecution in 1933. *Introduction* deals with another composition from what Eisler and Adorno called Schoenberg's "most radical period," the "Accompaniment to a Cinematographic Scene" (1930). The composition bears the simple inscription "Threatening Danger, Fear, Catastrophe," and Eisler and Adorno argue that the fear expressed in Schoenberg's dissonances "far surpasses the measure of fear conceivable to the average middle-class individual; it is a historical fear, a sense of impending doom."[3] Although fear and danger certainly apply to the atmosphere in Berlin when the music was written, Straub/Huillet's work also stresses a postwar, post-1968 perspective. As Jacques Aumont has written, "Straub and Huillet are working after the war; they know how the threat has become catastrophe, horror. Their reflection traverses the French colonial wars, Zionism and the Six Day War, May '68 and European leftism; they confront violence, the traces of which are borne by their German films."[4]

Both musical works featured in these films are outstanding examples of Schoenberg's attempt to write large-scale musical works using the twelve-note technique of composition he had developed a few years before. Dodecaphony, the twelve-note structure on which the technique rests, was Schoenberg's way of restoring a logical principle to composition once tonality had been abandoned in the early 1900s. Rather than being organized around a tonal center, twelve-tone composition places notes in a sequence that is then followed and varied only in relation to its own structure. Adorno and Eisler described such modern music in *Composing for the Films*: "In truly valid new music, everything is the direct result of the concrete requirement of structure, rather than of the tonal system or any ready-made pattern."[5]

Schoenberg's position as a musical innovator who failed to reach a wide audience is not unlike that of Straub/Huillet in the cinema. Although their works are radical in many respects, these modernists insist that their methods are derived from earlier forms. The principles of atonality, for instance, were found in tonality itself in the form of "alternative and subordinate means of creating the relation of dissonance and consonance" that developed more and more power in the nineteenth century. "Schoenberg's genius," as Charles Rosen puts it, was "to have recognized almost unconsciously the dispossession of the principal means of musical expression by the new force of what had been a subordinate and contributing element."[6] Straub/Huillet's use of cinematic materials against the grain of film convention resembles the atonal principle that no pitch is more important than any other. Their stress on the forgotten qualities of earlier cinemas as a basis for modernist filmmaking resonates with Schoenberg's discovery of twelve-tone composition by studying the submerged logic of earlier developments, culminating in the "emancipation of dissonance."[7] And finally Straub/Huillet, like Schoenberg, reject the idea that strict formal principles are more important to them than artistic expression: "It was never Schoenberg's intention to emphasize the technique."[8]

In discussing the Schoenberg films, I will begin to connect the Brechtian theories of a political avant-garde discussed so far to the insistence on critique and "negativity" found in Frankfurt school Critical Theory, particularly the work of Adorno. Straub/Huillet films have convinced me that Brecht and Adorno are not as far apart as is commonly assumed. Or, to put it another way, the contradictions between the two correspond to the aesthetic and theoretical tensions that Straub/Huillet films constantly explore. In *History Lessons*, the freedom of the audience was found in the separation of narrative and history from the film form in which they are contained. *Moses and Aaron* and *Introduction* explore further aspects of this separation of cinematic materials and the freedom it postulates. They thus correspond to the kind of modern "film music" Eisler and Adorno envisioned when they wrote, "A proper dramaturgy, the unfolding of a general meaning, would sharply distinguish among pictures, words, and music, and for that very reason relate them meaningfully to one another."[9]

## *Moses and Aaron*

In her study of "visual constructions of Jewishness," Gertrud Koch begins with a consideration of Adorno, Schoenberg's opera *Moses and Aaron*, and the Straub/Huillet film of that work.[10] Her discussion of the contradictions between mimesis and the "proscription of images" in Adorno's aesthetics relates closely to the aspects in Straub/Huillet's work I consider here in regard to Adorno and Brecht. The principal subject of Koch's book, however, is the difficulty the cinema has in creating adequate visual representations of Jews as Jews, particularly since such representations either tend to reproduce anti-Semitic stereotypes or are defeated by the unrepresentability of the *Shoah*. In the face of this, Koch stresses that Critical Theory's theoretical attempt to link the extremes of mimesis and the proscription of images is relevant to contemporary film.[11] Although Koch concludes that Straub/Huillet's *Moses and Aaron* is unsuccessful in resolving the extremes, I hope to show that this film and the short film *Introduction* productively explore the contradictions of politics and representation, anti-Semitism and identity. They carry on the task that Adorno valued in Schoenberg's opera, as Philippe Lacoue-Labarthe described it, "the offering of a work which explicitly thematizes the question of its own possibility as a work—this makes it modern—and which thereby carries in itself, as its most intimate subject, the question of the essence of art."[12]

Straub/Huillet's interest in Schoenberg as a basis for film is nearly as old as their Bach project. Plans to film *Moses and Aaron* stem from 1959, when they saw the first fully staged production at the Deutsche Oper in Berlin.[13] Their Schoenberg collaboration with the conductor Michael Gielen continues with plans for a film of *Von Heute auf Morgen* in 1996.

The action of *Moses and Aaron* is Schoenberg's retelling of the story of Moses' presentation of the Ten Commandments to the people of Israel and their worship of the Golden Calf (Exod. 3, 4, 30–32). The work breaks off at the resulting impasse between the invisible law of monotheism, for which Moses stands, and the more accessible religion Aaron represents, which includes miracles, sacrifices, and the worship of the Golden Calf. The unfinished third act occupied Schoenberg until his death in 1951, when he expressed the wish, carried out by Straub/Huillet in the film, that the final act "be staged merely spoken, in case I cannot complete the composition."[14] Schoenberg envisioned the opera more as a staged oratorio, and Straub/Huillet's exploration of this form in film extends from *Chronicle* to the Hölderlin films.

Since the temporal structure of *Moses and Aaron* is largely predetermined by the score of Schoenberg's opera, my main focus here is its relation to cinematic space. The themes of the opera's narrative are located by Straub/Huillet in separate planes of cinematic space, allowing the spectator to move with the camera within and between these planes. By contrast, the strongly two-dimensional nature of the short film *Introduction* draws our attention to its use of cinematic time and its relation to Schoenberg's innovations in composition. In conclusion, I will argue that this film asserts both artistic and political freedom through its thorough separation of art from politics.

Before examining the spatial drama of the opera film, I want to note briefly a few aspects of the relation between Schoenberg's score and the score and screenplay finally used in the film. As the musical conductor for the film, Michael Gielen, has pointed out, since Schoenberg only completed a draft of the score, the work involved in producing this complete production for the film provided the opportunity to "research and present a fundamentally authentic text, definitive for our time. Here, too, in this sense it was a premiere."[15] Gielen's published comments document the quality and the thoroughness of Straub/Huillet's preparation of the opera.[16] The resulting film has since been called "the standard-setting opera film, which leaves all the others behind" and "the most radical film-opera the cinema has given us."[17] The Philips studio recording made conjointly with preparation for the film is also considered definitive (record no. 6700 084) and was awarded the Prix Mondiale du Disque de Montreaux. Gielen's record diverges from the film in leaving off the recitation of the text of the third act, a decidedly different interpretation of the unity of the work, Koch has pointed out.[18]

The nature of the recording also differs from film to record: For the film a very "dead" recording was used, with as little resonance as possible, whereas the record has the "artificial resonance" typical of the recording industry. Gielen in some ways prefers the lack of resonance, because it emphasizes the structural relationships in the music, rather than tone.[19] This structural relationship carries over into the technical basis for the filming of the performances themselves. True to their principles, Straub/Huillet rely almost exclusively on live sound in this work, with the singers recorded on camera in the theater of Alba Fucense in the Abruzzi region of Italy. The orchestral accompaniment, however, comes from a studio recording, audible to the singers as they perform through earphones hidden by wigs and costumes. The technical separation, which takes on cinematic meaning in shots I will examine later, corresponds to Adorno's observation of the musical difference between the voices and orchestra: "The unity of *Moses and Aaron* is created by its strictly sustained dualism. [ . . . ] The function of the orchestra as a whole is that of an accompaniment."[20] In an acoustic as well as a visual sense, then, the film offers a dimension that other recordings of the work do not.

The other aspect, which will be largely excluded here, is the exactness with which the editing of the film follows the "movement" of the score as Gielen attests. This essay, like any analysis or viewing of the film, is thus partial inasmuch as its ignores this careful correlation of music and editing. Merely the phrase "musically necessary locations for cuts"[21] establishes the uniqueness of the Straub/Huillet approach. The relatively small number of shots in the film, seventy-seven shots over 110 minutes, arises from the difficulty of breaking between measures of twelve-tone composition. As Koch has observed, each series of notes could be related as well to the series coming after as that coming before; the cinematic consequence of this lack of hierarchy is much more camera movement than usual in a Straub/Huillet film.[22]

The emphasis of this chapter will thus be on the "cinematic space" of *Moses and Aaron* and its relation to the material of the opera/film, the constitution of a nation in and through history. The film takes as its starting point the assertion that "things could have been otherwise," even in regard to monotheism and the existence and nature of God. Straub/Huillet have in more recent films further investigated this interplay between myth and history, which Lacoue-Labarthe has called "the caesura of religion." Such a materialist project is not contradictory to that of humanist theology, since Martin Buber also has written, "We will not be able to reach the core of history . . . , the experience of events as miracles is itself history on a grand scale. It must be understood on the basis of history and placed within the historical context."[23]

The historical miracle at the center of *Moses and Aaron* is the development of monotheism among the Hebrew tribes, along with their emerging consciousness of nationhood. They created *their* God who chose them as *His* people. Even Catholic theologians describe this as a historical process, subject to change, which thus attests to the freedom of God.

> The God Moses is allowed to confront is not tied to a place. He proclaims himself "God of Abraham, God of Israel, God of Jacob," and thus the God of wandering nomads, with whom He has moved and whom He has led. He prophesies and promises that He will lead the people into the land of Canaan. An unrepresentable God is a free God—God in His unfathomable freedom, from which history emerges: history which will give meaning and a goal to the life of the peoples.[24]

The existence of such a God, however, is tied by covenant to that of His People: "It is the prophecy that God's Being will be revealed in His Being-with-and-for Israel."[25]

A materialist concept of history values the historical mobility the development of monotheism represents. For this reason, Danièle Huillet accompanied the published screenplay of *Moses and Aaron* with a "Little Historical

Excursus," based on a variety of historical sources.[26] The essay describes just how much the Israelite nomads had in common with the other tribes of the area and thus to what extent the historical development of their religion fit their needs for progress as a nation. The significant historical dimensions parallel those in Adorno's aesthetics, that is, memory of a past, motion toward a future, and thus constitution of a group identity, historical subjectivity. In her excursus, Huillet stresses the importance of the link between the "unrepresentable God" and the freedom and identity of the Israelites: "He [Moses] was convinced—and convinced his people—that a god fought on their side who was more powerful than all the gods of Egypt: Jahweh, the Elohim of the Sinai, who would not only free the oppressed Hebrew tribes, but also would make a People out of them."[27]

The radical concept here is the importance of historical change bound up with the central existence of God: a people comes to its God; its religious life is not unchanging but moves forward, has a history. The "unrepresentable" nature of God is the driving force, the thought, that pushes onward into the future.

> Thus Moses' task was a practical one: the creation of a People by means of a national religion: Jahweh is to be the God of Israel and Israel the People of God. This often-repeated formulation is Moses' guiding thought. A last trait of this national religion is its historical character.
>
> Most other Semitic peoples had worshiped their gods since time immemorial and felt bound to them through a natural, physically related image. But on a certain day, Israel was brought to Jahweh by Moses, a personality long to be remembered.[28]

At another time Straub asserts that although Schoenberg was "anti-Marxist," his "prudent" way of working makes the opera a suitable "object of Marxist reflection":

> When he talks about the "chosen people" there is a mystical idea there, which is not a Marxist idea, but which he neither takes as an end in itself. The idea of the chosen people is instrumental. It enables a step into history, as it were, as a means to something else. Subsequently, of course, the idea became an oppression. It became institutionalized. We have to start again every day, and when something becomes institutionalized it loses its revolutionary potential.[29]

The opera *Moses and Aaron* is centered on just this contradiction: the strength of the monotheistic idea rests on its link to a historical event, the liberation of the people of Israel from Egypt. This idea is new; it cuts a people off from its past in order to allow it to "step into history." But just this newness requires Moses' insistence that the old gods, with physical and geographic nearness to the people, be left behind. The new God cannot be seen in images.

This historical quality of God is inherently ambivalent, and here arises the conflict between Moses and Aaron. First, the newness of this God is based on "the complete, absolute separation of God, who is everything, from humanity, who is nothing."[30] This is the source of the power that could lead an oppressed people into the unknown; the power of God does not derive from any human characteristics but is something that can never quite be absorbed into human experience; "it is truly the 'completely Other.' "[31] But the fact that this power "chose" to free the Israelites and chose to speak to Moses contradicts its nature as "completely Other." Having created this nation, it is also somehow "represented" in it.

The contradiction between God as "unrepresentable" and separate from the world and God's existence *for* the chosen people is expressed clearly enough in the opera. Moses argues for the "unrepresentable Idea" while Aaron allows its physical representation in images. Moses expresses himself in *Sprechstimme*, Aaron in "melodic" tenor. The film *Moses and Aaron* is unique in two ways, however: first, the cinematic "representation" of the ambivalence of an unrepresentable God actively influencing reality; and second, the transformation of this historical conflict into an aesthetic experience for an audience. As Adorno's aesthetic theory suggests, the dilemma of art is similar to this contradiction. It points toward freedom, but it is by nature separate from the society in need of this freedom. It represents the unrepresentable.

Straub/Huillet's film balances this ambivalence by separating the kinds of narrative space created at each point of the dilemma. In the first place, all narrative action that involves either performance of the opera or the temptation of the people to return to religious images is tied very strictly to the physical space of and motion within the amphitheater of Alba Fucense. On one level, the entire opera is confined to this space; all the "images" created by Aaron *and* the people of Israel as represented in the opera are photographed there. The "unrepresentable," the mythical step into history that Moses "represents" as well as the implied aesthetic step into history for the spectator of all this, is provided only by the material means of the cinema that go beyond the opera's performance.

The early shots establish this contrast. As Moses receives his call to lead the people out of bondage, we see him and the space in which he will continue to be photographed in an extended shot tracing the extremes of the camera's mobility, shot 10. The shot moves from an extreme close-up of Moses by way of a 300-degree pan around the amphitheater that is to become the setting for the action, and during this pan it tilts from a high angle showing the ground from over Moses' left shoulder to a low angle showing the mountains in the distance outside the amphitheater.[32]

Shot 10 thus sets Moses within his sphere of action. As he receives his call from God, we see the amphitheater in which the "drama" of leading the people

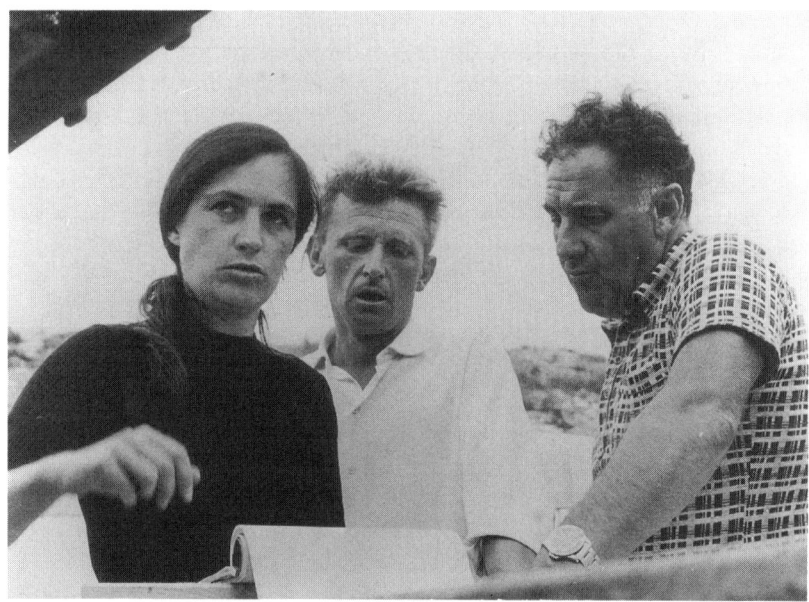

Straub/Huillet directing Schoenberg's *Moses and Aaron* with cinematographer Ugo Piccone, right. Courtesy Stiftung Deutsche Kinemathek.

will be enacted and, at the end of the pan, the mountain where the "idea" has originated. As yet the people are not visible, since the spiraling tilt has literally gone over the heads of the other singers. They do not exist until Moses (or God) addresses them through Aaron. Because this initial view of Moses is an oblique one from over his shoulder, the viewer does not take the place of speaker or listener at this stage but instead observes the camera's passage from Moses' position to the "goal" this idea represents. As Straub has said of this shot, "All the themes of the film are there." The pan halts on its long shot of the distant mountains with the words of the burning bush, "And this I promise to you: / I shall conduct you forward, / to where, with the Eternal Oneness, you'll be a model to every nation."[33] As in the rest of the film, the *Verheißung*, the otherness of God, the unrepresentable, is pointed to by way of cinematic techniques that are also "other" to the drama within the amphitheater.

Walsh links the historical and aesthetic/philosophical issues of the film in the following manner: "Co-extensive with Moses and Aaron's conflict over how to lead the people is the problem of how to 'represent the unrepresentable': how to realize the idea in an image without betraying the idea. In short, they are concerned with the ideology of representation, and the film may be read entirely on this level."[34] The "ideology of representation" is therefore a theme for both the people of Israel and the spectators of the film, but by different means.

The chorus in *Moses and Aaron*. Courtesy Museum of Modern Art.

The film's manner of separating these two "audiences" determines its structure to a great degree.

After the spatial tour de force of shot 10, the film sets up the "rules of the game," as Huillet calls them, for the drama within the amphitheater. These are the spatial relationships between Moses, Aaron, the chorus, the priest, the man, the young man, and the young girl. These relationships, like the motion of Moses from the theater to the mountain, are constructed through an external cinematic device. During these exchanges in Act I, leading to the liberation of the Israelites from bondage, the camera remains in the center of the ellipse. Thus every shot of one of the "roles" listed above has the amphitheater as its background. The choir is arranged in a square of six rows instead of the customary four, so that it, like the other actors, can always have space around it and usually the wall of the amphitheater in the background. The existence of the people is thus always accompanied by evidence of human history.

The effect of this arrangement is established in shots 19 and 22, which without editing include the positions of all the actors in the amphitheater. Since all the positions are photographed here in a single pan, the spectator and the camera do not identify with any single position. There is never a shot, for instance, that shows Moses from the point of view of the chorus whom he addresses. But the camera is still *within* this configuration. It never again stands behind Moses to reveal at once his position and the location of the listeners,

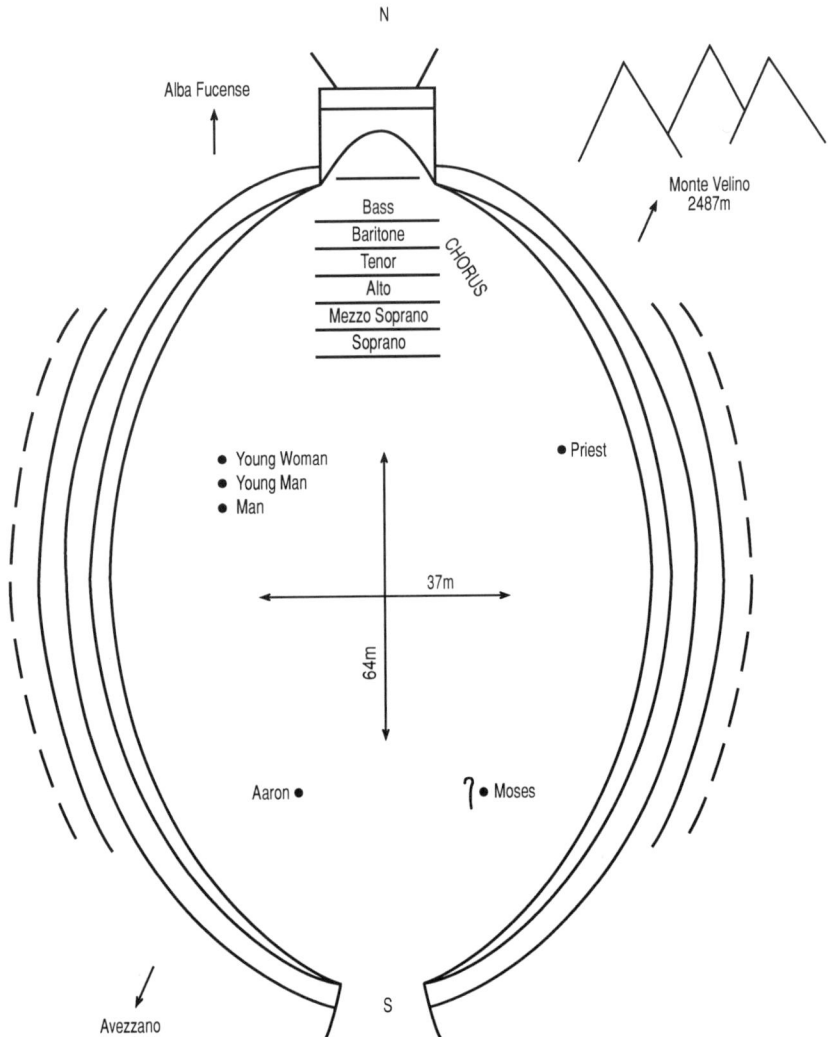

*Moses and Aaron*: The amphitheater at Alba Fucense showing arrangement of characters for Act I. Graphic: Andrew Reich.

which would make the spectator superior to this relation. Thus the spectator is not confined to a point of view but still senses the confinement of the theater space. This constant background serves to emphasize at the same time the static performance quality of the work, the separateness of this historical action from the present tense of the spectator and the camera movement, and the equality and interdependence of each of the musical and dramatic parts.

Walsh has noted the narrative structure in the way camera placement varies the positions of Moses and Aaron in the image: "insofar as shots 4 and 6 bracket shot 5, Aaron metaphorically surrounds Moses—is his voice."[35] What Walsh notes here is that changing camera placement shows Aaron in various positions with respect to Moses, while Moses remains static, photographed from the front. Walsh also notes the function of camera movement to provide the changing positions of Moses and Aaron in shot 24. Schoenberg has specified such shifts in distance between Moses and Aaron and between each of them and the audience.

> Straub/Huillet's mise-en-scène respects the sense of an oscillating power struggle that is here Schoenberg's concern, but instead of having Moses and Aaron move (they remain static throughout the shot), the camera moves, the relative sizes of Moses and Aaron shifting in the frame as the camera tracks around them, and back again. The shot thus functions narratively, but Straub/Huillet simultaneously accomplish more than this, since their materialist use of the medium becomes apparent once again, this time through the contrast between the rapidly shifting background of the amphitheater and the slowly changing relations between Moses and Aaron: this dramatic separation of foreground and background has a strong two-dimensionalizing effect.[36]

As in twelve-tone musical technique, then, the importance of the camera in this narrative thus equalizes its elements, flattens them out in visual space, and emphasizes their abstract interrelatedness, existing wholly in the past.

So far, we have seen that neither Moses' confrontation with God nor his (and Aaron's) persuading and leading the people is acted out. Instead, these events are represented through relationships of cinematic space and camera movement. A sharp contrast to this technique of "representation" is thus provided by those aspects of the opera that are acted out. These elements belong entirely to Aaron's transgression of the prohibition of images and are also largely confined in space to the amphitheater. We do not see Moses go to the mountain or return; we do not see his receiving the Ten Commandments. But in his absence, we do see the unification of the twelve tribes, whose princes arrive at the amphitheater on horseback. The adoration of the Golden Calf is acted out, as are the representations of decadence, the orgy, the animal and human sacrifices. These activities are thus aesthetically and thematically opposite to the stylized manner in which Moses received and conveyed his mission, "the unrepresentable." However, this is not to assert unequivocally that Aaron's transgression is condemned by the film. The expressions of worship involved with the Golden Calf do indeed arise from the real-life experience of the people of God. They also have history and are a way of joining history. Thus one must note that the Golden Calf is meant to represent the liberation from bondage and that it is made of the gold the people themselves had gathered (Aaron: "Ihr spendet diesen Stoff, / ich geb ihm solche Form";

Aaron (Louis Devos). Courtesy Museum of Modern Art.

shot 30). Even the destruction and the self-destructiveness acted out are desensationalized. They are not made more powerful by way of cinematic effects but are merely presented as "representations" of these transgressions. Gielen finds the "renunciation of the orgy" of great importance to the film, stressing, among other things, the "unprofessional" dance of the butchers, performed by professional dancers.[37] Koch also accurately observes that this method of presenting the ballet is part of the price Straub/Huillet have paid for treating the opera as a text, including this portion which approaches conventional film and theater spectacle. But she seems to underestimate the significance of her own crucial observation: "The naturalistic details and objects, recommended by the composer and potentially offering considerable visual spectacle, have the effect in the film as theatrical props in the literal sense."[38] A powerful shock is produced by the juxtaposition of music, theatrical spectacle, the athletic skill of the Cologne ballet dancers, direct sound, and "the frustrating precision of the framing." The final image of the ballet is of the gravel base of the amphitheater, a frame the dancers have left, filled only by the sound of their panting from such exertion.[39]

One could also argue that this distancing from the "pleasure of the spectacle" is necessary to historicize it. The dance of the butchers is not only the music most closely resembling traditional program music in Schoenberg's opera,[40] it is also the only portion ever performed during his lifetime. As such, it has already been "realized" in the past to a greater degree than the unfinished opera as a whole.

Concerning the separation of life and art and the question of representing the unrepresentable, the "artlessness" of these scenes becomes extremely complex. It seems particularly fitting that virtually all critics have been disturbed by the orgy scenes and the dance of the butchers as Straub/Huillet have filmed them, since they portray the transgressions of the people, who attempt to represent their religion in the forms of everyday life. Since both true art and true holiness are separate from everyday life, these scenes are neither artful nor reverent. Despite their lack of art, however, they do provide a contrast to the rest of the film by capturing some of the spirit of real human life in its physical richness and diversity and give some credence to the "demands of the people" as even Eisler and Adorno urged. The images of the night of the orgy are cool and comfortable compared to the stark bright heat of most of the film's settings. The image of the moon in shot 69, for all its associations with death in the shots preceding it, is an inviting one. And the life breathed into the amphitheater by the arrival of the animals for sacrifice is also attractive as a sign of everyday living; their surplus of sound temporarily overwhelms the music. Furthermore, the unconvincing depiction of the suicides in the orgy also has an affirmative, realistic note: self-destruction is not natural after all, and thus it is difficult to depict without the aid of professionals in the art.

The transgression against the unrepresentable God thus is represented without "art." It is merely acted out, quite literally following the libretto, set within the reality of human life. The cinematic art of this film thus is linked to the opposite element: the unrepresentable God, the idea of freedom, the negation of reality, otherness. The ultimate expression of this freedom occurs in the film when the cinematic apparatus leaves the realm of narrative representations to suggest something beyond them. Preparation for this liberation from the historical narrative is provided by the central placement of the camera in the amphitheater. All the narrative action is focused inward, but the camera's perception of it can escape. Suggestions of this possible escape reside also in the fact that Moses' journey is not seen, nor is his destruction of the stone tablets narratively completed. Most important, the destruction of the Golden Calf is not acted out but is achieved by the fade to white offered only by cinematic technique. Here the question of the audience rises again. Moses is able to destroy the image, but even this destruction is an image: "Auch die Zerstörung des Bildwerks war nur ein Zeichen, ein Bild."[41] But in the context of the film, the destruction of the Golden Calf and, more important, the liberation of the people from bondage are radically different kinds of images from those positive ones worshiped within the narrative drama. The destruction of the Golden Calf, for instance, is not acted out dramatically but occurs through the fade of the film image. This is not to say that the white film or black film is any less a "sign" than the calf, but it does have a different audience: the calf is an image for both the people of Israel and for the viewer of the film; the fade to a white screen is only an image for the viewer. Even more liberating is the travel of the camera outside the narrative space of the amphitheater. In this motion it follows none of the actors of the film, not even Moses. The two long panning shots of the Nile, shots 42 and 43, thus do much more than represent the escape of the Israelites from Egypt described in the accompanying text. To a great extent, it replaces this escape with an opportunity for the spectator to be both within and beyond the conflict of the film. At this point, we are on a different level from an audience reflecting on an "estranged" opera performance. The cinematic structure both confines and abandons the operatic performance. The audience for this pan across the Nile valley is also not the people of Israel, because they are enclosed in the space of the amphitheater and are not given the freedom of movement that the camera has. The chorus heard on the sound track is suddenly not present to the shot. The opportunity of freedom offered by this cinematic transformation is to become an audience for (and in) which the unrepresentable is brought into existence. As Jahweh is to the people of Israel, so is the authentic work of art to the audience that might exist for this film.

The final confrontations between Moses and Aaron also complete the separation of the formal structure of the film from the historical dilemma of their two ways of leading the people. As shot 10 united Moses' journey with the promise of the burning bush to free the people and to lead it, here the process is reversed. In shot 78, Moses destroys the stone tablets, the result of the foregoing struggle. Aaron and the people are no longer seen, and this is another parallel to the beginning. But Aaron's voice argues that the signs that lead toward the promised land, the pillar of fire by night and the pillar of clouds by day, are no less signs from God than the burning bush. A moving camera points to the distant sky outside the amphitheater as Aaron sings "Darin zeigt der Ewige nicht sich, / aber den Weg zu sich und den Weg ins gelobte Land" (shot 79). The same camera perspective that had inspired Moses to lead the people into the desert (into freedom) inspires Aaron to lead them out again. Act II ends as the opera began, with Moses alone, with only the arid ground around him.

The photography of Act III takes another step out of the context of the amphitheater. Like the long pans of the Nile, this shot is lush, fertile, and cool, with a mountain and a lake in the background. Lacoue-Labarthe has observed that by staging the first two acts in a Greek theater, Straub/Huillet have emphasized that this portion of the opera is the "tragedy" of Moses.[42] The modern dilemma enters with the opera's unfinished state, both a historical and a conceptual contradiction that cannot be resolved. This is the "caesura" that Lacoue-Labarthe locates in Straub/Huillet's approach to the third act.

> The dramaturgical choice of Straub and Huillet is particularly illuminating: for not only do they play this rarely spoken scene in the unbearable silence which succeeds the unfurling of the music, a silence that Adorno analyzes so well, but they have it played in a place other than that which, since the outset, was properly the stage or the theater. They do this in such a way that it is not only the tragic

apparatus as Adorno understands it that collapses in a single stroke, but the entire apparatus which kept *Moses* within the frame of opera or music-drama. And it is here, probably, that religion is interrupted.[43]

Again, Straub/Huillet allow the cinema to take over: Moses and Aaron are no longer in the desert; they have been transported to a new setting, not by their own action, but by the camera's. Here, too, they do not act; all motion is supplied by the camera. The camera takes in first both Moses and Aaron, who is bound and lying in the mud, insisting that his images served the survival of the nation: "for their freedom—so that they would become a nation." Then, without a cut, the camera pans to Moses, who has the last word. The lack of editing unifies the scene rather than breaking it up into its contrasting parts.

Originally, the escape into the desert had been an escape from bondage and the creation of a nation. Now Moses proclaims that the nation will always need to return to the desert, as punishment for the successes of its own creation.

> Whensoever you went forth amongst the people and employed these gifts—
> which you were chosen to possess
> so that you could fight for the divine idea—
> whensoever you employed those gifts for false and negative ends,
> that you might rival and share the lowly pleasures of strange peoples,
> and whensoever you abandoned the wasteland's renunciation
> and your gifts had led you to the highest summit,
> then as a result of that misuse you were ever hurled back
> into the wasteland.[44]

The separation of God from the people is the reality that makes it possible for this people to depart from and return to its covenant; the absoluteness of God's otherness makes possible a historical continuity for the "chosen people." The otherness of God is the basis of their freedom. But to "become a people," the images of Aaron were also necessary, and Straub/Huillet thus maintain the dissonance of this contradiction to the end. Aaron, who had been the man of melody and images, speaks his last words from offscreen; and the stage direction indicating that he falls down dead thus is negated. The only image at the film's end is Moses proclaiming the unity of the people and God without images.

The otherness of the cinematic structure in this film is the basis for the spectators' freedom. Since the audience is not *in* the cinematic space that confines the historical characters, it can see beyond them, can imagine the possibility of another liberation that cannot be represented because the people who could claim it do not exist. The film proposes an escape from its own images but does not depict either a leader or a nation that could carry out this escape. It returns to the limits of its own forms; since it is not the world, it cannot depict freedom in the world. Even the magnificent freedom of the panoramas of the Nile, freedom offered to an audience able to accept it, begins and ends in bondage, in the history of its own mechanical creation, its unreality. Visually, shot 43 encompasses the hopes and the limits of the entire film as well: it begins with the arid rocks at the left of the frame, moves to take in the glorious green expanse of the Nile valley, then returns to the same arid rocks at the right of the frame, just as the chorus repeats the word "free." This film thus does not unselfconsciously indulge the audience's desire to gaze at natural beauty and evades, I think, the trap Gertrude Koch has consigned it to: "Thus both shots of pure nature get caught up in the wake of the ambiguity of *Moses and Aaron*, including its Zionist, political-biographical aspect."[45] The film can escape the desert and point toward the promised land, but it cannot enter it; liberation in reality and liberation in the cinema are separate propositions. The proscription of images and cinematic pleasure are both upheld.

## *Introduction to Arnold Schoenberg's "Accompaniment to a Cinematographic Scene"*

The heterogeneity of elements seen at work in *Moses and Aaron* provides a link to the work of Schoenberg as presented in *Introduction*. "Accompaniment," composed in 1930, bears the simple inscription "Threatening Danger, Fear, Catastrophe." The piece is the only music heard in the Straub/Huillet film, one of a series of short films on composers commissioned by West Germany's Süd-West-Funk television station. The film is a collage of the following elements: a short introduction by Straub, showing him on a balcony in Rome and then shifting to images of Schoenberg's expressionistic self-portraits; excerpts from letters Schoenberg wrote to Wassily Kandinsky in which he confronts anti-Semitism and proclaims his rejection of politics (read on-screen into a microphone by two young men in the broadcasting studio);[46] a statement by Brecht on the connection of economics to fascism, from the year 1935 (recited by Huillet in her home); and finally, images of bombs being loaded onto B-52 aircraft and then dropped on the rice fields of Southeast Asia. Schoenberg's "Accompaniment" begins about halfway through the film, while the composer's letters are being read, and continues to the end.

The arrangement of such diverse elements into the temporal unity of a film is a film counterpart to Schoenberg's atonal compositions and his method of twelve-tone composition. Traditional tonality in music has a structural function parallel to that of traditional narrative in film. The overall structure of both is hierarchical, giving each note, image, or moment a "meaning" dependent on its relative place in the hierarchy. Dissonance in music, like the "lack" or "unreality" caused by the fragmentation of film, postulates a final resolution that restores and confirms equilibrium and completeness.

This sense of completeness based on hierarchical organization was rejected by Schoenberg. As Rosen puts it, "In Schoenberg, there is no voice, no note that is expressively neutral."[47] As noted above, however, this renunciation of a hierarchical structure is not a renunciation of structure or organization in itself. The composer still uses musical materials as a means of expression, but the value or meaning of certain expressions is no longer merely accepted as given by tradition. Thus other means of organization proposed by the nature of musical possibilities themselves are investigated; variations in sound were produced by changes in instrumentation rather than by the arrangement of notes. Rather than rest on a tonic chord, serial composition pushes toward the logical material limit of eventually using *all* the notes. "The saturation of musical space is Schoenberg's substitute for the tonic chord of the traditional musical language."[48]

Here is another parallel to the narrative tradition. A spectator of narrative cinema is held in position through the activity of filling the gaps in the narrative, restoring connections as time passes to synthesize the experience into a coherent memory. The gaps and dissonances in tonic composition serve the same purpose. They urge the listener to participate in the hierarchy by anticipating its formal coherence, knowing often what the next note will be, or at least feeling that each note fits comfortably into the structure.

Schoenberg's abandonment of the traditional principles of harmonic structure was not absolute. In fact, "relative degrees of stability" are still created but not on the basis of an external hierarchy. Schoenberg's atonal compositions of the pre–World War I period were thus both a step in the direction of his later twelve-note technique and a method of pushing the tensions within the earlier tonal system to their extreme. Stability is now internal to the music, *or* is implied by a reference to the traditional stability it *refuses* to provide. Rosen describes this relation of innovation to tradition as follows:

> Here we touch on the most delicate and most difficult to understand of all Schoenberg's innovations: his reconstruction of the relation of consonance and dissonance without the use of the perfect triad, which had been the ground of this relation for more than four centuries. . . . For the moment, we must concentrate on his reconstruction of relative degrees of stability, that subtly nuanced wavering between intense anguish and half-resolution which is so characteristic of *Erwartung*. The simplest and most localized device for achieving this is described by Schoenberg himself at the end of the *Harmonielehre*, but with a certain hesitation as if he did not himself quite understand the technique he had invented. It concerns an implied resolution that does not in fact take place. In a discussion of the attenuation of the harshness of dissonances by spacing the dissonant notes far apart, Schoenberg gives a chord from *Erwartung*, of thirteen notes, which embraces eleven different notes of the chromatic scale plus two octave doublings. He observes that a resolution of the two upper notes into consonances according to the rules of tonal harmony appears to be implied by the structure of the chord,

and that this allusion to older forms seems to have a satisfying effect even though the resolution does not actually occur. Schoenberg himself realized the important role that the older style was to play in his work.[49]

A parallel to Straub/Huillet and Brecht emerges here. There is no "resolution" in their work, according to the hierarchical rules of traditional organization of meaning, but the relation of the organization of its materials to these traditional forms implies a resolution outside the work itself. As noted in regard to *History Lessons*, the subject of this "resolution" is outside the work of art but implied by it—is its utopian aspect.

The two most important aspects of *Introduction* in this regard are the heterogeneity of its material elements, parallel to musical "saturation," and its arrangement of and its existence in time. Heterogeneity of elements is one of the aspects common to Schoenberg's music and to the Straub/Huillet film that is stressed by Martin Walsh. Contrast, as opposed to transition, was found by Adorno to be Schoenberg's formative technique. "The 'separation of elements,' a materialist articulation that resists homogenization—and hence resists the appeal to any single universal 'truth'—is common to Straub/Huillet and Brecht, as it is to Schoenberg."[50] But Walsh fails to include "politics" as an element not to be homogenized. If the work appeals to no "single, universal 'truth,'" must it then appeal to a single, particular political truth? Walsh cites the separation of art and politics in Schoenberg's view but places Adorno and Brecht side by side without reflecting on their philosophical differences. Therefore, my analysis of the film will refute his conclusion that "this conscious desire for total separation of music and politics is precisely opposed by Straub/Huillet's structuring of *Introduction*."[51] On the contrary, the separation of music and politics is intrinsic to the film.

As Walsh has said of *Bridegroom*, this short film, too, is almost a summary of film history, a chromatic scale of cinematic possibilities. Walsh compares the elimination of tonal harmony in Schoenberg's music with the "elimination of perspectival illusionism" in *Introduction*.[52] Although I would argue that the elimination is not absolute, the flatness of the images throughout the film is indeed striking and crucial to its structure. On the one hand, this flatness increases the relevance of time as a tool of visual composition, since there is virtually no movement within the images in most of the film. On the other hand, this flatness does lend the film an added level of "unreality," as desired by both Brecht and Schoenberg.[53] The shots of the film have a "still-photo quality,"[54] which Walsh locates as the distinction between "document" and "documentary." Each shot is in some respect a document, in addition to its content, of an aspect of film history and film's material possibilities.

On the material level, the film very simply runs through a broad range of possibilities, without organizing them in a traditional hierarchy. The film begins

Jean-Marie Straub in *Introduction to Arnold Schoenberg's "Accompaniment for a Cinematographic Scene."* Courtesy New Yorker Films.

with shots in color, with live sound, although most of the shots are in black-and-white or in color but of black-and-white subjects. The final shots of the film are entirely two-dimensional: the newspaper columns, announcing the acquittal of concentration camp architects; then the credits, white letters on red, the color of film leader, a nonverbal way of saying "the end" and perhaps a political statement. The only exterior color panorama, behind Straub in shot 2, is complemented at the end by the most extreme flatness of which film is capable. The live sound is complemented by the music, which is mechanically dubbed onto the film, like the printed titles, having no spatial relationship to the camera's presence. Even the number of shots, thirty-four, is supplied by the opus number of Schoenberg's work, a parallel to the composer's earlier *Pierrot Lunaire* opus 21, a setting of "thrice-seven" poems.

Between these two extremes are variations. For instance, although Straub/Huillet always use live sound, Schoenberg's letters to Kandinsky or Brecht's speech read by Straschek and Nestler are also "studio sound," since they were filmed in a studio of the broadcasting station that commissioned the film (Süd-West-Funk in Baden-Baden). The definition of this is therefore ambiguous because we "see" the recording of this studio sound; it is not dubbing, but if this very sound track were used to accompany another image, the event here recorded might still have looked the same.

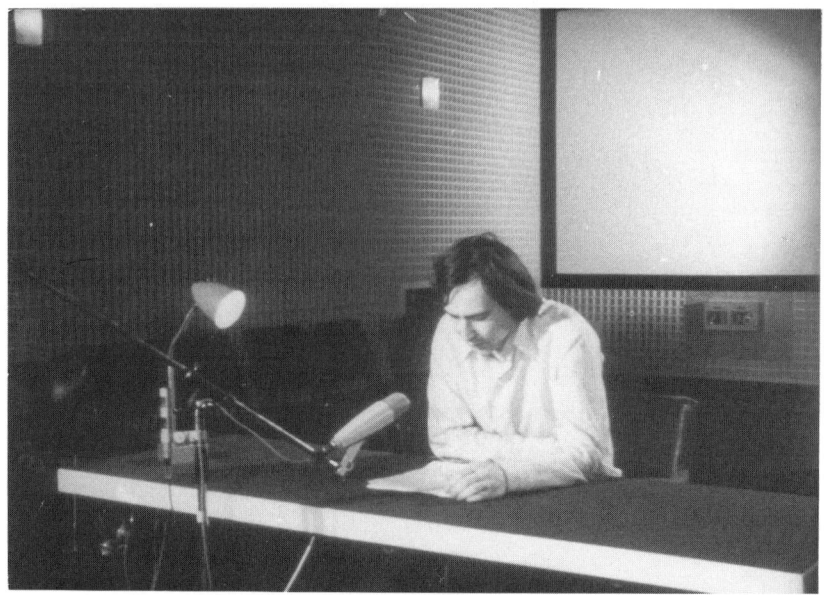

Günter Peter Straschek in *Introduction to Arnold Schoenberg's "Accompaniment for a Cinematographic Scene."* Courtesy New Yorker Films.

Visually as well, the film runs through a chromatic scale of possibilities. It begins with the fountain that ends *History Lessons,* but this time with only peaceful water sounds and not the Bach oratorio. The well-known diagonal composition is here, in shot 2 of Straub speaking from the Giannicolo, for instance, and in the shots of the studio. The two shots in the studio stand out, most prominently the empty movie screen in the background, spilling over the upper right corner of the image, leading away from this image; then the microphone, the reading lamp, and the readers' shirts and faces, which appear almost white. The rest of the image, a study in black and gray, is dominated by the tilted horizontal (black) line of the desk and the vertical but angled (gray) plane of the wall. In the second shot of the studio, which involves camera movement and a cut, the lines end up in a less diagonal and more "resolved" arrangement. But in a rare occurrence in a Straub/Huillet film, a person—Danièle Huillet—speaks squarely facing the camera. Of course, this extreme is mitigated by the unpredictable motion of the cat on her lap. Also, for further ambivalence, this shot, too, is in color, but it is very hard to remember it as such; it is very flat because of the angle, and the cat, as well as Huillet's dress, is black and white.

Although the entire film naturally consists of photography, variations are explored here as well. Photographs are seen, such as Man Ray's portrait of

Danièle Huillet in *Introduction to Arnold Schoenberg's "Accompaniment for a Cinematographic Scene."* Courtesy New Yorker Films.

Schoenberg or that of the murdered members of the Paris Commune "framed" by their coffins ("the first mass murder victims of modern capitalism").[55] Schoenberg himself is represented in four ways: in the quotations from his letters, in the photograph, in his self-portrait from the expressionist exhibition of "Der Blaue Reiter," and in his music. In addition to a sound studio, including the recording engineer, the film also documents the "documentary film": the sequence near the end shows bombs being constructed, loaded onto planes, and dropped, then exploding in flames. Film's two extremes are present in the black frames spliced in and the empty white screen in the studio. Camera movement is used sparingly, merely documenting its possibility. The camera pans in shot 16 from the engineer to Nestler reading the continuation of the Brecht text into the studio microphone. The camera tilts only twice, first over Schoenberg's self-portrait and second to allow the audience to read the newspaper excerpt in the final shot, 34. Now at the end of the film, the viewer either takes over the role of the actors, reading, or simply listens to the music (the eyes follow the camera movement in shot 34 in a way unlike the three-dimensional pan in shot 16: it cannot be "read").

Thus the film cites many of the major art forms of the twentieth century without homogenizing them. Further significance of this "separation of elements" derives from the content of the text. In a rare departure from their usual practice, Straub and Huillet here include words they have written. Hence, two shots actually contain "narration" in the strict sense of the word. It is another indication of the "material" significance of this, that when Straub and Huillet intervene between text and audience in words of their own, they film themselves. The only presence of the "voice" of Straub/Huillet in their work is also accompanied by their image. And here is a third ambivalence: the people who "narrate" in these two shots are and are not the filmmakers. They relegate themselves to a past by appearing on screen, while the role of filmmaker remains present to the whole film. When I quote myself, I am splitting my existence into two locations in time, and, of course, both are "past" in regard to the time and place in which I truly exist. On the one hand, this contradiction of past and present identity corresponds to the loss and re-creation of the subject called "suturing" in psychoanalytic terms.[56] On the other hand, it is a historical contradiction as well, as Franco Fortini discovered in the film in which he and a book written by him are the center of attention, *Fortini/Cani*. As Fortini wrote, "Now it is clear that the main character in *The Dogs of Sinai* [*Fortini/Cani*] is not exactly the author of that book, and also does not correspond to the person writing to you now. [ . . . ] The words that main character will say will stand in conflict with the real impotence . . . and with the countenance of the character himself."[57]

Straub's narration, aside from providing sketchy biographical information on Schoenberg, serves two purposes. Straub introduces the letters to Kandinsky as Schoenberg's response to an invitation to join the Bauhaus in Weimar. The letters themselves contain the reasons for Schoenberg's refusal, a refusal to accept an exceptional status above anti-Semitic discrimination against others. The letters read later in the film by Straschek reveal strongly Schoenberg's insight into the implications of the social forces that define him as a Jew in the first place, then grant him privileges as such.

The introduction, however, only mentions Schoenberg's exile and the reason for the letters. The main argument of Straub's speech is against the proposition that the "Accompaniment" can be dramatized. Straub quotes the reasons for Schoenberg's detailed stage directions in all his dramatic works, the desire "to leave as little as possible to the new rulers of the theatrical art, the producers."[58] The fact that the *Begleitmusik* has no such directions, other than the heading "Threatening Danger, Fear, Catastrophe," proves that the work is not meant to depict directly the events described or foreseen in the letters. The work has only an abstract relation to reality. Hence Straub's last assertion, before more neutral biographical narration continues in shot 3, "Otherwise unrepresentable, the cinematographic scene consists only of the so-called accompaniment."

Here, at least, the separation of music and politics is still maintained. The contents of the letters, too, although prompted by political realities, do not connect music and politics, or even suggest political action. Schoenberg drew the conclusions necessary for him from anti-Semitism, accepted the Jewishness society assigned him, and went into exile to survive. But he did not see political causes of these events or how things could have been otherwise. "To be against war is as pointless as to be against death," he writes.

The only other third-person narrator in the film is Danièle Huillet, and her narration introduces the quotation from Brecht just as Straub's introduces the Schoenberg letters. But now the narrative stance is limited to its simplest possible form. Huillet's speech begins, "'Aber,' fragt Brecht . . ."—and her position as someone talking about a Brecht text is defined only in these two words, "fragt Brecht." Clearly, only the two narrators, Straub and Huillet, are in the position to say the names Schoenberg and Brecht, for it is only they who are "quoting." Here the presentation of the texts they cite merges with their role as filmmakers. The other readers—Straschek and Nestler—remain as speakers on the same material level as the words they speak. They too are "quotations" made by the filmmakers and introduced by them. The status of the reader is clearly not "representing" Brecht or Schoenberg in reading their words, but he is also not simply representing someone who could say "I will now quote Brecht or Schoenberg." Only the filmmakers say this, as the continuation of Huillet's "Brecht asks" in Nestler's reading makes explicit. The process of quoting merges with the process of filmmaking, as it does in all Straub/Huillet films made only of preexisting texts. Filming themselves, they quote themselves.

The political argument of the film can be located between Schoenberg's indignation in response to anti-Semitism in Straschek's reading and Brecht's connection of fascism to capitalist property relations in the reading by Nestler. This argument between the two quotations also hinges materially and temporally on the word "but" (*aber*) spoken by Huillet in the connecting shot. The argument between Schoenberg and Brecht (a fiction) is thus imagined; indeed, a "story" has been generated by a single word.

All this says nothing about the relation between music and politics, as Walsh supposes. No indication is made that Schoenberg should, with more political consciousness, have made his *art* more political. Indeed, Brecht's argument in 1935 was not for political art but for political politics—addressing the real problem. He was not making an aesthetic point when he urged anti-Fascist artists to "talk of property relations." If anything, he was urging that art not be seen as a substitute for politics, because they are separate and distinct realms of activity. This stance is implicit in his exhortation, "Let us have pity for culture, but let us first have pity for humanity. Culture is saved only when humanity is saved."[59]

The achievement of *Introduction* has nothing to do with conveying a political message. Rather, it is its structural refusal to confuse politics with art, art with reality. The music of Schoenberg, as Straub insists, is not meant to generate images of "the world" or even an imaginary world. The film also does not present the music as a direct result of historical, political, or even narrative events. The music joins the film at its most abstract, material level, while the screen is black, an arrangement of sounds in time, just as the film is a temporal arrangement of sounds and images. The film thus is partly constructed out of and sustained by the *Accompaniment*; it is not superior to it, it does not quote it. There is no voice to say, "And now, here it is . . . ." The music is the only sound in the film that is not produced before the camera.

To oversimplify the relationship between the two, one might say that politics belongs to the fiction of the film, while the music makes up a part of its material reality. Peter Nau has pointed out the central importance of the manipulation of time to generate film fiction, to assert the real distinction between art and reality. The reading cadences of Straschek and Nestler are broken at points not corresponding to those of natural speech. These breaks (*Zäsuren*), combined with the next larger temporal break, the cuts in the film and black frames, make it possible for film time to distinguish itself from real time. The inserted title card dating the two letters also contributes: it steps out of chronology and locates in time both the letter it follows and the letter it precedes. Here again, the film reveals its relation to and its distance from reality in the nature of its construction. It does not represent a memory of events for the viewer; instead the consciousness of its own kind of time allows it to become an event itself. As Nau puts it, "Through the gaps created by the unfamiliar rhythm of speech the *time of the film* penetrates the text. Separated as fiction from the materials of reality and giving it meaning, the distinctiveness of the film expresses itself in the conscious perception of its duration."[60]

The imaginative activity of a spectator to affirm an ideological representation of reality requires an unconscious acceptance of the whole structure of the work as past, not as passing. The material separation of a work from reality makes it possible to perceive its existence in time and to give it meaning, rather than to get a meaning out of it. The temporal structures of *Introduction* have no meaning to transmit, and this they share with the structures of music. Here is where the relationship between the film, the music, and reality is most subtle and complex. Because the time of the film has separated itself from the "pastness" of narrative identification, it is able to move backward and forward among the documents of human history just as the renunciation of conventional narrative enables new arrangements of film materials to appear, or the renunciation of harmony makes new musical expressions possible.

The "history" with which the film began (the fountain from *History Lessons*) seemed to be confined to German fascism and anti-Semitism but is gradually expanded to include history of artistic forms as well. The documents from Schoenberg's lifetime are complemented by earlier and later evidences of capitalist barbarism—the victims of the Paris Commune, the bombing of Southeast Asia. As Benjamin put it, all documents of culture are documents of barbarism as well. And finally, a contemporary judgment of Schoenberg's time is also documented in the newspaper accounts in the final shots: concentration camp architects are found innocent. It is ironic that the textual narrative described earlier is complemented by visual narration in the bombing sequences; cause and effect, steps in a process, are shown, but not meaning. The final shot of the newspaper text is indeed a push out of the realm of art and into reality, for the viewer is at the same time watching a (two-dimensional, "unreal") film and reading a newspaper article of political significance. The political significance exists in the real world of the spectator but not so clearly in the fiction of the film. The link to the fictional structure of the film is now only provided by the carryover of the music. It is able to link present and past, art and reality, precisely because it does not explain that link. Its otherness, both in regard to the film and to the world, makes the spectator-listener capable of imagining a process of change in reality that does not exist, that has not been represented, "an implied resolution that does not in fact take place," a "liberation by default."[61]

# 8

## THE POWER TO NARRATE
*Class Relations* and Kafka's *Amerika*

The utopian force to be found in countering the "patriarchal orchestration of the look"[1] can be found in Straub/Huillet's film *Class Relations* (*Klassenverhältnisse*, 1983), based on the novel fragment *Amerika* by Franz Kafka. Unlike the films before and after it, *Class Relations* was widely admired by the critics, who called it perhaps their best film[2] and "probably . . . the only Kafka film that can stand the test of time."[3] It prompted the second of two mainstream film books on Straub/Huillet to be published in West Germany.[4] It was also the last of their films to be seen by sizable U.S. audiences (only *The Death of Empedocles* has been distributed in the United States since), as it was the last of their films to be shown at the New York Film Festival. It was an official German entry at the Berlin Film Festival, where Straub/Huillet were awarded an Honorable Mention "in recognition of their unique, sustained contribution to universal film art." The festival scheduled the film in the afternoon, however, reflecting the official segregation between "art films" and the mainstream. Straub expressed regret that the film thus missed the time when people ordinarily go to the movies but added that it may be an honor to join the films from the Third World in the same fate.[5]

As a black-and-white film photographed with artificial lighting by William Lubtchansky and based on a text of German prose, *Class Relations* reconnects with the style of the Böll films. Straub/Huillet compare the uncle to Machorka-Muff, for instance, and where the general's conquest of the capital is compared to Fritz Lang's *M*, Karl Rossmann's journey across America becomes the "journey into the land of vampires."[6] The text, broken into blocks of dialogue, is articulated with syncopated pauses and a range of speech registers again reminiscent of Schoenberg.[7]

Partly funded by the city of Hamburg, *Class Relations* was rehearsed and filmed there while Straub/Huillet were the city's guests as artists-in-residence. A Hamburg laboratory processed the film, and it was edited partly as an educational project with students at the Hamburg film school. With the exceptions of the final shots, then, the film parallels Kafka's description of America as being all too reminiscent of the oppressions of the Old World.

Despite this, however, we discover in *Class Relations* an example of the liberation from and through the cinema postulated by Benjamin in his writing on the apparatus of photography. Koch poses this utopia as an alternative to the renunciation urged by Laura Mulvey in the 1970s.

> If one follows Benjamin's utopia of the emancipated camera "eye," however, its implications seem to run counter to the distancing effect desired by Mulvey: "Thus, for contemporary life, the filmic representation of reality is incomparably more significant than that of the painter, since it offers, precisely because of the thorough-going permeation of reality with mechanical equipment, an aspect of reality which is free of all equipment."[8]

In regard to the novel *Amerika* and the film version *Class Relations*, Straub/Huillet subvert the Oedipal narrative, especially in spatial terms. In exploring how they do so, I will address the fundamental dilemma shared by Kafka, Straub/Huillet, and feminist (film) theory: how to envisage a realm of freedom for ourselves in this world when the language we have to describe it is itself one of the means of our enslavement.

Kafka sought to overcome this paradox in literature by challenging the mechanisms of narrative representation. As Klaus Ramm has demonstrated, Kafka reduced the presence of a narrator in his prose as much as possible, thus frustrating the reader's tendency to identify with either the narrator or the protagonist.[9] A similar strategy is developed in feminist theory, which seeks to find a space in cinema that is not entirely dominated by the Oedipal narrative. Feminists have raised the possibility that every narrative is inherently a repetition of the Oedipus drama, the struggle of the son to become the father. In this drama, woman has no space of her own but is seen only as an obstacle or as the currency of exchange.[10] The dilemma resides in the fact that in existing society, such narratives are a source of pleasure and social cohesion as well as oppression. Therefore, the task is to employ narrative and undermine it at the same time.

An example of Kafka's subversion of narrative can be illustrated briefly by considering the plot of the short story "Das Urteil" (The Judgment).[11] In this simple inversion of the Oedipus drama, Kafka constantly builds up in the reader an expectation of a narrative whole, a narrative trajectory. In the first few sentences, this trajectory is repeatedly traced from Georg Bendemann in his room, outside to the row of houses along the river, and then to the green hills beyond, and perhaps to the friend in Russia to whom Georg has just written. The plot of the story then proceeds to undermine the reader's expectations about all these elements. Finally, rather than taking him to the distant hills or to a reconciliation with his friend, Kafka cuts across Georg's expected trajectory, having him drop himself *off* the bridge instead of crossing it. Both the expected narrative movement and Georg's actual path have a fateful character. But by placing two narrative wholes in opposition to each other, Kafka has left for himself and the reader a structural gap promising freedom from the narratives' closed Oedipal logic.

The challenge to closed narrative structure articulated by feminist film theory echoes Kafka's narrative strategies. Much avant-garde and feminist work has tried to frustrate the impulse toward narrative wholeness in film but often at the expense of visual pleasure. This project was theorized most prominently by Mulvey in 1975 in her article "Visual Pleasure and Narrative Cinema." At its most extreme, this feminist theory calls for a renunciation of all the "satisfaction, pleasure and privilege" offered by the conventional cinema.

Partly on the basis of E. H. Gombrich's theories of perception, de Lauretis has more recently argued that Mulvey's "Brechtian-Godardian program" was unnecessarily brutal in its denial of pleasure and that it could not logically succeed without abolishing cinema entirely.[12] De Lauretis proposes an alternative analysis of conventional narrative, using Gombrich's theory of the "phantom percept." The phantom percept is an illusion present in all sensory perception. It is fundamental to human survival, since it allows us to reconcile the fragmentary data of our senses with the unified whole we expect to perceive. Hence we tend to see a whole circle even if a segment of it is obscured from view. The success of illusion in the visual arts rests on the exclusion of contradictory percepts that would not fit into the expected pattern, "the social contract by which external consistency is given up or traded against the internal coherence of the illusion."[13] De Lauretis believes that it must be possible to undermine conventional narrative without destroying the basis of visual pleasure. Therefore she asks, "With regard to avant-garde practices which foreground frame, surface, montage, and other cinematic codes or materials, including sound, flicker, and special effects; could contradictory or phantom percepts be produced not to negate illusion and destroy visual pleasure, but to problematize their terms in cinema?"[14]

A problematization of narrative illusion and the pleasure it affords is found in Kafka's works as well as in the films of Huillet and Straub. Let us now turn to Straub/Huillet's film *Class Relations*. Through a visual problematization of Karl Rossmann's subjectivity, Straub/Huillet's film achieves many of the goals of feminist film practice without destroying visual pleasure.

The first reel of *Class Relations* corresponds to "Der Heizer" ("The

Stoker''), the opening chapter of Kafka's novel. Kafka was less happy with "The Stoker" segment than with its companion piece, "The Judgment." He called it a "bald imitation of Dickens," perhaps because it at times seems to postulate a privileged narrator who reveals accurately Karl Rossmann's subjective perceptions.[15] For instance, when he first enters the ship captain's office, the seat of power and justice, Karl looks out at the majestic spectacle of ships in New York Harbor. The description concludes, "Yes, in this room one knew where one was."[16] Soon thereafter, as the stoker is clearly failing in his plea for justice, the view shifts to small motorboats darting about and "peculiar floating objects," and the description concludes, "A movement without end, a restlessness, carried over from the restless element onto helpless humanity and their works."[17] The subjective impressions are inconsistent but perfectly logical if we assume there is a superior narrator who is merely revealing Karl's state of mind.

Most film treatments of Kafka have seized precisely on this subjective identification and have tried to depict the images described. Straub/Huillet, however, use their film to explore the relations between the figure of Karl and the narratives within which he is placed. They do so solely on the basis of the pared-down utterances they have selected from the novel fragment, in a manner of speech that Wolfram Schütte has called "an arena where struggles of power and class take place."[18] It is clear at the beginning of both the film and the story that Karl's position in matters of class and power is very important. This position is explored by Straub/Huillet through Kafka's use of language and his method of narration as well as through their own construction of the narrative space of cinema.[19]

As Karl arrives by ship in New York, his narrative takes a sudden turn from his vision of the Goddess of Liberty back to the lower decks of the ship. He searches there for his lost umbrella (a connection to his family and the Old World) and finds a German-speaking ally and father figure in the person of the stoker. The conditions of this alliance are tenuous, however. Karl is drawn to the stoker only because they have suffered similar humiliations. But when the stoker says "there must have been a reason" for Karl's exile, Karl responds, "Now I could also become a stoker. To my parents it's quite indifferent now."[20] He refuses to reveal to the stoker the true basis of his sympathy, that his parents have disowned him for getting a servant pregnant. At the same time his reference to the stoker's job betrays his presumption of superiority.

Their solidarity continues to rely on this lack of communication. Karl explains why he does not expect to study in America with a series of speculations, concluding with the assumption, "Besides, people here have a prejudice against foreigners, I believe." Not only is the word "here" ironic, since he has not "arrived" anywhere, but the stoker heightens the irony by responding, "Have you learned that, too, already? Well, then that's good. Then you're my man."

In fact, Karl has not learned/experienced (the word is *erfahren*) anything new up to this point, and the stoker's ensuing complaints about his Rumanian supervisor on a German ship build up a nationalistic bond between them. Karl's invented solidarity betrays his presumption of superiority as he tells the stoker not to stand for such treatment and later impulsively speaks up for him in the captain's office. The speciousness of this solidarity is fully exposed in Karl's last theatrical attempt to impress the captain with its longevity: "To me you have always depicted it so clearly," he admonishes the stoker. Karl has attempted to fabricate a long-standing bond out of a shared feeling of victimization. Yet it becomes clear through the narrative that their two stories have nothing in common, since their social circumstances remain different.

In addition to social roles, the power to narrate is another means by which characters' relative positions are revealed. By transferring this power from figure to figure, Kafka reveals class relations and subverts narrative identification at the same time. The entire work is Karl's story, after all, but by the end of "The Stoker" sequence he is the one character with no story to tell. Karl himself raises the issue of narration, since he believes the stoker's failure lies in his inability to use his own tale of victimization effectively to gain sympathy. Yet Karl's support of the stoker has nothing to do with the stoker's story, either, despite Karl's lie. Karl's own narrative is more pertinent. In Kafka's novel, Karl's narrative is summarized in a dependent clause within the opening sentence but is narrated thoroughly only by the uncle, with Karl's comments revealed by internal monologue. In the film, both the initial summary and Karl's unspoken commentary are dropped. Only the uncle has the privilege of explaining Karl's journey and eliciting our sympathy for him. The uncle's narrative, one of the longest speeches of the film, takes the central position away from the stoker. It is delivered with polished theatricality by Mario Adorf, whose vocal style is one extreme of a broad spectrum of voices in the film. With this narrative, the uncle places Karl back into continuity with the past, in fact embedding Karl's exile into his own fantastic success story. Now that the relationship is clear, the uncle usurps Karl's right to speak by repeating his statements, almost mockingly. For example, "It did him no harm!"—referring to the ocean crossing below decks. The uncle also takes over the words that had propelled Karl in his actions—words such as "right" and "justice," which Karl has been repeating as in a school lesson but with the belief that they might have some power on their own. In the face of the uncle's impatience over the attention given the stoker, Karl insists, "But that isn't important in a matter of justice." The uncle then takes over the phrase "matter of justice," subordinates it to a "matter of discipline," and declares both subordinate to the judgment of the captain. The uncle finally uses his superior position and understanding to steer the plot of the story itself: "I understand perfectly your way of acting, but precisely that gives me the right to conduct you hence most quickly."

The power to narrate: Mario Adorf as Uncle Jacob in *Class Relations*. Courtesy New Yorker Films.

Karl responds to this assertion of power over him by turning to the stoker's oppression, not his own. Using the intimate form of address for the first time—as if talking to himself or to a family member—he asks the stoker why *he* does not resist. But since the relationship Karl has hoped for has been destroyed, Straub/Huillet cut the upper body of the stoker out of the frame as Karl kneels and holds his hand, telling him he must leave him on his own.

The final speech in this section of the film, closing "The Stoker" episode, again has the uncle as omniscient narrator: "You felt abandoned, there you met the stoker, and now you are grateful to him; that is very laudable. But don't push that too far, if only out of love for me, and learn to comprehend your place." The word *place* (*Stellung*) is the achieved end of the entire sequence. Lost in the ship, sent to America, Karl had only an assumed "place" in regard to the stoker. The slender legacy he has brought from home, however, has expanded to the point that it temporarily determines his identity and fate: it is a long tracking shot from a very low angle, showing the facades of Uncle Jacob's endless harbor warehouses. The father's power and Karl's dependence and vulnerability are given material substance in composition, montage, and duration. Straub/Huillet have no need to repeat Kafka's summation, "It was truly as if there were no stoker anymore."[21]

If there is no hope of freedom in Karl's narrative, is there at least hope for Karl? Or is there hope for the viewers of this film? Their task is not an easy one. By eliminating many of the familiar supports of film narrative, such as establishing shots and reverse angle shots, Straub/Huillet make it much more difficult to construct a complete narrative space out of the fragments filmed. Karl's inability to provide us with an intentional direction of the narrative is also an inability to present an overview of its locations. We are left with the fragile unifying function of Karl's mere presence, variously placed within the class relations of language and—as we will now examine—space. It is in the spatial gaps of this narrative construction that we will look for hope.

Karl's presence in the two locations of "The Stoker" segment is never comfortably established in terms of space. Most of the shots of him consist of only two quite two-dimensional compositions. In the stoker's cabin he is perched precariously on the edge of the bunk. We see none of his retreat below decks, only his knock at the stoker's cabin door. He does not move freely into the cabin but is conducted there. His confinement is emphasized when he rises to look for his suitcase and the stoker's arm enters the frame to push him back onto the bed. Similarly, in the captain's office we see Karl step forward out of the frame of the shot, to defend the stoker, but we have not yet seen the space into which the words are spoken. He steps into a void, a feeling instinctively shared by the audience since no "phantom percept" can be constructed.

The space of the captain's office—like that of most of the film—is never unified by conventional narrative use of the camera, which would establish an overview of the space and would unify it by movement from one shot to another or at least by solidly connected eye-line matches. Instead, the three positions occupied by the characters in the confrontation are carefully framed and prevented from overlapping. The stoker and later his foreman and others stand against the door or near it. The captain, the uncle, and the officers sit in easy chairs with windows behind them in a roomier shot of the interior. Karl stands alone along a paneled wall in the two-dimensional composition, a medium close-up. The only movement between these fragments of narrative space is the invasion of Karl's space by the uncle as he takes over Karl's right to speak.

Any unity attributed to the space of this office must be constructed through an effort by the viewer. But this effort calls attention to the undefined space between the three basic compositions, just as the rigidity of the frame and the delivery of the text call attention to the constructed nature of the language we hear. Who could inhabit this abstract, undefined space?

One possible answer would be Karl, and in a conventional bildungsroman this would be the audience's expectation. But despite the fact that the viewers must use Karl as a visual organizing principle, they are constantly reminded that other reference points often have greater influence on the connections between filmed spaces. By the end of the film, Karl loses all the external characteristics that make him a narrative hero. The family tie to his uncle is abruptly severed, he loses his only memento of his parents (their photograph), and finally he gives up his name for the label "Negro." But Straub/Huillet find

Christian Heinisch as Karl Rossmann in *Class Relations*. Courtesy Museum of Modern Art.

the optimism in Kafka's novel in the separation between its protagonist and the external narrative devices that make him "Karl Rossmann." It is one of the major achievements of this film—and one due primarily to Huillet, I believe—that the performance of Christian Heinisch is visually and acoustically so doggedly consistent. His measured, articulate recitation of Kafka's text functions as a tonic chord among the voices in the film, which range from professional stage rhetoric to the straining memorized speech of non-German speakers and lay actors including a number of film colleagues and friends. As his links to the past are cut, Karl also maintains the determined yet well-meaning appearance he had at the beginning. As a photo caption in *Der Spiegel* put it, "Not a hair is disturbed." And Kristie Foell has seen precisely in the beautiful, "fluid" composition of the image of Karl's body lying next to the balcony drainpipe an intimation of death and utopia.[22]

Throughout the film, Karl is carefully located in regard to the narratives of others, usually in an insecure position of his own. He speaks less and less until, in the final scene, he is completely silent. His narrative role diminishes—from protagonist to witness—but his importance to the film does not. Straub/Huillet often show Karl alone on screen, watching and listening. Most often his gaze is directed inward, toward the center of a room or any space to which he is confined. For example, later in the film Karl hears Robinson's story on the

Alf Bold as the waiter and Christian Heinisch as Karl Rossmann in *Class Relations*. Courtesy Museum of Modern Art.

balcony of Brunelda's apartment. Robinson and Delamarche are subservient to Brunelda, and they want to enslave Karl. As Robinson talks to Karl, the view from the balcony is never revealed. The space around the two is limited to a door, a low wall, and a drainpipe. Later, when Brunelda forces Karl to look out at a political parade through her opera glasses, Karl insists he does not see anything—and neither does the viewer. He sees enough already, Karl maintains. The effect of this is twofold. It implies that Karl's experiences do indeed contain sufficient political information to understand class relations. Furthermore, the frustration of the viewer's gaze exaggerates the illusion of confinement yet calls attention to the film frame as one source of this illusion.

So far, this might seem to be an example of the Brechtian frustration of visual pleasure as urged by Mulvey. But Kafka's aesthetic is not exhausted in revealing the unreliability or the fragmentary nature of his subjective narration. Similarly, since we are allowed to share Karl's position as witness, as listener, we are tempted to construct some future that would be implied by his experience, even if he does not. We know that he sees less than the camera can show, and this reminder disrupts conventional visual pleasure and provokes our escape from the narrative—to insist on seeing more, differently.

It is in basing the pleasure of their narrative on the impulse to escape the structural confines of cinema that I see the connection between Straub/Huillet

# The Power to Narrate: *Class Relations* and Kafka's *Amerika* 173

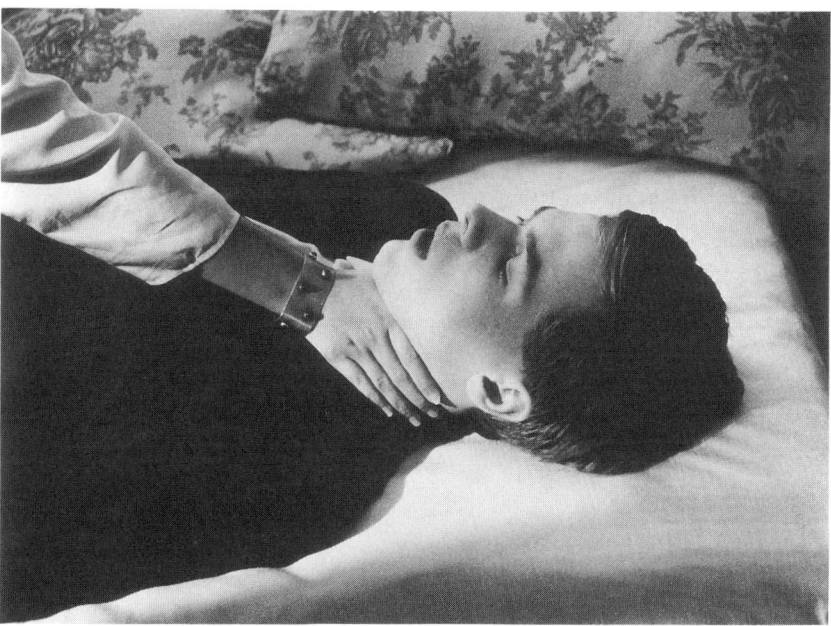

Christian Heinisch as Karl Rossmann in *Class Relations* (with hand of Anne Bold as Klara). Courtesy Museum of Modern Art.

and feminist theory. In this regard, I believe it would be a mistake to consider Straub/Huillet as predominantly "minimalist" or "structuralist" filmmakers, or to assume they have issued a "blanket condemnation of narrative and illusionism." It is important to distinguish the strategies of Straub/Huillet as described here from "the minimalist strategies of materialist avant-garde cinema," which de Lauretis criticizes for being "predicated on, even as they work against, the (transcendental) male subject."[23] Indeed, it is the desire for an alternative basis for the film practice and narrative structure that gives dramatic force to the composition of Straub/Huillet's work.

A decisive example of Straub/Huillet's separation of visual pleasure from (transcendental) male subjectivity occurs in the filming of the story told to Karl by Therese, the hotel secretary. Karl and Therese stand at a white window, beyond which is supposedly snow. Therese looks out, while Karl looks somewhat more toward her and the camera. As Therese begins her story, the camera tracks in from the shot of them both to a close-up of Karl listening. As the story is completed, the process is reversed: the camera tracks out from Karl to the initial shot of both figures together.

This sequence sums up the narrative lines of the film and reveals the possibility of freedom beyond them. First, the story Therese tells is simple, linear, and hopeless, and it is given an unforgettable delivery by Libgart

Libgart Schwarz as Therese in *Class Relations*. Courtesy New Yorker Films.

Schwarz, counterbalancing the bombastic rhetoric of Mario Adorf earlier in the film. After a night without shelter in winter, Therese's mother goes with her child to a building site where she is to obtain work. Immediately she climbs a scaffold and walks along it with miraculous agility to its end, where she topples over a pile of bricks and falls to her death. The physical separateness of Therese and Karl can also be described in terms of straight lines, since they face at oblique angles across the axis of the camera. Yet two devices imply a connection. In the only such shot in the film, the tracking camera has indeed set up a coherent narrative space that they share on equal terms. The use of reverse cuts during the story, although implying separateness, are nonetheless an acknowledgment of communication and are all the more powerful for their rarity in the work of Straub/Huillet. At the end of the sequence, the camera tracks out to rejoin Karl and Therese, again on equal terms in the composition.

The fact that their gazes cross the axis of the camera conveys both separateness and complementariness. There is no indication that Karl can do anything with this story except hear it. But there is one more element along the linear structure of this scene that gives it a hopeful balance. This is the empty window, which is at the center of the frame at both beginning and end, a counterpart to the camera and the screen themselves. The window lights Therese's face, in a composition reminiscent of earlier films by Straub/Huillet. Far from frustrating visual pleasure, this shot uses the subjective point of view

Christian Heinisch as Karl Rossmann, Harun Farocki as Delamarche, and Manfred Blank as Robinson in *Class Relations*. Courtesy Museum of Modern Art.

(so freely exploited in the empty promises of commercial cinema) to suggest unlimited possibility.

Whatever solidarity Karl and Therese achieve in this scene produces no concrete change in their fates as characters, but it is profoundly significant for the viewer. Nothing is visible in this white window, but as the mediating space between Therese speaking (remembering) and Karl listening (perhaps understanding), it stands as a potential realm where the justice Karl originally spoke of could truly be located. The Father and the Law, represented by Uncle Jacob and the captain in "The Stoker" sequence, are nowhere to be seen. Recalling Benjamin's utopian vision, the realm of freedom is outside the space the film can construct but is still a construction of the cinema.

The conclusion of the film resonates with this structure. In the last sequence, no more of Kafka's text is spoken at all. Karl and another elevator boy, Giacomo, are shown sitting next to each other on a train bound for Oklahoma. They exchange smiling glances, then a close-up shows Karl finally looking out the window. Then, with thoroughly conventional cinematic logic, we are allowed to see what Karl sees: the passing landscape of the Missouri River valley.

This subversion of the Oedipal narrative allows us to consider an alternative to the linguistic model adopted by feminist film theory from Lacan. Koch

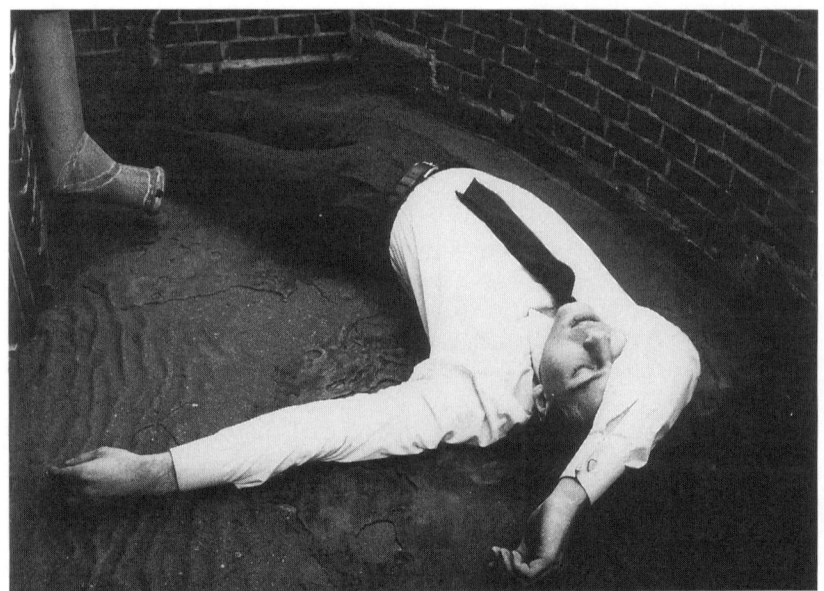

Christian Heinisch as Karl Rossmann in *Class Relations*. Courtesy New Yorker Films.

proposed exactly this type of attention to the "mimetic" impact of objects and landscapes in film, which will become even more important in Straub/Huillet's Hölderlin films.[24] As Huillet said of their film *Too Early, Too Late* (1980–1981), "But there are landscapes and they are treated exactly as if they were people."[25] I argue that *Class Relations* achieves what Koch admires in the "aesthetically most advanced films" of the feminist avant-garde: "They anticipate an expanded and radicalized notion of subjectivity . . . a type of subjectivity that transcends any abstract subject-object dichotomy."[26]

The final shot of the river and the initial few seconds' view of the Statue of Liberty are the only such "traveling" shots in the entire film, and the only shots filmed in America. The motion of the arrival in New York Harbor is negated by Karl's return to the narrative of his past. A Kafkaesque suspicion would be that the cycle would repeat itself in the second instance, but Straub/Huillet's construction of contradictory percepts reveals that neither metaphysical forces nor Karl's supposed "true nature" makes this unavoidable. In fact, an audience that refuses to let go of the memory of Therese at the window will finally see that although the film does not present an image of freedom, it does point to a freedom beyond its own structure. I do not believe this process involves the sacrifice of visual pleasure. Instead, I believe Straub/Huillet allow their audiences a fundamental joy in constructing the phantom percept of this

Straub/Huillet at the Berlin International Film Festival, 1984; press conference for *Class Relations*. Courtesy dpa/photoreporters.

freedom. In doing so, they meet the challenge of feminist cinema de Lauretis described as follows: "Not to deny all coherence to representation, or to prevent all possibility of identification and subject reflection, or again to void perception of all meaning formation; but to displace its orientation, to redirect 'purposeful attending' toward another object of vision, and to construct other ways of seeing."[27]

# 9

# LANGUAGE IN EXILE

Hölderlin's *The Death of Empedocles*

*Und immer*
*Ins Ungebundene gehet eine Sehnsucht.*
And always
Into the unbounded goes a longing.

Friedrich Hölderlin is perhaps the quintessential European author for an investigation of relations of politics to culture, Germanness to "other" cultural traditions, myth to everyday language. The broadest spectrum of twentieth-century thinkers have written about him: Georg Lukács, Theodor W. Adorno, Thomas Mann and Heinrich Mann, Martin Heidegger, Michel Foucault. Even the Nazis turned to the reclusive poet as a nationalist icon: the Hölderlin Society was founded under the patronage of Josef Goebbels.[1]

In their film of Hölderlin's *Death of Empedocles*, confronting the dense German poetry of the drama fragment with the intensity of the natural landscape near Mount Etna in Sicily, Straub/Huillet again displaced a German cultural icon. Despite the rhetoric of European unity and increased attention in many quarters to "the threatened destruction of the earth," the film encountered a generally hostile reaction, especially in West Germany. Huillet offered the following interpretation.

> I think the scandal of Hölderlin and of the film is that one attempts to avoid giving up anything, either in regard to the individual, or the subject as Hölderlin says, or the others, the people. That one doesn't give something up in order to gain something else, but tries to keep everything. And that in a time where people let themselves be closed in more and more, also with their feelings, with all their might. That is the scandal, somehow. I believe that is what led Hölderlin to the brink of madness; that is the madness of Empedocles and that is what makes the film an object of scandal. Because one can sense that everything tries to close people in and to separate them from life, and that here just the opposite is being

attempted: to open up and renounce nothing and neglect nothing or destroy in order to preserve something else.[2]

At the conclusion of his book *Antigones*, George Steiner writes of the balance of understanding and deed that work against the "action" implied by the word *drama* and toward a sense of stasis or suspension: "In reach of the tragedy as we know and experience it, there lies . . . an intimation of inaction of the deed arrested by the acknowledged gravity, density, and inhibitions of mutual insight."[3]

The "lasting hesitation" between understanding and action, which Steiner postulates to be possible only in music-drama, is perhaps the unbearable quality Danièle Huillet explains in regard to reactions to the Empedocles films. In these films, as in the more recent *Antigone*, there is an insistence on "having it all," a refusal to accede to the necessity of choosing supposedly enforced by "film language" and, in social living, the restrictions imposed by the increasing dehumanization of life.

Both in their cinematic structure and in the language of their narratives, Straub/Huillet's Hölderlin films capture the sense of Steiner's imagined music-drama, in "realiz[ing] the suspension of the existential compulsion to choose, to be partial, to narrow and sharpen consciousness toward action."[4] This is also the "haltingness" (*Stocken*) that Peter Handke writes about, which only now and then breaks free in the films of Straub/Huillet. The suspension also keeps the balance between the bright sunlit potential of air and landscape in Sicily and the dark facticity of Hölderlin's German words.

All four of Straub/Huillet's films made after *Class Relations* are connected to Hölderlin. The first two, *The Death of Empedocles* and *Black Sin*, are based on versions one and three of his fragmentary Empedocles drama. Straub/Huillet had originally considered the third version unfilmable, but while they were editing *The Death of Empedocles* at the film school in Hamburg, one of the students showed them a videotape of a Berlin stage production. Appalled by what they saw, Straub/Huillet decided to film the work after all, "to avenge Hölderlin," and the result was *Black Sin*. This project also allowed them to continue their work with a few of the actors from the Empedocles film and to push some of their methods to an extreme, for instance, the variation of the pauses in the rhythms of the lines, the harshness of the light.

After their Cézanne film, which includes an excerpt from *Empedocles*, Straub/Huillet returned to Sicily to film *Antigone*, based on Hölderlin's translation of the Sophoclean tragedy in the 1948 adaptation by Bertolt Brecht. This chapter concentrates on the significance of the choice of Hölderlin's dramas and their setting in the Sicilian landscape. For this reason, emphasis will be placed on the first Empedocles film, as the more complex "drama" of the two versions—in Straub's words, "a musical comedy compared to the second."[5] *Black Sin* can already be seen as a transition to *Antigone*, which is treated in a later chapter, since both films signal a return to some of the qualities of early silent cinema.

The exacting rehearsal and planning of the Hölderlin films allowed Straub/Huillet to undertake a long-held wish "to attack the originality of the work of art."[6] Each of the films has been edited in up to four distinct "original" versions, with the negatives distributed among the cities of Rome, Paris, Berlin, and Hamburg. In the shooting of *Empedocles*, for instance, 62,000 meters of 35 mm Eastmancolor film were exposed, of which 54,000 meters were printed.[7] "The only luxury the Straubs allow themselves," in Rembert Hüser's words (and a luxury even Hollywood directors do not have, Straub insists). This is unusual, since the industry usually does not process its raw footage to this extent. Printing this much footage made it possible to "check the progress and the concomitant loss" as the work went on. The light in Sicily, varying "from black to pulsating, pounding brightness,"[8] forced them to try even more takes than usual. As Hüser notes, "Getting the visual connections [*Bildanschlüsse*] for the editing outdoors, in the filmmakers' opinion, had only previously been achieved by Gregg Toland."[9] Most of the shots had been done in about twelve takes, although they ranged from half a dozen up to twenty-four.[10] In editing the four versions of *Empedocles*, then, Straub/Huillet had versions with takes that were both early and late in the sequence, and the versions also have different degrees of harshness in the light and sound. They are also using more of the printed footage that would otherwise be destroyed: "art against waste," in Straub's words.[11]

To distinguish the four negatives, one is called the "Lizard Version" because a lizard is seen scurrying across the ground in the scene where Empedocles takes leave of his slaves; in the second, "Paris Version," the colors are at first muted by the cloudy sky and then burst forth as the sun appears. In this version also, there is a long pause on the profile of Panthea in the garden before the cut to the "opulent images of the most diverse nuances of green on Etna." The third version, the sunniest of all, has a butterfly skimming in and out of the foreground of several shots, and a rooster crows as Empedocles says, "You have polluted the holiness." The fourth version is known as the "Cricket Version," since loud chirping accompanies the slave scene.[12]

Straub has also described the exact technical differences among the four negatives, including the exact length of each, whether they were done with wet or dry printing, where and when they were edited, where the titles are placed, and so on. They also differ according to whether most of the takes used were toward the beginning, middle, or end of a series of up to thirty-six takes.[13]

With these films, Straub Huillet took another turn in their work, farther away from "film language" and toward the origins of the cinema as well as the origins of Western and modern culture. In doing so, they lost the support of a number of critics and viewers, particularly in Germany (with the further result that U.S. critics did not even see the films in order to judge for themselves).

Language in Exile: Hölderlin's *The Death of Empedocles*   181

*The Death of Empedocles* (Empedocles' hand). Courtesy Edition Manfred Salzgeber, Berlin.

Those condemning the new work usually lamented the fact that after seeming to take a step toward more "accessible" or entertaining films with *Class Relations*, Straub/Huillet had gone off the deep end in the other direction with *Empedocles*. Strangely enough, this is seen as both a political as well as an aesthetic transgression.

*The Death of Empedocles* does abandon the track that *Class Relations* represented, but in doing so it returns to other themes Straub/Huillet had worked on in other films. It is a return to color, landscape, and the bright, "pitiless, cruel" light of Italy (Huillet)[14] after the artificially lit interiors and night scenes of *Class Relations*. A change in cinematographers corresponds to this, from the somber lighting of William Lubtchansky back to the Italian Renato Berta. For *Antigone* and *Black Sin*, they would return to Lubtchansky once again. According to Hüser, Berta and Lubtchansky are among the "great lighting experts in Europe," to whom Godard had turned, for instance, in his experiment of employing two chief cinematographers in *Sauve qui peut (la vie)*. Hüser summarizes the differing skills of the two cinematographers as follows: "While Lubtchansky prefers half-light and works with much contrast (preferably with artificial light) and is known for striking images, Berta is a specialist for optimal exploitation of the entire image plane, for extremely concentrated, 'simple' images reduced to the essentials. Berta prefers exterior shots with gentle light."[15]

*Empedocles* is also a return from the narrative flow of language (*Erzählung*), dense as it is in Kafka, to the more concentrated poetry of myth and legend. As such, it returns to the thematic, visual, and linguistic context of *Moses and Aaron* and *Othon*. The setting and theme also return to "classicism," which was represented in *Othon* and in the legends of Pavese, as well as some of the arrangements of speakers in oratorio fashion pioneered in *Moses and Aaron*. The character of Empedocles is in some ways a synthesis of Moses and Aaron: his wisdom and mystical powers of leadership both separate him from the people and lead them to offer him the title of King. The contradiction in this dilemma, however, leads him to spurn the people for their lack of comprehension and ultimately to his own destruction—the plunge into the volcano rather than life in exile. And these are all stories set on the borderline between democracy and tyranny, between myth and history. A main "character" of *Empedocles*, however, is the landscape, and here, too, earlier work is developed to a new level, particularly *Too Early, Too Late*.

As with other films, Straub/Huillet's choice of the Hölderlin texts follows that of the location and the filmmakers' mounting concern with the destruction of the natural environment—along with the humane environment. Straub/Huillet often stress that the impetus for a film arises from a feeling for a place: partly as a paraphrase of Renoir, Straub has defined film (or the "filmic") as "a slender dialectic between film, theater, and life."[16] In another interview, the terms of the equation were modified somewhat: "life" means experience, that of the actors or the filmmakers or even of the audience; "theater" means fiction, usually that provided by a preexisting text (in the strain of films from *Othon* to *Moses and Aaron* to Kafka to Hölderlin); and "film" means "location"—the documentation of a confrontation with a location. "The camera is nothing but an X-ray machine," Straub has stated.[17]

Straub has described the immediate impetus behind *The Death of Empedocles* in a threefold manner: first, after so much interior and night shooting for the Kafka film, the desire to make a film using daylight; second, a kind of dare from Huillet, who "had fallen in love with Sicily in 1971," scouting locations for *Moses and Aaron*;[18] and finally, Straub refers to a long history of reading other Hölderlin works, beginning in the 1950s, and to the chance discovery of *The Death of Empedocles* as they reached the conclusion—even before the catastrophes of Chernobyl or the poisoned Rhine at Basel—that the abuse of nature could not go on. And Empedocles was not only cursed for his defense of nature, Straub asserts, but also for trying to extend democracy: "He was reproached for having gone too far, a bit in the direction of what one called the '*fête permanente*' in 1968."[19]

The recollection of the 1960s corresponds loosely to the personal memories that Straub/Huillet reconstructed in the course of interviews. At first, Straub had claimed that he was not a reader of Hölderlin until recently, but Huillet reminded him that he had been "running around with a poem in his pocket" in the early 1950s. It was Hölderlin's *Der Frieden*, which she made him translate for her.[20] This was the period of the idea of the Bach project and of the nascence of what was to become the French New Wave. He also then recalls that he had thought for years of making a film based on fragments of *Hyperion* but abandoned the idea as "too literary and novelistic" for a film.[21] Parts of *Hyperion*, in fact, also refer to the character of Empedocles. Such figures as Hölderlin or the poet/hero Hyperion were fitting inspiration for the young male rebels who saw themselves both as misfits and as reformers/redeemers of the European cultural heritage. The image of a young filmmaker with Hölderlin in his pocket is reminiscent of the scene from *The 400 Blows* in which Antoine Doinel almost sets the house afire with candles lit to "honor Balzac." The romance between Straub and Huillet, reconstructed out of these memories, continues with Huillet's performance as the chorus in *Black Sin*, where part of the text she recites at the end of the film is one of those from Hölderlin Straub had been moved by in his youth.[22]

Another possible source of the interest in Hölderlin, which the filmmakers have not mentioned, is Böll's *Billiards at Half Past Nine*, the basis for their first long film. Böll invokes the name of Hölderlin along with the Sermon on the Mount as two expressions of a culture of resistance to Nazism that had to be stamped out. Hölderlin is the antithesis, in Böll, for the dangers expressed by the words "Hurrah" and "Hindenburg."

And finally, Hölderlin (along with Brecht) plays a role in Jean-Luc Godard's 1963 film *Contempt*, in which Fritz Lang plays a director making a film based on the Odyssey. That an early New Wave work by Godard had already juxtaposed classical myth, German "classic" poetry, and Hollywood as seen through Brecht's ironic gaze adds another layer to the archaeological work of both *Empedocles* and *Antigone*. In *Contempt*, Lang is brought to Italy to film *Ulysses*, since "only a German" can film Homer. In the screening room Lang quotes both Brecht and Hölderlin. From Brecht he quotes the poem "Hollywood," while from Hölderlin he recites contradictory versions of the poem "Dichterberuf" (The Poet's Calling):

> Yet if it must be man
> Without trepidation
> Remains alone before God
> His candor protects him
> He needs no weapons, no wiles
> Until the absence of God rescues him.

The last line had originally been "As long as God is there." Then Hölderlin wrote, "As long as God is near us." Lang continues, "For one thing, the line now, the last version contradicts the other two. It's not the presence—the *presence*—of God, it's the absence that rescues him. It's so odd. Ah well, that's all for now. How would one say 'it's so odd' in Italian?'' Lang also echoes a position often underscored by Straub/Huillet regarding realism and the blurring of myth and history: "The world that Homer knew was real. He mirrored his own times, a civilization that was developed in harmony with nature and not in opposition to it. That is one of the beauties of the *Odyssey*—the fate of Homer and things as they actually are, as they exist. Reality.''[23]

## Hölderlin and the German Left

The invocation of 1968 is not at all amiss in reference to Empedocles or to Hölderlin, since Straub/Huillet's Hölderlin films add to a long tradition of Hölderlin reception on the Left. Hölderlin is a romantic figure but a rather classical author in German literature. He was a friend and fellow student of Hegel and Schelling, was known for his talent as a philosopher and Hellenist, and was closely associated with the idealist philosophy of the period. Hölderlin is celebrated as a classical poetic genius and was praised by the romantics as well, especially Bettina von Arnim. He has been politically appropriated by both the Right and the Left in recent German history. Like many other German artists and intellectuals, he was inspired by the French Revolution and corresponded with the Swabian Republican movement as well. His first version of the Empedocles play, for example, has been seen as an explicit contribution to this political struggle.

Hölderlin attracts the romantic sensibility, however, partly due to his withdrawal for the last forty years of his life into a legendary state of mental illness (now believed to be schizophrenia) and silence pierced by flashes of lucidity and poetic insight. His last works before this withdrawal (from which Straub/Huillet have chosen their film texts) also distinguish Hölderlin from the classicism and the Hegelian idealism of his earlier allegiances. The poems of this period reveal what Eric Santner has called a loosening of ''narrative vigilance,'' and I argue that this quality exists in *Empedocles* as well (from the same period). The translations of Sophocles introduce a new attitude toward the nature of language itself and toward the nature of the essence of poetic expression. All of this might account for Straub/Huillet's choice of these works by Hölderlin for almost ten years of work.

After considering the role of Hölderlin in leftist positions on German cultural heritage, I examine the treatment of language in Hölderlin's *Empedocles* and *Antigone*, the importance of translation, and the relevance of these issues for Straub/Huillet's cinematic structures. As Hölderlin challenged the ability of language to communicate, Straub/Huillet question ''film language'' and confront head-on the dilemma of idealism and identity raised by the ''crisis of political modernism.''

The parallels between Straub/Huillet's reception of Hölderlin and their own position as contemporaries and inheritors of the New Left culture are striking. The demise of state socialism in Eastern Europe and the USSR, the crisis of the leftist intelligentsia in the First World since the 1970s, and the critical fragmentation brought about by the "postmodern condition" raise fundamental questions about the political position of leftist intellectuals and artists. As in their approach to German culture and history in other films, their work is not to be seen in isolation, however. In the 1930s, Ernst Bloch, Hanns Eisler, and Bertolt Brecht all maintained a need for an avant-garde in socialist art, which would have been consistent with retaining the sharp-edged contradictions between Hölderlin's national-poetic achievements and his political and formal radicalness. The work of placing Hölderlin in this context of intellectual and cultural archaeology is similar to the case of Kafka, treated in chapter 6, and the work of Gilles Deleuze and Felix Guattari to "rescue" Kafka from the canon.[24] Helen Fehervary has summarized Hölderlin's importance for the Left as follows: "More radically than any other German writer and in quintessential form, Hölderlin exposes the problematic of the intellectual caught between the utopian and tragic dimensions of history and between subjective consciousness and political engagement."[25]

As we will see, the political engagement Hölderlin's work represents in Straub/Huillet films diverges sharply from the reception of Hölderlin by both the conservative Right and the establishment Left. The Right has celebrated Hölderlin as a German nationalist and as the stereotypical poet of myth. The Nazis, for example, placed Hölderlin in the "German" tradition of Leibniz, Herder, and Goethe as counterpoised to the "'Western' degeneration" of the thought of Kant and Schiller. At the same time, however, leftist German exiles—particularly Lukács, Johannes R. Becher, and their heirs in the GDR—defended Hölderlin. They did so, however, by means that also reified him so that he could fit the canon of "good" German culture that was to be the alternative cultural heritage of the German Democratic Republic. As Fehervary concludes regarding this popularization of Hölderlin for socialism, "That he thereby represented a co-optation of the materialist moment in socialist culture is self-evident."[26]

Because of this establishment co-optation of Hölderlin by socialism since the 1930s, Straub/Huillet are again choosing an author for their films with a leftist relevance but a stifled or deformed reception by the Left. As part of their historical relation to the cultural and political legacy of the 1960s, their films reveal what Fehervary has termed the "schizophrenic character" of this reception.[27] The general inhibitions of cultural exploration in West Germany caused by the legacy of Nazism and the chill of the cold war had led avant-garde and Left-liberal artists and intellectuals to ignore Hölderlin for the most part. The primary Nazi image of Hölderlin as the poet of nationalistic myth persisted on the one hand, while on the other, the Stalinist reification of culture in the GDR occluded any productive Western reflection on the leftist tradition of the 1930s as well.[28] This stagnation in the reception of Hölderlin lasted in West Germany from 1945 well into the 1960s, according to Fehervary, typifying the attitude of both the "Group 47" and revolutionary writing in the student movement (Hans Magnus Enzensberger, for example): "Clearly Hölderlin would be irrelevant to this development [i.e., politicization à la Brecht after the Spiegel Affair]. If he had been anathema to avant-garde writers in the 1950s, in the tendentious-agitational literature of the 1960s he was virtually nonexistent."[29]

This stalemate in the West was broken by two influential speeches on Hölderlin, by Theodor W. Adorno in 1963 and by Pierre Bertaux in 1968,[30] the period when Huillet and Straub were living in Munich. Adorno's speech stressed Hölderlin's modernism, which meant for Adorno his tendency toward abstraction, especially in the late poems. This interpretation, as furthered by Santner, will be examined in the context of the Empedocles film shortly. Bertaux's speech reestablished the connection to the French Revolution, which the French had always assumed in their scholarship but which had become invisible to the West Germans. Without discounting the poetic greatness of Hölderlin's work, Bertaux argued that its formal radicalism was due to its "conscious, independent, and active political character." The "lyrical-Jacobin style" of *Empedocles*, Bertaux argued, was of "burning contemporary topicality." The Greek setting, according to him, was merely a Paris fashion of the time, and the real subject was "not a situation in Agrigent but the National Convention in Paris."[31]

Straub indicates his familiarity with this significance when he refers to the Empedocles drama as Hölderlin's "calling card" as an ambitious young "Poet of the Revolution" for the expected republic in Swabia.[32] Bertaux had emphasized the importance of the play to Hölderlin's politics, its revolutionary content even in the direction of François-Noël (Gracchus) Babeuf's agrarian communism, or what Straub has called "Hölderlin's 'Communist dream.'" Bertaux points out that the work on the fragment was abandoned when the French general, Jourdan, announced that revolutionary activities would not be permitted in Württemberg.[33]

The various emphases continue from that point on in Hölderlin's reception on the Left in Germany, with the controversial play by Peter Weiss that also presents Empedocles as a revolutionary character but once again removed from political efficacy.[34] In the 1970s as well, D. E. Sattler published a new "Frankfurt" edition of Hölderlin's works, the product of independent scholarship and appearing at the Red Star publishing house. Like Fritz Lang in *Contempt*, the Frankfurt edition placed value on the variants in Hölderlin's work rather than the search for a definitive reading.[35] And more recently, in a dialogue with himself (1976 and 1993) and with Hölderlin, Sattler has published sixty-six

"Theses on Statelessness."[36] The Empedocles film, calling on the Stuttgart edition and with Sattler as a consultant, thus relates to the Hölderlin debate on the Left and what Fehervary calls the schizophrenic position of left-wing intellectuals both in regard to high culture/poetic language and revolutionary political practice.

The plot of *The Death of Empedocles* begins after the hero's transgression and subsequent condemnation to exile. Thus, as Hans Hurch has put it, the play is "basically a long, grand leavetaking."[37] Because he has been swept along by his own visionary enthusiasm to call himself a god, Empedocles has been condemned to leave Agrigento—by his rival, the priest Hermocrates, and with the concurrence of his former friend Critias. Loyalty to Empedocles comes only from his young disciple Pausanias, Critias's daughter Panthea, and his three steadfast slaves. Pausanias insists on following Empedocles into exile and, at the play's conclusion, urges him to seek another country rather than death. Delia begins the play by praising Empedocles' aura to her older friend Delia, a visitor from Athens. Empedocles' ministrations had also once "healed" Panthea when she was close to death.

The only other characters in the piece are the "citizens," who vacillate between harsh condemnation of Empedocles at first and later the wish to crown him king as they fear the fate of their city under the leadership of Empedocles' tormentors. Finally, there is a peasant who refuses hospitality to the stranger Empedocles on his way to Etna.

The cyclic progression of Empedocles' relation both to the people and to the gods (or, represented by Nature in the abstract, the metaphysical realm in general) parallels the "spiral" of the movement of the spirit postulated by German idealism. Therefore, one could say that the "plot" of *Empedocles* has both an idealist and a political side. Empedocles' drama shares with Hegel's phenomenology the cyclical structure Santner observes uniting the sacred narrative with human history: "For, according to Hölderlin, the sacred narrative unfolds only within the historical space of mortals, indeed, history is nothing other than the story of the union, alienation, and imminent reunion of gods and mortals."[38]

Santner also describes this idealist narrative in the context of the extinction of various heroes in the "heavenly fires" after they have surpassed the boundaries between the human and the divine: "This longing for dissolution, for merging with the fires of heaven—the theme of the ode 'Stimme des Volks'—is portrayed throughout Hölderlin's oeuvre as the distinctive trait of the heroic individual; the hero's fate describes the tragic path . . . 'away from this earth.'"[39]

The narrative path of Empedocles is indeed this: because he has broken the bounds that separate humans from nature, Empedocles is impelled out of human society and into the heights of Mount Etna, since "the hero's tragedy is always that of incineration by the heavenly fires."[40] The progression of locations and camera angles in Straub/Huillet's film reflects this same impetus toward the heights that Santner describes in the poems. Only at the beginning of the film do we look down toward the sea. And although we learn in the first lines of the piece that "this is his garden," we are following the gaze of the young Panthea and not Empedocles. On the contrary, as the film progresses, we see less and less of the ground, especially in shots of Empedocles. Instead, he is framed most often with the branches of a tree, shot from slightly below, with more and more light and sky appearing. And finally, the two images of the heights of Mount Etna itself are accompanied only by Empedocles' implied gaze and his disembodied voice. They are further separated from the rest of the film by the fact that the text is *read* offscreen, not recited from memory.[41]

What Santner does not examine is the other aspect of this dialectic of the hero's alienation: from the people. This is implied by the fact that the hero's "longing for dissolution" is expressed most clearly in the poem "Voice of the People." Thus it is not only the alienation from the gods and nature that the hero longs to overcome by the dissolution of his own identity, it is also the alienation of the individual from society.

Here we have returned to the political context of the human history on which a metaphysical narrative is inscribed: the longing for dissolution is connected by the longing of a political revolutionary for his own dissolution, the dissolution that would be implied by the very success of the revolutionary enterprise. The intermediate step between the impulse for identity impelled by popular revolutionary fervor and the impulse for dissolution that would be its logical fulfillment is the hubris of the revolutionary becoming a king, the impulse to reify the revolution into a bureaucratic state.

Schütte summarizes the connection of the film's plot with the hubris of Hölderlin's time.

> Hölderlin's fragment . . . reflects the bitter experience of failure into which the French Revolution—welcomed by the German Jacobins—seemed to be turning. It places the Sicilian natural philosopher Empedocles at the center of a consideration of the themes of human greatness, society, religion, nature, and res publica.
>
> At first Empedocles had been banned from society by the citizens of Agrigento (led and "seduced" by the priest Hermokrates) because the onetime favorite of the gods had raised himself too far above the people and was therefore punished by the gods. Later he is begged to return by the same citizens, but after having just been spurned by a peasant and offered a crown, he has long since decided to retreat into a union with Nature.[42]

For the late twentieth century, one has the brief solidarity of students, intellectuals, and workers in 1968 contrasted with the long list of co-optations of revolutionary inspiration and alienation of left-wing intellectuals from the "masses." Fehervary stresses the importance of this aspect for the reception of Hölderlin by the Left after 1968: "Thus the history of Hölderlin's reception on the Left during this time [the 1960s] was also coming to terms with the relationship between the poetic word and concrete political practice. If the writers' image of Hölderlin was an ambivalent one, it only articulated their own ambivalence to their craft."[43] It's important to note, too, that the two sides of this schizophrenia, as Fehervary describes, relate to cultural production as well as political leadership: the contradiction between praxis and manipulation of the audience as an artistic method.

How one interprets Hölderlin's relation to the French Revolution depends exactly on one's interpretation of this dilemma: in short, the choice between a "realist" (Lukács) or "modernist" Hölderlin. One who belongs in the past tradition of bourgeois revolutions, or one who spurs on contemporary revolts with the unfulfilled longings of his poetic practice.

Lukács clearly felt that Hölderlin needed to be used to manipulate people, rather than spur them along to autonomous revolutionary undertakings. Therefore, while exploiting Hölderlin as a synthesizer of German idealism and the ideas of the French Revolution, he discounted Hölderlin's Jacobinism because it came too close to the modernism of 1920s and 1930s avant-garde movements and the "radical 'sectarianism'" of that time.[44] Therefore, the "modernism" of Hölderlin, as that of Kafka, is transformed into "realism" for socialist consumption, and the progressive impetus of Hölderlin is confined entirely to the past. Hölderlin was seen as "a unique poet, who did not and could not have a *Nachfolge*."[45]

### Language, Nature, and Progress

The Straub/Huillet film uses this narrative skeleton as its basis but decidedly takes it in the modernist direction, in part by suspending the various "strides" of the narrative, a modernist separation of elements, and in part by cinematographic means. Helmut Krebs describes the suspension and explosion of the two sides of the plot.

> In Hölderlin's first version the death of Empedocles follows, on the one hand, from the will to revolt, to a break of the barrier between nature and human arising from the divisions among people themselves; and on the other hand, from individual hubris, the blind obsession with reason, domination of nature rather than to shape a relation to it. The first brings upon him the curse of the priest caste, for the second he curses himself. [ . . . ]
> 
> The tragedy explodes in the last moment this interweaving of suicide and martyrdom, of revolution and guilt. Granted, it is in the moment where the play breaks off, in the break between the lines, as a fragment.[46]

This fragmentary, contradictory quality is the essence of the "modernism" of Hölderlin and the Straub/Huillet films, which exists at both the thematic and formal level. At the thematic level, the film shares with *Othon* the juxtaposition of a "classical" text with the present reality, in Straub's words, "We live in a world of ruins and an empire that cannot be governed."[47] Part of the contemporary malaise is the contradiction of progress and oppression, both seen in the context of the French Revolution and the socialist experiments of the twentieth century,[48] and also the contradiction between social and industrial-scientific "progress" and destruction of the environment. As Hurch puts it, Hölderlin "had sensed something of, as Benjamin says, 'what we call progress' and what was in reality an incessant consequence of great desolation and destruction that passes over this earth."[49] Dominique Païni has also traced to the turn of the nineteenth century and the work of Hölderlin the origin of the "modern" sense of these contradictions.

> The modern feeling of nature—and its representation that would culminate in Cézanne—was invented at the dawn of the nineteenth century. Hölderlin is the exact contemporary of this audacious representation of nature that dispenses with the justification of a prerequisite and explicit discourse (religious, philosophical, or poetic). Also it is not by the accident of a vague intellectual attraction that drove the Straubs to direct this *Death of Empedocles* by Hölderlin and to *draw* the text—without forcing it very much—toward a cry of anguish in regard to the outrages to which nature submits today.[50]

Both in thematic and formal terms, the narrative of Empedocles, then, can be seen to correspond to this "original sin of the modern."[51]

The indictment of the devastation of nature is combined with the political revolutionary content of Empedocles to produce a challenge to the ideology of progress. The result, however, is not elegiac, which I would say it was in the case of Lukács's hope to harness Hölderlin to the wagon of socialist state formation. Instead, the radical challenge proposed by Empedocles arises precisely from the suspension of choice between the utopian ideals of the past, sensuous joy in the "thereness" of the world in the present, and revolutionary zeal insisting on the contemporary possibility of this unity and plenitude. But since it refuses to make any *sacrifices* to achieve unity, the resolution of this dichotomy remains "paratactic."

The refusal to make a choice in the Empedocles film arises in part from the fact that virtually none of the political references critics have seen in Hölderlin or the film is made explicit. There is no document in the film from the period following the French Revolution except for Hölderlin's language; there is no document of the twentieth-century resonance with the theme and politics of the film except for the voices, bodies, and faces of the actors (aside from Hölderlin's text, literally *all* that is German in the film) and the contemporary look and sound of the Sicilian hills. Beyond that, a contemporary reality the film documents is the invisible efficacy of its own cinematic technology.

This *distance*, which I examine later on the level of language and film structure, is seen by Krebs as a major prerequisite for the critical force of the film.

> Although it refrains from any contemporary updating, precisely in the distance and foreignness of this film lies a moment of historical truth that touches our "End-of-Time" [*Endzeit*] more than any Star Wars film.
> The present is recognizable here as the German malaise of an unfulfilled promise, which perpetuates the connection between violence and history.[52]

Krebs sees precisely the *lack* of optimism or contemporary relevance as the source of the "utopian powers" of literature and film, which bear elegiac testimony of a humane culture as it becomes ever more distant and disappears. Although I agree that the distance to the text is one aspect of the film's critical force, I do not agree that the entire attitude of Straub/Huillet is elegiac. The explicit reference to Benjamin in this regard as well as the overtly political interpretation Straub/Huillet give to the plot of the Empedocles drama speak more toward militancy than elegy. Krebs's own contrast of the world of Empedocles with Germany's "unfulfilled promise" and the "preclusion of all social change since 1789" seems to share this militancy.

Straub included in a collage of texts from Hölderlin and Cézanne the following résumé of the revolutionary hope of [Hölderlin's] poetry: "And poetry should give the children of the earth the courage to turn their backs on so-called progress, so-called science—the courage of revolution, which according to Benjamin is the tiger's leap, not into the future, but into the past, a tiger's leap 'under the free sky of history.'"[53] But this "redemptive" view of the sense of poetry, in the context of Empedocles' fate, can have another interpretation— one that suspends the choice, even the choice of a *specific* redemption.

Wilhelm Schmid stresses that the power of the Empedocles film derives in part from its simplicity. "[Straub and Huillet] do not load Hölderlin's language with meaning, but exclude the question of interpretation as much as possible. They gain thereby a multifaceted, crystal-clear figure of Empedocles. All that is to be said is on the surface of the celluloid; there is no subject 'beneath the surface.'"[54] Part of this simplicity arises simply from the modest yet radical undertaking of putting Hölderlin on film at all: again a work for "a mass medium" that generally is thought to be a difficult event for the educated and thus reserved for the enjoyment of a small elite. Just to make a film of Hölderlin "for the people who don't have time to read him" is a utopian assault on the culture industry—that is, both the restrictions it places on high culture and its watering-down of mass culture.

### The Paratactics of Cinematic Space

The refusal to choose also accepts the fragmentary nature of the Hölderlin text, both as a narrative and as language. Here we see in the narrative of the film one of the signs of Hölderlin's modernism as Santner has described it in regard to the late poetry. The ideal narrative to which Hölderlin aspired was that of a spiral development, with a Hegelian progression from unity through alienation to a higher unity. As we have seen here, however, the fragmentary nature of *Empedocles* suspends the narrative before it can be resolved. In addition to this, Straub/Huillet cut off the narrative spiral in terms of the film as well. They delete the last scenes in which Pausanias, Delia, and Panthea converse about what may have happened to the hero. Instead, the film ends with the image of Mount Etna and the voice-over of Empedocles' last hymn to nature. Thus the contradictory tension present throughout the film is perpetuated: the absence of Empedocles, his ascent as a hero into the flames of oblivion, is contradicted by the verdant presence of nature, particularly in the form of the repeated long shot over the valleys toward Mount Etna.

Another way of putting it would be that the unity that is achieved at the conclusion of the narrative does not take place in the narrative at all but rather in language and image alone. The character of Empedocles is gone, and all that remains is Hölderlin's language and the documentary capability of the cinema. Rather than a conclusion, therefore, I argue that this is a suspension of the narrative. As such, it corresponds very closely to those "anxieties" Santner points out in Hölderlin's narratives, which point to his modern, if not postmodern, quality.

> The primary function of the circular/spiral narrative (and perhaps, in a certain sense, of narrative *as such*) was, for Hölderlin, the paradoxical one of guaranteeing a seamless continuity across spans of separations, gaps of space and time. The problematic that seems to loom in the background of Hölderlin's theoretical enterprise (a problematic that has become a postmodern preoccupation) is the structure of representation itself, the gap that emerges between signified and signifier in the exteriority of any expression. [ . . . ] The very structure of expression seems to involve a primary experience of alienation, rupture, difference. The circular/spiral narrative tells the story of this rupture and its redemption.[55]

In the poetry of Hölderlin, Santner finds the most exciting, modern quality precisely "where the energy of the language outstrips the narrative of redemption."[56] The breakdown of this narrative closure, what Santner prefers to call the "loosening of narrative vigilance," is described in his book on the basis of a number of seeming imperfections in Hölderlin's later poetry. Of interest to our examination of the Empedocles film are two areas, the separation of elements and poetic parataxis.

The separation of elements results in part from the anxious self-consciousness or exaggerated concentration on stages of the narrative progression or on images and states of mind in Hölderlin's work. For instance, although critics have seen in Hölderlin's narrative the idealist unification of opposites, "the

Hegelian identity that manages to comprehend alterity," Santner is uncomfortable with "this subordination of the strides of Hölderlin's verse to the cadences of spirit." For, he concludes, "The space between the strides seems, at times, infinite."[57]

The particular evidence of this interruption of the narrative impetus is found in parataxis, the quality that Adorno found to be the most modern in Hölderlin's poetry. Santner's definition of parataxis applies equally well to Straub/Huillet's film as to Hölderlin's poetry: "Paratactic composition will tend to juxtapose images, let them stand side by side, without subordinating them to any overarching narrative syntax."[58]

The effect of this is not necessarily "minimalist," however, to use a word often found in Straub/Huillet criticism. Instead, the tension created by the contradiction between paratactic composition and narrative expectation, as we have seen, produces powerful aesthetic effects, closely related to those of early cinema. Again, this contradiction is seen by Santner as part of Hölderlin's modernism: "Often troublesome in Hölderlin's 'paratactics' is our inability to decide which of the two forms we are confronted with: absence may begin to look like excess, abject silence may become the promise of infinite possibilities. But what is more, both absence as well as excess of signification may prove to be psychologically intolerable. Such a reading of Hölderlin places him squarely within current debates about the redemptive vs. repressive aspects of narrative."[59]

We will presently look at the connection between Hölderlin's parataxis and Straub/Huillet's composition, editing, and treatment of nature. But the issue of the narrative of redemption should first be examined more closely. The narrative in the Empedocles film is presented in the context of a rather strict separation of elements: each character or group of characters (who act with a common purpose) is photographed in rather long takes against a vivid and carefully composed (or rather, "selected") natural background. Very seldom are dialogue exchanges edited in a version of shot-countershot, and when this is done, only the camera angle (and perhaps the distance) is changed, not the camera position.

One example is illustrated in the figures on pages 194 and 195. The camera placement indicated is from the original screenplay sketch, while the arrangement of figures has been revised in the actual shooting.[60] The sequence is a dramatic interchange between three citizens, Critias, and Hermocrates, on the one hand, and Pausanias and Empedocles, on the other hand, when Empedocles is implored to return to Agrigento. The shots consist of the entire group of Agrigentines, including Critias and Hermocrates, two-shots of Pausanias and Empedocles, and close-ups of each of the imploring citizens, Critias, Hermocrates, and Empedocles. The narrative is indeed partly reflected in the editing: the delegation is heard to approach, and Pausanias looks offscreen to the left to see them. This anticipation is confirmed by the appearance of the

194    Language in Exile: Hölderlin's *The Death of Empedocles*

The citizens implore Empedocles to return to Agrigento: from left, as citizens, Frederico Hecker, Peter Boom, Giorgio Baratta; William Berger as Critias; Howard Vernon as Hermocrates. Courtesy New Yorker Films.

group, looking to the right at Empedocles and Hermocrates. At first, Hermocrates, the priest, speaks alone in a medium close-up. Then a longer shot reveals all five Agrigentines in a row, with Critias and Hermocrates farthest to the right, closest to Empedocles. There are close-ups of Empedocles and Hermocrates during a short interchange and close-ups of each citizen as well. As they reach the point of saying "we are reconciled," we see all the Agrigentines in a group again, this time in a four-shot minus the villainous priest Hermocrates. He remains invisible for the rest of the seen, "not reconciled" and "unforgiven." At this point the dramatic space is interrupted by the first of the two panoramic views across the foothills to Etna, while Empedocles addresses the gods once again.[61] After this, we again see the citizens, an exchange in close-up reconciling Critias and Empedocles, which ends the scene: Empedocles looks left in profile close-up; Critias turns from profile (looking at Empedocles) and exits to the left of the screen.

Clearly the narrative space, with the exception of the somewhat ambiguous view of Etna, is unified to an extent by the dialogue, the eye-line matches, and the single camera position, to the side and between the two parties. The compositional elements are separated, however; no master shot reveals the relative location of the two groups, and each shot is composed as resting in itself

# Language in Exile: Hölderlin's *The Death of Empedocles* 195

The three citizens from the same camera position but isolated by a change of lens. Courtesy New Yorker Films.

rather than implying any overlap of space. With the exception of the rather emotional reconciliation between Critias and Empedocles, the space between the two groups could be infinite, and no thought of motion from one to the other is suggested by the composition; quite the opposite.

The background of the compositions also separates them visually: the citizens are on a path with a group of birches behind them, and aside from the white verticals of these tree trunks, the background is a curtain of bright, yellowish green. Pausanias and Empedocles, by contrast, are standing at the base of an old pine tree where Empedocles had been resting. Juxtaposed with the lightness and nuance of the long shots of the Agrigentines, the shots of Empedocles and Pausanias have much more contrast, ranging from full black of the shadows under the pine to the white of Empedocles' hair.[62] The close-ups and extreme close-ups of Empedocles, especially at the end of the scene, intensify the "expressionist" quality of this composition as the light of sun and cloud shifts, producing sharply contrasting fields of color. The close-up lens turns the distant background into a bright wash of yellow-green and bright blue sky, while it shocks with the clarity of the black shadows, the dark brown pine branch, the rich green of the individual pine needles, the flesh tones of the face, and the blue of the costume and the white of his hair.

196  Language in Exile: Hölderlin's *The Death of Empedocles*

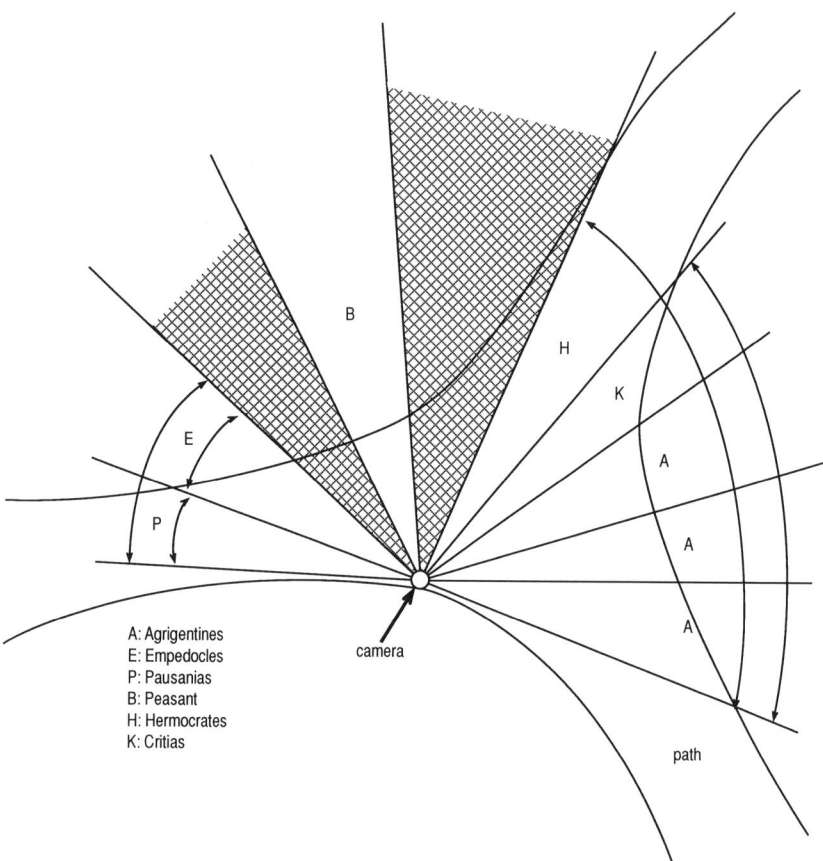

Camera position for Act II of *The Death of Empedocles*, based on Straub's screenplay sketch. The arrangement was altered in final shooting. Graphic: Andrew Reich.

The still, extreme long shot of Etna is a third element, which may bear a relation to this space if we assume it is seen by Empedocles as he speaks to the gods. But in color and composition, it, too, remains fundamentally "other."

The force of this scene arises not only from its paratactics but also from its drama and narrative, which is defeated by the isolation of Empedocles in his grandeur and of Etna in its remoteness. This duality may correspond to Santner's description of Hölderlin's narrative, contrasting it with the "epic" prescriptions of Schiller and Goethe, following the tradition of Homer. Their definition of "epic" does suggest a rather modern "separation of elements," where images succeed each other while remaining separate and without hierarchy. In Santner's words, "The deictic gesture of epic, the 'photographic' quality of its comportment vis-à-vis the things of the world, is in turn mirrored in the relative independence of units in the text."[63]

But the difference between Hölderlin and the idealist tradition is the questioning of the overarching basis that previously provided security for such independence. Santner terms this "the quality, more than any other, which makes Hölderlin an early modern—the use of an epic *style* in the absence of 'epic space' and 'epic security,' the absence of a 'public square' that would encompass and give human and social meaning—a depth dimension—to concrete particulars."[64] After we consider once more the "infinite possibilities" suggested by the absence of "epic security" in the Empedocles film, we will consider how both this film and more significantly *Antigone* investigate the problem of the absence of a "public square" in contemporary culture.[65]

The result of using this "epic style" is a form of modernism that equalizes the importance of compositional elements to develop structures of interaction between them. Therefore, it is quite appropriate to think of Schoenberg's twelve-tone composition in regard to Straub/Huillet's Hölderlin films, as Santner does in writing of Hölderlin's parataxis.[66] Aside from the lack of hierarchical organization on the level of language, the various levels of narrative, history, and what Huillet would call "archaeology" also characterize Straub/Huillet's treatment of "film language." Here we are again in close proximity to the role of the poet in the context of Hölderlin: "No longer authorized to narrate the grand myth of redemption, he [the poet] must choose a more modest task: discovering relations, correspondences, constellations of meaning within the field of history—understood as a field of dispersed events rather than the plot of *Heilsgeschichte*—amid 'the millionfold hydra of the empirical world,' and, finally, within language itself."[67]

The first manifestation of this approach to meaning is the simplification and rendering equal of elements of composition that Straub/Huillet undertake. We have already noted that the shots are of long duration; each is a composition that is complete in itself, and there is no camera movement in the Empedocles film. In other words, it is a step in Straub/Huillet's return to some of the qualities of silent film. As noted above, also, the compositions gain individual weight as camera position does not alter: there is thus no redundancy in the space that they reveal, so all the information in a shot is significant and will not be supported or confirmed by another perspective. Ignoring the industry conventions regarding the consistency of light or sound is part of this as well, as Alain Philippon has written: "The absolute submission of the method to the reality of a landscape or a climate (if a cloud passes, the camera captures a noticeable variation in luminosity) arises from a vision of the world where *everything* counts, without hierarchy." As Straub/Huillet are fond of quoting Rosa Luxemburg in this context, "The fate of an insect is not less important than the fate of the revolution."[68] Other aspects of the equal significance of the elements include the way that all the characters are photographed and the recording of their speeches. Regardless of how insignificant a character's role might be, that person is photographed with as much compositional clarity and respect as any other. The duration of their speeches or their relative position may be conveyed through editing, but the "portraits" of them are all of equal dignity. And the landscape, too, is a character, or a drama. Describing her work on the cinematography for *Too Early, Too Late*, Caroline Champetier has written, "Certain shots are the interpretation of a movement of the sky on the earth; while filming, those were instants of true joy."[69]

# 10
# FILM AS "TRANSLATION"

### The Deterritorialization of Language

The "impossibility of translation" has produced an apparently opposite realization that the translation of a text actually reveals an alienation from its own language that was already there. The gap between what words say and what they mean, between signifier and signified, may be invisible in one's own language, but the inevitable failure of translation brings it to the fore. Straub/Huillet's methods of distancing texts from their performance in film has a similar effect. Particularly in regard to German literary works, the films reveal that these works are not necessarily at home with conventional German diction, nor do they necessarily belong to Germany at all.[1] As Louis Seguin put it, "the film is the exodus of the text."[2]

Since the double impossibility and virtue of translation were major concerns for Hölderlin, presentation of his work by Straub/Huillet adds additional layers to the displacement of language from its function as transparent communication. To alienate the German language and to make its textual quality evident, Straub/Huillet employ a number of devices other than the "scoring" of the delivery. If a "truthfulness" of language arises from its being spoken by non-native speakers, this certainly is a method that Straub/Huillet have by now used in a majority of their films, with special consistency since *Othon*. In *Class Relations*, as we have seen in relation to Brecht's *Saint Joan of the Stockyards*, a differentiation is added between both native and foreign accents and the degree of theatrical training of the speakers, plus extreme variations of style, pitch, and speed. *The Death of Empedocles* broadens the spectrum of voices even further (including Sprechstimme, as in Schoenberg's opera), while a triple impossibility of translation is enacted in the film of Brecht's adaptation of Hölderlin's translation of Sophocles' *Antigone*.

In *Empedocles*, each word of Hölderlin's text is recited so that it can be understood; the text is as clear as if it were printed on the page. However, the speed of the recitation makes it impossible for the audience to always comprehend the text. Because of the density of Hölderlin's text and the suspension of meaning through parataxis, even if individual words are understood, the pace prohibits the hearer from always remaining in control of the meaning, or even the associations the text produces. The result of this is not that there is a loss of meaning but that each viewer will have different associations, and that associations arising from the combination of sound and image will be different with each viewing. Here again the comparison to twelve-tone music would be appropriate, although Peter Buchka resorted to an earlier musical metaphor. "But precisely when concentration wanes, the sensuality of proceeding reservedly proves itself: Hölderlin's text suddenly becomes a musical score, and the sounds of nature play the *basso continuo*."[3]

The mode of delivery that Straub/Huillet have perfected over the years is carried to a rhythmic extreme with the Hölderlin text, where the author's straining of German syntax threatens to make individual elements break off and stand for themselves. By emphasizing rhythm and intonation, but never "psychologizing"[4] or "romanticizing"[5] language, the filmmakers allow the words of the text to resonate beyond the conventions of syntax and to connect with the visual image in unpredictable ways. For instance, the actor of the Empedocles role cited the example of the line, "Und schönes stirbt in traurig stummer Brust nicht mehr" (And beautiful dies in sorrowing silent breast no more): "At first I was tempted to develop the psychological aspect and said, 'in *sorrowing* silent breast'; I emphasized 'sorrowing.' And I remember that Danièle Huillet immediately insisted on following the rhythm exactly and thus to give both words equal weight, sorrowing and silent. That actually makes one aware of the actual meaning for the first time, that sorrow is silent, that it cannot be spoken."[6]

The effect on the language here is twofold. On the one hand, the precise work on the rhythm and intonation, almost to the extent that the script becomes a musical score, is meant to be wholly in service to making the fundamental rhythmic quality of the Hölderlin text audible, nothing more. On the other hand, to make Hölderlin's unique manipulation of German syntax audible, a Brechtian "alienation effect" is also introduced.

Determinant for the Hölderlin text is the pause at the end of each line, which was carefully orchestrated by Straub/Huillet according to the rhythm of the words. This corresponds to a "classical" aspect of Hölderlin, that the caesura is the essence of the spirit that the work conveys. As Bettina von Arnim wrote, citing Hölderlin, "The laws of the Spirit are metrical."[7] However, the stylized manipulation of speech in the service of the rhythm of the words functions simply to distance the hearer from both the meaning and the delivery, again so that the elements can be appreciated in their separation.

The hostility of the reception of this method, especially in Germany, is quite telling. As Huillet has observed, experimentation with sound and speech is much less acceptable in the cinema today than visual experimentation. An analogy with atonal music is again appropriate, since twentieth-century music in the mainstream cinema is almost entirely banned to the horror genre (in Stanley Kubrick's *The Shining*, for example). Critics have generally not accepted either the analogy to rap music, proposed by Harun Farocki,[8] or the filmmakers' insistence that such rhythms do indeed occur in natural speech: they have related the story of a child approaching them as they walked their dog in Hamburg with an "unnatural" caesura in the question "Beißt / der Hund?"[9] One critic even trotted out Alexander Kluge's objection, that one cannot treat language as an object, without noting that it dated from 1965.[10] And even Brecht insisted on the "unnatural" emphasis on the caesura in his Hölderlin adaptation, rather than "psychological" readings of the text, comparing it to the syncopation of jazz.[11]

Huillet and Straub of course do not endear themselves to German critics by asserting that, on the contrary, this is the first time Hölderlin has ever really been *heard* in Germany. In saying this, they are continuing the Brechtian tradition, shared apparently by Renoir, that accents and foreigners' difficulty in speaking a language actually reveal a truthfulness not available in "normal" speech. The revelatory power of this foreignness is also to be found in Hölderlin, as Santner points out: "Hearing our own language from the mouth of a foreigner (or, perhaps, of a poet) is much like framing the language with a kind of Brechtian *Verfremdungs-Effekt*; our own language is made strange, is objectified. This can secure for us the necessary distance from our mother tongue so that we may then use it 'more freely.'"[12] By alienating the German language, Straub/Huillet are both "wresting it from the control of the bourgeoisie," to use the rhetoric of the 1960s, and regaining a new access to it for contemporary Germans (who, it seems, generally do not appreciate it). But the principle Straub/Huillet employ seems at least consistent with Hölderlin's position: "But what is proper to oneself must be as well learned as what is alien. Therefore the Greeks are indispensable to us."[13]

As in their other films, but to a more theatrical degree, the Empedocles is thus what Raphaël Bassan calls a "creative documentary" of the performance. Against the background of the careful scoring of the text, the film documents the quality of spontaneity that shines through because each actor has a particular manner of speaking that has its own history. As Andreas von Rauch put it, it could even take some detective work to discover how certain Rhineland pronunciations came into the speech of young Germans raised in Rome, or to explain why a scholar of German literature in Italy might have a Bavarian accent (the peasant in Empedocles). The personal history, although not manifest, does play a role in the "character" of the figures, however. For example, Pausanias is indeed a young man gradually gaining more self-confidence (both in the German of the text and before the camera) as he works through the drama of Empedocles' fate. As an Italian speaker of German, he is also documented as he learns what is proper to himself, to paraphrase Hölderlin.[14]

The difficulty of non-native speakers with language combines with the inherent difficulty of the text itself to produce this document of the creation of sense from words. For that reason, Straub has admitted to choosing this version of Empedocles, as with other texts, because it is "impure" and because it "resists" being filmed.[15] We have seen that modern interest has arisen from the "loosening" of syntactic structures in Hölderlin's later works, and the Hölderlin edition by Sattler (a consultant on the films) reveals the indeterminacy of variants rather than striving for a "definitive" reading.[16] Straub/Huillet purposely demonstrate that this is an "impure" text, not a completely polished one. This is reminiscent of their removal of Max Brod's "polishing" from the Kafka text. In this case they even acquired photocopies of unfinished material from Sattler and made their own choices.[17] Although a single performance of the play cannot place textual variants side by side, as in the Frankfurt edition, the distancing of the performance makes it clear that it is a product existing *between* the words on the page and the meaning that either was intended or is received. Here the "archaeology" so often apparent in Straub/Huillet's work functions on the textual level. Their mortification of the body of the text by delivery and choice of speakers is consistent with another concept of Benjamin's, as elucidated by Paul de Man, and that is the "task of the translator."[18]

Translation and its impossibility are of great importance to both Hölderlin and Benjamin. What we will see is that the problems and virtues of translation form much of the interest that Straub/Huillet bring to bear in the cinema, both in the area of so-called adaptation and in the question of fiction versus documentary and the ontology or truth of the cinematic/photographic image. If we examine the scarring of the text by translation, we will get closer to the issues that these texts and these films raise.

We turn here to Benjamin's essay "The Task of the Translation" as well as Paul de Man's reading of it in *The Resistance to Theory*. In general, we can postulate that Straub/Huillet's method of filmmaking is quite analogous to the act of translating as Benjamin describes it. De Man points out that Benjamin's text is in fact a "poetics," investigating the relationship of poetic language, intentionality and meaning, and history. Many of Benjamin's observations about poetic language, as revealed through the task of the translator, apply directly to the filmmaking of Straub/Huillet.

First of all is Benjamin's insistence that the translation, as de Man puts it, "per definition fails."[19] It is not the task of the translator to express anything but merely to demonstrate the relationship between languages. This, in turn, does not reveal the meaning of the original but instead shows its "temporary" quality: the original, too, is "foreign."

To give honor to this reality, Benjamin proposes a number of rather provocative "givens." The first is the categorical assertion that a work of art has nothing to do with an audience. Benjamin reduces the postulation of an audience to the postulation that humans exist at all, which becomes meaningless. Straub/Huillet's persistent refusal to manipulate the grammar of "film language" to reach a bigger audience is entirely consistent with Benjamin's position.

Straub/Huillet's position on the translation of the subtitles for their films reveals both their affinity for Benjamin's position on translation and its relevance for their cinematic adaptation of texts as well. In her own translations into French and in her requests to me in making the English translation of the subtitles beginning with *Class Relations*, Huillet insisted, as does Benjamin, that "the word is the primary element of translation."[20] Using word-for-word translation and respecting the original syntax wherever possible, metaphor and equivalent expressions in the second language were to be avoided at all times.[21] The translation was to be neither a replacement of the original nor an "interpretation" of it. This method pushes comprehensibility to its limits, since, as de Man points out, the German word for *translate* is a version of the word *metaphor*: "It is a curious assumption to say *übersetzen* is not metaphorical, *übersetzen* is not based on resemblance, there is no resemblance between the translation and the original."[22] Indeed, the French of Huillet's subtitles (for *Antigone*), in the view of Laurence Giavarini, lets the verse form of the German and the Greek show through.[23]

Concomitant with the utopian force of Hölderlin's poetry, this method of translation also threatens to take a step from the secure world of existing language into the void. Benjamin cites Hölderlin's translations as an example: "A literal rendering of the syntax completely demolishes the theory of reproduction of meaning and is a direct threat to comprehensibility."[24] The danger of this step is described further on. "For this very reason Hölderlin's translations in particular are subject to the enormous danger inherent in all translations: the gates of a language thus expanded and modified may slam shut and enclose the translator with silence. Hölderlin's translations from Sophocles were his last work; in them meaning plunges from abyss to abyss until it threatens to become lost in the bottomless depths of language."[25]

The "expansion and modification of language" referred to here is the effect that the act of translation has on both the second language and, indirectly, on the original. Translation, being a relationship between languages, reveals the incomplete, fragmentary nature of each. In exploring Benjamin's description of the relation between translation and original as that between broken shards of a vessel, de Man cites Carol Jacobs's observation that not only do these pieces not resemble each other but they are never to be put together to form a vessel, either. "Benjamin insists that the final outcome is still 'a broken part.' "[26]

Just as Straub/Huillet insist that the subtitles cannot replace or even resemble the spoken text in a film, so does their work with the speakers of these texts reveal that the filming is also a translation: as such, it reveals the "foreignness" of one's own language, for instance, by revealing the nature of Hölderlin's German to the Germans. This process, by way of their direction of the actors and the choice of a variety of marked accents and manners of speech, corresponds to the "suffering" of the translator's language that comes about in its transformation by the act of translation. If Hölderlin said "What is proper to oneself must be learned," part of that learning of the nature of one's own language arises when confronted by the reality of one's alienation from it. The "pains of one's own" (*Wehen des eigenen*) reveal that one's supposed comfort in one's native language was an illusion: "We think we are at ease in our own language, we feel a coziness, a familiarity, a shelter in the language we call our own, in which we think that we are not alienated. What the translation reveals is that this alienation is at its strongest in our relation to our own original language, that the original language within which we are engaged is disarticulated in a way which imposes upon us a particular alienation, a particular suffering."[27]

In addition to revealing the alienation inherent in the second language, the translator's "native" language, it also reveals the damaged nature of the original. Benjamin describes this damage in a number of ways: the original is, like the translation, only a "fragment" of what he postulates as "the pure language." The translation, by fixing some aspect of the original in a second language and thus freezing it at a point in time, reveals that the original was also always in motion, incomplete. The reference to the "afterlife" of the original, via translation, also suggests the original's death.[28] This afterlife, however, is not incidental to literature but essential to it, which is why the task of the translator is to be compared to a poetics in general: the translation puts the original into historical motion. "Once you have a translation you cannot translate it anymore. You can translate only an original. The translation canonizes, freezes, an original and shows in the original a mobility, an instability, which at first one did not notice. The act of critical, theoretical reading performed by a critic like Friedrich Schlegel and performed by literary theory in general—by means of which the original work is not imitated or reproduced but is to some extent put in motion, de-canonized, questioned in a way which undoes its claim to canonical authority—is similar to what a translator performs."[29]

This is also similar to what the filmmaker performs, in the treatment of "texts" by Straub/Huillet. The alienation of cultural artifacts and texts has a threatening, nihilistic side and a utopian side, for Straub/Huillet as for Benjamin. On the one hand, the act of translation/filmmaking dislocates what one thought of as secure: what was thought to be the reassuring voice of the mother, language, appears as a structure to which we are subject but which is not itself *human at all*.[30] "The relationship of the translator to the original is the relationship between language and language," de Man writes, wherein the problem of meaning or the desire to say something, the need to make a statement, is entirely absent.[31] The realm of language has in the modern age come to replace the realm of the spirit since the time of Hegel and Hölderlin.[32]

Translation thus dislocates us into a "nonhuman" realm, which rather than the sacred narrative of religion or the cyclic narrative of idealism, Benjamin describes as a history that is outside both Nature and human experience. This realm, which de Man describes with the term *nihilism*, is one where human endeavor is no longer the measure of all things; in other words, it is the fulfillment of the desire for dissolution as found in Hölderlin.

Benjamin, in describing the translation as relating to the "afterlife" (*fortleben*) of the original, separates this concept of "life" from human life and memory: "One might, for example, speak of an unforgettable life or moment even if all men [*sic*] had forgotten it."[33] Memory, in this case, could become "God's remembrance"—or photography, as Susan Sontag and John Berger have observed. In the case of literary works, however, Benjamin places them into a concept of history that neither bears the security of human agency nor the action of spirit. It is instead a very neutral process, comparable to the linguistic relations he is describing; but this, he insists, is also a kind of life: "The concept of life is given its due only if everything that has a history of its own, and is not merely the setting for history, is credited with life. In the final analysis, the range of life must be determined by history rather than by nature, least of all by such tenuous factors as sensation and soul."[34]

This expansion of the concept of life beyond human memory and sensation is the "nihilistic moment that is necessary in any understanding of history," according to de Man.[35] He does not see this as a paralyzing nihilism, however, but as a prerequisite for any historical act.[36] Rather than a messianic impulse, it has a materialist basis: "Understand by nihilism a certain kind of critical awareness which will not allow you to make certain affirmative statements when those affirmative statements go against the way things are."[37]

The task of the translator, this poetics of relationships between language, thus ends up describing the particular suffering and alienation of humans in both language and in history. Neither is stable and in our control, not linguistic structures, relationships to nature, or even relationships between people, de Man concludes, "since there is, in a very radical sense, no such thing as the human."[38]

### The "Look of the World" and Redemption

In the face of this nihilism, what kind of hope can there be? In the first place, if one sees things as they are, that should certainly be more hopeful than false consciousness, which would conceivably be even more helpless in the face of the world. Second, the motion that is brought into awareness by translation, the instability of the original text, brings with it a sense of potential—like the contradictory potential of Hölderlin's abysmal silences, or Fortini's assertion that the working class have no homeland. It is a process of learning to take possession of what is properly one's own, and this process is not one of stasis but one of movement. By becoming aware through translation of an original's distance from Benjamin's postulated "pure language," one comes to know one's own unstable position. De Man cites Benjamin's contradictory position within and against the tropes of language.

> Benjamin, who is talking about the inability of trope to be adequate to meaning, constantly uses the very tropes which seem to postulate the adequation between meaning and trope; but he prevents them in a way, displaces them in such a way as to put the original in motion, to decanonize the original, giving it a movement which is a movement of disintegration, of fragmentation. This movement of the original is a wandering, an *errance*, a kind of permanent exile if you wish, but it is not really an exile, for there is no homeland, nothing from which one has been exiled. Least of all is there something like a *reine Sprache*, a pure language, which does not exist except as a permanent disjunction which inhabits all languages as such, including and especially the language one calls one's own. What is to be one's own language is the most displaced, the most alienated of all.[39]

Although this quality of homelessness in language is inescapable, that does not mean that meaning is impossible. On the contrary, the purpose of this nihilism is to understand history in order to be able to live in it as it is. Understanding consists of recognizing the instability of meaning and being aware of one's own relationship to it. De Man cites Gadamer as seeing "understanding . . . as a process between author and reader in which the reader acquires an understanding of the text by becoming aware of the historicity of the movement that occurs between the text and himself" [*sic*].[40]

Being aware of one's position in an impersonal motion is not far removed from Brecht's *Lehrstücke* (learning plays) or the tentativeness of Hölderlin's images. The awareness that relations of this kind are tentative and not determined by any preexisting or transcendent authority can lead to the silence of the abyss or to a sense of unlimited potential. The absence of transcendent justification also gives to the smallest detail of everyday life the same importance as great events of history or theology. In Santner's analysis of Hölderlin's poetry, this is the comfort that is discovered beyond the "narrative of redemption." "The poet begins to find a place and a comfort within the errancy and drift that in 'Hälfte des Lebens' had appeared so horrifying. [ . . . ] [T]he poet begins to discover the pleasures of 'die Tageszeichen,' or 'signs of the day.' [ . . . ] They connote the things, the concrete particulars that populate one's immediate life world; unassuming objects that may give the poet a sense of calm, security, equipoise. It is as if the poet had discovered, for the first time, the possibility of a life in nonsacred, mundane space and time."[41]

Santner goes on to connect this attention to "concrete particulars" to John Berger's description of the "look of the world" from an essay on photography. "The look of the world is the widest possible confirmation of the *thereness* of the world, and thus the look of the world continually proposes and confirms our relation to that thereness, which nourishes our sense of Being."[42]

With Santner's repeated invocation of criticism of film and photography in regard to Hölderlin's images, we return to the juxtaposition of those poetic images with the "look of the world" in Straub/Huillet's films. As we have seen, the connections between Hölderlin's poetic and narrative strides, as between the shots in the film, is a tenuous one. The term "tenuousness" or "temporariness" (*Vorläufigkeit*), has been applied to Benjamin's translation, Hölderlin's verse, and Straub/Huillet's mise-en-scène. Benjamin writes, "This, to be sure, is to admit that all translation is only a somewhat provisional [*Vorläufig*] way of coming to terms with the foreignness of languages."[43] In the case of Hölderlin, the fragmentary nature and parallel variants in his work, made visible by the Frankfurt edition, reveal a similar quality. "But rather than simply destroying the 'illusion' of the completed poem and demonstrating the provisional character—the *Entwurfscharakter*—of the later Hölderlin, which the editors set as their goal, the Frankfurt edition suggests something even more radical: a certain undecidability between the draft or working sketch, on the one hand, and the finished work of art, on the other. This sort of undecidability becomes chronic in the later work, indeed it seems to be at the core of Hölderlin's poetic practice at this time."[44]

Since the recitation of the poetry in film cannot preserve the tenuousness of the verse, it is placed in a tenuous relation to the "thereness" of the speakers themselves and the look of the world. The endeavor is to "empty the image" of all intention and meaning, so that the impersonal "life" that Benjamin envisions is a result of extremely controlled structuring juxtaposed with complete openness to "the signs of the day." Straub/Huillet consciously structure their films rigidly, so that accident or chance can be perceived as such.[45] As Krebs writes,

> When Straub/Huillet have the actors recite in this way . . . and when the editing confronts shots of landscape, earth, faces and persons with each other, a dialectic of image and language is constructed that resembles the experimental structure [*Versuchsaufbau*] of Brecht's *Lehrstück*. The text itself is an experimental structure, i.e., both in recitation and in the film image, it repeatedly enters new constellations. . . . It may appear that this is off-putting and "clumsy," the experience of the friction between actor and costume, gesture and language,

208    Film as "Translation"

Ute Cremer as Delia and Martina Baratta as Panthea in *The Death of Empedocles*. Courtesy Edition Manfred Salzgeber, Berlin.

space and figure, speaker and text. But in this friction, far from all sterility and stringency, dwells the anarchic power and joy [*Lust*] of speaking and seeing.[46]

Krebs uses terms very similar to Benjamin's as he argues that his structuring of the text as an "experiment" shows "solidarity with literature," for which a reading "makes up a position of the work in its own history." The tension between the speakers, the text, and the image of them reciting is also one of anarchic potential: "In them [the images] the actors appear tenuously, experimentally arranged while yet giving a thoroughly 'classical,' stable and determinate impression."[47]

The method of opening up wide avenues by way of rigorous structure is perhaps one of the things that Peter Handke had in mind when he emphasized Straub/Huillet's nearness to the Greeks. Straub also has indicated such an affinity in his unwillingness to choose, for instance, between comedy and tragedy in the drama of Empedocles.

*Straub:*   In life, one can never say at what point it's tragic, but one can also never say at what point it's funny; and a film isn't interesting unless

Delia (Ute Cremer) kneeling to Panthea (Martina Baratta) in *The Death of Empedocles*. Courtesy Edition Manfred Salzgeber, Berlin.

> one senses these two things *at the same time*, I mean at each second and not in alternating strokes à la Tchaikovsky . . .
>
> *Huillet:* The Greeks, with their myths, knew that already.[48]

Straub's description of their films as having the shape of "a fan" is an appropriate one at this point. The reference to a fan (regarding *Othon*) concerned the range in actors from polished native speakers (theatricality) to lay actors and non-native speakers, for whom Straub did use the term "authenticity."[49] If the rigorous structuring of the text, the placement of the actors, and the composition and editing of the shots make up Straub/Huillet's "classicism," here is their "romanticism": in the conviction that through the "documentary" aspect of their cinema, directed at young lay actors laboring with a well-memorized linguistic text or recording the play of wind, light, and shadow on a landscape, some sort of authenticity can be perceived.

On the one hand, the authenticity that the camera gives us access to is merely the "thereness" of the world, the "signs of the day" that, for all the concern for the destruction of Nature, still conveys the striking impression that, as Jean Narboni quotes Straub, "the world is still habitable."[50] At another screening Straub had said that the only "Aussage" (message) of *The Death of Empedocles* is that the world is a cradle, an invocation of the Communist utopia,

Empedocles (Andreas von Rauch) on Etna, in *Black Sin*. Courtesy Edition Manfred Salzgeber, Berlin.

"Das Einfache, das schwer zu machen ist" (The simple thing that is hard to do).[51]

The word *expressionism* has already been mentioned in regard to the extreme visual contrasts in the Empedocles films, but it could apply to other aesthetic aspects as well. Indeed, Expressionism is one modern connection between Romanticism and formal rigor (see Schoenberg). But the emphasis placed on the equal value of all elements in the film, as structures with their own logic and their own history, also has an expressionistic effect. Nature, photographed with a neutral, contemplative camera without narrative motivation, is not human. The words of the texts, in their careful, rhythmic delivery, are also not human; or at least, as Benjamin's "translation" reveals, they are part of the afterlife of something that is already dead. Against this background, the *live* performance of the actors, the presence of any living human bodies is almost a striking contradiction, an impossibility.

Hence the powerful effect of the spectacle of the actors breathing in order to deliver this dead text: "What one hears, as never before, is breath, and the body with its gestures is like the seismograph, the point of application: it redistributes the essential focus [*focalisation essentielle*], accompanies it, prolongs it: the body, this musical instrument."[52]

Straub's description of how meaning arises not from the text itself or from the interpretation by the actor but in the actor's physical production of the words that make meaning is yet another version of Benjamin's assertion that a translation can only approach an original's "Art des Meinens"—its manner of indicating—and not what it indicates. After so much rehearsal, Straub says, the actors "understand what they are speaking so well that they no longer need to understand the sense of each word: the sense (meaning) becomes bodies that think and breathe [*des corps qui pensent, qui respirent*]."[53] Distancing himself somewhat from Brechtian acting as "quotation" (cited in the opening titles of *Not Reconciled*), Straub sees this manner of speaking a thoroughly memorized text as creating moments "where actors simply explode. But not by blowing up like fireworks—which has nothing to do with the text. But rather the text itself becomes an explosion—just what no one attempts anymore."[54]

Against the severe structural restraint of the text and against the narrative impetus of the revolutionary leader into "death in the heavenly fires" (without a tomb), it is youth that stands as the hope of the future. (De Man: in spite of everything, hope.) Panthea and Pausanias, young amateur actors who are sister and brother, expressing their perhaps fragmentary, perhaps intuitive understanding of the hero's worth, are the future. Delia kneels to Panthea in one of the most striking gestures of the physically restrained film. And it is Panthea who introduces the film, "This is his garden," and describes the harmony between Empedocles and Nature in the most beautiful poetry. And Pausanias, in his loyalty to Empedocles as the young friend, concludes through the course of the narrative what Straub has called a "school of freedom."[55] When the citizens say they will not know what to do without Empedocles' counsel (*ratlos verläßt du uns?*), he instructs them, "Ask this youth!" Similarly, the young woman who would play Antigone was spotted by Straub and Huillet (independently of each other) by chance at an acting school in Berlin; her sister plays the role of Ismene. Despite their supposed "asceticism" and "classicism," Straub/Huillet have the romanticism to look to the young and unspoiled for authenticity. And despite all the "redemptive" concern with history and Nature, one strain of expressionism remains: what is old must pass away and be replaced by something completely other.

Extreme expressionistic abstraction is placed alongside documentary simplicity and a romantic vision of "authenticity." It is my contention that this juxtaposition of opposites in Straub/Huillet is an example of the "Stillegung" (arresting) of thought, as proposed by Benjamin and Adorno. It is not the "unification of opposites" of idealism or even a "Marxist redemption myth" that abolishes all division and alienation[56] but the confrontation or even forcing of division. Divisions in the audience, in the layers of textual signification, in the cinematic ways of producing meaning are also not to be confused with a postmodern position: instead, it is utopian.

As in Adorno's view of Hölderlin's parataxis, the utopian force lies not in Hölderlin's ideas but "in the primacy of abstraction, in the purity of form itself."[57] Rather than blemishes, the disruptions caused in "narrative vigilance'' by these pure forms are gestures toward this utopia. As Santner has concluded, "The *harte Fügung* so typical of Hölderlin's later poetry becomes the emblem of the poet seer; the rifts of silence become the openings where the Unnamable can only be circumscribed."[58] The mortification of language points toward utopia with the force of both religion and revolution but without the "redemptive myth" of either. Like Benjamin, Straub/Huillet look to Hölderlin with a "combination of nihilistic rigor with sacred revelation."[59]

Nihilism, expressionism, revolution—how are they combined in the conclusion of *The Death of Empedocles* where the "poet-seer" speaks for the last time in a utopian hymn to nature? Like a coda, the end of the film repeats its themes, and the question is whether they are resolved in one direction or another. The repetition of the visual of Etna links the shot to the earlier exchange in which Empedocles personally renounced his opportunity to return to the city. The narrower angle of the lens removes some of the verdant foreground of the view of the volcano, continuing the geographic ascent through the course of the film: mountain, clouds, and sky are the main compositional elements. Since the entire speech is delivered in voice-over, there is a sense in which Empedocles is already dead as it is spoken; perhaps the higher view of the volcano suggests his impending plunge. However, since so much of the film has been directed to nature and to the future of civilization without the poet-seer, there is a sense in which the absence of Empedocles is not threatening but is a liberation. Given the expressionistic tension present through most of the film by way of the live image of actors performing the text, the final hymn accompanied only by the view of the mountain, with its long duration and the fact that it is already somewhat familiar, is an image of peace. The disruption of the human presence between these words and this landscape is removed, and we witness only the juxtaposition of these two "inhuman" abstractions. This juxtaposition continues after the image of Etna has disappeared as well, since the sound track continues with two different cuts: first, the opening of the Bach violin concerto that had been quoted at the beginning of the film (the first instance was the ending, so the result is a sort of reverse framing; second, following closely on this highly structured sound, a recording of sounds from nature, birds twittering on the mountainside and the thunder of an approaching storm. If the thunder promises rain (one is tempted to think of T. S. Eliot's *The Wasteland*), both this and the Bach are beginnings, promises of a future, one with a structure and one without.

Straub has said that he had three precedents in mind in thinking about the ending: Eisenstein's *Alexander Nevsky* (1938), Hitchcock's *Foreign Correspondent* (1940), and Chaplin's *The Great Dictator* (1940).[60] All three films end with a male voice addressing some version of posterity. In the Eisenstein film, the message is to all potential enemies of Russia, present and future. The vow to defeat all attackers is spoken by Nevsky, then repeated in text superimposed over a shot of armored soldiers bearing spears. Both Chaplin and Hitchcock use the radio, one of Hitler's own effective propaganda weapons, to appeal to "the people" to resist fascism in Europe. *Foreign Correspondent*, filmed before the United States entered the war, uses abstract terms to appeal to people in "America" to keep the lights burning while Europe has been plunged into the darkness of war. Rather than this anti-isolationist message, Chaplin's message is to the little people, urging them to maintain their hope in the face of Nazi aggression. Chaplin, like Eisenstein, visualizes "the people" as this message is being conveyed, but in the form of an idyllic Alpine family scene rather than soldiers on their guard.

Striking in each case is the withdrawal of the speaking voice into helplessness and the appeal "an die Nachgeborenen"—to those born after—as Brecht repeatedly varied it. The stress on the apparatus of communication in each case—superimposed type in the Russian and the radio of the American examples—extinguishes the character of the speaker and breaks the message out of the narrative that went before. Indeed, the humanistic earnestness of Chaplin's appeal is almost unbearable in contrast to the irreverent comedy that has gone before.

Empedocles' voice is similarly disembodied, and, to a subtle extent, the cinematic apparatus is emphasized by the switch from recitation to reading of the voice-over text.[61] Consistent with all the other utopian moments in Straub/Huillet films is the absence of "the people" to whom this speech might be addressed; if the text is revolutionary, the revolution cannot be depicted, and the point of Empedocles' drama is that his kind of "revolutionary leader" is no longer needed, must no longer be needed. What remains are the two poles between which the drama has unfolded: the ability of the camera to record, in this case the somber beauty of the peak of Mount Etna, and the reality of the world, which like the text read by a voice from the dead past, outlives human history.

The sense of this final shot is certainly the extinguishing of the subject and the loss of identity in the unbounded. For the first time in the film it reconciles language and nature,[62] but at the expense of the human. As Benjamin wrote, "meaning plunges from abyss to abyss until it threatens to become lost in the bottomless depths of language."[63] "Aber es gibt ein Halten," Benjamin asserts in spite of everything: "There is, however, a stop."[64] For Benjamin, it is to be found in no text but in Holy Writ, "in which meaning has ceased to be the watershed for the flow of language and the flow of revelation."[65] The space between the filmed image of nature and the disembodied text is Straub/Huillet's way of indicating this "Halten" as well. It is a "space between" much as Benjamin's "interlinear" commentaries on the Scriptures; it is stressed at the film's conclusion by its repetition in two forms: between the text about nature and the "look" of nature and between the sound of Bach and the sound of thunder.

Hüser has objected that the thunder at the conclusion does not succeed. He considers it too great a resolution and validation of Empedocles, because his speech is about death. I do not agree, since the effect of the film has been to erase any regret about Empedocles' death, or about time in general. The fact that the sound track "outlives" the visual track, as it often does in Straub/Huillet films, is a further step away from the temporality of the body. The "inhuman" is what lives on, in the text or in the inhuman history of nature, and only if it does will human life still be possible on the earth.

# 11

# ANTIGONE

*Antigone* incorporates in many ways the return to mythic origins suggested by films such as *Moses and Aaron* or *From the Cloud to the Resistance*. It returns to the aesthetic origins of contemporary film and theater in its use of the visual simplicity of the silent cinema and the staging of Sophocles' play in a Greek theater of his era. It also returns to the mythic origins of civil society in the death of the heroic individual: Antigone's voluntary self-sacrifice parallels Moses' sojourn in the desert and Empedocles' plunge into volcanic fire. And its visual images, like its language, straining to be both German and Greek, mark the border between Europe and the other continents: the "African sun" shines on Sicily, as Huillet has put it.

Danièle Huillet's love for the light and landscape of Sicily, the fascination with the Teatro de Segesta (a Greek theater in Sicily dating from the fourth century B.C.E. and one of the best-preserved Greek theaters of antiquity, discovered by Straub/Huillet some twenty years earlier while scouting locations for *Moses and Aaron*) led her and Straub to conclude their ten-year consideration of Hölderlin while returning to Brecht's political aesthetics. Brecht's version of the Hölderlin *Antigone* translation is rather obscure among his works and seldom performed, but Straub has emphasized that the text is "very much Brecht," including some of the strongest writing he ever did for the theater.[1] The lack of scholarly or critical work on Brecht's adaptation probably arises from its political and production history rather than its intrinsic quality—a situation not irrelevant to Straub/Huillet films as well.

Strangely enough, some of the most positive responses to the film reject its politics (or at least and especially Straub's polemical political position adjacent to the film) and do so partly by downplaying Brecht in favor of Hölderlin. This

*215*

*Antigone* (Danièle Huillet's hands). Courtesy Edition Manfred Salzgeber, Berlin.

is partly true in the case of the positive French reception of the film, building on an already more favorable view than in Germany of the "pure" Hölderlin texts in the previous films. Peter Handke's political argument with Straub/Huillet leads him to emphasize Hölderlin's formal modernism and Greek tragic forms over Brecht's more political concerns.[2]

This even leads Handke to a disregard for the facts: He writes of Antigone as if it were very little changed by Brecht's adaptation, when in fact the opposite is the case. He describes the paradoxical balance among the various levels of text as "Sophocles in the language of Hölderlin brought into suspicious motion by Brecht's rhetoric and brought down to earth again by strophes of Pindar inserted by Straub."[3] In adapting Hölderlin, he notes, "Brecht was modest for once," when in fact Brecht kept only 20 percent of Hölderlin's text without change, "modestly" adapted another 30 percent, and freely transformed the remaining half (not to mention the cutting of about one hundred verses).[4] The insertions of lines from Pindar, not to mention from Goethe and others, are all Brecht's, not the filmmakers'.

By leaving Brecht out of the picture to this extent, Handke can dismiss Straub/Huillet's political statements about the film as a perhaps quaint but silly personal tic of theirs. Handke accuses Straub/Huillet of "trying to close in or prop up their wonderful old militancy, which works freely in every shot of their film language, in the sloganistic framework of antiquated class struggle."[5]

Astrid Ofner as Antigone. Courtesy Edition Manfred Salzgeber, Berlin.

Handke is most upset by the impact of the "moralizing-prophesying" Brecht quotation at the end of *Antigone*. The text placed at the end of the film and connected to the Theater of Segesta only by the sound of a military helicopter recorded there is the following, delivered by Brecht at the Peoples' Congress for Peace (Völkerkongress für den Frieden) in Vienna in 1952.[6]

> The memory of humanity for sufferings borne is astonishingly short. Its gift of imagination for coming sufferings is almost even lesser. For humanity is threatened by wars compared to which those past are like poor attempts, and they will come without any doubt if the hands of those who prepare them in all openness are not broken.

For Handke, the "petty spirit of explicit thinking" runs counter to the openness of the rest of the film. We will consider the political import of the Brechtian aspect of *Antigone* later on, which Handke is clearly avoiding here by emphasizing the formal impact of Straub/Huillet's work and their closeness to the power of Greek tragedy: "The Straubian cinema and ancient Greek theater are for me virtually one in the same, of like form."[7] We will also see that where he does stress the connection to Greek drama, Handke does indeed identify powerful effects of the cinematic simplicity of Straub/Huillet's treatment of text and space. But at this point, in objecting to the explicitness of the printed text at the end of the film, Handke is excluding one of the "textual levels" of the film: its place in the postwar history of Germany.

The printed Brecht text and seemingly extradiegetic sound fit with the opening of the film as a frame that places the action in the archaeological layers of its development. On the screen at the beginning of the film are seen the titles along with the logo of the Theater of Segesta (with its age)—the only image in the film revealing its full shape. The title of the film spans all four levels of its history, *Die Antigone des Sophokles in der hölderlinschen Übertragung für die Bühne bearbeitet von Brecht 1948 (Suhrkamp Verlag)*. Beyond the references to Sophocles, Hölderlin, and Brecht, the contemporary intervention of Straub/Huillet and the film's material conditions of existence appear in the words "1948 (Suhrkamp Verlag)" appended to the title used in Chur, Switzerland. The date places the Brecht adaptation in historical time, while the naming of the publisher both gives them credit and reminds the audience that the Brecht rights had to be bought. In interviews, Straub has made a point of mentioning that, as with many other films, it was not easy to get the rights to this text: it took the personal help of the publisher Unseld to get Barbara Brecht Schall's approval, for which she demanded DM 50,000.[8]

Over these titles is heard an excerpt from the *Musique pour les soupers du roi Ubu* (1966), composed by Bernd Alois Zimmermann (1918–1970) and conducted and recorded by Michael Gielen. Zimmermann also composed the opera *Die Soldaten*, which is, according to *The New Grove Dictionary of Music and Musicians*, "widely acknowledged as the most important in German since those of Berg."[9] Like Straub/Huillet, Zimmermann worked with collage from a wide variety of sources, with a dose of atonality added, and maintained his "roots firmly in history" rather than associating with the avant-gardism of "the fashionable schools of the 1950s and 1960s."[10] The excerpt introducing Antigone is particularly ominous with its atonal weavings around Wagner's "Ride of the Valkyries" driven by an unremitting tympani rhythm against the trills of the flutes. The music has been ignored by the German critics, however, with the exception of one who ridiculed it (without reference to Zimmermann) as "Wagner's 'Ride of the Valkyries' intercut with the 'Symphonie Fantastique' by Berlioz," as if it were the work of a studio sound technician.[11]

The music embodies both similarity and difference to Brecht's production: Brecht had used rhythms and music (e.g., recordings of rhythms struck directly on piano strings)[12] during the performance to accompany the text and movement, while Straub/Huillet avoid movement and rely solely on the language for rhythm and music. However, one aspect of Brecht's adaptation was to smooth out the flow of the play, and in this Straub/Huillet have followed him: as Straub noted in the program for the stage version, Brecht's pace was very fast, and the structure of the film is also one of a single ineluctable arc of destruction.[13] The race with time as the warnings turn into messages of devastation is almost increased by the interruption of the dark poetry of the choruses, which bear the fewest changes in Hölderlin's verse.

Brecht's adaptation of *Antigone* was significant to his transition back into German culture after being "hounded out of the U.S. by the House Un-American Activities Committee."[14] Waiting for opportunities to be solidified in Berlin, Brecht adapted *Antigone* in the winter of 1947–1948 for a small theater in Chur. Brecht chose *Antigone* from a number of plays suggested by Hans Curjel, who was in charge of the theater, and used Hölderlin's translation at the urging of his stage designer, Caspar Neher. The play was also a favorite of Helene Weigel, for whom the role was a preparation for *Mother Courage and Her Children* and a reintroduction to acting in German after more than a dozen years in exile. Ruth Berlau has asserted that the *Antigone* production might never have been done had there been a role for Weigel in *Mr. Puntila and His Man Matti*, one of Brecht's first projects on his return to Berlin.[15]

Brecht's attitude toward Hölderlin was anything but reverent, as it was for all that is "classical"[16]: "Even if one felt obligated to do something for a work like *Antigone*, we can only do that by letting it do something for us."[17] But he had come to admire some of Hölderlin's work that Hanns Eisler had set to music in California, "chiseling the plaster off it," as Eisler put it.[18] Brecht found Hölderlin's translation the "most forceful and amusing"[19] of those available (Straub also cited the "amusing," ironic quality of Hölderlin and, like Brecht, contrasted him with Goethe and Schiller, who he thought "deadly serious."[20]

Most important to Brecht was Hölderlin's language, as he wrote in his work journal: "Hölderlin's Antigone language would deserve deeper study than I could devote to it this time. It is astonishingly radical."[21] Curjel stresses that Brecht's changes deal with the narrative flow and the nature of fate in the play but that he kept Hölderlin's rhythmic arrangement, even intensifying it in its "mercilessness."[22]

The aspect of Hölderlin's language that he expanded on even as he adapted it is the Swabian folk influence. The examples he cites from Hölderlin include "Und die Sache sei / nicht wie für nichts"; "Denn treulos fängt man *mich* nicht"; and "Hochstädtisch kommt, unstädtisch / zu nichts er, wo das Schöne / mit ihm ist und mit Frechheit."[23]

An example of this kind of language, added by Brecht, is Antigone's "paratactic" retort to Creon's "hypertactic" question about the reasons for her stubbornness: "Halt für ein Beispiel (As an example)."[24] Brecht shortened Hölderlin's longer speeches somewhat and made the stychomythic exchanges more complex, for example, where he has the elders enter into the debate between Haemon and Creon.

*DIE ALTEN:* Doch frißt's viel Kraft, auf grausam Strafen denken.
    *KREON:* Den Pflug zu Boden drücken, daß er pflügt, braucht Kraft.

| | |
|---|---|
| DIE ALTEN: | Doch milde Ordnung, spielend schafft sie viel. |
| KREON: | Der Ordnungen sind viel. Doch: wer ordnet? |
| HÄMON: | Wäre ich auch nicht dein Sohn, ich sagte, du. |
| KREON: | Doch wär's mir auferlegt, müßt ich's auf meine Weis' tun. |
| HÄMON: | Auf deine Weis', doch sei's die richtige Weis'. |
| KREON: | Nicht wissend, was ich weiß, könntest du's nicht wissen. Bist du mir Freund, wie ich auch handeln mag? |
| HÄMON: | Ich wollt, du handeltest, daß ich dir Freund sei. |

(ll. 640–648)[25]

Here we see one result of Brecht's substantial changes in the plot and emphasis of the play. With Hitler and Stalingrad in mind,[26] Brecht has made Creon's motives for the war with Argos into imperialistic ones in search of metal ore. He orders victory celebrations before victory is assured and turns weapons against his own troops to drive them into hopeless battle. One of these, not a traitor but a deserter in the senseless effort, is Antigone's brother Polyneices. Through the series of messengers who arrive on the stage, including Antigone and Haemon but also Tiresias (the seer become acute observer), the messenger from the front, and the maid, Creon is faced with a single series of truths about the disastrous effects of his actions: a threatened rebellion among his own people, the death of his entire family by his unwillingness to hear reason, and ultimately the destruction of the entire city of Thebes as the consequence of his militaristic obsessions.

The "topical" situations introduced by Brecht into the play provide some of its strongest poetry. For instance, there is Antigone's refusal to be swayed by Creon's appeal to *Heimat*, one of the most emotionally charged words in German (to say nothing of New German Cinema):

> Falsch ist's. Erde ist Mühsal. Heimat ist nicht nur
> Erde, noch Haus nur. Nicht, wo einer Schweiß vergoß
> Nicht das Haus, das hilflos dem Feuer entgegensieht
> Nicht, wo er den Nacken gebeugt, nicht das heißt er Heimat.
>
> (ll. 447–450)[27]

Antigone's call to the citizens of the city to resist tyranny illustrates Brecht's further secularization of Sophocles, begun by Hölderlin.[28] Hölderlin had given the specific gods named in the original more general names, indicating people's metaphysical predicament: "Vater der Zeit" for Zeus, for example. Brecht's Antigone urges a return to naming names but this time under the rubric, "The fate of humanity is humanity." Brecht's thinking of Weigel and the pain of exile (a kind of death, like Antigone's) is revealed by the echo between Antigone's rejection of "fate" and a similar rhetorical twist in "The Jewish

Wife." Antigone says at the beginning of her last speech before "fleeing into the grave,"

> Nicht, ich bitt euch, sprecht vom Geschick.
> Das weiß ich. Von dem sprecht
> Der mich hinmacht, schuldlos; dem
> Knüpft ein Geschick!
> (ll. 834–837)[29]

In "The Jewish Wife," performed by Weigel in Paris in 1935 (directed by another exile, the maker of the film *Kuhle Wampe*, Slatan Dudow), Judith Keith rehearses an "honest" reckoning with her non-Jewish husband before she leaves him to flee Nazi Germany. Concluding the last of these "honest" speeches, which she never says to him in person, are the words, "Reden wir nicht von Unglück. Reden wir von Schande" (Let's not talk about misfortune. Let's talk about shame).[30]

The poetry of the two reports of defeat and destruction that seal Creon's downfall is also some of Brecht's most powerful. The speech by the maid, delivered by Libgart Schwarz (Therese in *Class Relations*), is partly adapted from that of Eurydice, whom Brecht has replaced. Instead, the speech is able to add to the compression of events and text, relating all the deaths one after another from the viewpoint of one who lives on. The messenger who tells of the disasters of war does not live on but "is glad to be gone" as he dies at the end of his speech. In this speech, in almost unbearably bitter German verse, are the "explicit parallels" to Stalingrad Brecht had recorded in his "working notes."[31]

> [Bote]
> Und, Herr, das Argosvolk focht abgefeimt.
> Die Weiber fochten und die Kinder fochten.
> Eßkessel, lang schon ohne Eßbares
> Von ausgebrannten Firsten wurden sie mit kochendem
> Wasser auf uns gestürtzt; selbst heilgebliebene Häuser
> In unserm Rücken angefeuert, so als dächte
> Keiner mehr jemals wo zu hausen. Denn zu Schanzzeug
> Und Waffe wurde Hausgerät und Wohnung.
> (ll. 1143–1150)[32]

Brecht here creates a counterpart to Antigone's willingness to die and to side with the enemies of Thebes rather than bend to tyranny; the Argives risk annihilation of all domestic foundations for life in order to ward off the invasion from without.

In the example of three-way dialogue cited above, one can observe a significant departure from Hölderlin, and no doubt Sophocles: the isolation of characters and the power of language *in itself* to embody action is altered to a degree. George Steiner has emphasized the complete separateness of Creon and Antigone, despite their dialogue.[33] Hölderlin's abyss threatens to swallow up both words and characters. This "tödlichfaktisch" power of the word in isolation for Greek drama is emphasized by Hölderlin, in a passage cited by Straub in the *Antigone* program for Berlin: The word "collects what poetry wishes to say, not lyrically or hymnically, but rather it moves in real actions and conflicts [*Zwisten*], like fate itself. But in Greek tragedy this factic word is deadly, it *is* physical death."[34]

The separation of the worlds of Antigone and Creon is in part achieved by their long, lyrical speeches juxtaposed with passages of verbal sparring where each speaks one line at a time. Brecht complicates the effect by shortening the longer speeches and weaving the elders as well as the political plot into the dialogue. The separate "semantic codes" Steiner speaks of become a difference in diction, with Creon preening himself with the elaborate rhetoric of power and Antigone confronting him with harsh, almost vulgar phrases.[35] As in other films, Straub/Huillet have also separated the roles in the diction of the actors: Antigone is played by a young and inexperienced actor, while Creon's role is taken by a "Schmierenschauspieler wie er im Bilderbuch steht" (a picturebook version of a hammy, provincial actor).[36] Werner Rehm's prowess in pulling out the rhetorical stops corresponds to "the professionalism of power."[37]

Brecht's goal here was to increase the flow of the play, whereas the effect of Hölderlin that Straub/Huillet rediscover is one of stasis, where the action exists in the words themselves. This is one of the Greek qualities in their work that Handke so much admires, the shock of their incomparable editing in concert with the text so that "each and every transition of image and sound has the fineness and electricity of the end or beginning of a film."[38] Because each of their compositions has such sovereignty, a cut does indeed bear in it an intimation of the abyss (remembering "narrative space" and the need for some "unreality" in order for editing to be possible).

Straub/Huillet's method for achieving these eye- and ear-opening shocks is quite simple: they rely only on the text to motivate an edit, rather than a "theatrical" perception of action. The result is a shock caused by the simultaneous appearance of speaker and word that can only be achieved by the cinema. In the text, the approach of a character is often anticipated by a few lines from someone on stage. When this is done in the conventional theater, unless there are special lighting or stage effects, the person's approach is visible as it is being described. But in the Straub/Huillet film, the cut only occurs when the approaching figure begins to utter words, so that it seems as if the preceding text, as an incantation, had caused this image to appear. Because the speakers are usually isolated in space as well and do not share the frame, this apparition quality of cinematic space is ominous, even violent. As Giavarini writes, "The millimeter-fine practice of shot-countershot reproduces the agonistic logic of tragic dialogue, a shot-to-shot [*plan à plan*] that rediscovers the exaltation of stichomythia, this verse-to-verse, verse-against-verse. What one sees and hears very well in *Antigone* is that the unresolved opposition is equivalent to a midpoint where life and death merge."[39]

Since the norm in the film is the separateness of the compositions, emphasized by the cuts from character to character, the few gestures within the frame become all the more powerful. The shift of the eyes with a gesture in the text, a special concern of Huillet's direction, also takes on deadly force of the words. The few pans of the camera in the film, which are done with wrenching speed, also have the effect of revealing some horrible result of violence or guilt; Handke compares them to Hitchcock.[40] One pan follows the threat Creon poses to the hesitant messenger as he spits out the line "Gibst du mir Rätsel auf, du durchsichtiger?"[41] while another turns to the arid emptiness of the ground before the chorus as they ponder the "monstrousness" of mankind: "Ungeheuer is viel. Doch nichts / Ungeheurer als der Mensch" (ll. 268–269).[42]

Handke has asserted that the action of the film is all the more powerful, more rhythmic, more filmic, even "hallucinatory," because it is invisible—"threatened by Creon, retold by messengers, commented on by the chorus, prophesied by Tiresias."[43] It exists only in the words.

The gradual effect is a physical one, however, which moves from Brecht back to Hölderlin and the Greeks' belief in the corporeality of language. Steiner emphasizes this "presence" of language for both the Greeks and for Hölderlin's period, since "we speak organic vestiges of myth when we speak."[44] Whereas they were able to synthesize such concepts as truth and beauty, subject and object, Steiner writes, "nothing is more taxing for the modern reader than to seek to recapture the substantive intensity, the almost carnal presentness which these abstract terms carry for the thinkers and poets of the Revolutionary period and nineteenth century."[45] The corporeal and mythical quality of words becomes evident in the "event" of their being spoken. For this reason, Steiner further argues, "we do not experience, except metaphorically, the 'athletic, plastic' (Hölderlin's adjectives) immediacy of physical destruction through an act of speech."[46] In writing about the film *Antigone*, Handke describes how the actors, as a result of the editing and statuesque mise-en-scène, "increase wonderfully...in massivity, physicality, presence, volume, purely through their exaltedly fervent speaking, so that in the end...one has seen an athletic film."[47]

Here again we are reminded of the significance of the actors' physical struggle with the text and the act of breathing as part of the production of the meaning. Straub/Huillet carefully set the caesuras in *Antigone*, and a caesura for them is connected with the act of breathing. Hölderlin furthermore believed, "The caesura makes out of the mere alternation of tones the actual tragic law."[48] The idea that a filmic documentation of an actor's breathing, producing words and meaning, would carry intimations of life and death brings Straub/Huillet also a bit away from Brecht. Indeed, Straub has recently distanced himself somewhat from the Brecht quotation at the outset of *Not Reconciled* that describes acting as *Zitieren* (quoting, citing). In any case, Straub is categorical in his statement, "I do not believe that the so-called alienation [*Verfremdung*] is transferable to the film."[49] He stresses instead that Brecht, like Straub/Huillet, was trying to develop a mechanism to deal with the limitations of his medium. Like their cinematic investigation of the relation of text and speech to space and time, Straub argues, Brecht's theories were "a concrete reflection about a concrete piece of craftwork."[50] John Fuegi has also noted that the late 1940s brought Brecht again somewhat closer to the Aristotelian theater.[51]

By concentrating on the specific manifestations of supposed theoretical precepts, Straub/Huillet are indeed bringing an aspect of Brecht in proximity to the radicality of Hölderlin's translation. Steiner has already asserted such a connection, where the Shwabian *Volksgestus* is concerned: "Coercing German into a word order and pace as close as possible to Sophoclean Greek, Hölderlin gives to the famous 'unwritten laws' . . . a tremendous physical weight. Throughout, Antigone's diction, so elevated in the original, is on the borderline of a rough and populist colloquialism. It invokes ultimate values in a key of almost perfunctory, vulgate speech. The turn of phrase, '*Das eins der sterben muß*'(A creature, an anyone, which must die), is already Brechtian."[52] And Paul de Man, in his discussion of Benjamin and Hölderlin, has even argued that popular speech shares the corporeal metaphor of myth.[53]

Handke cites two examples where the description of unseen, disastrous events takes on the most physical weight. In both cases, near the film's conclusion, Straub/Huillet add to the mise-en-scène a physical signal of this life and death force. When the military messenger speaks, then collapses in death, it is at the border between proscenium and stage. As Giavarini observes, "No crossing [*franchissement*] is possible, nothing but the entering and leaving of the field [*champ*], which reaches an incredible violence in this absoluteness."[54]

The case of the maid telling of the suicides of Antigone and Haemon, with Creon powerless to stop them, is the inverse of this. As she tells of the unseen horrors, her entire body and head are shrouded in a brown garment. But when finally her head is revealed, Handke notes, this "has all the more the effect of an event."[55] With Brecht's transfer of this role from the queen to a humble woman, the messenger of war has a counterpart. But he spoke only of senseless death and defeat and falls forward to die as soon as the words are out. The maid speaks of voluntary deaths, however, with dignity and meaning; the revelation of her face as she speaks recalls the images of the defiant Antigone and rekindles hope.

In his admiration for Straub/Huillet, while ridiculing their politics, Handke values most the "originary" force by which their films redeem the presence of the world. He speaks of his walks home after the films, "which rejuvenate—me and the world."[56] But the mythical force of Antigone does not evoke a world without history, and myth itself is always also a form of history. So the depoliticization of *Antigone* is both false and unnecessary.

A final example of this is found in the comparison of *Antigone* to the myths of origins typified by the American Western film. It is certainly true that Antigone relates such a myth, and Hölderlin saw it as such. For him, Steiner writes, it was "a play set in and representative of a moment of 'national reversal and revolution' [*vaterländische Umkehr*]. The hour is that of a dramatic revaluation of moral values and political power relations."[57]

It is appropriate, then, that *Antigone* be discussed along with such films as Clint Eastwood's *Unforgiven*, which continues the tradition of the mythic West. The *Cahiers du cinéma* did just that with the cover feature in the summer of 1992. Citing Louis Deluc's 1927 article "From Orestes to Rio Jim," Giavarini observes that both Westerns and myths "tell of the origins, the beginnings of civilization, the birth of nations."[58]

Both *Antigone* and *Unforgiven* present a frontier where the laws of civilization have lost their credibility. The borderline between civilization and barbarism traced by the Western is seen in both spatial and linguistic terms. In a Western, this boundary is represented by the boulder behind which a man with a gun might shield himself. In *Antigone*, Giavarini writes, "the break with an old order, the antagonism of two worlds, is marked by the limit represented by the line of stone separating the ancient chorus from the actors." Compared to *Unforgiven*, Giavarini finds *Antigone* the more violent, where words are the weapons, "naked and lacerating." "There is nothing of a resolution."[59]

But Creon's courting of disaster, in Brecht's interpretation of it, is both a transgression of civilization and an extreme of the logic of capitalism. Tiresias sums up the connection in the lines

> Mißwirtschaft schreit nach Großen, findet keine.
> Krieg geht aus sich heraus und bricht das Bein.
> Raub kommt von Raub, und Härte brauchet Härte
> Und mehr braucht mehr und wird am End zu nichts.
> (ll. 1010–1013)[60]

Creon's whipping up of war until it brings destruction home recalls another precedent in film history to which Straub/Huillet often return, D. W. Griffith's *A Corner in Wheat*. Griffith's film has very few camera positions—at the end of the farmer's wheatfield, at the farmer's barn, and theatrically framing the bakery, the grain trading floor, and the office and granaries of the grain speculator. The capitalist, after trying to corner the market and thereby ruining the farmer, is in the end accidentally buried under a flood of that self-same wheat. Like words, the "staff of life" can also become a weapon of retribution.

The temptation to depoliticize *Antigone* gains some support from the idea that such myths of origin attain a resolution. Steiner writes, citing Heidegger, that each classical variant is "a literal homecoming: to the *Lichtung* [the clearing] in which Being made itself manifest."[61] This evocation of origins does have its hopeful, forward-looking, utopian element, since "in myth there is always an 'awaiting' of meaning, messianic or antimessianic."[62]

In addition to the juxtaposition of poetic language, myth, and politics, the placement of the drama in cinematic space is the most striking connection between *Antigone* and *Empedocles*. As we have seen, the progressive experimentation in regard to framing and camera placement (for which Empedocles represents a major step) was a search for the "elect position" from which all characters could be shot.

In Alain Philippon's analysis, this method of surgically dividing up the space rather than creating the illusion of space consists of treating space as something sacred. The space is divided to reveal the actors, but it is not divided according to their points of view. And above all, the space where the camera stands can never be shown: it is the fundamental taboo in the structure. Philippon uses the example of the exchange between Delia and Panthea at the opening of the Empedocles film, where Panthea looks left and is also framed left. Contrary to convention, no "air" is left in the direction of her gaze, with the result that the two women appear not to be looking at each other. "What could have been a classical shot-countershot . . . introduces what is to become the stylistic law of the film: less the arrangement of the characters in space than a veritable *partition*. To each, her/his frame, in an impossible seaming of the narrative fabric and of the spatial continuum."[63]

Both the concept of a sacred space, which was so central to Hölderlin's poetic criticism of the modern world, and the narrative division of space among characters become the "law" of the film *Antigone*. Straub/Huillet here again step into new cinematic territory by constructing the entire film from a single camera position, at two tripod elevations: one at approximately eye level on the ground and one on a platform four meters straight above this point: "That developed out of our earlier films, but we're doing it this way for the first time, and this has never been tried by anyone else."[64] The camera is placed near the border between the stage and theater in the Teatro de Segesta, dating from approximately the same period as Sophocles' play. All the drama and composition of the film are thus based on the options available from these positions: change of lenses and camera motion on its stable footing. The result is again the construction of an artistic tension between narrative and space that returns self-consciously to the powerful discovery of cinematic space in the silent cinema. As Hans Hurch has put it, "Perhaps the Straubs are the last great primitives of a cinema that began with Griffith and Stroheim. Further than that, says Jacques Rivette, we have never come."[65]

As in Empedocles, each character or group of characters has their own space. They are connected only by the work of the camera, never by theatrics until the few dramatic moments of Antigone's dispatch to the tomb or Creon's

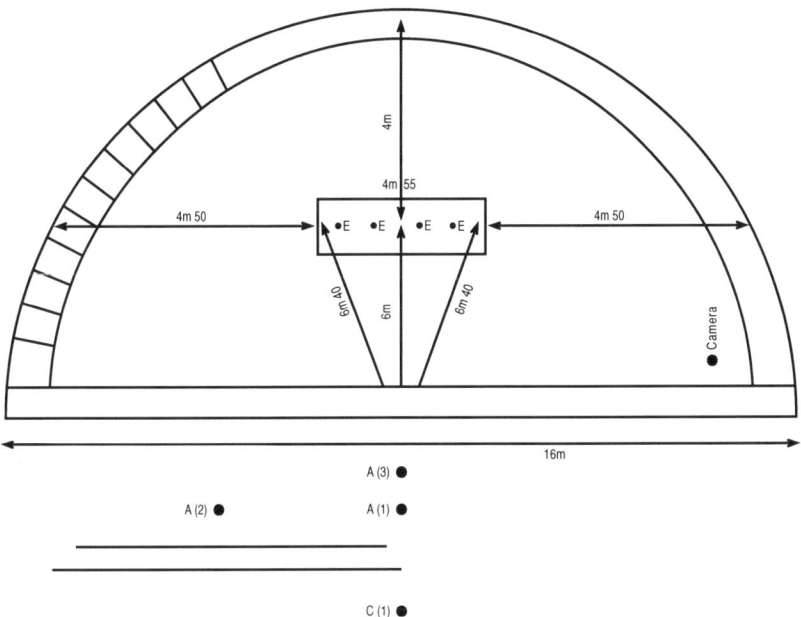

*Antigone*: The single camera position in the Theater of Segesta, with Antigone's positions in each act (A1–A3), that of Creon in Act I (C1), and that of the elders (E). Based on Huillet's screenplay sketch. Graphic: Andrew Reich.

presentation of the sword of war to the elders. The camera divides the theater into three views, somewhat more than 180 degrees, which correspond to the three backdrops that had been used in the stage version. Creon is almost always seen at the left, on the stage portion of the ruin with the landscape behind him. He enters from the left and below, from a space that is not seen. Antigone and allied characters enter from the path onto the stage between the stage and amphitheater, seen from a longer shot with more detail: to the left is a view of some of the landscape; to the right are the huge stones rising at right angles into the amphitheater; straight ahead is a small nettle tree (nearly the only living thing in the film) and to its right a path gently sloping up the hill behind and away from the theater. Between the camera and this edge of the theater is a straight line formed by stones set in the ground, separating the theater/stage area from the "public" area. Creon and Antigone are always to the left of this line; the chorus, representing the citizens of Thebes, are always to its right. On the long stone dividing line an elder places the wine and millet that Antigone is to take to her living grave.

The single point of view across or down onto the "stage" of the ancient theater is also a liberation from the long history of photographic framing and "theatrical" staging in the cinema. Both the narrative implications of per-

Straub/Huillet directing *Antigone* (Lars Studer as the guard). Courtesy Edition Manfred Salzgeber, Berlin.

spective produced by framed still photographs and the "naturalist" sense of distance from conventional film compositions imitate the position of the spectator in the theater that has been the norm since the Renaissance. The proscenium and the photographic frame enclose the film image in a box and confine the viewer to a position corresponding to a theater spectator. In *Antigone*, the camera takes up a position that no spectator in this theater could have, thus placing every shot of the film at an oblique angle to the sight lines suggested by the theater itself. Indeed, only the logo seen at the outset reveals the complete, rounded shape of the theater, and no shot is directed from the camera position to the seating area to inscribe the returned gaze of an implied theatrical spectator. Only the *knowledge* that this is a classical theater identifies the stones behind the elders as risers for seating or the vertical dividing line formed by rocks on the ground as the suggestion of a proscenium.

The result is that each shot has two perspectives: that of the camera and that of the implied spectator in this theater. And the second is entirely imaginary and without visual support from the camera. The result of this separation from visual expectation is to underscore the "thereness" of the space we see: as Straub puts it, the point is not to *create* space but merely to show it.[66]

There are three spaces, then: Creon's, with his own entrance to the theater and the wide majesty of the landscape behind him (in one of the most shocking shots of the film, near the end as the destruction of his obsession with total victory becomes clear, a modern, curving highway bridge is revealed gleaming behind him); the chorus's, which has no open background and no entrance or exit and consists only of the sun-baked stones of the amphitheater, "which attest to the luster of old Thebes but are also an eloquent indication of the fall of Creon and the city";[67] and Antigone's, which is a combination of the two, with a more flexible space for entrance and exit, a more flexible array of compositional elements: mountain, sky, tree, path, gateway, amphitheater, and ground. The most significant part here is played by the nettle tree (French: *micocoulier*), a "thoroughly Mediterranean tree" [Straub] also common in France but now being replaced by plane trees, which are more economically useful.[68] The tree not only frames "those who do not bend to power,"[69] it also provides color and shadow, reveals the movement of light and wind, and frames the view toward the sea, the "hole in the hills" that had attracted the filmmakers in the beginning. "Antigone is not abandoned, as long as this tree is near her," writes Dietmar Schings.[70]

Schings claims the filmmakers see this tree as "one with the stones" that make up the amphitheater,[71] and Handke writes that the wind in its leaves near Antigone evoke the *Verschwindenstod* that she has in common with Empedocles.[72] But Narboni has pointed out that Straub/Huillet films deal not only with those who vanish, or with the ill-buried dead (such as *From the Cloud to the Resistance*, *Fortini/Cani*, or the Mallarmé short), but also with those who live on, the young people in *Empedocles*, but already in *Not Reconciled* (or the Bach and Kafka films).[73] But here, since again "the people" are absent, the tree acts as a mediator between the audience and the extremes of the film's composite parts: the dramatic action, the language, the ancient stones are all quite distant, timeless, and abstract. But this tree is not very old: in photographs of the theater taken in the 1950s, it is not even there. Its time is our time.

But if *Antigone* refers to a myth of origins, Brecht's time reminds us that, for European culture, the destruction wrought by Nazism is the "common crime" that marks the historical border-crossing into identity.[74] After this point, and also in the light of Stalinism, there is no homeland anymore.[75] If one refuses to make propaganda, as Straub asserts an intellectual must, then the "journey homeward" is a journey into exile.[76] Along with reminding of the destructive threat of fascism, Straub also raises doubts about the belief in "progress," especially in Marxism. The working class has been bought, he argues, by the promise of technical progress. Such faith in progress is there in Sophocles' choruses, too, he notes, which "all have the tone of the first chapter of the Communist Manifesto." "For me," Straub goes on, "industrial society is barbarism. For Hölderlin, too, I believe."[77] But once such evil is launched, there is no stopping it without exile to the desert: "For Schoenberg, the idea was nomadism. An absolute nomadism without the possibility of

Jean-Marie Straub and Danièle Huillet, Berlin, 1990. Photo: Ekko von Schwichow.

property."[78] For Straub/Huillet, Moses, Empedocles, and Antigone turn toward a utopian future with no hope of progress and no security of meaning. They face what Steiner calls in *Antigones* "the third, most terrible, alternative: that the gods are unjust or impotent, that mortal man [*sic*], if he insists on acting ethically, according to reason and conscience, must leave the gods 'behind.' "[79] Steiner also quotes Schelling on tragedy in a similar vein: "But man's [*sic*] defeat crystallizes his freedom, the lucid compulsion to act, to act polemically, which determines the substance of the self." "The fate of humanity is humanity."[80]

Here Straub/Huillet have placed alongside each other the utopian force of myth and the "Communist utopia" Straub finds best described in Hölderlin, a description Brecht would not have been capable of: "reach one another your hands / again, give the word and share the goods"—"you are born to the clear day."[81] But the step into this utopia means leaving all constraints of the past behind.

> EMPEDOCLES
> You have thirsted very long for the unusual,
> and as from a sick body the spirit
> of Agrigent longs to leave the old track.
> So venture it! what you have inherited, what you have acquired,
> what your fathers' mouth has told you, taught you,
> law and custom, the names of the ancient gods,
> forget it boldly and raise, as newborn,
> your eyes to godly Nature

Although one would suspect that Brecht also leaned toward the "productivism" of Sophocles and Marx, Straub sees in him a gesture toward doubt when he includes in *Antigone* such lines from Pindar's "Bacchanal Utopia" as "verwüstet / Nicht das Erdreich mit der Gewalt der Hände" (ll. 739–740).[82]

"What intellectuals must introduce is doubt," Straub concludes. And the Brecht text that concludes *Antigone*, which Handke sees as too explicit, can actually be seen as a signal of doubt. For it is a document of Brecht's misgivings not many years after *Antigone*, and after the foundation of the two German states. The mistrust of the powerful has a utopian element equal to the self-destruction of the tragic figures of Empedocles and Antigone. It is "business as usual" that gives real cause for pessimism. As Brecht remarked in 1949, "It's this continuity, this going-on, that makes for destruction."[83] With the unification of Germany has come a reassertion of continuity, to which the film *Antigone* responds. Or can we trust the planet to the care of those who have power?

The ending of the film is another example of the "suspension" of meaning and form that marked Hölderlin's translation: Brecht's warning bears the date 1952, making it already historical, yet the helicopter noise forces us to imagine a contemporary threat as well. But the terms of the Brecht text are reminiscent of Tiresias's last lines, where he bases his dire predictions merely on his witnessing of past events and leaves it to others to "shudder" at the thought of the future: "Und hab ich so zurückgeschaut, und um mich / Schaut ihr voraus und schaudert" (ll. 1014–1015).[84]

The terms of Brecht's description of Tiresias's powers are only "looking back" and "looking around," which in the film's epigraph become "memory" and "imagination"—powers the films of Straub/Huillet strive to activate. The suspension of hope and dread, looking forward and looking back, equalizes the elements of the film one last time to prevent a sense of resolution. While reading the text and hearing the helicopter, the audience is denied the beauty of the images that had gone before, which had projected a future for the world. Hurch describes how the Maid's report embodies this concrete utopia.

> A dress fluttering in the wind, a voice bemoaning the death of an innocent woman, a wall of stone with a broad plain stretching deep below it toward the sea, a hand straightening a veil, sunlight on the sandy ground. It is all there in this wide nonhierarchical ensemble of forms, shaped and unshaped, free and equal under the heavens. Nothing need mean more or stand for something else. It is the anticipatory glimpse of a world where "nothing is done for acquisition." That is the concrete dream that moves this film, and all films of the Straubs to this day.[85]

# 12

# REAL HISTORY AND THE NONEXISTENT SPECTATOR

Brecht, Adorno, and Straub/Huillet

If one is not satisfied with the flippant claim that Straub/Huillet merely have the perverse intention of "making films for intellectuals who hate the movies," the challenge that their films and their artistic stance presents to aesthetic theory must be answered. They do not see the lack of a large audience for their films as the fault of the films themselves but rather as the result of the domination of the media market by products of the culture industry. They do not respond to this by compromising with the conventions that would make their films more accessible, by resorting to an "art-for-art's-sake" posture, or by accepting the ungroundedness of signification posited by postmodernism. They are, however, very critical of filmmakers who have compromised, as they see it, to reach a mass audience, for example, Fassbinder and Wenders. However, they do not criticize Godard's films, even though they might have disagreements, because his work also has difficulty getting distribution ("If all films were like that," perhaps they would even criticize Godard).[1] For their part, Straub/Huillet insist on a documentary accuracy, resolute commitment to a redemptive view of history, and a search for a liberated spectator who could become the historical subject that until now has been obliterated by various modes of oppression. Here is the point at which their work intersects with recent discussions of the contemporary relevance of Brecht, Benjamin, and Adorno. As Andreas Huyssen has put it, "If Adorno's critique of the capitalist culture industry is combined with the theories of Brecht and Benjamin, it is still valid."[2]

Adorno saw no need to develop a specific theory of the art of the cinema, due no doubt to his general disapproval of the film industry. Yet a number of his works do indeed add up to a theoretical position on film that has earned considerable contemporary attention. Miriam Hansen reintroduced Adorno into the discussion of the New German Cinema in 1981 with her discussion of his essay "Transparencies on Film."[3] In this 1966 essay, he did indicate a certain recognition of the critical potential in the Young German Cinema of the time. And Huyssen's essay on Adorno's *In Search of Wagner* shows that this critique of mass culture applies to film as well as other media.[4] Adorno's "emphasis on ruptures and breaks" and his attacks on "the traditional epistemological preference for identity," as Peter U. Hohendahl has written, have also been the basis for a poststructuralist appropriation of Adorno.[5] By working at the points at which Brecht and Adorno conflict, however, I believe Straub/Huillet represent a method by which modernism can continue its formal dialogue with history without sacrificing their utopian hopes to the historical skepticism of postmodernism. As Michael P. Steinberg put it in his essay on Adorno's music theory, "The disappearance of the subject, rather than protect against the hegemony of the strong and the official, threatens the dignity of the persecuted."[6] Straub/Huillet's combination of Adorno's emphasis on the negativity of art and Brecht's political militancy preserves a contemporary connection of the cultural and political struggles of the 1960s and the 1930s.

The materialist self-discipline Straub/Huillet exercise in making films has made it difficult to categorize them among the other filmmakers of the "New German Cinema." Many critics are unable to reconcile Straub/Huillet's professed radical politics with the lack of explicit political messages in their films. Martin Walsh writes, for instance, "Straub/Huillet do, it seems to me, manage to 'suspend meaning,' but that very suspension eliminates the possibility of any didactic political statement—and this perhaps begins to explain the gap between the vision of their films encountered in interviews with them, and an actual experience of certain of their films."[7] This "gap" is inherent to the political honesty of Straub/Huillet's aesthetics. Merely to satisfy the audience that exists would abandon both aesthetic and political progress. Yet even the negation of what is, in aesthetic or political terms, is "a necessary but not sufficient condition." Therefore Straub insists, "I don't believe in the cinema."[8] Joel Rogers summed up the challenge to theory posed by Straub/Huillet as follows:

> When Straub/Huillet "answer" their critics, they make implicit appeal to a certain analysis of capitalist society and the possibilities of autonomous production within it. Without the analysis, the answers remain incoherent, but the articulation of the analysis is not something they themselves have pursued in print. Instead they make films. It would remain a useful project to try to reconstruct a theory contemporary with their film practice. Such a theory would draw heavily from Adorno's aesthetics. As justification it would not try to put Straub/Huillet's work beyond the reach of critical discussion. On the contrary, it would aim to make that discussion more sensible, by specifying what is up for grabs, or what would be required of an immanent critique of their work. The more modest and immediate hope would be to demonstrate the sheer *plausibility* of

what they are doing within argument unbounded by the context of their work alone.[9]

It is not necessarily elitist arrogance, then, that makes the films of Straub/Huillet appear inaccessible but the fact that the context within which they hope to operate has not been created in either politics or criticism. It has been a project of this book to help to generate that forum for discussion, which would necessarily first require that the films themselves be seen by more people. The relative unfamiliarity of most U.S. audiences with Straub/Huillet also has necessarily colored the critical tone of this book: It is difficult to explore and analyze the shortcomings of artists whose strengths have not yet been recognized. This is also a contradiction faced by any critic writing about foreign artists whose work is not part of the commercial system of cultural transmission in the United States. Such critics necessarily replace the public relations effort that for commercial work is done by specialists. The additional dilemma for U.S. critics writing about state-subsidized German art is that they might merely aid in the image building for the German state that such art supports. Straub/Huillet's confrontation of German history and their "Europeanization" of German culture seem to work against this tendency.

A potential context for such a critical discussion is presented by the work of Brecht and Adorno. For Brecht and Adorno and for Straub/Huillet as well, a political and historical context is necessary to any critical or aesthetic discussion. The following will attempt to show the plausibility of creating such a context around Straub/Huillet's films in order to overcome the impasses of "political modernism."

In his testimony before the House Un-American Activities Committee, Brecht declared that he was unaware of any influence he might have had on the American film industry.[10] Brecht's statement need not be taken as a flippant evasion. Indeed, where the dominant narrative cinema is concerned, virtually none of the developments Brecht either expected or desired has appeared. Some techniques derived from Brecht's theater have, however, become merely fashionable, stripped of their original purpose or forcefulness. In some regards, the self-reflexive aspects of the arts were developing long before Brecht began writing, with Baudelaire and the Symbolist poets, for example. By now, calling attention to the "deceptions" of artistic media is most often a superficial cliché. Serious questions of Brecht's relevance will therefore be directed not at his concrete technical suggestions but at his philosophical considerations. Klaus-Detlef Müller writes, "Brecht's innovation in theater is fundamentally philosophical and not—as was often assumed—a formal technique, linked to a political stance and ultimately interchangeable with it."[11] If this can be said of Brecht's main area of activity, it must be even more important to considerations of his direct or indirect relevance to film theory. What is important is not a list of formal criteria for "political art" but thoughts on the nature of theater and film and their relations to society.

Brecht's most important contribution to film theory derives indirectly from his deliberations on epic theater. Before turning to these, however, let us consider the context of the dominant narrative cinema and how its development neutralized Brecht's direct prognosis for the medium. For both Brecht and Benjamin, the most important aspect of the cinema was its unreality. A result of its technical nature, the obvious gap between cinema and "the world" was welcomed by both theorists, who considered it inherent to the medium.[12] In many respects, these descriptions of the nature of the medium are valid enough, but they become paradoxical when it comes to a positive, liberating potential. They no doubt arise from the same attraction the early cinema holds for the avant-garde. But the actual development of the cinema goes directly against the hopes that Brecht and Benjamin had for it.

Of the two, Benjamin was the more open to the fact that film would be a part of a transformation of the function of art in society. His deliberations consider the changes that might be brought about by the very nature of the new, mechanically reproduced art, while Brecht seems more inclined to try to master the new medium to further his previous intentions in theater. Thus we find Brecht unable to work creatively in the cinema. He saw parallels between the technical possibilities of cinema and his ideas of epic theater but was unable to concretely unite the two. Hence his famous "fundamental reproach" against the cinema.[13]

There are identifiable reasons for this. The initial hopes Brecht had for the cinema were based on its newness, its unreality. In the "Dreigroschenprozess," he asserts that the bourgeois worldview based on the perspective of the individual is overthrown by the film. Motivation does not come from the "character" or the "inner life" of persons, but instead, people are seen from the outside. Brecht's wishful thinking led him to believe that this evaluative, concrete, didactic way of looking at reality (see Benjamin as well) would be put to use by the masses, who measure things by their practicality for the real world. Furthermore, Brecht was optimistic about the unreality of film images. "Precisely because it represents reality with such an abstract effect, it is well suited to confrontations with reality."[14] Burkhardt Lindner also attributes Brecht's concept of the "social gestus" in epic theater to the photographic reproduction of reality. The abstract isolation of individual human relationships and attitudes was thought to reveal their broad social and historical significance.[15] Brecht's mistake here is to assume that this abstract quality and the resulting critical view of reality via art were inherent in film and photography. He concludes, "In reality, film requires external action and nothing introspectively psychological. And in this tendency, capitalism has a thoroughly revolutionary effect, in that it multiplies, organizes and automates certain needs on a mass scale."[16]

The actual development of cinema has sought to overcome the technical newness of film in favor of novelistic realism. Exactly the psychologizing individual perspective that Brecht detested in the bourgeois novel has triumphed in the film as in the culture industry in general. Brecht polemicized against Thomas Mann's approach to film as a way of revitalizing the novel, insisting that the novel was dead and had nothing to do with film: "Thus one uses every new (or to be newly defined) thing to support the old, by using the old as the basis of the definition."[17] But Brecht makes the same mistake himself in looking to film for solutions to problems of the theater. More important, the battle to keep film from serving the needs of the supposedly moribund bourgeois novel was lost long ago. As Gidal has asserted, the realist novel lives on today largely in the disguise of the commercial narrative cinema.

The political and social basis for the survival of this nineteenth-century bourgeois art form need not be dwelled on here. Its formal aesthetic basis, however, precisely in technical areas noted by Brecht and Benjamin, is of great interest. The so-called realist novel has always had more of a prescriptive than a descriptive relation to the reality of the middle class it addressed. In a sense, the "unreality" of the world seen on film is no greater than the artifices of nineteenth-century realism; it is merely technically different. The function of this novelistic world in legitimating bourgeois ideology has proved superior to the liberating potential of new media. One reason for this is that ideology derives its force from imaginary constructs rather than from the "reality" Brecht expected the masses to prefer. As Heath put it, "In ideology, it is said, is represented the imaginary relation of individuals to the real relations in which they live."[18] Brecht proclaimed that aesthetics must be derived from the needs of the class struggle, but he did not sufficiently consider that the ruling class would follow the same precept. The legitimation of bourgeois ideology begins with the very same "unreality" in cinema that Brecht saw but uses it to strengthen, rather than reveal, the power of its novelistic representations of imaginary social relations.

Brecht's most significant misconception about film and photography in general is the assumption that the stasis[19] and unreality of the image were contradictory to bourgeois narrative forms. Eisler and Adorno explained the function of film music to contain this disruptive potential.[20] And Heath has maintained that the editing devices that make it possible to imitate the individual perspective of novelistic narrative are actually based on the "partial unreality of the film picture." As Heath goes on to note in this context, "If film photographs gave a very strong spatial impression, montage probably would be impossible."[21] Thus the imaginary social relations of the novel and its readers are matched by an imaginary spatial relation of the viewer to the film. The energy required of the spectator to maintain this relation to the film, despite and because of its unreality, in turn has fundamental psychological and ideological relevance. Heath has described the process from both points of view. Regarding the film's effect on the viewer, Heath writes, "In its movement, its framings, its cuts, its intermittencies, the film ceaselessly poses an absence, a lack, which is ceaselessly recaptured, for—one needs to be able to say 'forin'—the film, the process binding the spectator as subject in the realization of the film's space."[22] To state the dilemma most extremely, one could say that even Brecht's Verfremdungs-Effekt could be used formally for reactionary purposes, repelling a spectator at certain points only to strengthen the desire for a "meaning" that can reunite the work. Heath also asserts that the narrative strategies of classical cinema are not as transparent as to render the spectator passive through ignorance of the production of the work. It would be more accurate to say that, rather than a passive consumer, the spectator becomes a willing accomplice in the artifice of the narrative film. As Heath puts it, "Classical cinema does not efface the signs of production, it contains them."[23]

Here we can relate aesthetic effectiveness to the essential genius of the culture industry. Since capitalism cannot meet the "real" needs of the masses (this even implies that one knows they have real needs), or rather, since the masses must not be allowed to unpredictably discover or express their needs, the culture industry creates needs that it is able to satisfy. The unreality, incompleteness, motion, confusion, the "lack" exists in cinema both in its technical makeup and its often sensational (threatening) content. Yet the unity and aesthetic distance of each film and the serene existence of the artistic institution itself automatically neutralize these internal threats or deficiencies, while binding the spectator to a society that contains these dynamics.

Thus the insufficiency of art in the face of reality (as Brecht might see it) allows it to be used to imply another reality to which it is sufficient. The preservation of the social fabric rests on the existence of this social fabric (a sense of community) in the imagination—the definition of ideology. The bourgeois individual, as imagined in the realist novel, is still imagined as the basis for narrative cinema and "real" society. Heath must here be quoted at length on the social significance of this process in the institutions of art.

> "When the bourgeoisie had to find something else besides painting and the novel to disguise the real to the masses, to invent, that is, the ideology of the new mass communications, its name was the photograph." Godard's remark serves to emphasize this at least: the film is developed and exploited from the photograph as an alternative and successor to the novel for the production-reproduction of the *novelistic*; the novelistic is the ideological category of the narrative elaborated in the film, as it is of that in the novel. The title of the novelistic is *Family Romance* (or *Family Plot*, as the recent Hitchcock film would have it); the problem it addresses is that of the definition of forms of individual meaning within the limits of existing social representations and their determining social relations, the provision and maintenance of fictions of the individual; the historical reality it

encounters [is] a permanent crisis of identity that must be permanently resolved by remembering the history of the individual-subject. Narrative lays out—lays down as law—a film memory from the novelistic as the re-imaging of the individual as subject, the very representation of identity as the coherence of a past safely negotiated and reappropriated.[24]

Brecht was right about this much: real history, real individual and class interests would have destroyed capitalism by now. Herbert Marcuse asserted that all history is revolutionary.[25] But the history of the individual, which legitimates the existing social order, is a fabricated history. The spectators of the narrative film share in a memory, thus resolving the crisis of identity of the individual and of a society of individuals. The presence/absence ambivalence in film representation allows even the most threatening content to become part of a nonthreatening past, which has been conquered by the (imaginary) community that shares this past. Thus, to expect reality in film, or a confrontation with reality via the film, ignores the very function of conventional narrative. Its unreal representation of social relations defines them in reality and places the spectator within them. A spectator who could exist within these relations yet compare them to another "reality" is a social contradiction.

Here the dilemma of Brecht's own aesthetics reappears. We have already noted that an audience or a "historical subject" adequate to his innovations did not exist. The fact is that it cannot exist, for if it did, the premise of the aesthetics would invalidate itself. A sense of this resides in Brecht's remark that his ideal audience would be Karl Marx, or at least Marxists.[26] Adorno applies the phrase, "preaching to the saved."[27] However, the technical innovations Brecht achieved are based on the bourgeois traditions that also do not at present belong to the intended audience. Brecht's audience was and is imaginary.

Furthermore, the above description of the function of the unreal aspect of film leads to the conclusion that any "audience" is imaginary. The work of art, by implying a collective history (and this can be done by means of Heath's "novelistic" or merely by the use of language or music, as Benjamin, Eisler, and Adorno have noted), necessarily says "We."[28] Through the culture industry, this aspect becomes the tool of ideology.

Here we can begin to see possibilities for liberating art from servitude to ideology and for pointing toward social liberation beyond the theories of Brecht and Adorno. The ideological function of art lies not in its content but in its constitution of the individual. The ideological function cannot be transformed by replacing the content of art with a rival ideology but only by transforming the relation of the work of art to its subject.

Adorno points the way with his concept of the "authentic" work of art. Such a work can have none other than a negative relation to reality, and its separation from reality is absolute. Otherwise it would necessarily become a tool of ideology. Art can desire neither action nor communication: "The criticism practiced a priori by art is criticism of activity as the cryptogram of domination. By its very form, praxis tends toward that which its goal would be to abolish."[29] And further, "That works renounce communication is a necessary but by no means sufficient condition of their nonideological nature. The central criterion is the power of expression. [ . . . ] In expression they expose themselves as a social wound."[30] In precisely this withdrawal from reality, Adorno sees the utopian, liberating aspect of art. By insisting on its negation of things-as-they-are, art proves the possibility that things can be changed. Yet it does not contradict itself by "representing" that change, because this would merely destroy the utopian future by repeating the violence of the past. The condemnation of the world in art is inherent and absolute. The similarity of the world and the "novelistic" dictates that the world must remain as it is, or the promise of the culture industry cannot be fulfilled. For Adorno, the gap between art and the world revives the possibility of change in the world; and this possibility arises from a non-nostalgic relation to the past.

> Ultimately mimesis would be reversed; in a sublimated sense, reality should imitate works of art. But the fact that works of art exist indicates that nonbeing could be. The reality of works of art testifies to the possibility of the possible. What is implied by the desire in works of art—the reality of that which is not—is transformed for it into remembrance. In it are fused what is, as past (*Gewesenes*), and nonbeing, because the past is no more. Since the Platonic Anamnesis, the not-yet-being has been dreamed of in remembrance, which alone concretizes utopia without betraying it into Being.[31]

This is indeed the crucial description of the liberating potential of art, but it, too, must be overcome. Otherwise, it applies to the art that Heath describes as the novelistic as well as to any other, since such art affirms society by negating it. It uses the very same utopian impulse to provide a tenuous social system with the imaginary past it needs to legitimate its future. Adorno indeed appears too neutral in his description of just this process: "The process which every work of art completes within itself becomes a model of possible practice affecting society as well, a model in which something like a subject-community [*Gesamtsubjekt*] constitutes itself."[32] This is very similar to the process of "the reimagining of the individual as subject" which Heath describes. The "model of possible practice" as Adorno describes it could very well be an affirmative one; it might pose as a utopian possibility the survival of the existing system of domination. Since this system is so unstable that it negates itself, even negative works of art could conceivably preserve it through their utopian force.

Adorno's application of his insights begins to contradict itself in the following: "All works of art, including affirmative ones, are a priori polemical. The idea of a conservative work of art is self-contradictory. Inasmuch as they emphatically divorce themselves from the empirical world, their Other, they proclaim that this world itself should be altered, [are] unconscious schemes for its transformation."[33] Thus Adorno would like to see both affirmative and negative works of art as utopian. Yet the culture industry is perfectly capable of seducing both impulses to serve its ideological purposes. Negative art, by proving that the possible is possible, may merely channel the despair already generated by "empirical reality." But if affirmative art presents an image that is at odds with the bleakness of empirical reality, that image provides no proof that empirical reality could be changed to measure up to it. There is in this no concrete reason to believe that this separation will ever be overcome, or that empirical reality will even enter consciousness. The affirmation, like the negation, requires a renunciation of practical intervention. Adorno finally seems to vacillate between an unsubstantiated optimism about the inherent revolutionary nature of art and the conclusion that art, to remain true to itself, must make its self-definition narrower and narrower, so that it merely observes the decline of civilization in silent protest.

Another application of Adorno's theoretical insights is necessary to reunite his definition of artistic utopia with forces for social transformation existing outside of art. It is this latter that Adorno neglected. Having postulated the survival and viability of art in its separation from reality, he seemed to cease to take the dynamic potential of reality seriously. Thus he writes, "Art respects the masses by confronting them as that which they could be, instead of conforming to them in their degraded state."[34] As in the demand that reality should imitate art, Adorno seems to have concluded that not only does the culture industry deflect or absorb potential for change but it has also obliterated it completely. Of the two separate realms, art and reality, only in art can progress be imagined. Thus Lindner criticizes Critical Theory in general for confusing technical and economic-political domination. Critical Theory assumes that the need for a culture industry to manage impulses for change has disappeared and that the culture industry has become what the people want. Lindner sees the Critical Theorists' analysis of society as too cynical in its assumption that rational principles of technical domination have become so all-pervasive as to need legitimation no longer.

> Culture industry "refers to the standardization of the thing itself" and thereby to its technical characteristics. The basic structure of the culture industry—the relationship of tangible details to the totalitarian whole—is described in terms such as "cataloging, classification, quantification, interchangeability, administration, stereotyping." The relationship between the blind masses and central steering is characterized as technical rationality. The masses respond to the "omnipresence of stereotypes" with blind worship of technology. The pleasure of "being an appendage of the machinery" apparently hardly needs any content which legitimizes domination any longer. Civilization, which began as "self-preservation" against powerful natural necessities, continually increases its

rationality in the form of "domination of nature." Domination of nature includes domination of people. The total transformation of literally every aspect of existence into a realm of means to an end leads to the liquidation of the subject which is to make use of them.[35]

These terms, which Lindner has drawn from Adorno and Max Horkheimer, do indeed imply that social reality, the "subject," no longer offers any resistance to the culture industry. Therefore, the culture industry is not seen as an instrument of domination of some segments of humanity by others or as a means of holding a system together which the "real needs" of humanity threaten to break apart. Humanity no longer has "real needs" according to this technological scheme, and political-economic oppression is abolished, not merely hidden, in the oppression of consciousness.

An alternative to this one-dimensional view of the culture industry can be found in Adorno's own description of utopia in art but with a less abstract application than he gives it. After all, even Adorno did speak of "what the masses could be" as one dimension of art. The key aspects of this utopian future, where the masses are concerned, lie in two elements that have constantly resurfaced in these investigations: these are the elements of time (history, memory, a past) and of the subject, that nexus of social relations that exist in and through time, history, language, and art. Thus, as we have seen, Straub/Huillet, Hölderlin, and Benjamin push language and history to the borders where it threatens to cease even to be human.

Brecht, too, defines the subject as demanding a new relation between theater and time or process.

> Today, when the human being must be conceived as "the ensemble of all social relations," the epic form is the only one which can grasp those processes that serve drama as the material for a comprehensive worldview. The individual human being, too—the flesh-and-blood human being—is only tangible through the processes in which and as a result of which it exists. The new drama must methodologically incorporate the "experiment" into its form. It must be able to use connections in all directions; it must make use of statics; it will have a tension reigning between its individual parts, mutually charging them.[36]

If this quotation is compared to Heath's description of the "novelistic" in cinema, we see the shift that has taken place, away from Brecht's intentions. Brecht wrote of the human being in the work of art as "only tangible through the processes in which and as a result of which it exists." The spectator, as subject, is meant to evaluate (in this "experiment") both the human being and the social processes. According to Heath, the social processes are presented in the film with the spectator as their point of unification. Rather than the static quality Brecht sought (and expected cinema to possess) in order to permit reflection, the cinema's images, with their fragmentations and constant motion, uncontrollable from beginning to end, bring about "the holding of the spectator as the unifying position—the subject—of their relation in time."[37]

Just as the fixed point of the subject/spectator is necessary to make sense of the film (and to affirm its social relations), so also is the subject the fixed point that makes sense of the fragmentations and fabrications of the culture industry. The social relations postulated by ideology, the collective past in which they exist, are imaginary, artificial. It does not logically follow, however, that real social relations, a real past, do not exist. Instead, it seems the purpose of ideology to obscure them, to rob them of their disruptive force.

Let us assume for a moment that both a "real past" and a real "historical subject" might exist apart from the imaginary ones that legitimate the culture industry. How might they relate to art? As Adorno described it, the work of art as Other merges with pastness, that which is no longer, to prove the reality of that which does not (yet) exist: utopia. This is similar to the manipulative function of the imaginary past of the novelistic, which forges an artificial community. But what if the Other were a link with a real past that is denied its future expression by the culture industry? This is the utopian aspect of Brecht's epic theater.

The cinema's unreality poses an incompleteness that demands that a subject fill it in by accepting an affirmative position within its social relations. But historical reality, which is Brecht's aesthetic material, is also incomplete and postulates a future subject that can claim it as its own past. Müller writes of Brecht's concept of the work of art, "It takes on a decidedly new dimension: its completion lies outside itself in a future reality. Contemporary reality, the work of art, and future reality form a whole. Therefore, the work of art is necessarily incomplete, since the not-yet-being (to borrow a term from Ernst Bloch) is a part of its existence."[38] Here we are not far from Hölderlin and Benjamin's "the task of the translator," but Adorno notes this utopian strain even in Brecht's work. Thus he repeatedly comes back to Brecht as an authentic-artist-in-spite-of-himself, while denying the direct relation of Brecht's work to reality. Brecht's failure in his commitment to change reality becomes for Adorno a stronger critique of reality than any success: "In his plays, the theses took on an entirely different function than their content intended. They became constitutive, molded the drama into an anti-illusionist one, and contributed to the collapse of its unity and meaning."[39] Here is the other side of the coin. Where cinema resorts to unreality and fragmentation to captivate a real addressee, Brecht's epic theater insisted on reality and its fragmentation even though this meant losing its addressee. Rather than an imaginary subject-community (Gesamtsubjekt) in the present, Brecht's work—like the cinema of Straub/Huillet—points toward a real transformation in the future.

This potential in Brecht's theory and practice rests on a concept of the separation of art and reality similar to Adorno's—but on a more diversified, concrete inclusion of reality as a contributing element. To simplify the culture industry as described by Critical Theory as well as Heath's more psychoanalytic description of aesthetic manipulation, one would say that the working class that Brecht sought to address simply does not exist. It does not constitute a historical subject capable of responding to a Marxist critique of political economy or to sophisticated transformations of bourgeois art forms. The working class clearly does not exist today as the subject of the imaginary social relations presented by the culture industry. Nevertheless, there is reason to assert that the working class does indeed exist, but merely in reality, not in imagination. Its real existence has been purged from history, so that it cannot even remember itself.

Adorno does not pursue the importance of history to imply resistance on the part of the subject, but it is implicit in his description of concrete utopia and of the objective potential for resistance in *Composing for the Films*. Imaginary pastness is the power behind the social cohesion of the culture industry. But real pastness—the real history of real subjects—preserves the artistic yearning for that which does not yet exist: a future for those very subjects.

One must decide whether or not the reality of capitalist society would indeed destroy itself if only imagination could consent to it. If technical rationality truly means capitalism is no longer self-destructive, then these arguments are foundationless. But real human suffering and oppression, a collective past that could point toward a different future, persists as a basis for art, even for Adorno. The final sentence of his *Aesthetic Theory* is, "But what kind of history writing would art be if it were to shake off the memory of accumulated suffering."[40] Brecht's utopian impulse retains its social basis by anchoring itself in "real" history, that is, history as subject to analysis of social processes that would lead to revolution if only a historical subject were there to imagine it. Like Adorno, Brecht recognizes that the role of art is only to record (imagine) the past sufferings that prepare the way for a future that cannot be imagined. Even the present is a part of this "historicization." Adorno separates art and reality; Brecht unites art and past reality (which, as Adorno says, is thus nonbeing) while also refusing to include future reality or the future subject that is its necessary condition. The material of art is reality; its implications are utopian. Müller describes the utopian aspect of this historical materialism.

> *Verfremdung* in a strict sense implies familiarity and thus finds its true materials in the present. But since Verfremdung and historicizations are interchangeable terms, a point of view is necessary which can make the structure of the present visible as a historical phenomenon. This point of view must lie "further ahead in developments." This means that Verfremdung is undertaken from the basis of the recognized meaning of history, that is, from utopia. Utopia provides for the present what historically later periods can give to every phase of history: the consideration of phenomena as past, insight into their interrelationships from a

historical distance. By implication, of course, this means no less than a transformation of the present.[41]

Even if one rejects the "recognized meaning of history" as a final possibility, this entire description matches Adorno's claim for art of the power to imagine the world other than it is. This indeed revolutionizes the present, "concretizing utopia without betraying it into being."

This aesthetic humility does not assert the uselessness of socioeconomic or historical analysis. But such activities belong to the world as it is, not as it might be. They can have no direct relationship to revolutionary reality, for, as Fortini wrote, "revolutionary reality, when it emerges, will be such as to render even the most imaginative models unrecognizable."[42]

Not only would revolution render limited intellectual speculation irrelevant, it would also rearrange the structures and processes of all of history retroactively through the shift of power. Thus, inversely, the aesthetic reclaiming of history postulates such a shift of power to a different historical subject. Benjamin describes the radical significance of seizing a history to constitute a revolutionary force.

> The French Revolution viewed itself as Rome reincarnate. It evoked ancient Rome the way fashion evokes costumes of the past. Fashion has a flair for the topical, no matter where it stirs in the thickets of long ago; it is a tiger's leap into the past. This jump, however, takes place in an arena where the ruling class gives the commands. The same leap in the open air of history is the dialectical one, which is how Marx understood the revolution.[43]

In light of the foregoing analysis, one might assert that what passes for "Brechtian" in political art—especially the cinema of political modernism—has more in common with Adorno than with Brecht. In stressing the political purpose of exclusively formal innovation without linking it to the frustrated aspirations of real people and real history, such an approach implies with Adorno that reality is too thoroughly administered to offer any hope. Politics in art becomes an alibi, a substitute for politics lacking in reality. As Colin MacCabe put it in the 1970s, "That the breaking of the imaginary relation between text and viewer is the first prerequisite of political questions in art has, I would hold, been evident since Brecht. That the breaking of the imaginary relationship can constitute a political goal in itself is the ultra-leftist fantasy of the surrealists and of much of the avant-garde work now being undertaken in the cinema."[44] Indeed, there is a tendency to hold up such "political" art as almost a moral imperative. Since reality is frustrating, the only possible expression of freedom is self-denial in art as well. Hence a certain moralistic tone is inescapable in the way Walsh cites Straub as claiming that viewers who cannot watch the long traveling shots from within an automobile in *History*

*Lessons*, who cannot "engage with activity in the street, cannot have an advanced political position."[45] Instead of moralistically claiming such involvement as a prerequisite for "an advanced political position," one might see the relationship Straub outlines as merely descriptive. The systematic manipulation of viewers as subjects for novelistic reality keeps them from seeing their own reality, their own history. Straub/Huillet films are not an indictment of viewers whose viewing habits are otherwise but an offer of an alternative that points to potential for freedom in other aspects as well—the tiger's "leap" under the clear sky of history.

Peter Gidal criticizes Straub/Huillet from just such an ultra-leftist point of view. For him, the subversion of traditional narrative in their films is not radical enough. Rather than dwell on the location of the spectator in relation to the film, which is the main aesthetic and utopian thrust of these films, Gidal sees a political imperative in the complete overthrow of representation. For him, the use of black leader to call attention to deletions is a false claim of equivalency. "Black leader = emptiness" is just as odious to him, apparently, as the devices of representing the bourgeois individual personality. The filmic unity of the works also strikes Gidal as a mystification. "The point is," he writes, "that the mystification of procedures into a coherent line, into a rightness about sound, image, continuity, uninterrupted by the material (film), is in fact a basic illusionist project."[46] Furthermore, he sees in the films an "unseen center, . . . a persecuted character. The persecuted outsider is never far from the center of thought. The romantic, mystical artist as outsider, communist, Jew, may be the figure of Jean-Marie Straub, judging by the strongly identificatory manner in which it is set up. This may be the central problem as well, the inability of the films to produce themselves as material operations. They always end up as stories."[47] He concludes as well that this positing of a persecuted character ends up confirming the "patriarchal male [Hegelian] subject."[48] But in her essay on the relevance of Hegel to psychoanalytic film criticism and the Left, Julia Kristeva stressed a point made evident again and again in Straub/Huillet films: "the fact that these aesthetic forms constitute, along with the history of religions, a different series from that of the forms of the state and the juridical superstructures."[49] But to preserve some political and aesthetic purity in art, it is not enough to offer alternative structures to the "stories" that define and imprison the viewer as subject. Instead, art can propose a return to the fundamental purpose of aesthetic innovation: to rediscover reality that has been obscured by forms based on manipulation. Schoenberg, for instance, was irritated by those who refused to see serial composition as composition, as more freedom for artistic expression, not less. Hölderlin found joy in sorrow and discovered what was his own in the German language by exploring its foreignness.

At some point, the political avant-garde or political modernism implies an acceptance of capitalism's technical rationality of progress and reserves theory and culture to the work of "experts." A certain respect for the audience, implied even by Adorno, is lacking here. Authentic art does not presume to offer experience that is useful in the context of needs generated by the culture industry, but it does attempt to offer what might be useful if the future subject implied by its formal and historical development were to arrive, if the masses became "what they could be." This is why Straub/Huillet, for all their formal radicality, insist that they are working in the popular tradition of cinema, rather than in a marginal, avant-garde subcategory for initiates. Serge Daney has described the uniqueness and difficulty of their stance.

> With their well-oiled war machine, their sacred egoism, their fine vitality, too, and the clear ideas they have concerning their work, the Straubs are probably the last to create a cinema for loners that can nevertheless be brought into regular theaters. They are squarely in cinema and I would have given up on them long ago with their garbled political ideas, had I not understood that they were the last great film-makers of the history of modern cinema, perhaps of the history of cinema, period. I harbor no illusions about the receptability of their work; they set out to teach people something and people will always hate them for that.[50]

But despite the public's resistance, Straub/Huillet have not withdrawn into the political self-protection in such aesthetic dogmatism, an inability to accept that reality can and will change, perhaps positively, without an artist's design. Instead, they turn toward the world to find the traces of such change. Their belief in change rather than aesthetic puritanism echoes Brecht's argument that artistic self-obsession can actually hinder any frightening changes.

> The world is thus nailed up with barricades for many leftist writers. The barricade hides their opponents from them, and protects the opponents more than themselves. The world then consists of two worlds, distant from each other, not within one another. So a large number of people are petty-bourgeois and petty-bourgeois are just nothing but petty-bourgeois, belonging to an unchanging, natural category. [ ... ] Contempt protects them from all demands. So, too, industry is soulless and the courts unjust, as the trees are green, and it would seem more reasonable for industry to be soulless than for us therefore to criticize it. [ ... ] The commodity character of literature increases and the laws of competition force our writers always to produce something new, nothing familiar or already forgotten. An injustice, getting on in years, thus remains unchallenged; a great outrage becomes after two weeks a minor irregularity; and capitalism, which is after all only "material," becomes dull material, yesterday's news.[51]

The fear behind these obsessions, whether they are with static conceptions of political art, separate from politics, or with compulsory newness in form, regardless of real social needs, is seen by both Fortini and Adorno. It is the fear of death. If art dares to want something real, if it dares to express a yearning based on real history or the artist's real involvement with the materials of art and life, it runs the risk of getting what it wants. People naturally resist art that makes them uncomfortable, since, as Eisler and Adorno put it, "The fact that music is alien to industrious people reveals their alienation in regard to one another."[52] The end of this alienation would mean a kind of death: the end of the world as we know it. The figures of Empedocles and Antigone embody this utopian leap. For art to dare to assert an identity in this context is to face the necessity of its extinction.

# Notes

### Introduction

1. On a letter accusing the film *Machorka-Muff* of insulting the nation and the city, Straub added the annotation, "We love this nation and the city of Bonn." Cited in Reinhold Rauh, ed., *Machorka-Muff: Jean-Marie Straubs und Danièle Huillets Verfilmung einer Satire von Heinrich Böll* (Münster: MAKS, 1988), 67. Unless otherwise noted, all translations are my own.

2. Vincent Nordon also speaks of a "nomadic gaze": "Violence et passion (Straub, encore)," *Ça cinéma* 9 (1976):26.

3. Jean-Claude Bonnet, "Trois Cinéastes du texte," *Cinématographe* 31 (October 1977):2–6.

4. See the special issue on Alexander Kluge, *October* 46 (Fall 1988), and Raymond Bellour and Mary Lea Bandy, eds., *Jean-Luc Godard: Son + Image, 1979–1991* (New York: Museum of Modern Art, 1992).

5. Helmut Färber, "Im Anschluß an das Protokoll der *Chronik der Anna Magdalena Bach*," *Filmkritik* 10 (1966):695–703.

6. "Enretien avec Jean-Marie Straub et Danièle Huillet," in *Der Tod des Empedokles/La mort d'Empédocle*, ed. Jacques Déniel and Dominique Païni (Dunkerque: Studio 43/Paris: DOPA Films/Ecole régionale des beaux-arts, 1987), 41.

7. Cited in Sylvia Harvey, *May '68 and Film Culture* (London: British Film Institute, 1978), 97.

8. Gilles Deleuze, *Cinema 2: The Time-Image,* trans. Hugh Tomlinson and Robert Galeta (Minneapolis: University of Minnesota Press, 1989), 215–216.

9. Thomas Elsaesser, *New German Cinema: A History* (New Brunswick: Rutgers University Press, 1989); Anton Kaes, *From Hitler to Heimat: The Return of History as Film* (Cambridge: Harvard University Press, 1989) [revised, translated version of *Deutschlandbilder. Die Wiederkehr der Geschichte als Film* (Munich: edition text und

kritik, 1987)]; Eric L. Santner, *Stranded Objects: Mourning, Memory, and Film in Postwar Germany* (Ithaca: Cornell University Press, 1990).

**Chapter 1. Straub/Huillet and the Cinema: Tradition and Avant-garde**

1. *Filmkritik* 1 (1977): inside front cover, n.p.
2. Walter Benjamin, *One-Way Street and Other Writings*, trans. Edmund Jephcott and Kingsley Shorter (London: NLB, 1979), 67; excerpted in *Film* (March 1956):137. Bitomsky, referring here to *Othon*, is cited by Karsten Witte, "*Moses und Aron* von Straub/Huillet," in *Im Kino. Texte vom Sehen und Hören* (Frankfurt am Main: Fischer, 1985), 124.
3. Hanns Eisler, *Composing for the Films* (New York: Oxford University Press, 1947), 120–121. Co-authored by Theodor W. Adorno, who is not cited in this edition.
4. Ibid., 36.
5. See Bertolt Brecht, "Der Dreigroschenprozeß," in *Versuche 1–12* (Berlin: Suhrkamp, 1958), 280–281; and Eisler, *Composing*, 121.
6. Richard Roud, *Jean-Marie Straub* (London: Secker and Warburg/British Film Institute, 1971; New York: Viking, 1972), 15; Peter W. Jansen and Wolfram Schütte, eds., *Herzog/Kluge/Straub* (Munich: Carl Hanser Verlag, 1976), 241, cited hereafter as *HKS*.
7. Michael Klier, *Porträts der Filmemacher: Jean-Marie Straub*, WDR, Cologne, 1970. Film.
8. *HKS*, 241; "Erstes Lexikon des Jungen Deutschen Films," *Filmkritik* 1 (1966): 44–48.
9. See Roy Armes, "Jean-Marie Straub: Strict Counterpoint," in *The Ambiguous Image* (London: Secker and Warburg, 1976), 208–215; and Roud, *Jean-Marie Straub*, esp. 7–27.
10. "Lexikon," 47.
11. Ibid.
12. "Antigone nue," *Libération*, 1 September 1992.
13. Helge Heberle and Monika Funke Stern, "Das Feuer im Innern des Berges" [Interview with Danièle Huillet], *Frauen und Film* 32 (June 1982):4–12.
14. Ibid., 6.
15. Ibid., 5–7.
16. Ibid., 5.
17. Ibid.
18. Ibid., 9.
19. Ibid., 10.
20. Ibid., 12.
21. Ibid., 11, 12.
22. Gertrud Koch, "Ex-Changing the Gaze: Re-Visioning Feminist Film Theory," *New German Critique* 34 (Winter 1985):140–141.
23. Elin Diamond, "Brechtian Theory/Feminist Theory: Toward a Gestic Feminist Criticism," *TDR/The Drama Review* 32 (1988):82–94.
24. Koch, "Ex-Changing," 142.
25. Teresa de Lauretis, *Alice Doesn't: Feminism, Semiotics, Cinema* (Bloomington: Indiana University Press, 1984), 60.

26. *HKS*, 241–242.
27. Heberle and Stern, "Feuer im Innern des Berges," 5.
28. "Notes on Gregory's Work Journal by Danièle Huillet," *Enthusiasm* 1 (December 1975):32–54.
29. See, e.g., Peter Gidal, "Straub/Huillet Talking and Short Notes on Some Contentious Issues," *Ark/Journal from the Royal College of Art* (January 1976):90.
30. "Enretien avec Jean-Marie Straub et Danièle Huillet," in *Der Tod des Empedokles/La mort d'Empédocle,* ed. Jacques Déniel and Dominique Païni (Dunkerque: Studio 43/Paris: DOPA Films/Ecole régionale des beaux-arts, 1987), 44.
31. See Barbara Bronnen, "Jean-Marie Straub (interview)," in *Die Filmemacher. Zur neuen deutschen Produktion nach Oberhausen,* eds. Barbara Bronnen and Corinna Brocher (Munich: Bertelsmann, 1973), 25–45; Maureen Turim, "*Ecriture Blanche*: The Ordering of the Filmic Text in *The Chronicle of Anna Magdalena Bach,*" *Purdue Film Studies Annual* (1976):177–192; Maureen Turim, "Jean-Marie Straub and Danièle Huillet: Oblique Angles on Film as Ideological Intervention," in *New German Filmmakers,* ed. Klaus Phillips (New York: Ungar, 1984), 335–358; and Gertrud Koch, "*Moses und Aron*: Musik, Text, Film und andere Fallen der Rezeption," in *Die Einstellung ist die Einstellung: Visuelle Konstruktionen des Judentums* (Frankfurt am Main: Suhrkamp, 1992), 30–52.
32. See David Caldwell, "Personal and Political Bonding in the Work of Straub/Huillet," in *Sex and Love in Motion Pictures: Proceedings of the Second Annual Film Conference of Kent State University,* ed. Douglas Radcliff-Umstead (Kent: Romance Languages Department, 1984), 80–84; and Whitney Chadwick and Isabelle de Courtivron, eds., *Significant Others: Creativity and Intimate Partnership* (London: Thames and Hudson, 1993).
33. Kaja Silverman, *The Acoustic Mirror: The Female Voice in Psychoanalysis and Cinema* (Bloomington: Indiana University Press, 1988); Martin Jay, *Downcast Eyes: The Denigration of Vision in Twentieth-Century French Thought* (Berkeley, Los Angeles, and London: University of California Press, 1993); David Michael Levin, ed., *Modernity and the Hegemony of Vision* (Berkeley, Los Angeles, and London: University of California Press, 1993). Even Eisler and Adorno refer to the traditional idea that hearing was passive and feminine and seeing was active and masculine; see Eisler, *Composing*, 20–21.
34. André Bazin, "*Le Journal d'un curé de campagne* and the Stylistics of Robert Bresson," in *What Is Cinema?* ed. Hugh Gray (Berkeley, Los Angeles, and London: University of California Press, 1967), 133.
35. See Andreas Huyssen, "The Vamp and the Machine: Fritz Lang's *Metropolis*," in *After the Great Divide: Modernism, Mass Culture, Postmodernism* (Bloomington: Indiana University Press, 1986), 65–81.
36. Bazin, "*Le Journal* and Bresson," 133.
37. Siegfried Kracauer, *Theory of Film: The Redemption of Physical Reality* (New York: Oxford University Press, 1960), e.g., ix.
38. See Roland Barthes, *The Grain of the Voice: Interviews 1962–1980,* trans. Linda Coverdale (New York: Hill and Wang, 1985), esp. "From Speech to Writing," 3–7.
39. Mark Nash and Steve Neal, "Film: 'History/Production/Memory,'" *Screen* 18, no. 4 (Fall/Winter 1977–1978):87–91.

40. See Cesare Pavese, *Dialogues with Leucò,* trans. William Arrowsmith and D. S. Carne-Ross (Boston: Eridanos, 1989).

41. See George Steiner, *Antigones* (New York: Oxford University Press, 1984), 136.

42. Marc Chevrie, "Le retour d'Empédocle. J.-M. Straub et D. Huillet: entre deux films," *Cahiers du cinéma* 418 (April 1989):64. For the conversations quoted in the film, see *Joachim Gasquet's Cézanne: A Memoir with Conversations,* trans. Christopher Pemberton (London: Thames and Hudson, 1991).

43. Hans Hurch, "Von Steinen und Menschen," *Falter* 16 (1992):24.

44. Peter Handke, "Kinonacht, Kinotiernacht," *Die Zeit,* 20 November 1992.

45. *Film at the Public* program, ed. Jonathan Rosenbaum, November 1982. The program also contains excerpts from interviews with the filmmakers under the heading, "Straub and Huillet on Filmmakers They Like and Related Matters," 5–8.

46. "Erde, Raum und Menschen: Aus einem Gespräch mit Jean-Marie Straub über das Theater- und Filmprojekt der *Antigone,*" *Frankfurter Rundschau,* 22 April 1991.

47. Cited in Dietmar Schings, "Eine Frau im Licht," *Deutsches Allgemeines Sonntagsblatt,* 14 February 1992.

48. Handke, "Kinonacht."

49. Laurence Giavarini, "Puissance des fantômes," *Cahiers du cinéma* 460 (1992):74.

50. Manfred Blank, *L'insistence du regard/Die Beharrlichkeit des Blicks,* Hessischer Rundfunk/Arte, 1993. Film.

51. Alain Bergala, "Le plus petit planète du monde," *Cahiers du cinéma* 364 (1984):27–31. Translation by Thom Andersen and Bill Jones.

52. Cited in Winfried Günther, "*Antigone,*" *epd Film* 11 (1992):29.

53. Among the first films exhibited to the public were the Lumière brothers' *La Sortie des Usines Lumière, L'Arrivée d'un train en gare de la Ciotat,* and *L'Arroseur arrosé,* all made in 1895. Straub/Huillet "quote" *Workers Leaving the Lumière Factory* with a shot of an Egyptian factory in *Too Early, Too Late.*

54. Kracauer, *Theory of Film,* ix.

55. Sylvia Harvey, *May '68 and Film Culture* (London: British Film Institute, 1978), 66.

56. See "Die Größe des Films, das ist die Bescheidenheit, daß man zur Fotografie verurteilt ist," *filmwärts* [Straub/Huillet issue] 9 (December 1987):10–11.

57. Roswitha Mueller, "Introduction," *Discourse* [Special issue: German Avant-Garde Cinema: The Seventies] 6 (Fall 1983):8.

58. Rosalind E. Krauss, *The Originality of the Avant-Garde and Other Modernist Myths* (Cambridge: MIT Press, 1984), 14.

59. "Andi Engel Talks to Jean-Marie Straub," *Cinemantics* 1 (1 January 1970):19.

60. Blank, *L'insistence du regard.*

61. Robert Bresson, "Zum Selbstverständnis des Films V," *Filmkritik* 9 (1966): 527–528.

62. Ibid., 528.

63. See, e.g., David Bordwell's description of the visual "theatricalization" of *Moses and Aaron* as against Bazin: *The Films of Carl-Theodor Dreyer* (Berkeley, Los Angeles, and London: University of California Press, 1981), 149.

64. "The Film as Art," Jean Renoir interview, *Pacifica Radio Archive,* 1960 [copyright 1983].

65. Ibid.

66. Brecht, cited in Wilhelm Große, *Bearbeitungen des Johanna-Stoffes* (Munich: R. Oldenbourg, 1980), 90.

67. See Große, *Johanna-Stoff*, 64.

68. Bertolt Brecht, *Die heilige Johanna der Schlachthöfe*, in *Die Stücke von Bertolt Brecht in einem Band* (Frankfurt am Main: Suhrkamp, 1978), 285.

69. David Bordwell, *Narration in the Fiction Film* (Madison: University of Wisconsin Press, 1985), 271–273.

70. Thomas Elsaesser, *New German Cinema: A History* (New Brunswick: Rutgers University Press, 1989), 295.

71. Ibid., 40–41.

72. On Brecht and the cinema, see also Dana Polan, *The Political Language of Film and the Avant-Garde* (Ann Arbor: UMI Research Press, 1985); Martin Walsh, *The Brechtian Aspect of Radical Cinema*, ed. Keith M. Griffiths (London: British Film Institute, 1981); Pia Kleber and Colin Visser, eds., *Re-interpreting Brecht: His Influence on Contemporary Drama and Film* (Cambridge: Cambridge University Press, 1990); Sylvia Harvey, "Whose Brecht? Memories for the Eighties," *Screen* 23, no. 1 (May/June 1982):45–59; and Peter Wollen, "The Two Avant-Gardes," *Edinburgh '76 Magazine* 1:77–86.

73. D. N. Rodowick, *The Crisis of Political Modernism: Criticism and Ideology in Contemporary Film Theory* (Urbana: University of Illinois Press, 1988), 5.

74. Colin MacCabe, "Class of '68: Elements of an Intellectual Autobiography 1967–81," in *Tracking the Signifier: Theoretical Essays, Film, Linguistics, Literature* (Minneapolis: University of Minnesota Press, 1985), 15.

75. Rodowick, *Crisis of Political Modernism*, 158.

76. Thomas Elsaesser, "General Introduction: Early Cinema from Linear History to Mass Media Archaeology," in *Early Cinema: Space/Frame/Narrative*, ed. Thomas Elsaesser and Adam Barker (London: British Film Institute, 1990), 18.

77. Rodowick, *Crisis of Political Modernism*, 272.

78. Ibid., 280.

79. Cited in ibid., 289–290.

80. See Nash and Neal, "Film," 87–88.

81. Cited in Rodowick, *Crisis of Political Modernism*, 296–297.

82. See Harvey, *May '68 and Film Culture*, 47.

83. MacCabe, "Class of '68," 31.

### Chapter 2. Straub/Huillet, the New Left, and Germany

1. Thomas Elsaesser, *New German Cinema: A History* (New Brunswick: Rutgers University Press, 1989), 93. Cited hereafter as *NGC*.

2. On various aspects of the frustration of political action and a resulting melancholy withdrawal since the 1960s, see, e.g., Todd Gitlin, *Years of Hope, Days of Rage* (New York: Bantam, 1987), 246; Russell Berman, *Modern Culture and Critical Theory: Art, Politics, and the Legacy of the Frankfurt School* (Madison: University of Wisconsin Press, 1989), 43, 98; and Richard W. McCormick, *Politics of the Self: Feminism and the Postmodern in West German Literature and Film* (Princeton: Princeton University Press, 1991), 17. Since Straub/Huillet's political engagement arose in the "apolitical"

1950s, they could represent what Gitlin refers to as the "missing radical generation"; see Gitlin, *Years of Hope*, 176.

3. "Entretien Dominique Païni–Jean Narboni," in *Der Tod des Empedokles/La mort d'Empédocle*, ed. Jacques Déniel and Dominique Païni (Dunkerque: Studio 43/ Paris: DOPA Films/Ecole des beaux-arts régionale, 1987), 62. This book is hereafter cited as *Dunkerque*.

4. Both Kluge and Wenders criticize Straub/Huillet for not reaching a wider audience. See Robert Phillip Kolker and Peter Beicken, *The Films of Wim Wenders: Cinema as Vision and Desire* (Cambridge: Cambridge University Press, 1993), 32; Alexander Kluge, "Gespräch mit Alexander Kluge," *Filmkritik* 12 (1976):588–589; and Tim Corrigan, *A Cinema Without Walls: Movies and Culture after Vietnam* (New Brunswick: Rutgers University Press, 1991), 121. Peter Handke's similar inclination to depoliticize Straub/Huillet's aesthetic radicalism will be discussed in chap. 11.

5. Cited in Anton Kaes, *From Hitler to Heimat: The Return of History as Film* (Cambridge: Harvard University Press, 1989), 101.

6. Gilberto Perez, "Bell-Bottom Blues," *Nation* (18 February 1991):211.

7. Martin Schaub, "Bilderarbeit," *Cinema* 3 (1976):43.

8. Ibid.

9. Walter Benjamin, *Illuminations*, ed. Hannah Arendt, trans. Harry Zohn (New York: Schocken, 1978), 231, 241, 251n.

10. See Elsaesser, *NGC*, 49.

11. D. B. Polan, "Brecht and the Politics of Self-Reflexive Cinema," *Jump Cut* 17 (April 1978):30.

12. "Andi Engel Talks to Jean-Marie Straub," *Cinemantics* 1 (1 January 1970):21.

13. "Balayez-moi tout ça!" [Interview], *Les Lettres Françaises*, 13 January 1971.

14. Rolf Aurich, " 'Irgendwo muß ein Punkt sein, daß man sieht, da brennt etwas': Versuch darüber, was der Neo-Realismus, André Bazin, Roberto Rossellini und eine Moral mit den Filmen von Danièle Huillet und Jean-Marie Straub zu tun haben könnten," *filmwärts* [Straub/Huillet issue] 9 (December 1987):9.

15. See Peter Wuss, *Die Tiefenstruktur des Filmkunstwerks: Zur Analyse von Spielfilmen mit offener Komposition* (Berlin: Henschel, 1990), and *Filmanalyse und Psychologie: Strukturen des Films im Wahrnehmungsprozeß* (Berlin: Edition Sigma, 1993).

16. Norbert Elias, "Gedanken zur Bundesrepublik," *Merkur* 9/10 (1985):733–755.

17. Rolf Aurich, "Magazin: Eine letzte Anmerkung," *filmwärts* 3 (May 1986):16.

18. Klaus-Detlef Müller, *Die Funktion der Geschichte im Werk Bertolt Brechts* (Tübingen: Niemeyer, 1967), 29.

19. Brecht, *Arbeitsjournal*, 2 vols., ed. Werner Hecht (Frankfurt am Main: Suhrkamp, 1973), 1:18 (3 March 1938).

20. Ibid., 1:144 (9 August 1940).

21. "After *Othon*, before *History Lessons*: Geoffrey Nowell-Smith Talks to Jean-Marie Straub and Danièle Huillet," *Enthusiasm* 1 (December 1975):31.

22. Cited in "A Work Journal of the Straub/Huillet Film *Moses and Aaron* by Gregory Woods," *Enthusiasm* 1 (December 1975):48.

23. Cited in K.-D. Müller, *Funktion der Geschichte*, 29.

24. See Timothy Corrigan, *New German Film: The Displaced Image* (Austin: University of Texas Press, 1983); James Franklin, *New German Cinema: From Oberhausen to Hamburg* (Boston: Twayne, 1983); Eric Rentschler, *West German Film in*

*the Course of Time: Reflections on the Twenty Years since Oberhausen* (Bedford Hills, N.Y.: Redgrave, 1984); John Sandford, *The New German Cinema* (London: Oswald Wolff, 1980), 27–36; and Maureen Turim, "Jean-Marie Straub and Danièle Huillet: Oblique Angles on Film as Ideological Intervention," in *West German Filmmakers*, ed. Klaus Phillips (New York: Ungar, 1984), 335–358.

25. See Kaes, *From Hitler to Heimat*; Eric L. Santner, *Stranded Objects: Mourning, Memory, and Film in Postwar Germany* (Ithaca: Cornell University Press, 1990); and Elsaesser, *NGC*.

26. Kaes, *From Hitler to Heimat*, 9, 18–20.

27. See Elsaesser, *NGC*, esp. 8–35; Elsaesser downplays the importance of politics in the decade before 1967, however. Perhaps the audience was not as political as later, but the motives and positions among young filmmakers and critics certainly were. See also Rentschler, *West German Film*.

28. Franklin, *New German Cinema*, 35.

29. See Elsaesser, *NGC*, 24, 27.

30. Harun Farocki, unpublished interview with the author, February 1992.

31. Elsaesser, *NGC*, 20.

32. "Le cinema du Papa est mort" had been the title of a French review of *Last Year at Marienbad*. See Hans-Dieter Roos, "Brief aus Paris: Papas Kino ist tot," *Filmkritik* 1 (1962):7.

33. Sylvia Harvey cites the importance of Brecht and Benjamin for French film theory in the 1960s as well, especially in *Cahiers du cinéma* and *Cinétique*: *May '68 and Film Culture* (London: British Film Institute, 1978), 69.

34. See *Filmkritik* 5 (1968).

35. Enno Patalas, "Herr K. erobert Venedig," *Filmkritik* 10 (1966):547.

36. Wilhelm Roth, "Nachlese in Mannheim," *Filmkritik* 11 (1968):740.

37. *Frankfurter Rundschau*, 30 November 1965.

38. On the importance of the festival to the New German Cinema, see Rentschler, *West German Film*, 75, and Franklin, *New German Cinema*, 21.

39. See the discussion in chap. 4.

40. Peter W. Jansen and Wolfram Schütte, eds., *Herzog/Kluge/Straub* (Munich: Carl Hansen Verlag, 1976), 13.

41. Franklin, *New German Cinema*, 47–48, 130, 136, 141.

42. Enno Patalas, "Ansichten einer Gruppe," *Filmkritik* 5 (1966):247.

43. In a 1980 interview, Straub/Huillet name the following as those whose work they admired while in Germany: Vlado Kristl, Peter Nestler, Rudolf Thome, Klaus Lemke, Max Zihlmann, Hellmuth Costard, Werner Nekes. See Jochen Brunow, "Der Maschine Widerstand leisten," *Filme* 1 (1980):31–32. On the marginality of Thome and Lemke and their alternative to Oberhausen, cf. Elsaesser, *NGC*, 120, 136.

44. See Elsaesser, *NGC*, 43–44, 74.

45. Ibid., 78.

46. Ibid., 73.

47. See, e.g., Schaub, "Bilderarbeit," 33, 43; Ulrich Greiner, "Achtung Liebe! Vorsicht Kino!" *Die Zeit*, 2 March 1984.

48. The groundbreaking work for many of these interpretations was Alexander Mitscherlich and Margarete Mitscherlich's *The Inability to Mourn* (London: Tavistock, 1975).

49. Santner, *Stranded Objects*, 30.

50. Jochen Brunow, "Der Maschine Widerstand leisten: Begegnung mit Danièle Huillet und Jean-Marie Straub," *Filme* 1 (1980):31.

51. Ibid.

52. Peter Gidal, "Straub/Huillet Talking and Short Notes on Some Contentious Issues," *Ark/Journal from the Royal College of Art* (January 1976):97.

53. "Andi Engel Talks to Jean-Marie Straub," 21.

54. Ibid.

55. Cited in "Straub and Huillet on Filmmakers They Like and Related Matters," *Film at the Public* program, ed. Jonathan Rosenbaum, November 1982, 5.

Straub/Huillet returned to this example in the press conference after the Berlin premiere of *Antigone* in 1992, this time identifying with Artur Brauner, the Jewish producer of those films, whose *Europa, Europa* (directed by Agnieszka Holland) was refused the imprimatur of a "German" film.

56. Kaes, *From Hitler to Heimat*, 19, 114.

57. See B. Ruby Rich's criticism of this tone in Kluge's authorial voice: "She Says, He Says: The Power of the Narrator in Modernist Film Politics," *Discourse* [Special issue: German Avant-Garde Cinema: The Seventies] 6 (Fall 1983):31–46.

58. "Andi Engel Talks to Jean-Marie Straub," 21.

59. Kaes, *From Hitler to Heimat*, 120, 239.

60. Cited in Elsaesser, *NGC*, 136.

61. Ibid.

62. Kaes, *From Hitler to Heimat*, 132.

63. Santner, *Stranded Objects*, xiii.

64. *Brechts Antigone des Sophokles*, ed. Werner Hecht (Frankfurt am Main: Suhrkamp, 1988) 100, ll. 447–450. Since the subtitles have not been translated, I have left the original German in the text. For a rather free translation of Brecht's version, see Judith Malina, *Sophocles' Antigone, Adapted by Bertolt Brecht, Based on the German Translation by Friedrich Hölderlin* (New York: Applause Theatre Book Publishers, 1990). A more literal rendering:

> It's false. Earth is a burden. Home is not only
> Earth, not house only. Not where one has poured out sweat
> Not the house that helplessly sees the approaching fire
> Not where he bowed his neck, not that calls he home.

65. I discuss this issue in more detail in the chapters on *Not Reconciled* and *History Lessons*. See also James E. Young, "The Counter-Monument: Memory Against Itself in Germany Today," *Critical Inquiry* 18 (Winter 1992):267–296.

66. Martin Walsh, *The Brechtian Aspect of Radical Cinema*, ed. Keith M. Griffiths (London: British Film Institute, 1981), 59.

67. *Antigone*, press materials courtesy Edition Manfred Salzgeber, Berlin.

68. Elsaesser, *NGC*, 298; Corrigan, *New German Film*, 22–23. See also Pierre Sorlin, "Challenging Hollywood," in *European Cinemas, European Societies 1939–1990* (London: Routledge, 1991), 138ff.

69. Peter Zach, "Vom Unglück in einer Maschine zu sein, die viele Freiheiten beinahe hat, aber in sich das Glück nur ab und zu zeigt" [Interview with Straub/Huillet], *Blimp* (March 1985):16; "Entretien avec Jean-Marie Straub et Danièle Huillet," in *Dunkerque*, 34.

70. Elsaesser, *NGC*, 284–289.

71. Kuby wrote a number of works critical of rearmament and the West German Right, particularly Franz Josef Strauss. See his *Das ist des Deutschen Vaterland: 70 Millionen in zwei Wartesälen* (Stuttgart: Scherz and Goverts, 1957), and *Franz Josef Strauss: Ein Typus unserer Zeit* [with Eugen Kogon, Otto von Loewenstern, and Jürgen Seifert] (Vienna: Kurt Desch, 1963). Howard Vernon is perhaps best known for his roles in Godard's *Alphaville* and Lang's *The Thousand Eyes of Dr. Mabuse*.

72. Straub/Huillet criticize this abandonment of Germany and the German language by Fassbinder and Wenders, arguing it diminished the space for their own films to function. See Zach, "Vom Unglück in einer Maschine zu sein," 16.

73. Zach, "Vom Unglück in einer Maschine zu sein," 20.

74. Michael Klier, *Porträts der Filmemacher: Jean-Marie Straub*, WDR, Cologne, 1970. Film.

**Chapter 3. Traces of a Life: *Chronicle of Anna Magdalena Bach***

1. *Chronicle* won the German film critics' prize (Bambi), was screened at "critics' week" in Cannes, and won the Grand Prize at the festivals in London and Prades (all 1968).

2. Anticipating the continued use of siblings in acting roles, as in *Empedocles* and *Antigone*, this actor is the sister of Renate Lang, who played Inn in *Machorka-Muff*.

3. Roy Armes, "Jean-Marie Straub: Strict Counterpoint," in *The Ambiguous Image* (London: Secker and Warburg, 1976), 211, 212.

4. For English translations of such documents, see Hans T. David and Arthur Mendel, eds., *The Bach Reader: A Life of Johann Sebastian Bach in Letters and Documents* (New York: W. W. Norton, 1966).

5. See Esther Meynell, *The Little Chronicle of Anna Magdalena Bach* (Boston: E. C. Schirmer, 1934). The book was first published anonymously in 1925 and was also published in Germany without the author's name: *Die kleine Chronik der Anna Magdalena Bach* (Reutlingen: Bertelsmann, 1957). Examples of events from Meynell's chronicle that appear in the film include Bach's discourse on the virtues of the *basso continuo* (113); the acoustic marvels of the *Apollo-Saal* in the Berlin Opera (118); the co-rector who "turned out Krause in the middle of a hymn and put Küttler in his place" (127); the wording of Bach's intransigence—"He would not retract anything in the matter, let it cost what it might" (128); the origins of "A Musical Offering" during Bach's visit to Potsdam, where the monarch played a theme for him "and Sebastian proceeded to develop it in his own learned and incomparable manner, to the great astonishment and admiration of the King" (170–171). Although these are documents used by both Meynell and Straub/Huillet, it is plausible that the 1957 publication brought the filmmakers to think of using them in the film.

6. Peter W. Jansen and Wolfram Schütte, eds., *Herzog/Kluge/Straub* (Munich: Carl Hanser Verlag, 1976), 205. Cited hereafter as *HKS*.

7. Most of the information on the attempts to produce *Chronicle*, *Machorka-Muff*, and *Not Reconciled* is drawn from the following: Rainer Rother, "Das mühsame Geschäft des Filmemachens: Zur Entstehungsgeschichte von *Machorka-Muff* und *Nicht versöhnt oder Es hilft nur Gewalt, wo Gewalt herrscht*," in *Machorka-Muff: Jean-*

*Marie Straub und Danièle Huillets Verfilmung einer Satire von Heinrich Böll*, ed. Reinhold Rauh (Münster: MAKS, 1988), 65–78; "Andi Engel Talks to Jean-Marie Straub," *Cinemantics* 1 (1 January 1970):16–23; and Uwe Nettelbeck, "Plädoyer für ein Projekt: Der Fall Jean-Marie Straub," *Die Zeit*, 14 October 1966.
  8. *Cahiers du cinéma* 180 (July 1966):57.
  9. Ibid.
  10. See "Andi Engel Talks to Jean-Marie Straub and Danièle Huillet Is There Too," *Enthusiasm* 1 (December 1975):1.
  11. "Engel Talks to Straub," 17.
  12. Ibid.; "Engel Talks to Straub and Huillet," 2.
  13. "Engel Talks to Straub," 16.
  14. See Nettelbeck, "Plädoyer für ein Projekt"; *Filmkritik* 12 (1966):662; and *Filmkritik* 3 (1967):122.
  15. "*Chronik der Anna Magdalena Bach*" [Interview with Jean-Marie Straub], *Film* (April 1968):25. Hereafter cited as *Film*.
  16. Ibid.
  17. Ibid.
  18. See Philippe Sollers on anti-Fascism and pop culture in the 1950s: "Why the United States?" in *The Kristeva Reader*, ed. Toril Moi (New York: Columbia University Press, 1986), 283–284.
  19. Klaus Eder, "Der wiedergefundene Barock," *Film* (April 1968):28; Straub refers to the "Gesetzeshüter" in the video portrait by Michael Klier.
  20. "Engel Talks to Straub and Huillet," 1.
  21. *Film*, 25.
  22. Ibid.
  23. Ibid., 27.
  24. Michael Gielen has described the care with which Straub/Huillet planned the cuts from shot to shot in *Moses and Aaron* (see chap. 7).
  25. For the screenplay, see Jean-Marie Straub, *Chronik der Anna Magdalena Bach* (Frankfurt am Main: Verlag Filmkritik, 1969).
  The excerpts from the works performed are the following:

  1. Brandenburg Concerto no. 5 (BWV 1050), Allegro I, measures 147–227, harpsichord and orchestra, 1720–1721
  2. Clavierbüchlein for Wilhelm Friedemann Bach, Prelude VI (BWV 928), clavichord, 1720
  3. Clavierbüchlein for Anna Magdalena Bach, Minuet II of the Suite in D Minor (French Suite I, BWV 812), spinet, 1722
  4. Adagio of the Sonata no. 2 in D Major (BWV 1028), viola da gamba and harpsichord obligato, c. 1720
  5. Largo of the Trio Sonata no. 2 in C Minor (BWV 526), organ, 1727
  6. "Magnificat" in D Major (BWV 243), nos. 11 and 12 to measure 19, 1728–1731
  7. Clavierbüchlein for Anna Magdalena Bach, Tempo di gavotta of the Partita in E Minor (BWV 830), spinet, 1725

8. Cantata (BWV 205), "Der zufriedengestellte Äolus," 1725
9. Trauer Ode (BWV 198), final chorus, 1727
10. Cantata (BWV 244a), "Funeral Music for Prince Leopold," measure 25 to the end, 1729
11. St. Matthew Passion (BWV 244), initial chorus, 1736
12. Cantata (BWV 42), introductory sinfonia (Da capo of measures 1–53 and recitative for tenor: "Am Abend aber desselbigen Sabbats"), 1725
13. Prelude for organ in B Minor (BWV 544), first part, 1727–1731
14. First Kyrie of the B Minor Mass for Chorus and Orchestra (BWV 232), measures 1–30, 1731–1733
15. Cantata (BWV 215), "Preise dein Glücke, gesegnetes Sachsen," initial chorus, measures 1–181, 1734
16. Ascension Oratorio (BWV 11), final chorus, second part, 1735
17. Usual Latin Sunday motet for the 11th Sunday after Trinity, from the Florilegium Portens of Erhard Bodenschatz, in eight parts, by Leone Leoni
18. Chorale "Kyrie, Gott heiliger Geist" (BWV 671), from the third part of the Clavierübung, organ, 1739
19. Italian Concerto (BWV 971), andante, 1735
20. Cantata (BWV 140), "Wachet auf, ruft uns die Stimme," first duet, measures 1–36, 1731
21. Goldberg Variations (BWV 988), 25th variation, clavecin, 1741–1742
22. Cantata (BWV 82), "Ich habe genug," last recitative and last aria, 1727
23. Musical Offering (BWV 1079), Ricercar a 6, measures 1–39, harpsichord, 1747
24. Art of the Fugue (BWV 1080), Contrapunctus xix, measures 193–239, harpsichord, 1750
25. Chorale (BWV 668), "Vor deinen Thron tret ich," first part, organ, 1750

26. Maureen Turim, "*Ecriture Blanche*: The Ordering of the Filmic Text in *The Chronicle of Anna Magdalena Bach*," *Purdue Film Studies Annual* (1976):177.
27. Ibid.
28. I have adjusted Turim's shot numbers to correspond to the published screenplay.
29. Turim, "*Ecriture Blanche*," 180.
30. Turim cites Eisenstein's essay "The Music of Landscape," published in installments in *Cahiers du cinéma*, 211 (April 1969) to 219 (April 1970), as the best theoretical source for analysis of the "counterpoint" of this film but also argues that the tension created by Straub/Huillet's editing exceeds Eisenstein's "montage of attractions"; Turim, "*Ecriture Blanche*," 184–185. See Sergei Eisenstein, "The Music of Landscape and the Fate of Montage Counterpoint at a New Stage," in *Nonindifferent Nature*, trans. Herbert Marshall (Cambridge: Cambridge University Press, 1987), 216–396.
31. Turim, "*Ecriture Blanche*," 189.

32. Joachim Kaiser, "Respekt, Spiel, Freiheit: Zu drei Filmen über Musik: *Chronik der Anna Magdalena Bach, Eika Katappa, Ludwig van* . . ." *Fernsehen und Film* 2, no. 2 (August 1970):28.

33. Friedrich Hommel, "Le Martyr de Saint-Jean-Sébastien: Anmerkungen eines Musikkritikers zu Straubs *Chronik der Anna Magdalena Bach,*" *Film* (May 1968):31.

34. Kaiser, "Respekt, Spiel, Freiheit," 28.

35. Ibid.

36. Hommel, "Le Martyr de Saint-Jean-Sébastien," 31.

37. Kaiser, "Respekt, Spiel, Freiheit," 28.

38. Hommel, "Le Martyr de Saint-Jean-Sébastien," 31.

39. *Texte zu den Kirchenkantaten von Johann Sebastian Bach / The Texts to Johann Sebastian Bach's Church Cantatas,* trans. Z. Philip Ambrose (Neuhausen-Stuttgart: Hänssler-Verlag, 1984), 339.

40. Hommel, "Le Martyr de Saint-Jean-Sébastien," 31.

41. Kaiser, "Respekt, Spiel, Freiheit," 28.

42. Hommel, "Le Martyr de Saint-Jean-Sébastien," 31.

43. Turim, "*Ecriture Blanche,*" 183–184.

44. Frieda Grafe, "Ein deutsches Selbstporträt?" *Filmkritik* 2 (1966):144.

45. See shot 37, BWV 205, Straub, *Chronik,* 33.

46. "Gespräch mit Danièle Huillet und Jean-Marie Straub," *Filmkritik* 10 (1968): 688; Meynell, *Little Chronicle,* 59.

47. See Herbert Linder, "Kinder, aufgepaßt!" *Filmkritik* 10 (1968):710. On the Mitchell camera, see *Film,* 26.

48. This effect is reminiscent of Fritz Lang, for instance in the film *Hangmen Also Die,* with a script co-authored by Bertolt Brecht. A professor and Czech anti-Fascist, played by Walter Brennan, awaits execution in a prison cell. He is visited by his daughter, to whom he gives a moving speech on how he wants his death to be remembered, much in the tone of Brecht's poem "An die Nachgeborenen" (To Those Born After). The action into and out of the scene moves to and from a door seen to the left of the simple wooden chair in the center of the cell, where Brennan recites the speech. After his daughter leaves in this direction, the sound of soldiers approaching is heard, and one assumes they will soon arrive at this door (to the left) to take Brennan away. But at the end of the scene, the camera pans to the *right* to reveal a window, the presence of which was unknown before. The shock of this revelation gives the scene a powerful effect of the possibilities held by the unknown future—and even death.

49. *Chronik der Anna Magdalena Bach, Kleine Filmkunstreihe* 81, ed. Herbert Linder (Frankfurt am Main: Neue Filmkunst, 1969), n.p. Hereafter cited as *Kleine Filmkunstreihe.*

50. "Gespräch," 689.

51. *Film,* 25.

52. Helmut Färber, "Im anschluß an das Protokoll der *Chronik der Anna Magdalena Bach,*" *Filmkritik* 10 (1968):695–703.

53. "Gespräch," 689–690.

54. Ibid., 690.

55. *HKS,* 210.

56. Meynell, *Little Chronicle,* 42.

57. Eder, "Der wiedergefundene Barock," 28.

58. Jörg Peter Feurich, "Tagebuch," *Filmkritik* 8 (1968):529.
59. Hommel, "Le Martyr de Saint-Jean-Sébastien," 31.
60. Feurich, "Tagebuch," 529.
61. Wolfram Schütte, *Frankfurter Rundschau*, 6 April 1968.
62. Ibid.
63. Feurich, "Tagebuch," 529.
64. *Kleine Filmkunstreihe*, n.p.
65. "Gespräch," 690.
66. Ibid.
67. Straub, *Chronik*, frontispiece.
68. *Film*, 26.
69. *Kleine Filmkunstreihe*, n.p.

**Chapter 4. Formal and Political Radicalism in the Short Films of the 1960s**

1. Michel Delahaye, "Pornographie et cinéma à l'état nu" [Interview with Jean-Marie Straub], *Cahiers du cinéma* 180 (July 1966):56.
2. Ibid.
3. See "Straub and Huillet on Filmmakers They Like and Related Matters," *Film at the Public* program, ed. Jonathan Rosenbaum, November 1982, 5.
4. Michael Klier, *Porträts der Filmemacher: Jean-Marie Straub*, WDR, Cologne, 1970. Film.
5. "Andi Engel Talks to Jean-Marie Straub," *Cinemantics* 1 (1 January 1970):17. Straub/Huillet eventually made the newsmagazine *Der Spiegel* for traveling all the way from Munich to Bonn to record the sound of the trolleys, insisting that they do not sound at all alike.
6. "Engel Talks to Straub," 18. Thomas Elsaesser relates the Karajan anecdote with Artur Brauner as the producer, but refers to Straub and not a published source. Brauner did, however, make a small donation to the Filmfonds for the Bach film; Straub does not mention him in the interviews as a possible producer. Elsaesser, *New German Cinema: A History* (New Brunswick: Rutgers University Press, 1989), 68; cited hereafter as *NGC*.
7. Rainer Rother, "Das mühsame Geschäft des Filmemachens: Zur Entstehungsgeschichte von *Machorka-Muff* und *Nicht versöhnt oder Es hilft nur Gewalt wo Gewalt herrscht*," in *Machorka-Muff: Jean-Marie Straubs und Danièle Huillets Verfilmung einer Satire von Heinrich Böll*, ed. Reinhold Rauh (Münster: MAKS, 1988), 66–67.
8. *Machorka-Muff* thus relates to *Not Reconciled* in the same way that a number of short Straub/Huillet films serve as "studies" for larger works. Other examples would be the Schoenberg short (made close to *History Lessons* and in preparation for the major project *Moses and Aaron*), the Mallarmé film (the first film with William Lubtchansky as cinematographer), and *En Râchâchant* (made before *Class Relations*). This often allowed Straub/Huillet and some new crew members to become acquainted with working together and to try out sets, locations, or lighting before going on to a larger project.
9. The leaflet read, "Since the all-wise Gentlemen from the selection committee had no eyes, no ears, no sense for the cinematographic newness of *Machorka-Muff*—or

no sense for democracy (?), *Machorka-Muff* will be shown *elsewhere* in Oberhausen this week, to which you are invited." See Rother, "Das mühsame Geschäft," 65.

10. Ibid., 68; "Engel Talks to Straub," 18.

11. "Engel Talks to Straub," 18.

12. The letter from Stockhausen, published in *Film* 1, no. 2 (June/July 1963):52, and reprinted in Rother, "Das mühsame Geschäft," 69–70, reads as follows:

[2 May 1963]
Dear Mr. Straub,
First I want to congratulate you on the film I recently saw in Cologne. You yourself will know that you are following the difficult path. Therefore I am writing you so you will know that in this film you have done good work. In the realm of the spirit [*Geist*] it is not quantity that counts, but the truthfulness and the creative accomplishment.

The subject is taken from our time. It is true, precise and of general validity. Whoever censures exaggeration knows nothing of the artistic necessity of pushing an idea to the limit so that it really comes across. Give such grumblers Greek dramas or Shakespeare to read. What interested me most in your film is the composition of time, which is—as it is to music—particular to film. You have achieved good proportions in the duration of scenes, between those which almost stand still—how astonishing is the courage to be still, to a slow tempo, in such a relatively short film!—and extremely fast events—brilliant, to choose for this the newspaper citations in all angles to the vertical of the screen. Furthermore, the relative density of the changes in the varied tempos is good. Where one would have to work further would be on giving equal rights to the characters and locations: "main characters," "climaxes" (the speech at the laying of the cornerstone) would gradually have to disappear: Let each element have *its* own irreplaceable and indispensable moment; no decoration. "Everything is the main thing," said Webern in such cases (but each in its own time, one would have to add). Also good is the openness, the continuation of thinking in the heads of the spectators, dispensing with any gesture of overture or finale. There is much I could still add: the total lack of pedantics, do-gooding [*das Weltverbessernde*], illusion, symbolism, the false as-if: you didn't need it and chose facts instead; but not as flat reporting, but in that exaggeration, the uncanny sheet-lightning of the camera work, in the streets, in the hotel (very good is the empty wall of the hotel room that stands for a long time; one can't get away from its staleness), out the window. And in addition, this "unrealistic" condensation in time, without being rushed. On this tightrope between truth, concentration and exaggeration (which burns itself into perception) one can go further. Nowhere else. For we know today that even the shredded illusion is an illusion. You don't want to "change" the world, but rather engrave in it the trace of your presence and thereby say that you have seen a part of this world, have unfolded it as it gives itself to you. That has pleased me. All negative criticism must stand back behind these criteria. I look forward with anticipation to your work to come. Let in a little calmness, much stillness, much space and cheerfulness of heart—it broadens the scale.

13. "Engel Talks to Straub," 18.

14. Rother, "Das mühsame Geschäft," 72.

15. Delahaye, "Pornographie et cinéma," 53.

16. Reinhold Rauh, "Vorwort," in *Machorka-Muff: Jean Marie Straubs und Danièle Huillets Verfilmung einer Satire von Heinrich Böll*, ed. Reinhold Rauh (Münster: MAKS, 1988), 9.

17. Ibid., 7.

18. Heinrich Böll, "Bonn Diary," in *Absent Without Leave and Other Stories*, trans. Leila Vennewitz (London: Weidenfeld and Nicolson, 1967), 300–312. The story first

appeared in *Aufwärts* (Cologne) on 15 September 1957. Straub mistakenly cited publication in *Welt der Arbeit*, probably because its editor had been Gottfried Bold, who played the politician in *Not Reconciled* and the banker in *History Lessons*. For a leftist view of the political steps toward remilitarization of West Germany, cf. Martin Kampe, *SPD und Bundeswehr: Studien zum militärisch-industriellen Komplex* (Cologne: Pahl-Rugenstein, 1973), 42–43 and passim.

19. Böll, "Bonn Diary," 304.
20. Peter Nau, "Filme Lesen," *Filmkritik* 6 (1979):263–272.
21. Ibid., 266.
22. Ibid., 268–269.
23. Böll, "Bonn Diary," 310–311.
24. Ibid., 312.
25. Ibid., 308.
26. Ibid., 303.
27. Ibid.
28. Ibid., 300, 305, 306, 307.
29. Ibid., 304.
30. Ibid., 307.
31. Ibid., 303–304. Absurdly, this line was given as part of the justification for the official restriction of the film to adult viewers, thus damaging the film's access to both audiences and additional funding. See Rother, "Das mühsame Geschäft," 68.
32. Böll, "Bonn Diary," 308.
33. Ibid., 309.
34. Nau, "Filme Lesen," 270.
35. Eric Rentschler, "The Use and Abuse of Memory: New German Film and the Discourse of Bitburg," *New German Critique* 36 (Fall 1985):76.
36. Karsten Witte, cited in Rentschler, "Use and Abuse of Memory," 76.
37. Rentschler, "Use and Abuse of Memory," 76.
38. Böll, "Bonn Diary," 305.
39. See Nau, "Filme Lesen," 266.
40. Böll, "Bonn Diary," 305.
41. Cited in Reinhold Rauh, "*Machorka-Muff*—Thema and Form," in *Machorka-Muff: Jean-Marie Straubs und Danièle Huillets Verfilmung einer Satire von Henirich Böll*, ed. Reinhold Rauh (Münster: MAKS, 1988), 60.
42. Helmut Färber, "Machorka Muff" [*sic*], *Filmkritik* 1 (1964):36.
43. Jean-Marie Straub, Letter to Editor, *Filmkritik* 4 (1964):221.
44. Ibid.
45. See Karsten Witte's description of the film's broadcast without either the dedication or director's credits: *Im Kino. Texte vom Sehen und Hören* (Frankfurt am Main: Fischer, 1985), 120. The letter protesting the television censorship appeared in *Filmkritik* 5/6 (1975):253.
46. "Engel Talks to Straub," 20.
47. See, e.g., Franz Wille, "Griechische Puppenstube," *Frankfurter Allgemeine Zeitung*, 7 May 1991. Another specific political dedication was not reported in most reviews: to "Georg von Rauch, who was murdered by the police." Wille notes that von Rauch was a member of the June 2 Movement who died under uncertain circumstances in police custody in 1971. He was the brother of Andreas von Rauch, the actor of the

role of Empedocles in the Straub/Huillet films. See Wilhelm Schmid, "Auf der Bühne steht nur der Diskurs," *die tageszeitung*, 7 May 1991.

48. Straub uses the German term *Filmkunstgetto* in the *Cahiers* interview in 1966; see Delahaye, "Pornographie et cinéma," 52. See the discussion of the New German Cinema's relation to Hollywood in chap. 2.

49. Straub, Letter to Editor, 221.

50. On the "authors' cinema" in West Germany, see Elsaesser, *NGC*, esp. 74–116.

51. See Elsaesser, *NGC*, 111, 237.

52. Wilhelm Roth, "Tagebuch," *Filmkritik* 11 (1968):740.

53. The script of the film is published in *Filmkritik* 10 (1968):681–687.

54. BWV 11, see *Texte zu den Kirchenkantaten von Johann Sebastian Bach / The Texts to Johann Sebastian Bach's Church Cantatas*, trans. Z. Philip Ambrose (Neuhausen-Stuttgart: Hänssler-Verlag, 1984), 48. The same work is excerpted in *Chronik* as well, shots 59–61.

55. Peter Handke, "Kinonacht, Kinotiernacht," *Die Zeit*, 20 November 1992.

56. Bruckner was strongly influenced by the expressionist playwright Carl Sternheim, then moved into a style of "radical naturalistic objectivity." See Ferdinand Bruckner, *Pains of Youth*, trans. Daphne Moore (Bath: Absolute Press, 1989).

57. "Post-scriptum de J.-M. Straub," *Cahiers du cinéma* 212 (May 1969):10.

58. Bernd Eckhardt, *Rainer Werner Fassbinder: In 17 Jahren 42 Filme—Stationen eines Lebens für den deutschen Film* (Munich: Heyne, 1982), 84. On Fassbinder's theater work, see also Fassbinder's *Antiteater: Fünf Stücke nach Stücken*, afterword by Michael Töteberg (Frankurt am Main: Verlag der Autoren, 1986); and "Die Sachen sind so, wie sie sind," *Fernsehen und Film* (December 1970):18ff.

59. Wilfried Wiegand, "The Doll in the Doll: Observations on Fassbinder's Films," in *Fassbinder* (New York: Tanam, 1981), 26. [Translation by Ruth McCormick of the 1974 Hanser *Reihe Film* volume.]

60. Wilfried Wiegand, "Interview with Rainer Werner Fassbinder," in *Fassbinder* (New York: Tanam, 1981), 63–64.

61. St. John of the Cross, "Romance on the Gospel," ll. 145–149, in Antonio T. de Nicolás, *St. John of the Cross: Alchemist of the Soul* (New York: Paragon House, 1989), 95. The texts spoken in the film are the following: "Romance on the Gospel," ll. 145–156; "Spiritual Canticle," stanza 22 (first version) or stanza 29 (second version).

62. Peter W. Jansen and Wolfram Schütte, eds., *Herzog/Kluge/Straub* (Munich: Carl Hanser Verlag, 1976), 78.

63. Ibid., 78–79.

**Chapter 5. Time and Memory in Postwar Germany: *Not Reconciled***

1. James E. Young, "The Counter-Monument: Memory Against Itself in Germany Today," *Critical Inquiry* 18 (Winter 1992):267–296.

2. Ibid., 273.

3. Thomas Elsaesser, *New German Cinema: A History* (New Brunswick: Rutgers University Press, 1989), 258. Elsaesser writes that this film shares this quality in German cinema only with the films of a few Jewish exiles and feminist filmmakers.

4. Peter Handke, "Kinonacht, Kinotiernacht," *Die Zeit*, 20 November 1992.

5. See Heinrich Böll, *Querschnitte aus Interviews, Aufsätzen und Reden von Heinrich Böll*, ed. Viktor Böll and Renate Matthaei (Cologne: Kiepenheuer and Witsch, 1977).

6. As Klaus Jeziorkowski has noted, the longest sequences dedicated to the past are given to the three characters, Robert, Heinrich, and Johanna, filling most of chapters 3, 4, and 5, respectively. All three characters recount the past as their own way of avoiding the present. To this extent, these accounts are more than exposition. See Klaus Jeziorkowski, *Rhythmus und Figur: Zur Technik der epischen Konstruktion in Heinrich Bölls "Der Wegwerfer" und "Billard um halbzehn"* (Bad Homburg: Gehlen, 1968), 110.

7. Heinrich Böll, *Billiards at Half Past Nine* (New York: McGraw-Hill, 1962), 9; *Billard um halbzehn* (Cologne: Kiepenheuer and Witsch, 1959), 5. Cited hereafter with the page numbers from the English edition first, followed by those of the German.

8. Ibid., 157/173.

9. Ibid., 32/41.

10. Ibid., 41/50.

11. Ibid., 63/73.

12. Ibid., 35/44.

13. Ibid., 50/60.

14. Manfred Durzak assumes that the characters *have* been reconciled by the narrative and considers this a flaw in the novel's execution. For my interpretation, especially in regard to the film, this apparent reconciliation becomes less significant than the breaking open of temporal structures, which Durzak also stresses. See Manfred Durzak, *Der deutsche Roman der Gegenwart* (Stuttgart: Kohlhammer, 1971), 69.

15. Böll, *Billiards*, 149/164.

16. Ibid., 151/166.

17. Ibid., 239/260.

18. Ibid., 241/262.

19. Ibid., 245/266.

20. Ibid., 275/299.

21. Ibid., 251/273.

22. Cited in Marcel Reich-Ranicki, ed., *In Sachen Böll: Ansichten und Aussichten* (Cologne: Kiepenheuer and Witsch, 1968), 331.

23. Straub/Huillet were here contrasting the attitude toward violence in Nicholas Ray with that of Buñuel and Hawks. See "Straub and Huillet on Filmmakers They Like and Related Matters," *Film at the Public* program, ed. Jonathan Rosenbaum, November 1982, 7.

24. Richard Roud, *Jean-Marie Straub* (London: Secker and Warburg/British Film Institute, 1971; New York: Viking, 1972). All screenplay notes given by shot number in the text refer to the translation published on pp. 124–170 of the London edition.

25. On the Holocaust Memorial Museum, see, e.g., Phillip Lopate, "Resistance to the Holocaust," Yehuda Bauer, "Don't Resist," and Deborah E. Lipstadt, "What Is the Meaning of This to *You*?" [Critiques of Phillip Lopate], *Tikkun* 4, no. 3 (1990): 55–69. On the use of an enlarged casting of a Käthe Kollwitz pietà for the Central Memorial in Berlin, see "Mutter im Regen," *Der Spiegel* 46 (15 November 1993): 268–270.

26. Peter W. Jansen and Wolfram Schütte, eds., *Herzog/Kluge/Straub* (Munich: Carl Hanser Verlag, 1976), 212.

27. Böll, *Billiards*, 44/53.
28. Ibid., 241/262.
29. See Stephen Heath, "Narrative Space," *Screen* 17, no. 3 (Autumn 1976):68–112.
30. "Er blickte auf . . ."—in the billiard room; "Er sah sich auf den Uferwiesen stehen . . ."—in habitual action in the unspecified past; and finally, "Sie zappelten vorn an der Linie herum . . ."—past action on the specific day, 14 July 1935. Böll, *Billiards*, 32–34/41–43.
31. Böll, *Billiards*, 228–229/248–249.
32. Ibid., 279/303.
33. Michel Delahaye, "Pornographie et cinéma a l'état nu" [Interview with Jean-Marie Straub], *Cahiers du cinéma* 180 (July 1966):56.
34. Ibid.
35. Ibid., 55.
36. Ibid., 57.
37. Suite no. 2 in B Minor (BWV 1067).
38. Roud, *Jean-Marie Straub*, 62.
39. Roud, in *Jean-Marie Straub*, speaks of "Baroque" diagonals.
40. Roud, *Jean-Marie Straub*, 11.
41. Delahaye, "Pornographie et cinéma," 55.
42. Ibid., 56.
43. Ibid., 54.

**Chapter 6. *History Lessons* and Brecht's *The Business Affairs of Mr. Julius Caesar***

1. An earlier version of this chapter appeared in *Essays on Brecht = Versuche über Brecht*, Brecht Yearbook, vol. 15, ed. Marc Silberman et al. (Madison: International Brecht Society/University of Wisconsin Press, 1990), 125–149.
Bertolt Brecht, *Die Geschäfte des Herrn Julius Caesar* (Berlin: Gebrüder Weiss, 1957), 51. See Walter Busch, *Caesarismuskritik und epische Historik: Zur Entwicklung der politischen Ästhetik Bertolt Brechts 1936–1940* (Frankfurt am Main: Peter Lang, 1982), 43; Herbert Claas, *Die politische Ästhetik Bertolt Brechts vom Baal zum Caesar* (Frankfurt am Main: Suhrkamp, 1977), 167; Wolfgang Dieter Lebek, "Brechts Caesar-Roman: Kritisches zu einem Idol," in *Bertolt Brecht—Aspekte seines Werkes, Spuren seiner Wirkung*, ed. Helmut Koopmann and Theo Stammen (Munich: Verlag Ernst Vogel, 1983), 173–174; Harro Müller, "Anmerkungen zu Brechts historischem Roman *Die Geschäfte des Herrn Julius Caesar*," *Zeitschrift für deutsche Philologie* 104, no. 4 (1985):602.
2. The novel fragment is relatively obscure among Brecht's works, despite its being held in high regard by a number of critics. The segments included in Straub/Huillet's screenplay remain the only English translation: see *"History Lessons,"* *Screen* 17, no. 1 (Spring 1976):54–76.
3. Claas, *Die politische Ästhetik*, 137.
4. Maureen Turim, "Textuality and Theatricality in Brecht and Straub/Huillet: *History Lessons* (1972)," in *German Film and Literature: Adaptations and Transformations*, ed. Eric Rentschler (New York: Methuen, 1986), 235. Turim concentrates on

the theatricality, which makes the film an excellent example of "political modernism," rather than examining the method of narration.

5. Sylvia Harvey, "Whose Brecht? Memories for the Eighties," *Screen* 23, no. 1 (May/June 1982):57.

6. See Martin Walsh, "Brecht and Straub/Huillet: The Frontiers of Language, *History Lessons*," *Afterimage* 7 (Summer 1978):12–32. Reprinted (abridged) as "*History Lessons*: Brecht and Straub/Huillet," in Martin Walsh, *The Brechtian Aspect of Radical Cinema*, ed. Keith M. Griffiths (London: British Film Institute, 1981), 60–77.

7. See Peter Gidal, *Materialist Film* (London: Routledge, 1989), 36–41, 90. The reification of Brecht's ideas into a prescriptive theory is discussed at length in D.N. Rodowick, *The Crisis of Political Modernism: Criticism and Ideology in Contemporary Film Theory* (Urbana: University of Illinois Press, 1988), esp. chaps. 6 and 7.

8. See Christopher Roos, "The Adventures of the Signifier: The Driving Sequences in *History Lessons*," *Purdue Film Studies Annual* (1980):250–255; Gilberto Perez, "Modernist Cinema: The History Lessons of Straub and Huillet," *Artforum* 17, no. 2 (October 1978):46–55; Maureen Turim, "Jean-Marie Straub and Danièle Huillet: Oblique Angles on Film as Ideological Intervention," in *New German Filmmakers*, ed. Klaus Philips (New York: Ungar, 1984), 335–358.

9. Harvey, "Whose Brecht?" 56.

10. Martin Walsh, "Frontiers of Language," 21.

11. See Hans Jürgen Syberberg, *Hitler—ein Film aus Deutschland*, 1977.

12. H. Müller, "Anmerkungen zu Brechts historischem Roman," 602; and Claas, *Die politische Ästhetik*, 11.

13. Bertolt Brecht, *Arbeitsjournal*, 2 vols., ed. Werner Hecht (Frankfurt am Main: Suhrkamp, 1973), 1:72 (7 December 1939). All translations are my own.

14. Brecht, *Arbeitsjournal*, 1:42 (26 February 1939).

15. Ibid., 1:11 (23 July 1938).

16. Klaus-Detlef Müller, *Die Funktion der Geschichte im Werk Bertolt Brechts: Studien zum Verhältnis von Marxismus und Aesthetik* (Tübingen: Max Niemeyer Verlag, 1972), 31.

17. Ibid., 113.

18. Bertolt Brecht, *Die Geschäfte des Herrn Julius Caesar* (Berlin: Gebrüder Weiss, 1957), 51.

19. Ibid., 50.

20. Ibid., 217.

21. Ibid., 232.

22. K.-D. Müller, *Die Funktion der Geschichte*, 113.

23. Brecht, *Geschäfte*, 208.

24. Ibid., 211–212.

25. Walsh, "Frontiers of Language," 21.

26. Wolfram Schütte, "Gegenwartskunde oder Citizen C.," *Frankfurter Rundschau*, 12 October 1972.

27. Jan Kopf, *Bertolt Brecht: Ein kritischer Forschungsbericht: Fragwürdiges in der Brecht-Forschung* (Frankfurt am Main: Athenäum, 1974), 57.

28. Brecht, *Arbeitsjournal*, 1:76 (24 December 1939).

29. Werner Mittenzwei, *Brechts Verhältnis zur Tradition* (Berlin: Akademie-Verlag, 1973), 133.

30. Klaus Völker, *Bertolt Brecht: Eine Biographie* (Munich: Carl Hanser Verlag, 1976), 219.
31. Brecht, *Arbeitsjournal*, 1:16 (25 July 1938).
32. Völker, *Bertolt Brecht*, 304.
33. Franco Fortini, "The Writers' Mandate and the End of Anti-Fascism," *Screen* 15, no. 1 (Spring 1974):41. The poem referred to is "Die Literatur wird durchforscht werden."
34. Ibid.
35. Colin MacCabe, "The Politics of Separation," *Screen* 16, no. 4 (1975–1976):51.
36. Peter W. Jansen and Wolfram Schütte, eds., *Herzog/Kluge/Straub* (Munich: Carl Hanser Verlag, 1976), 209.
37. All screenplay notes are given by shot number in the text and refer to the following translation: "*History Lessons*," *Screen* 17, no. 1 (1976):54–76.
38. Walsh, "*History Lessons*: Brecht and Straub/Huillet," 65.
39. Walsh, "Frontiers of Language," 21.
40. Brecht, *Arbeitsjournal*, 1:18 (3 March 1938).
41. Walsh, "Frontiers of Language," 23.
42. Ibid.
43. Ibid., 24.
44. Ibid., 21.
45. Brecht, *Arbeitsjournal*, 1:72 (7 December 1939).
46. Walsh, "Frontiers of Language," 17.
47. Walter Benjamin, *Illuminations*, ed. Hannah Arendt, trans. Harry Zohn (New York: Schocken, 1978), 262.
48. Walsh, "Frontiers of Language," 23.
49. On Renoir and offscreen space, see Perez, "Modernist Cinema," 55.
50. MacCabe, "Politics of Separation," 52.
51. "Andi Engel Talks to Jean-Marie Straub and Danièle Huillet Is There Too," *Enthusiasm* 1 (December 1975):19.
52. Walsh, "Frontiers of Language," 17.
53. These two terms from 1970s film theory are cited in Rodowick, *Crisis of Political Modernism*, 281.

### Chapter 7. Musical Modernism and the Schoenberg Films

1. Theodor W. Adorno, *Prisms*, trans. Samuel and Shierry Weber (London: Neville Spearman, 1967), 34.
2. See Theodor W. Adorno, *Philosophy of Modern Music*, trans. Anne G. Mitchell and Wesley V. Blomster (New York: Continuum, 1985).
3. Hanns Eisler, *Composing for the Films* (New York: Oxford University Press, 1947), 36. Since Eisler was subject to McCarthyist attacks for his Communist affiliations when the book appeared, Adorno chose not to be credited as co-author until 1969.
4. Jacques Aumont, "Sur le Mont Sinaï," *Cahiers du cinéma* 430 (April 1990):52.
5. Eisler, *Composing*, 33.
6. Charles Rosen, *Arnold Schoenberg* (New York: Viking, 1975), 61.

7. See Carl Dahlhaus, *Schoenberg and the New Music*, trans. Derrick Puffett and Alfred Clayton (Cambridge: Cambridge University Press, 1988), 120.

8. Ibid., 102.

9. Eisler, *Composing*, 122.

10. Gertrud Koch, *Die Einstellung ist die Einstellung: Visuelle Konstruktionen des Judentums* (Frankfurt am Main: Suhrkamp, 1992).

11. Ibid., 29.

12. Philippe Lacoue-Labarthe, "The Caesura of Religion," in *Opera Through Other Eyes*, ed. David J. Levin (Stanford: Stanford University Press, 1993), 55.

13. See Koch, *Einstellung*, 32–33; and Aumont, "Sur le Mont Sinaï," 52.

14. Cited in Koch, *Einstellung*, 42.

15. Wolfram Schütte, "Aus einem Gespräch mit Michael Gielen," *Filmkritik* 5/6 (May/June 1975):281.

16. Michael Gielen, "Bericht über die Wiener Tonaufnahmen im April/Mai 1974: Schönbergs *Moses und Aron*," *Filmkritik* 5/6 (May/June 1975):276–278.

17. Liz-Anne Bawden, ed., *rororo Filmlexikon* 2 (Reinbeck bei Hamburg: Rowohlt, 1978), 427; "*Moïse et Aaron*," *Avant-scène cinéma* [Special issue on cinema and opera] 360 (May 1987):75.

18. Koch, *Einstellung*, 43.

19. Gielen, "Wiener Tonaufnahmen," 276.

20. Theodor W. Adorno, "Sacred Fragment: Schoenberg's *Moses and Aaron*," in *Quasi una Fantasia: Essays on Modern Music*, trans. Rodney Livingstone (London: Verso, 1992), 246.

21. Schütte, "Gespräch," 282.

22. Koch, *Einstellung*, 44.

23. Cited in Hans-Joachim Kraus, "Moses und der unvorstellbare Gott," in *Moses und Aron: zur Oper Arnold Schonbergs*, Bensberger Protokolle, no. 28 (Bensberg: Thomas-Morus-Akademie, 1979), 24.

24. Ibid., 15.

25. Ibid., 14.

26. Danièle Huillet, "Kleiner historischer Exkurs," *Filmkritik* 5/6 (May/June 1975):194–202. Compiled in preparation for the film, the sources for the information in the essay are not cited.

27. Ibid., 195.

28. Ibid., 202.

29. Joel Rogers, "Jean-Marie Straub and Danièle Huillet Interviewed: *Moses and Aaron* as an Object of Marxist Reflection," *Jump Cut* 12/13 (30 December 1976):62.

30. Huillet, "Kleiner historischer Exkurs," 201.

31. Kraus, "Moses," 16.

32. Both Koch and Walsh provide excellent interpretations of the camera movement and editing. Koch connects the motion of the camera to the musical annotations, and Walsh emphasizes the shifting image composition. See Koch, *Einstellung*, 44–45; and Martin Walsh, "*Moses and Aaron*: Straub and Huillet's Schoenberg," in Martin Walsh, *The Brechtian Aspect of Radical Cinema*, ed. Keith M. Griffiths (London: British Film Institute, 1981), 91–107, or *Jump Cut* 12/13 (30 December 1976):57–61.

33. "*Moses und Aron*: Beschreibung und Texte," *Filmkritik* 5/6 (May/June 1975): 203–252. Translations are not those of the subtitles but are taken from the libretto

published with the Philips recording: Arnold Schoenberg, *Moses und Aron. Oper in drei Akten*, Philips phonograph recording 6700 084, libretto trans. Allen Forte (Mainz: B. Schott's Söhne, 1974), 19.

34. Walsh, "*Moses und Aaron*," *Jump Cut*, 58.
35. Ibid., 59.
36. Ibid.
37. Schütte, "Gespräch," 282.
38. Koch, *Einstellung*, 51.
39. See Aumont, "Sur le Mont Sinaï," 52.
40. See Lacoue-Labarthe, "Caesura of Religion," 62–63: "That *Moses* is an opera, this is particularly difficult to dispute. From the dramaturgical point of view, it has all the faults of the genre. Among other things, I am thinking of the episode of worshiping the Golden Calf . . . which, in the style of an 'obligatory ballet' (in the second act, of course), lacks nothing of the lascivious absurdity of the 'flower maidens' in *Parsifal*."
41. Eugen Biser, "Der unvorstellbare Gott: Das Geheimnis ins Bild gebracht," in *Moses und Aron: zur Oper Arnold Schönbergs*, Bensberger Protokelle, no. 28 (Bensberg: Thomas-Morus-Akademie, 1979), 28. "Even the destruction of the graven image was only a sign, an image."
42. Lacoue-Labarthe, "Caesura of Religion," 65.
43. Ibid., 74.
44. Schoenberg, *Moses und Aron*, 20; shot 82.
45. Koch, *Einstellung*, 50.
46. See *Arnold Schoenberg, Wassily Kandinsky: Letters, Pictures and Documents*, ed. Jelena Hahl-Koch, trans. John C. Crawford (London: Faber and Faber, 1984).
47. Rosen, *Arnold Schoenberg*, 46.
48. Ibid., 57.
49. Ibid., 44–45.
50. Martin Walsh, "*Introduction to Arnold Schoenberg's 'Accompaniment for a Cinematographic Scene'*: Straub/Huillet: Brecht: Schoenberg," *Camera Obscura* 2 (Fall 1977):40.
51. Ibid., 37.
52. Ibid., 40.
53. Ibid., 42.
54. Ibid., 45.
55. Ibid., 37. Martin Jay also notes that the aftermath of the Paris Commune marks the beginning of the use of photos for police purposes. See Jay, *Downcast Eyes: The Denigration of Vision in Twentieth-Century French Thought* (Berkeley, Los Angeles, and London: University of California Press, 1993), 143.
56. Stephen Heath, *Questions of Cinema* (Bloomington: Indiana University Press, 1982), 13–15; see also Jacques-Alain Miller, "Suture," *Screen* 18, no. 4 (Winter 1977–1978):34.
57. Franco Fortini, "Brief an Jean-Marie Straub," *Filmkritik* [special issue] 1 (1977):2–3.
58. Straub/Huillet, "*Introduction to Arnold Schoenberg's 'Accompaniment for a Cinematographic Scene*'" [Screenplay], *Screen* 17, no. 1 (Spring 1976):77–83; shot 2.

59. Cited in Franco Fortini, "The Writers' Mandate and the End of Anti-Fascism," *Screen* 15, no. 1 (Spring 1974):56.

60. Peter Nau, "Drohende Gefahr, Angst, Katastrophe," *Filmkritik* 3 (1978):140.

61. A phrase used in the context of the creation of meaning in Hölderlin's poetry by Lacoue-Labarthe, in "Caesura of Religion," 73.

**Chapter 8. The Power to Narrate: *Class Relations* and Kafka's *Amerika***

1. Gertrud Koch, "Ex-Changing the Gaze: Re-Visioning Feminist Film Theory," *New German Critique* 34 (Winter 1985):142.

2. Dan Walworth, "A Partial Report from the 34th International Berlin Film Festival," *Millennium Film Journal* 14/15 (Fall/Winter 1984–1985):169.

3. Ulrich Greiner, "Achtung Liebe! Vorsicht Kino!" *Die Zeit*, 2 March 1984.

4. Wolfram Schütte, ed., *Klassenverhältnisse. Von Danièle Huillet und Jean-Marie Straub nach dem Amerika-Roman "Der Verschollene" von Franz Kafka* (Frankfurt am Main: Fischer, 1984).

5. Walworth, "A Partial Report," 170.

6. "Wie will ich lustig lachen, wenn alles durcheinandergeht" [Interview with Danièle Huillet and Jean-Marie Straub on *Class Relations*], *Filmkritik* 9/10 (1984):278.

7. "Wie will ich lustig lachen," 276.

8. Koch, "Ex-Changing the Gaze," 143–144.

9. Klaus Ramm, *Reduktion als Erzählprinzip bei Kafka* (Frankfurt: Athenäum, 1971).

10. See Teresa de Lauretis, *Alice Doesn't: Feminism, Semiotics, Cinema* (Bloomington: Indiana University Press, 1984), 103–157.

11. Franz Kafka, "The Judgment," in *The Basic Kafka* (New York: Washington Square Press, 1979), 54–66.

12. de Lauretis, *Alice Doesn't*, 60.

13. Ibid., 62.

14. Ibid., 63.

15. Franz Kafka, *Tagebücher 1910–1923* (New York: Schocken, 1949), 535.

16. Franz Kafka, *Amerika* (Frankfurt: Fischer, 1973), 12.

17. Ibid., 16.

18. Wolfram Schütte, "Arbeit, Gerechtigkeit, Liebe," *Frankfurter Rundschau*, 24 February 1984.

19. "Narrative space" is a concept developed by Stephen Heath. It describes the way in which narrative cinema leads viewers to construct a unified sense of space out of the fragments offered by the shots of a film. Common devices employed are establishing shots, point-of-view shots, reverse angle shots, and eye-line matches. For a fuller explanation, see Heath, "Narrative Space," *Screen* 17, no. 3 (Autumn 1976):68–112.

20. Citations from the subtitles refer to *Class Relations*, distributed in the United States by New Yorker Films.

21. Kafka, *Amerika*, 30.

22. Helmuth Karesek, "Niemandsland Amerika," *Der Spiegel* 38 (27 February 1984):181–184; Kristie A. Foell, "The Lyrical as Opposition in Straub/Huillet's Film Version of Kafka's *Amerika*," *Journal of the Kafka Society of America* 17, no. 2 (December 1993):8.

23. de Lauretis, *Alice Doesn't*, 68.
24. Koch, "Ex-Changing the Gaze," 144–145, 148.
25. Helge Heberle and Monika Funke Stern, "Das Feuer im Innern des Berges" [Interview with Danièle Huillet], *Frauen und Film* 32 (June 1982):9.
26. Koch, "Ex-Changing the Gaze," 151.
27. de Lauretis, *Alice Doesn't*, 63.

### Chapter 9. Language in Exile: Hölderlin's *The Death of Empedocles*

1. Helen Fehervary, *Hölderlin and the Left: The Search for a Dialectic of Art and Life* (Heidelberg: Carl Winter Universitätsverlag, 1977), 249.
2. Hans Hurch and Stephan Settele, "Der Schatten der Beute: Gespräch mit Danièle Huillet und Jean-Marie Straub," *Stadtkino Programm* [Vienna] 121 (October 1987): n.p.
3. George Steiner, *Antigones* (New York: Oxford University Press, 1984), 299.
4. Ibid., 300.
5. Marc Chevrie, "Le retour d'Empédocle. J.-M. Straub et D. Huillet: Entre deux films," *Cahiers du cinéma* 418 (April 1989):61.
6. Straub/Huillet issue, *filmwärts* 9 (1987):11.
7. Rembert Hüser, "Stummfilm mit Sprache: *Der Tod des Empedokles oder Wenn dann der Erde grün von Neuem euch erglänzt* von Danièle Huillet und Jean-Marie Straub," *filmwärts* 9 (1987):20. Also cited, with conflicting figures, by N.M., *Frankfurter Rundschau*, 27 May 1988.
8. Hüser, "Stummfilm mit Sprache," 20.
9. Ibid., 21.
10. Hans Hurch, " 'Habt ihr die Raben gehört?' Notizen zur Arbeit am *Tod des Empedokles*/ Dreharbeiten von Straub-Huillet," *Frankfurter Rundschau*, 23 December 1986. Hereafter cited as "Dreharbeiten."
11. "Kunst gegen Verschwendung," comment during public discussion at Filmmuseum Potsdam, 21 February 1992.
12. Wilhelm Schmid, "Im Garten am Rande des Abgrunds: Hölderlins *Empedokles* und der Versuch seiner Verfilmung," *die tageszeitung*, 6 August 1990. Schmid's descriptions are, however, inconsistent with those of Straub in *filmwärts* 9 (1987):11.
13. Straub/Huillet issue, *filmwärts* 9 (1987):11.
14. "Entretien avec Jean-Marie Straub et Danièle Huillet," in *Der Tod des Empedokles/La mort d'Empédocle*, ed. Jacques Déniel and Dominique Païni (Dunkerque: Studio 43/Paris: DOPA Films/Ecole regionale des beaux-arts, 1987), 47. This volume is cited hereafter as *Dunkerque*.
15. Hüser, "Stummfilm mit Sprache," 21.
16. "Erde, Raum und Menschen: Aus einem Gespräch mit Jean-Marie Straub über das Theater- und Filmprojekt der *Antigone*," *Frankfurter Rundschau*, 22 April 1991.
17. Public discussion, Filmmuseum Potsdam, 21 February 1992.
18. Carole Desbarats, "Jean-Marie Straub: Respecter le moment qui passe" [Interview], *Cinéma* [Paris] 423 (6 June 1988):8.
19. Ibid., 8.
20. Chevrie, "Le retour d'Empédocle," 61.

21. Desbarats, "Jean-Marie Straub," 8.
22. Chevrie, "Le retour d'Empédocle," 61.
23. Jean-Luc Godard, *Le Mépris* (Contempt), 1963.
24. See Gilles Deleuze and Felix Guattari, *Kafka: Toward a Minor Literature*, trans. Dana Polan (Minneapolis: University of Minnesota Press, 1986).
25. Fehervary, *Hölderlin and the Left*, 11.
26. Ibid., 27, 48. On the established leftist response to Hölderlin, see ibid., 44–48.
27. Ibid., 192.
28. There are striking parallels between the difficulties in the Hölderlin reception and the case of Kafka and much of the 1920s avant-garde. East and West Germany had different reasons for their cultural inhibitions, but they also failed to help each other break them down. In the East, the antidote to the aversion to avant-garde and modernist interpretations of Hölderlin, Kafka, and the arts of the 1920s was the ongoing theoretical investigation of Brecht, as a counterweight to Lukács. See, e.g., Gudrun Klatt, *Vom Umgang mit der Moderne: Ästhetische Konzepte der dreißiger Jahre* (Berlin: Akademie-Verlag, 1985); Karlheinz Barck, Dieter Schlenstedt, and Wolfgang Thierse, eds., *Künstlerische Avantgarde. Annäherungen an ein unabgeschlossenes Kapitel* (Berlin: Akademie-Verlag, 1979); and Dieter Schlenstedt, "Veto gegen die Trollwelt—Georg Lukács zur Kunstfeindlichkeit des Kapitalismus," *Weimarer Beiträge* 2 (1986): 275–286.
29. Fehervary, *Hölderlin and the Left*, 187.
30. Ibid., 187–191, 200–206.
31. Ibid., 202, 203.
32. Hurch and Settele, "Schatten der Beute."
33. Fehervary, *Hölderlin and the Left*, 203–204.
34. Peter Weiss, *Hölderlin* (Frankfurt am Main: Suhrkamp, 1971); see also Fehervary, *Hölderlin and the Left*, 206, 214.
35. On the Frankfurt vs. Stuttgart editions of Hölderlin, see Fehervary, *Hölderlin and the Left*, 233–239.
36. D. E. Sattler, *Thesen zur Staatenlosigkeit* (Bremen: Neue Bremer Presse, 1993).
37. "Dreharbeiten."
38. Eric Santer, *Friedrich Hölderlin: Narrative Vigilance and the Poetic Imagination* (New Brunswick: Rutgers University Press, 1986), 92–93.
39. Ibid., 127.
40. Ibid.
41. Hüser, "Stummfilm mit Sprache," 22.
42. Wolfram Schütte, "Priester, Philosoph, Volk: Straub-Huillet's Hölderlin-Film *Tod des Empedokles*," *Frankfurter Rundschau*, 7 May 1987.
43. Fehervary, *Hölderlin and the Left*, 193.
44. Ibid., 63.
45. Ibid., 110.
46. Helmut Krebs, "*Der Tod des Empedokles*," *Filmfaust* 60/61 (July/September 1987):51–52.
47. Michael Klier, *Porträts der Filmemacher: Jean-Marie Straub*, WDR, Cologne, 1970. Film.
48. Fehervary, *Hölderlin and the Left*, 1–10.
49. "Dreharbeiten."

50. Dominique Païni, "Straub et Cézanne ou l'insistence du regard," in *Dunkerque*, 19. That Hölderlin stands at a starting point for the modern sensibility is stressed by Foucault and Steiner as well: Foucault, cited in Hüser, "Stummfilm mit Sprache," 17. See also Steiner, *Antigones*, 67.

51. Schmid, "Im Garten."
52. Krebs, "Der Tod des Empedokles," 53.
53. Jean-Marie Straub, in *Cicim* 22/23 (June 1988):9.
54. Schmid, "Im Garten."
55. Santner, *Friedrich Hölderlin*, 45–46.
56. Ibid., 94.
57. Ibid., 25, 26.
58. Ibid., ix.
59. Ibid., x.
60. For a detailed description of how Straub/Huillet chose the camera position and lenses for the Act I confrontation of the same characters, see Jean-Marie Straub and Danièle Huillet, "Conception d'un film," *Théâtre/Public* 100 (July/August 1991):67–73.
61. The first of the two speeches is connected to a long shot of Etna taken with an 18 mm wide-angle lens; a lot of the foothills and little sky can be seen. The sides and foreground are reduced in the second shot of Etna that concludes the film, taken with a 25 mm lens. See Hüser, "Stummfilm mit Sprache," 22.
62. Straub/Huillet chose a very dense film stock, which produced a wide range of contrast in the harsh Sicilian light. See Hüser, "Stummfilm mit Sprache," 21.
63. Santner, *Friedrich Hölderlin*, 78.
64. Ibid., 76.
65. Both *Empedocles* and *Antigone* explore this public space, which Louis Seguin traces to the architecture of Jacobin spectacles. These gathered people "in the indivisible space of civic ardor and the transparency of hearts" but also designed the origins of the political distinction between Left and Right. See Louis Seguin, *"Aux Distraitement désespérés que nous sommes . . ." (Sur les films de Jean-Marie Straub et Danièle Huillet)* (Toulouse: Editions Ombres, 1991), 47.
66. Santner, *Friedrich Hölderlin*, 102, 146 n. 74.
67. Ibid., 90.
68. Alain Philippon, "Le secret derrière les arbres: *La mort d'Empédocle* par J.-M. Straub et D. Huillet," *Cahiers du cinéma* 400 (October 1987):42.
69. Caroline Champetier, "Tournage: *Trop Tôt, Trop Tard* (Straub-Huillet)," *Cahiers du cinéma* 316 (October 1980):ix.

### Chapter 10. Film as "Translation"

1. See also Adorno on this point: "On the Question 'What Is German?'" preceded by Thomas Y. Levin's essay "Nationalities of Language: Adorno's *Fremdwörter*; An Introduction to 'On the Question: "What is German?"'" *New German Critique* 36 (Fall 1985):121–131, 111–119.
2. Louis Seguin, *"Aux Distraitement désespérés que nous sommes . . ." (Sur les films de Jean-Marie Straub et Danièle Huillet)* (Toulouse: Editions Ombres, 1991), 76.

3. Peter Buchka, "Der gute Mensch von Agrigent: Die Straubs verfilmen Hölderlin," *Süddeutsche Zeitung*, 5 December 1987.

4. Hans Hurch, " 'Habt ihr die Raben gehört?' Notizen zur Arbeit am *Tod des Empedokles*/Dreharbeiten von Straub-Huillet," *Frankfurter Rundschau*, 23 December 1986. Hereafter cited as "Dreharbeiten."

5. Raphaël Bassan, "*La mort d'Empédocle*: Approche plastique du texte d'Hölderlin," *Revue du cinéma* 431 (October 1987):50.

6. Harun Farocki, "Den Text zu Gehör bringen: Gespräch mit Andreas von Rauch," *Stadtkino Programm* [Vienna] 121 (October 1987): n.p. Reprinted in *die tageszeitung*, 19 November 1987.

7. See *Der Tod des Empedokles/La mort d'Empédocle*, ed. Jacques Déniel and Dominique Païni (Dunkerque: Studio 43/Paris: DOPA Films/Ecole regionale des beauxarts, 1987), hereafter cited as *Dunkerque*; and Philippe Lacoue-Labarthe, "The Caesura of the Speculative," in *Typography: Mimesis, Philosophy, Politics* (Cambridge: Harvard University Press, 1989), 208–235.

8. Farocki, "Den Text zu Gehör bringen."

9. Cited in Rembert Hüser, "Stummfilm mit Sprache: *Der Tod des Empedokles oder Wenn dann der Erde grün von neuem euch erglänzt* von Danièle Huillet und Jean-Marie Straub," *filmwärts* 9 (1987):17. "Does the dog / bite?"

10. Ulli Müller-Schöll, "Heil'ge Natur," *Film/Video Logbuch* 12 (May 1987):7.

11. *Brechts Antigone des Sophokles*, ed. Werner Hecht (Frankfurt am Main: Suhrkamp, 1988).

12. Eric Santner, *Friedrich Hölderlin: Narrative Vigilance and the Poetic Imagination* (New Brunswick: Rutgers University Press, 1986), 58.

13. Cited in Santner, *Friedrich Hölderlin*, 59.

14. See Farocki, "Den Text zu Gehör bringen"; and Bassan, "*La mort d'Empédocle*," 50. Hüser also writes of Straub/Huillet's avoidance of trained actors and its effects: "For the two [Straub/Huillet] it is a disadvantage, since they consider professional actors as an independent group sociologically uninteresting ('In the early Hollywood films one can still see that the actor is a farmer or something'). The choice of actors is correspondingly mixed. Next to each other appear a Dutch opera singer, an Italian philosophy professor (and Gramsci specialist) next to a German ballet dancer and Goethe Institute teacher; an almost 80-year-old Melville/Lang/Godard actor next to a pair of Italian siblings. A majority of the actors speak German as a second language. Melodically that is very interesting. The Empedocles actor is Andreas von Rauch, a former teacher from Hamburg-Altona. The Bach violin sonata in the opening credits is played by him." Hüser, "Stummfilm mit Sprache," 20–21.

15. Hans Hurch and Stephan Settele, "Der Schatten der Beute: Gespräch mit Danièle Huillet und Jean-Marie Straub," *Stadtkino Programm* [Vienna] 121 (October 1987): n.p.

16. On the Frankfurt edition by D. E. Sattler, see Helen Fehervary, *Hölderlin and the Left: The Search for a Dialectic of Art and Life* (Heidelberg: Carl Winter Universitätsverlag, 1977), 235.

17. Hüser, "Stummfilm mit Sprache," 18.

18. I am grateful to Catherine Russell for calling my attention to this term from Benjamin.

19. Paul de Man, "Conclusions: Walter Benjamin's 'The Task of the Translator,'" in *The Resistance to Theory* (Minneapolis: University of Minnesota Press, 1986), 80. The troubling revelations, after de Man's death, of his wartime journalism in Belgium have produced much published discussion of questions of guilt, collaboration, anti-Semitism, and the relation of de Man's silence about his past to his practice as a critic. Although it is poignant that de Man's last essay treats Walter Benjamin, who committed suicide in 1940 while fleeing Nazi persecution as a Jew and a Marxist, I believe one can find de Man's interpretation of Benjamin useful without either demonizing its author or stylizing him as a tragic brother figure of Benjamin. For a discussion of these issues, see Shoshana Felman, "Paul de Man's Silence," *Critical Inquiry* 15, no. 4 (Summer 1989):704–744 (followed by a group of related essays in the same journal); and *Responses: On Paul de Man's Wartime Journalism*, ed. Werner Hamacher, Neil Hertz, and Thomas Keenan (Lincoln: University of Nebraska Press, 1989).

20. Walter Benjamin, *Illuminations*, ed. Hannah Arendt, trans. Harry Zohn (New York: Schocken, 1969), 79 (translation altered); *Illuminationen* (Frankfurt am Main: Suhrkamp, 1955), 66. Cited hereafter with page numbers from the English edition first, followed by those of the German.

21. See Joël Magny, "Lecture d'Empédocle," *Cahiers du cinéma* 402 (December 1987):xiv.

22. de Man, *Resistance to Theory*, 83.

23. Laurence Giavarini, "Antigone, sauvage!" *Cahiers du cinéma* 459:38–40.

24. Benjamin, *Illuminations*, 78/65.

25. Ibid., 81–82/69.

26. de Man, *Resistance to Theory*, 90.

27. Ibid., 84.

28. Ibid., 85.

29. Ibid., 82–83.

30. See ibid., 87: "Benjamin says, from the beginning, that it is not at all certain that language is in any sense human."

31. Ibid., 83–84.

32. Ibid., 76, citing Gadamer.

33. Benjamin, *Illuminations*, 70/57.

34. Ibid., 71/58. Vincent Nordon similarly stressed the "impersonality" of semiotic relations in his analysis of *Bridegroom*: see Nordon, "Notes sur un travelling," *Ça cinéma* 2 (October 1973):66–70, esp. 69.

35. de Man, *Resistance to Theory*, 92.

36. Ibid., 103.

37. Ibid., 104.

38. Ibid., 96.

39. Ibid., 92.

40. Ibid., 75.

41. Santner, *Friedrich Hölderlin*, 119.

42. Cited in ibid., 121.

43. Benjamin, *Illuminations*, 75/62.

44. Santner, *Friedrich Hölderlin*, xi.

45. "Dreharbeiten."

46. Krebs, "*Der Tod des Empedokles*," *Filmfaust* 60/61 (July/September 1987):52.
47. Ibid., 51.
48. *Dunkerque*, 53.
49. Michael Klier, *Porträts der Filmemacher: Jean-Marie Straub*, WDR, Cologne, 1970. Film.
50. *Dunkerque*, 60, 61.
51. Public discussion, Filmmuseum Potsdam, 21 February 1992.
52. Philippe Arnaud, "Strauboscopie: *La mort d'Empédocle*: Le Tournage," *Cahiers du cinéma* 394 (April 1987):51.
53. Straub, quoted by Magny, "Lecture d'Empédocle," xiv.
54. "Erde, Raum und Menschen: Aus einem Gespräch mit Jean-Marie Straub über das Theater- und Filmprojekt der *Antigone*," *Frankfurter Rundschau*, 22 April 1991.
55. Giorgio Baratta and Dagmar Kamlan, "Zärtliche Nähe von Herz und Vernunft," *Deutsches Allgemeines Sonntagsblatt* [*Kulturmagazin*], 3 April 1987.
56. Santner, *Friedrich Hölderlin*, 147.
57. Cited in Fehervary, *Hölderlin and the Left*, 189.
58. Santner, *Friedrich Hölderlin*, 84. *Harte Fügung*, which could be translated as "syntactical disjointedness," refers to the harshness or abruptness of syntactical relationships in the poetry.
59. de Man, *Resistance to Theory*, 79.
60. Charles Tesson, "L'heure de vérité," *Cahiers du cinéma* 394 (April 1987):50.
61. Hüser, "Stummfilm mit Sprache," 22.
62. Alain Philippon, "Le secret derrière les arbres: *La mort d'Empédocle* par J.-M. Straub et D. Huillet," *Cahiers du cinéma* 400 (October 1987):42.
63. Benjamin, *Illuminations*, 82/59.
64. Ibid.
65. Ibid.

**Chapter 11. *Antigone***

1. "Erde, Raum und Menschen: Aus einem Gespräch mit Jean-Marie Straub über das Theater- und Filmprojekt der *Antigone*," *Frankfurter Rundschau*, 22 April 1991.
2. Peter Handke, "Kinonacht, Kinotiernacht," *Die Zeit*, 20 November 1992. A renowned "post-Brechtian" playwright, Handke is also a screenwriter and filmmaker in his own right. He adapted his novel *The Goalie's Fear of the Penalty Kick* for the film directed by Wim Wenders (1971) and directed *The Left-handed Woman* (1978).
3. Handke, "Kinonacht."
4. Hiroshi Yagi, "*Antigone* von Brecht und das Theater im Osten," in *Brechts Antigone des Sophokles*, ed. Werner Hecht (Frankfurt am Main: Suhrkamp, 1988), 278. See also Jochanaan Christoph Trilse, "Brechts Verständnis der Antike," 238, and, on the Pindar insertions, Rainer Pohl, "Strukturelemente und Pathosformen in der Sprache," 249, in the same volume.
5. Handke, "Kinonacht."
6. Winfried Günther, "*Antigone*," *epd Film* 11 (1992):29.
7. Handke, "Kinonacht."

8. See "Erde."

9. *The New Grove Dictionary of Music and Musicians*, vol. 16, ed. Stanley Sadie (London: Macmillan, 1980), 687.

10. Ibid., 687, 688.

11. Rüdiger Schaper, "In Styropor gemeißelt: Straub/Huillet inszenieren *Antigone* an der Schaubühne," *Süddeutsche Zeitung*, 7 May 1991.

12. *Brechts Antigone des Sophokles*, ed. Werner Hecht (Frankfurt am Main: Suhrkamp, 1988), 127.

13. Thanks to Jonathan Rosenbaum for calling my attention to this unity.

14. John Fuegi, "The Metamorphosis of an Aristotelian Classic: *Antigone*," in *The Essential Brecht* (Los Angeles: Hennessey and Ingalls, 1972), 65.

15. *Brechts Antigone*, 185.

16. See also Helen Fehervary, *Hölderlin and the Left: The Search for a Dialectic of Art and Life* (Heidelberg: Carl Winter Universitätsverlag, 1977), 30, 41–42.

17. *Brechts Antigone*, 49.

18. Cited in Ulrich Weisstein, "Imitation, Stylization and Adaptation: The Language of Brecht's *Antigone* and Its Relation to Hölderlin's Version of Sophocles," *German Quarterly* 46 (1973):597.

19. Ruth Berlau, "Erinnerungen," in *Brechts Antigone des Sophokles*, ed. Werner Hecht (Frankfurt am Main: Suhrkamp, 1988), 184.

20. "Erde."

21. *Brechts Antigone*, 12–13.

22. Hans Curjel, "Die Bühnenbearbeitung Bertolt Brechts," in *Brechts Antigone des Sophokles*, ed. Werner Hecht (Frankfurt am Main: Suhrkamp, 1988), 177.

23. *Brechts Antigone*, 13. "And the matter be / Not as for nothing"; "For disloyal will one not catch *me*"; and "High-citied comes he, uncitied / To nothing, where the beautiful / With him is and with impudence." See Weisstein, "Imitation," 587.

24. Weisstein, "Imitation" [citing Pohl], 588; also *Brechts Antigone* [Pohl], 248.

25. *Brechts Antigone*, 116.

| | |
|---|---|
| Elders: | Yet it eats much force, to think of cruel punishment. |
| Creon: | To push the plow to earth so it plows takes force. |
| Elders: | Yet mild order, playing, achieves much. |
| Creon: | Orders are manifold. Yet: Who orders? |
| Haemon: | Were I even not your son, I would say, you. |
| Creon: | Yet were it lain to me, I must do it in my way. |
| Haemon: | In your way, yet be it the right way. |
| Creon: | Not knowing what I know, you could not know it. Are you my friend, however I may act? |
| Haemon: | I would that you acted so that I were your friend. |

26. See *Brechts Antigone*, 23: "und Argos wird ein Stalingrad von heute—die Parallele ist deutlich"; "and Argos becomes a Stalingrad of today—the parallel is clear."

27. *Brechts Antigone*, 100. "It's false. Earth is a burden. Home is not only / Earth, not house only. Not where one has poured out sweat / Not the house that helplessly sees the approaching fire / Not where he bowed his neck, not that calls he home."

28. See Weisstein, "Imitation," 593.
29. *Brechts Antigone*, 132. "Do not, I bid you, speak of fate. / That I know. Speak of him / Who does me in, guiltless: him / Knots a fate!"
30. Bertolt Brecht, "Die jüdische Frau," in *Furcht und Elend des Dritten Reiches*, in *Die Stücke von Bertolt Brecht in einem Band* (Frankfurt am Main: Suhrkamp, 1978), 452.
31. See *Brechts Antigone*, 23.
32. Ibid., 154.

> [Messenger]
> And, Lord, the Argos folk fought with villainous cunning.
> The women fought and the children fought.
> Kettles, long without edible contents
> From burned-out rooftops were they hurled
> Upon us with boiling water; even houses left whole
> Were set afire in our backs as if no one
> Thought of ever more living anywhere. For entrenchments
> And weapons were made of household goods and dwelling.

33. George Steiner, *Antigones* (New York: Oxford University Press, 1984), 247. Steiner translates *tödlichfaktisch* as "factually-deadly."
34. Programmheft, Schaubühne [Berlin], 3 May 1991, n.p. Cited also in Steiner, *Antigones*, 95.
35. See Steiner, *Antigones*, 93–94; Weisstein, "Imitation," 588–590.
36. Günther, *"Antigone,"* 29.
37. Wilhelm Schmid, "Auf der Bühne steht nur der Diskurs," *die tageszeitung*, 7 May 1991.
38. Handke, "Kinonacht,"
39. Laurence Giavarini, "Antigone, sauvage!" *Cahiers du cinéma* 459 (1992):41.
40. Handke, "Kinonacht."
41. "Are you giving me riddles, you transparent one?" Winfried Günther sees this pan as expressing an unspoken threat from Creon. See Günther, *"Antigone,"* 29.
42. "Much is monstrous. But nothing / More monstrous than humanity." *Brechts Antigone*, 86.
43. Handke, "Kinonacht."
44. Steiner, *Antigones*, 304.
45. Ibid., 14.
46. Ibid., 95.
47. Handke, "Kinonacht."
48. Schmid, "Auf der Bühne."
49. "Erde."
50. Ibid.
51. Fuegi, "Metamorphosis of an Aristotelian Classic," 65.
52. Steiner, *Antigones*, 93–94.
53. Paul de Man, "Conclusions: Walter Benjamin's 'The Task of the Translator,'" in *The Resistance to Theory* (Minneapolis: University of Minnesota Press, 1986), 102.
54. Giavarini, "Antigone, sauvage!" 41. Giavarini compares this violence to the "almost unbearable" vertical cutting of the frame by the snake in *Moses und Aron*.

55. Handke, "Kinonacht."
56. Ibid.
57. Steiner, *Antigones*, 81.
58. Laurence Giavarini, "Puissance des fantômes," *Cahiers du cinéma* 460 (1992):72.
59. Ibid., 73.
60. "Mismanagement cries for greatness, finds none. / War comes out of war and breaks its leg. / Robbery comes from robbery, and hardness needs hardness / And more needs more and comes in the end to nothing."
61. Steiner, *Antigones*, 132. Steiner presents a number of interpretations of *Antigone* that point toward a reconciliation or an idealist synthesis; see pp. 5, 14, 31, 74.
62. Steiner, *Antigones*, 303.
63. Alain Philippon, "Le secret derrière les arbres: *La mort d'Empédocle* par J.-M. Straub et D. Huillet," *Cahiers du cinéma* 400 (October 1987):41.
64. Peter Kammerer, "Worte gegen Wind und Steine: Straub/Huillet haben die *Antigone* Hölderlins und Brechts auf Sizilien gedreht," *Frankfurter Rundschau*, 20 January 1992.
65. Hans Hurch, "Von Steinen und Menschen," *Falter* 16 (1992):24.
66. "Erde."
67. Kammerer, "Worte gegen Wind."
68. Dietmar Schings, "Eine Frau im Licht," *Deutsches Allgemeines Sonntagsblatt*, 14 February 1992.
69. Günther, "*Antigone*," 29.
70. Schings, "Eine Frau im Licht."
71. Ibid.
72. Handke, "Kinonacht."
73. "Entretien Dominique Païni–Jean Narboni," in *Der Tod des Empedokles/La mort d'Empédocle*, ed. Jacques Déniel and Dominique Païni (Dunkerque: Studio 43/Paris: DOPA Films/Ecole regionale des beaux-arts, 1987), 64.
74. I have written elsewhere about the "fantasm" represented by Nazism, the Holocaust, and Hiroshima in the context of *Divided Heaven* and *Hiroshima mon amour*; see "Geschichte, Trauer und weibliche Identität im Film," in *Zwischen gestern und morgen: Schriftstellerinnen der DDR aus amerikanischer Sicht*, ed. Ute Brandes (Berlin: Europäischer Verlag der Wissenschaften/Peter Lang, 1992), 95–112.
On the "common crime" as a founding break of the symbolic order, see Julia Kristeva, "Revolution in Poetic Language," in *The Kristeva Reader*, ed. Toril Moi (New York: Columbia University Press, 1986), 119. On the "fantasm" in the context of the atomic bomb and the Nazi Holocaust, see Sharon Willis, *Marguerite Duras: Writing on the Body* (Urbana: University of Illinois Press, 1987), 95; and Madeleine Borgomano, *L'Ecriture filmique de Marguerite Duras* (Paris: Albatros, 1985), 47–48.
75. See Franco Fortini, "The Writers' Mandate and the End of Anti-Fascism," *Screen* 15, no. 1 (Spring 1974):41.
76. Steiner, *Antigones*, 31.
77. "Antigone nue," *Libération*, 1 September 1992.
78. Ibid.
79. Steiner, *Antigones*, 281–282.

80. Ibid., 3.
81. "Antigone nue."
82. *Brechts Antigone*, 126. "Do not / Lay waste the earthly realm with the violence of hands."
83. Cited in Holger Teschke, unpublished ms., 1993, 15.
84. *Brechts Antigone*, 144. "And have I thus looked back, and around myself / You look ahead and shudder."
85. Hurch, "Steinen."

**Chapter 12. Real History and the Nonexistent Spectator: Brecht, Adorno, and Straub/Huillet**

1. Peter Zach, "Vom Unglück in einer Maschine zu sein, die viele Freiheiten beinahe hat, aber in sich das Glück nur ab und zu zeigt" [Interview with Straub/Huillet], *Blimp* (March 1985):16.
2. Andreas Huyssen, *After the Great Divide: Modernism, Mass Culture, Postmodernism* (Bloomington: Indiana University Press, 1986), 157.
3. Miriam B. Hansen, "Introduction to Adorno, 'Transparencies on Film' (1966)," and Theodor W. Adorno, "Transparencies on Film," trans. Thomas Y. Levin, *New German Critique* 24/25 (Fall/Winter 1981–1982):187–198, 199–205. See also Hansen's essay, "Mass Culture and Hieroglyphic Writing: Adorno, Derrida, Kracauer," *New German Critique* [Adorno issue] 56 (Spring/Summer 1992):43–73.
4. Andreas Huyssen, "Adorno in Reverse: From Hollywood to Richard Wagner," in *After the Great Divide: Modernism, Mass Culture, Postmodernism* (Bloomington: Indiana University Press), 16–43. See Theodor W. Adorno, *In Search of Wagner*, trans. Rodney Livingstone (London: NLB, 1981).
5. Peter U. Hohendahl, "Introduction: Adorno Criticism Today," *New German Critique* [Adorno issue] 56 (Spring/Summer 1992):6.
6. Michael P. Steinberg, "The Musical Absolute," *New German Critique* [Adorno issue] 56 (Spring/Summer 1992):19.
7. Martin Walsh, "*Moses and Aaron*: Straub and Huillet's Schoenberg," *Jump Cut* 12/13 (30 December 1976):60.
8. Joel Rogers, "Jean-Marie Straub and Danièle Huillet Interviewed: *Moses and Aaron* as an Object of Marxist Reflection," *Jump Cut* 12/13 (30 December 1976):63.
9. Ibid., 61.
10. Bertolt Brecht, *Schriften zur Politik und Gesellschaft*, Vol. 20, *Gesammelte Werke* (Frankfurt am Main: Suhrkamp, 1967), 305.
11. Klaus-Detlef Müller, "Der Philosoph auf dem Theater: Ideologie-kritik und 'Linksabweichung' in Bertolt Brechts 'Messingkauf,' " in *Bertolt Brecht*, ed. Heinz Ludwig Arnold (Sonderband aus der Reihe Text + Kritik; Munich: Boorberg, 1972), 55.
12. This similarity between the two theorists' perceptions of the medium was first called to my attention by Marcus Bullock.
13. See Ben Brewster, "The Fundamental Reproach (Brecht)," *Ciné-Tracts* 1 (1977):44–53. The translation of the word *Grundeinwand* as "fundamental reproach" could be an exaggeration of Brecht's rejection of the medium, since it could be rendered as something much milder, such as "main objection."

14. Cited in Burkhardt Lindner, "Brecht/Benjamin/Adorno: Über Veränderungen der Kunstproduktion im wissenschaftlich-technischen Zeitalter," in *Bertolt Brecht*, ed. Heinz Ludwig Arnold (Sonderband aus der Reihe Text + Kritik; Munich: Boorberg, 1972), 20.
15. Ibid.
16. Ibid.
17. Bertolt Brecht, "Der Dreigroschenprozess," in *Versuche 1–12* (Berlin: Suhrkamp, 1959), 298.
18. Stephen Heath, *Questions of Cinema* (Bloomington: Indiana University Press, 1981), 5.
19. Lindner, "Brecht/Benjamin/Adorno," 9.
20. Hanns Eisler, *Composing for the Films* (New York: Oxford University Press, 1947), 54, 59.
21. Stephen Heath, "Narrative Space," *Screen* 17, no. 3 (Autumn 1976):76.
22. Heath, *Questions of Cinema*, 52.
23. Ibid., 51.
24. Ibid., 124–125.
25. See Herbert Marcuse, *Eros and Civilization* (New York: Vintage, 1962), 213 and passim.
26. Hans Meyer, *Brecht in der Geschichte: Drei Versuche* (Frankfurt am Main: Suhrkamp, 1971), 236.
27. Theodor W. Adorno, *Ästhetische Theorie* (Frankfurt am Main: Suhrkamp, 1973), 360.
28. Ibid., 250. The same has been said of music, a quality Straub/Huillet exploit even as they deny it in narrative.
29. Adorno, *Ästhetische Theorie*, 358–359.
30. Ibid., 353.
31. Ibid., 199–200.
32. Ibid., 359.
33. Ibid., 264.
34. Ibid., 356.
35. Lindner, "Brecht/Benjamin/Adorno," 25.
36. Bertolt Brecht, "Anmerkungen zur Dreigroschenoper," in *Versuche 1–12* (Berlin: Suhrkamp, 1959), 226–227.
37. Heath, *Questions of Cinema*, 125.
38. Klaus-Detlef Müller, *Die Funktion der Geschichte im Werk Bertolt Brechts: Studien zum Verhältnis von Marxismus und Ästhetik* (Tübingen: Max Niemeyer Verlag, 1972), 173.
39. Adorno, *Ästhetische Theorie*, 366.
40. Ibid., 387.
41. Müller, "Philosoph," 60.
42. Franco Fortini, "The Writers' Mandate and the End of Anti-Fascism," *Screen* 15, no. 1 (Spring 1974):60.
43. Walter Benjamin, *Illuminations*, ed. Hannah Arendt, trans. Harry Zohn (New York: Schocken, 1978), 261.
44. Colin MacCabe, "Theory and Film: Principles of Realism and Pleasure," *Screen* 17, no. 3 (Autumn 1976):21.

45. Martin Walsh, in discussion following Colin MacCabe's "The Politics of Separation," *Screen* 16, no. 4 (Winter 1975/1976):60.

46. Peter Gidal, "Straub/Huillet Talking, and Short Notes on Some Contentious Issues," *Ark/Journal from the Royal College of Art* (January 1976):90.

47. Ibid.

48. Peter Gidal, "Identifying Non-Narrative," *Film Form* 1, no. 2 (Autumn 1977):70.

49. Julia Kristeva, "Signifying Practice and Mode of Production" ["Hegel, the East and Us"], *Edinburgh '76 Magazine* 1:74.

50. Jacques Henric and Dominique Païni, "Serge Daney: Cinephilia" [Interview], trans. J. O'Toole, *art press* [Paris] 182:E29–30.

51. Brecht, "Dreigroschenprozess," 280–281.

52. Eisler, *Composing*, 132.

# Selected Bibliography

The following is a listing of publications on and by Straub/Huillet, organized by year of publication.

Färber, Helmut. "Machorka Muff" [sic]. *Filmkritik* 1 (1964):36.
Straub, Jean-Marie. Letter to Editor. *Filmkritik* 4 (1964):221.

Delahaye, Michel. "Allemagne ciné zero." *Cahiers du cinéma* 163 (February 1965):58–67.

Delahaye, Michel. "Pornographie et cinéma a l'état nu" [Interview with Jean-Marie Straub]. *Cahiers du cinéma* 180 (July 1966):52–57.
Nettelbeck, Uwe. "Plädoyer für ein Projekt. Der Fall Jean-Marie Straub." *Die Zeit*, 14 October 1966.

"Bach war kein Masochist" [*Chronik der Anna Magdalena Bach*] [Interview with Jean-Marie Straub]. *Film* (April 1968):23–28.
Färber, Helmut. "Im Anschluß an das Protokoll der *Chronik der Anna Magdalena Bach*." *Filmkritik* 10 (1968):695–703.
Hommel, Friedrich. "Le Martyr de Saint-Jean-Sébastien: Anmerkungen eines Musikkritikers zu Straubs *Chronik der Anna Magdalena Bach*." *Film* (May 1968):30–31.

*Chronik der Anna Magdalena Bach*. Kleine Filmkunstreihe 81. Ed. Herbert Linder. Frankfurt am Main: Neue Filmkunst, 1969.
Galle, Mischa, and Florian Hopf. "Jean-Marie Straub verließ die Bundesrepublik. Ein Gespräch zum Abschied." *Frankfurter Rundschau*, 26 April 1969.
Mengershausen, Joachim von. "'Und jetzt mache ich mich fort.' Zerstörte Hoffnung: Jean-Marie Straub und sein Film über Bach." *Christ und Welt*, 11 April 1969.

Schütte, Wolfram. "Präsens—Futur—Präteritum (zur 34. Einstellung der *Chronik*)." *Neue Züricher Zeitung*, 13 December 1969. Reprinted in *Visuelle Kommunikation*, ed. H. K. Ehmer (Cologne: DuMont Schauberg, 1971), 293–298.

Straub, Jean-Marie. *Chronik der Anna Magdalena Bach*. Frankfurt am Main: Verlag Filmkritik, 1969.

"Andi Engel Talks to Jean-Marie Straub." *Cinemantics* 1 (1 January 1970):16–24.

Benayoun, Robert. "Les Enfants du paradigme." *Positif* 122 (December 1970):7–26.

Engel, Andi. "Jean-Marie Straub." In *Second Wave*, ed. Ian Cameron et al. (London: Studio Vista, 1970), 128–132.

Kaiser, Joachim. "Respekt, Spiel, Freiheit: Zu drei Filmen über Musik: *Chronik der Anna Magdalena Bach, Eika Katappa, Ludwig van . . .*" *Fernsehen und Film* 8, no. 8 (August 1970):26–29.

Klier, Michael. *Porträts der Filmemacher: Jean-Marie Straub*. WDR, Cologne, 1970. Film.

Narboni, Jean. "Vicarious Power" [Translation by Leigh Hafrey of 1970 essay]. In *Cahiers du Cinéma, 1969–1972: The Politics of Representation*, ed. Nick Browne (Cambridge: Harvard University Press, 1990), 150–162.

Straub, Jean-Marie. "Doppiare e un assassino." *Paese Sera*, 13 March 1970.

"Balayez-moi tout ça!" [Interview]. *Les Lettres Françaises*, 13 January 1971.
"Jean-Marie Straubs *Othon*." *Filmkritik* 1 (1971):12–29.
Roud, Richard. *Jean-Marie Straub*. London: Secker and Warburg/British Film Institute, 1971; New York: Viking, 1972.

Bitomsky, Hartmut. *Die Röte des Rots von Technicolor: Kinorealität und Produktionswirklichkeit*. Neuwied/Darmstadt: Luchterhand, 1972. On *Othon*: 44–46; on *Chronik*: 76–79.

Pasolini, Pier Paolo. "The Unpopular Cinema" [1972]. In *Heretical Empiricism*, ed. Louise K. Barnett, trans. Ben Lawton and Louise K. Barnett (Bloomington: Indiana University Press, 1988), 267–275.

Schütte, Wolfram. "Gegenwartskunde oder Citizen C." *Frankfurter Rundschau*, 12 October 1972.

Bronnen, Barbara. "Jean-Marie Straub" [Interview]. In *Die Filmemacher. Zur neuen deutschen Produktion nach Oberhausen 1962*, ed. Barbara Bronnen and Corinna Brocher (Munich: Bertelsmann, 1973), 25–45.

Nordon, Vincent. "Notes sur un travelling." *Ça cinéma* 2 (October 1973):66–70.

Bitomsky, Hartmut. "'Geschichtsunterricht' . . . seit seiner Herstellung: Ein Film und seine kommerzielle Zensur." *Filmkritik* 5 (1974):210–223.

Pflaum, Hans Gunther. "Die Kunst des Augenblicks." *Süddeutsche Zeitung*, 18 June 1974.

Schoenberg, Arnold. *Moses und Aron. Oper in drei Akten.* Philips phonograph recording 6700 084. Libretto trans. Allen Forte. Mainz: B. Schott's Söhne, 1974.

Walsh, Martin. "Political Formations in the Cinema of Jean-Marie Straub." *Jump Cut* 1 (December 1974):12–18.

"After *Othon*, before *History Lessons*: Geoffrey Nowell-Smith Talks to Jean-Marie Straub and Danièle Huillet." *Enthusiasm* 1 (1975):26–31.

"Andi Engel Talks to Jean-Marie Straub and Danièle Huillet Is There Too." *Enthusiasm* 1 (1975):1–25.

Gielen, Michael. "Bericht über die Wiener Tonaufnahmen im April/Mai 1974: Schoenbergs *Moses und Aron*." *Filmkritik* 5/6 (May/June 1975):276–278.

Huillet, Danièle. "Kleiner historischer Exkurs." *Filmkritik* 5/6 (May/June 1975):194–202.

Jeremias, Brigitte. "Ein sakraler Monolith, mitten in die Landschaft gestellt: Jean-Marie Straubs *Moses-und-Aron*-Verfilmung." *Frankfurter Allgemeine Zeitung*, 27 February 1975.

Schütte, Wolfram. "Aus einem Gespräch mit Michael Gielen." *Filmkritik* 5/6 (May/June 1975):280–283.

———. "Bilder sammeln Musik." *Frankfurter Rundschau*, 29 March 1975.

Seguin, Louis. "La famille, l'histoire, le roman." *Cahiers du cinéma* 260/261 (October/November 1975):57–68.

Ungari, Enzo. "Sur le son: Entretien avec J.-M. Straub et D. Huillet." Trans. Marianne Di Vettimo. *Cahiers du cinéma* 260/261 (October/November 1975):48–53.

Woods, Gregory. "A Work Journal of the Straub/Huillet Film *Moses and Aaron* by Gregory Woods." *Enthusiasm* 1 (1975):32–54. With "Notes" by Danièle Huillet.

Armes, Roy. "Jean-Marie Straub: Strict Counterpoint." In *The Ambiguous Image* (London: Secker and Warburg, 1976), 208–215.

Buchka, Peter. "Die Treue zum verweigerten Glück: Deutsche Filmemacher V: Jean-Marie Straub und Danièle Huillet." *Süddeutsche Zeitung*, 4–5 December 1976.

Dermody, Susan. "The Politics of Film Practice." *Cinema Papers* 10 (September/October 1976):127–130, 184–185.

Gidal, Peter. "Straub/Huillet Talking, and Short Notes on Some Contentious Issues." *Ark/Journal from the Royal College of Art* (January 1976):89–97.

Jansen, Peter W., and Wolfram Schütte, eds. *Herzog/Kluge/Straub*. Munich: Carl Hanser Verlag, 1976.

Nordon, Vincent. "Violence et Passion (Straub, encore)." *Ça cinéma* 9 (1976):25–26.

Rogers, Joel. "Jean-Marie Straub and Danièle Huillet Interviewed: *Moses and Aaron* as an Object of Marxist Reflection." *Jump Cut* 12/13 (30 December 1976):61–64.

Turim, Maureen. "*Ecriture Blanche*: The Ordering of the Filmic Text in *The Chronicle of Anna Magdalena Bach*." *Purdue Film Studies Annual* (1976):177–192.
Walsh, Martin. "*Moses and Aaron*: Straub and Huillet's Schoenberg." *Jump Cut* 12/13 (30 December 1976):57–60.
Witte, Karsten. "Straubs Publikum." *Kirche und Film* 19, no. 3 (1976):1–2. Reprinted in *Frankfurter Rundschau*, 19 October 1976.
"Pressekonferenz in Pesaro mit Danièle Huillet, Franco Fortini und Jean-Marie Straub zu *Fortini/Cani*." *Filmkritik* [special issue] 1 (1977):4–13.
Bonnet, Jean-Claude. "Trois Cinéastes du texte." *Cinématographe* 31 (October 1977):2–6.
Fortini, Franco. "Brief an Jean-Marie Straub." *Filmkritik* [special issue] 1 (1977):2–3.
Nash, Mark, and Steve Neal. "Film: 'History/Production/Memory.' " *Screen* 18, no. 4 (Fall/Winter 1977–1978):77–91.
Walsh, Martin. "*Introduction to Arnold Schoenberg's 'Accompaniment for a Cinematographic Scene'*: Straub/Huillet: Brecht: Schoenberg." *Camera Obscura* 2 (Fall 1977):34–49.
Bennett, Edward. "The Films of Straub Are Not 'Theoretical.' " *Afterimage* 7 (Summer 1978):5–11.
Nau, Peter. "Drohende Gefahr, Angst, Katastrophe." *Filmkritik* 3 (1978):138–145.
Perez, Gilberto. "Modernist Cinema: The History Lessons of Straub and Huillet." *Artforum* 17, no. 2 (October 1978):46–55.
Walsh, Martin. "Brecht and Straub/Huillet: The Frontiers of Language, *History Lessons*." *Afterimage* 7 (Summer 1978):12–32. Reprinted (abridged) in Martin Walsh, *The Brechtian Aspect of Radical Cinema*, ed. Keith M. Griffiths (London: British Film Institute, 1981), 60–77.
Blank, Manfred. "Mond, Sonne, Wasser, Feuer; Blut auf den Feldern: Eine Materialsammlung." *Filmkritik* 4 (1979):158–173.
Nau, Peter. "Filme Lesen." *Filmkritik* 6 (1979):263–272.
"Aus einem Kolloquium: Mythologie und Widerstand." *Filmkritik* 12 (1980):529–545.
Brunow, Jochen. "Der Maschine Widerstand leisten. Begegnung mit Danièle Huillet und Jean-Marie Straub." *Filme* 1 (1980):29–35.
Champetier, Caroline. "Tournage: *Trop Tôt, Trop Tard* (Straub-Huillet)." *Cahiers du cinéma* 316 (October 1980):viii–ix.
Fieschi, Jean-André. "Jean-Marie Straub." In *Cinema: A Critical Dictionary*, ed. Richard Roud, trans. Michael Graham (New York: Viking, 1980), 969–973. Also in French: *Ça cinéma* 9 (February 1976):20–24.
Fortini, Franco. "Warum ein Film verstehen hilft, was in den letzten zwanzig Jahren geschehen ist. Und was werden soll [*Dalla Nube alla resistenza* di Jean-Marie Straub e Danièle Huillet]." Trans. Manfred Blank. *Filmkritik* 12 (1980):520–528. Reprinted from *La Nouvelle Revue Française*, 1 November 1979.

Magisos, M. "*Not Reconciled*: The Destruction of Narrative Pleasure." *Wide Angle* 3, no. 4 (1980):35–41.
Roos, Christopher. "The Adventures of the Signifier: The Driving Sequences in *History Lessons*." *Purdue Film Studies Annual* (1980):250–255.
Sandford, John. "Jean-Marie Straub." In *The New German Cinema* (London: Oswald Wolff, 1980), 27–36.

Feddermann, Klaus, and Helmut Herbst. *Zwischen den Bildern. 3. Teil. Über die Trägheit der Wahrnehmung*. Stiftung Deutsche Kinemathek/ZDF, Berlin (West)/Mainz, 1981. Film.

Heberle, Helge, and Monika Funke Stern. "Das Feuer im Innern des Berges" [Interview with Danièle Huillet]. *Frauen und Film* 32 (June 1982):4–12.
Mariani, Phil. "An Interview with Jean-Marie Straub and Danièle Huillet." *Wedge: An Aesthetic Inquiry* 1 (Summer 1982):22–29.
Rosenbaum, Jonathan. "Introduction: Once It Was Fire . . ." In "The Cinema of Jean-Marie Straub and Danièle Huillet, November 2–14, 1982." *Film at the Public* program tabloid. Also contains: Filmography, "Straub and Huillet on Filmmakers They Like and Related Matters," "Film Is Only a Reflection of the Class Struggle" (Luc Moulet), "Modernist Cinema: The History Lessons of Straub and Huillet" (Gilberto Perez), "Synopsis and Review of *Every Revolution Is a Throw of the Dice*" (Tony Rayns), Bruce Jenkins on *Every Revolution . . .* and *From the Cloud to the Resistance*, Rosenbaum on *From the Cloud . . .* , and Serge Daney on *Too Early, Too Late*.

Brewster, Ben. "Too Early/Too Late: Interview with Huillet and Straub. Translation and Notes by Ben Brewster." *Undercut* 7/8 (Spring 1983): 28–33.
Budney, Mildred, and Yehuda Safran. "The Lay of the Land." *Undercut* 7/8 (Spring 1983):34–36.
Farocki, Harun. "Einfach mit der Seele, das gibt es nicht" [Interview]. *Filmkritik* 5 (1983):242–247.
———. "Guten Tag, Herr Rossmann." *Die Zeit*, 1 July 1983.
———. *Jean-Marie Straub und Danièle Huillet bei der Arbeit . . .* Harun Farocki Filmproduktion/WDR, Berlin (West)/Cologne, 1983. Film.
Franklin, James. "Jean-Marie Straub/Danièle Huillet." In *New German Cinema: From Oberhausen to Hamburg* (Boston: Twayne, 1983), 74–88.
Lange, M., et al. "Wie kann man Hitchcocko-Hawkesianer sein?" *Filmkritik* 1 (1983):9–32.
Rosenbaum, Jonathan. "Jean-Marie Straub and Danièle Huillet." In *Film: The Front Line* (Denver: Arden, 1983), 187–199.

*Les Films de Jean-Marie Straub/Danièle Huillet: Amerika/Rapports de classes/Klassenverhältnisse*. Toulouse: NEF Diffusion/Ombres, 1984.
Special issue on *Class Relations*: KLASSENVERHÄLTNISSE. *Filmkritik* 9/10 (1984).
Bergala, Alain. "Le plus petit planète du monde." *Cahiers du cinéma* 364 (October 1984):27–31.

Greiner, Ulrich. "Achtung Liebe! Vorsicht Kino!" *Die Zeit*, 2 March 1984.
Hoberman, J. "Class Relations." *Art Forum* 23 (September 1984):75–77.
Karesek, Hellmuth. "Niemandsland Amerika." *Der Spiegel* (27 February 1984): 181, 184.
Schütte, Wolfram, ed. *Klassenverhältnisse. Von Danièle Huillet und Jean-Marie Straub nach dem Amerika-Roman "Der Verschollene" von Franz Kafka.* Frankfurt am Main: Fischer, 1984. Also contains essay and interview by Schütte and an article on the shooting of the film by Dietrich Kuhlbrot.
Turim, Maureen. "Jean-Marie Straub and Danièle Huillet: Oblique Angles on Film as Ideological Intervention." In *New German Filmmakers*, ed. Klaus Phillips (New York: Ungar, 1984), 335–358.

Rentschler, Eric. "The Use and Abuse of Memory: New German Film and the Discourse of Bitburg." *New German Critique* 36 (Fall 1985):67–90.
Witte, Karsten. Essays on *Moses and Aaron*, *Fortini/Cani*, and *Every Revolution Is a Throw of the Dice*. In *Im Kino: Texte vom Sehen und Hören* (Frankfurt am Main: Fischer, 1985), 120–131.
Zach, Peter. "Vom ünglück in einer Maschine zu sein, die viele Freiheiten beinahe hat, aber in sich das Glück nur ab und zu zeigt" [Interview with Straub/Huillet]. *Blimp* (March 1985):16–23.

Duras, Marguerite. "*Othon*, by Jean-Marie Straub." In *Outside: Selected Writings*, trans. Arthur Goldhammer (Boston: Beacon Press, 1986), 155–157.
Hurch, Hans. "'Habt ihr die Raben gehört?' Notizen zur Arbeit am *Tod des Empedokles*/Dreharbeiten von Straub-Huillet." *Frankfurter Rundschau*, 23 December 1986.
Turim, Maureen. "Textuality and Theatricality in Brecht and Straub/Huillet: *History Lessons* (1972)." In *German Film and Literature: Adaptations and Transformations*, ed. Eric Rentschler (New York: Methuen, 1986), 231–245.

"*Moïse et Aaron*." *Avant-scène cinéma* [Special issue on cinema and opera] 360 (May 1987):75.
Special issue on Straub/Huillet: Die Grösse des Films, das ist die Bescheidenheit, dass man zur Fotografie Verurteilt ist. *filmwärts* 9 (December 1987).
Arnaud, Philippe. "Strauboscopie: *La mort d'Empédocle*: Le Tournage." *Cahiers du cinéma* 394 (April 1987):51.
Baratta, Giorgio, and Dagmar Kamlan. "Zärtliche Nähe von Herz und Vernunft." *Deutsches Allgemeines Sonntagsblatt* [*Kulturmagazin*], 3 May 1987.
Buchka, Peter. "Der gute Mensch von Agrigent: Die Straubs verfilmen Hölderlin." *Süddeutsche Zeitung*, 5 December 1987.
Farocki, Harun. "Den Text zu Gehör bringen: Gespräch mit Andreas von Rauch." *Stadtkino Programm* [Vienna] 121 (October 1987). Reprinted in *die tageszeitung*, 19 November 1987.
Hurch, Hans, and Stephan Settele. "Der Schatten der Beute: Gespräch mit Danièle Huillet und Jean-Marie Straub." *Stadtkino Programm* [Vienna] 121 (October 1987).

Hüser, Rembert. "Stummfilm mit Sprache: *Der Tod des Empedokles oder Wenn dann der Erde Grün von Neuem euch erglänzt* von Danièle Huillet und Jean-Marie Straub." *filmwärts* 9 (1987):20.
Krebs, Helmut. "*Der Tod des Empedokles.*" *Filmfaust* 60/61 (July/September 1987):51–52.
Magny, Joël. "Lecture d'Empédocle." *Cahiers du cinéma* 402 (December 1987): xiv.
Philippon, Alain. "Le secret derrière les arbres: *La mort d'Empédocle* par J.-M. Straub et D. Huillet." *Cahiers du cinéma* 400 (October 1987):40–42.
Schütte, Wolfram. "Priester, Philosoph, Volk: Straub-Huillets Hölderlin-Film *Tod des Empedokles.*" *Frankfurter Rundschau*, 7 May 1987.
Straub, Jean-Marie, and Danièle Huillet. *Der Tod des Empedokles/La Mort d'Empédocle*. Ed. Jacques Déniel and Dominique Païni. Dunkerque: Studio 43/Paris: DOPA Films/Ecole regionale des beaux-arts, 1987. Contains the essay "Straub et Cézanne ou l'insistence du regard" by Dominique Païni, an interview with the filmmakers, and one by Païni with Jean Narboni.
Tesson, Charles. "L'Heure de vérité." *Cahiers du cinéma* 394 (April 1987):50.

Esser, Michael W. *"Das ist eben das Leben, das das Leben nicht ist"* [*Black Sin*]. *filmwärts* 12 (1988):30–34.
Rauh, Reinhold, ed. *Machorka-Muff: Jean-Marie Straubs und Danièle Huillets Verfilmung einer Satire von Heinrich Böll*. Münster: MAKS, 1988.
Rosenbaum, Jonathan. "The Sound of German." *Chicago Reader* (2 December 1988):10, 12.

Chevrie, Marc. "Le retour d'Empédocle. J.-M. Straub et D. Huillet: Entre deux films," *Cahiers du cinéma* 418 (April 1989):59–64.
Gidal, Peter. *Materialist Film*. London: Routledge, 1989. (See pp. 36–41, 90.)
Witte, Karsten. "Der Preis der Melancholie" [*Black Sin*]. *Frankfurter Rundschau*, 14 March 1989.

*Jean-Marie Straub/Danièle Huillet. Hölderlin/Cézanne*. Lédignan: Editions Antigone, 1990. Includes the text "Avoir une idée en cinéma" by Gilles Deleuze.
"La preuve par Straub et Huillet." *Cahiers du cinéma* 430 (April 1990):48–53.
Hoh, Katharina, and Fritz von Klinggräff. "Die guten Götter Hölderlins. Ein Gespräch mit Danielle [*sic*] Huillet und Jean-Marie Straub über ihren neuesten Streifen *Cézanne* und die Zernichtung ihres Sujets." *die tageszeitung*, 5 May 1990.
Petley, Julian. "Etna and Ecology: Straub/Huillet's *Empedocles.*" *Sight and Sound* 59 (Summer 1990):150.
Schmid, Wilhelm. "Im Garten am Rande des Abgrunds: Hölderlins *Empedokles* und der Versuch seiner Verfilmung." *die tageszeitung*, 6 August 1990.
Straub, Jean-Marie, and Danièle Huillet. *Moïse et Aaron*. Toulouse: Editions Ombres, 1990.
———. *Empédocle sur l'Etna*. Toulouse: Editions Ombres, 1990.

"Erde, Raum und Menschen: Aus einem Gespräch mit Jean-Marie Straub über das Theater- und Filmprojekt der *Antigone*." *Frankfurter Rundschau*, 22 April 1991.

Schmid, Wilhelm. "Auf der Bühne steht nur der Diskurs." *die tageszeitung*, 7 May 1991.

Seguin, Louis. *"Aux Distraitement désespérés que nous sommes . . ." (Sur les films de Jean-Marie Straub et Danièle Huillet)*. Toulouse: Editions Ombres, 1991.

Straub, Jean-Marie, and Danièle Huillet. "Conception d'un film." Ed. Anne Benhaïem. *Théâtre/Public* 100 (July/August 1991):67–73.

"Antigone, Antigone" and "Straub par Straub." *L'Armateur* 4 (November/December 1992):5–13.

"Antigone nue." *Libération*, 1 September 1992.

Giavarini, Laurence. "Antigone, sauvage!" *Cahiers du cinéma* 459 (1992):38–41.

———. "Puissance des fantômes." *Cahiers du cinéma* 460 (1992):72–75.

Handke, Peter. "Kinonacht, Kinotiernacht." *Die Zeit*, 20 November 1992.

Hurch, Hans. "Von Steinen und Menschen." *Falter* 16 (1992):24.

Koch, Gertrud. "*Moses und Aron*: Musik, Text, Film und andere Fallen der Rezeption." In *Die Einstellung ist die Einstellung: Visuelle Konstruktionen des Judentums* (Frankfurt am Main: Suhrkamp, 1992), 30–52.

Schings, Dietmar. "Eine Frau im Licht." *Deutsches Allgemeines Sonntagsblatt*, 14 February 1992.

Settele, Stephan. *Play Antigone*. Deutsche Film- und Fernsehakademie Berlin, 1992. Film.

Blank, Manfred. *L'insistence du regard/Die Beharrlichkeit des Blicks*. Hessischer Rundfunk/Arte, 1993. Film.

Foell, Kristie A. "The Lyrical as Opposition in Straub/Huillet's Film Version of Kafka's *Amerika*." *Journal of the Kafka Society of America* 17, no. 2 (December 1993):4–12.

Seguin, Louis. "L'histoire et la géographie." *Quinzaine Littéraire*, 15 November 1994.

# Filmography

1962  *Machorka-Muff*
18 minutes
Photography: Wendelin Sachtler (35 mm)
Sound: Janosz Rozner, Jean-Marie Straub
Actors: Erich Kuby (Erich von Machorka-Muff), Renate Lang
  (Inniga von Zaster-Pehnunz)
Based on the story "Bonn Diary" by Heinrich Böll
Filmed in ten days on location in Bonn and Munich, September 1962

Published screenplays: *Cinema e Film* [Rome] (Summer 1968); Reinhold Rauh, ed., *Machorka-Muff: Jean-Marie Straubs und Danièle Huillets Verfilmung einer Satire von Heinrich Böll* (Münster: MAKS, 1988)

1964–1965  *Nicht versöhnt oder Es hilft nur Gewalt, wo Gewalt herrscht (Not Reconciled)*
55 minutes
Photography: Wendelin Sachtler (35 mm)
Sound: Lutz Grübnau, Willi Hanspach
Actors: Henning Harmssen (Robert Fähmel, age 40), Ulrich Hopmann
  (Robert Fähmel, age 18), Ernst Kutzinski (Schrella, age 15),
  Ulrich von Thüna (Schrella, age about 35), Martha Ständner
  (Johanna Fähmel, age 70), Danièle Huillet (Johanna Fähmel as a
  young woman)
Based on the novel *Billiards at Half Past Nine* by Heinrich Böll
Filmed in six weeks on location in Cologne and Munich,
  August–September 1964, and two weeks in spring 1965

Published screenplays: *Filmkritik* 2 (1966):65–70 (excerpts); Richard Roud, *Jean-Marie Straub*, trans. Misha Donat (London: Secker and Warburg, 1971), 124–171; *Cinema e Film* [Rome] (Winter 1966–1967):79–97; *Ça cinéma* (October 1973):30–57

1967  *Chronik der Anna Magdalena Bach* (*Chronicle of Anna Magdalena Bach*)
93 minutes
Photography: Ugo Piccone, Saverio Diamanti, Giovanni Canfarelli (35 mm)
Sound: Louis Hochet, Lucien Moreau
Actors: Gustav Leonhardt (Johann Sebastian Bach), Christiane Lang-Drewanz (Anna Magdalena Bach); with the Concentus Musicus (Vienna), the concert group of the *Schola Cantorum Basiliensis* (Basel), and the Hanover Boys' Choir
Filmed in eight weeks on location in Preetz, Stade, Hamburg, Eutin, Lüneburg, Lübeck, Nürnberg, Freiberg/Sachsen, East Berlin, Regensburg, and Haseldorf, August–October 1967

Published screenplays: *Chronik der Anna Magdalena Bach*, ed. Helmut Färber (Frankfurt am Main: Verlag Filmkritik, 1969); *Cahiers du cinéma* (April/May 1968):200–201; *Cinema e Film* [Rome] (Summer 1968):56–90

1968  *Der Bräutigam, die Komödiantin und der Zuhälter* (*The Bridegroom, the Comedienne, and the Pimp*)
23 minutes
Photography: Klaus Schilling, Hubs Hagen (35 mm)
Sound: Peter Lutz, Klaus Eckelt
Actors: Rainer Werner Fassbinder, James Powell, Lilith Ungerer, Hanna Schygulla, Irm Hermann, Peer Raben
Filmed in five days on location in Munich, April–May 1968

Published screenplays: *Filmkritik* 10 (1968):680–687; *Cinema e Film* [Rome] (Winter/Spring 1969)

1969  *Les yeux ne veulent pas en tout temps se fermer ou Peut-être qu'un jour Rome se permettra de choisir à son tour* (*Othon*)
88 minutes
Photography: Ugo Piccone, Renato Berta (16 mm, Eastmancolor)
Sound: Louis Hochet, Lucien Moreau
Actors: Olimpia Carlisi (Camille), Adriano Aprà (Othon), Anne Brumagne (Plautine), Ennio Lauricella (Galba), Marilù Parolini (Flavie), Jean-Claude Biette (Martian), Jean-Marie Straub (Lacus), Edoardo de Gregorio (Atticus)
Based on the play *Othon* by Pierre Corneille

Filmed in four weeks on location at the Palatine Hill and in the gardens of the Villa Doria Pamphili in Rome, August–September 1969

Published screenplays: *Othon*, drama by Pierre Corneille (1664), trans. Herbert Linder and Straub/Huillet (New York: Herbert Linder, 1974 [privately issued]); *Bianco e Nero* (January/April 1970); *Cinema e Film* (Summer/Fall 1970):203–239

1972     *Geschichtsunterricht (History Lessons)*
85 minutes
Photography: Renato Berta, Emilio Bestetti (16 mm, Eastmancolor)
Sound: Jeti Grigioni
Actors: Gottfried Bold (The Banker), Johann Unterpertinger (The Peasant), Henri Ludwigg (The Lawyer), Carl Vaillant (The Writer), Benedikt Zulauf (The Young Man)
Based on the novel fragment *Die Geschäfte des Herrn Julius Caesar (The Business Affairs of Mr. Julius Caesar)* by Bertolt Brecht
Filmed on location in Rome, Frascati, Terenten (Alto Adige), and on the island of Elba, June–July 1972

Published screenplays: *Screen* 17, no. 1 (Spring 1976):54–76; "Leçons d'histoire," trans. Straub/Huillet, *Cahiers du cinéma* 241 (September/October 1972):46–66; *Filmcritica* (February/March 1974)

1972     *Einleitung zu Arnold Schoenbergs "Begleitmusik zu einer Lichtspielscene" (Introduction to Arnold Schoenberg's "Accompaniment to a Cinematographic Scene")*
Photography: Renato Berta (16 mm, Eastmancolor); Horst Bever (black & white Gevaert)
Sound: Jeti Grigioni, Harald Lill
Actors: Günter Peter Straschek, Danièle Huillet, Jean-Marie Straub, Peter Nestler
Filmed in Rome and Baden-Baden, July–September 1972

Published screenplays: *Filmkritik* 2 (1973):80–87; *Screen* 17, no. 1 (Spring 1976):77–83; *Filmcritica* (January/February 1973):34–40; *Ça cinéma* 1, no. 2 (October 1973):58–65

1974–1975     *Moses und Aron (Moses and Aaron)*
105 minutes
Photography: Ugo Piccone, Saverio Diamanti, Gianni Canfarelli, Renato Berta (35 mm, Eastmancolor)
Sound: Louis Hochet, Ernst Neuspiel, Georges Vaglio, Jeti Grigioni
Actors: Günter Reich (Moses), Louis Devos (Aaron), Eva Csapò (Young Woman), Richard Salter (Man); Choir and Symphony

Orchestra of the ORF (Vienna), under the musical direction of Michael Gielen
Based on the opera *Moses and Aaron* by Arnold Schoenberg
Filmed on location in the amphitheater of Alba Fucense and at Lago Matese, August–September 1974

Published screenplays: *Moïse et Aron*, trans. Straub/Huillet (Toulouse: Editions Ombres, 1990); *Filmkritik* 5/6 (1975):203–252; corrections follow in *Filmkritik* 10 (1975); *Cahiers du cinéma* 260/261 (October/November 1975):69–84 (Act I) and 262/263 (January 1976):79–94 (Acts II and III) [trans. Straub/Huillet]; *Filmcritica* (March 1975):92–99 (excerpts); English translation of the libretto, not supervised by Straub/Huillet, accompanies Philips recording no. 6700 084

1976  *Fortini/Cani*
83 minutes
Photography: Renato Berta, Emilio Bestetti (16 mm, Eastmancolor)
Sound: Jeti Grigioni
Actors: Franco Fortini, Franco Lattes, Luciana Nissim, Adriano Aprà
Based on the book *I cani del Sinai/The Dogs of Sinai* by Franco Fortini

Published screenplays: *Screen* 19, no. 2 (Summer 1978):9–40; *Filmkritik* 1 (1977):14–35; *Les Chiens du Sinai—Fortini/Cani* (Paris: Dossiers Cahiers du Cinéma, March 1979)

1977  *Toute révolution est un coup de dés* (*Every Revolution Is a Throw of the Dice*)
11 minutes
Photography: William Lubtchansky (35 mm, Eastmancolor)
Sound: Louis Hochet
Actors: Danièle Huillet, Marilù Parolini, Dominique Villain, Andrea Spingler, Helmut Färber, Michel Delahaye, Manfred Blank, Georges Goldfayn, Aksar Khaled
Based on the poem *A Throw of the Dice Will Never Abolish Chance* by Stéphane Mallarmé
Filmed on location in the Père Lachaise Cemetery, Paris, May 1977

1978  *Dalla nube alla resistenza* (*From the Cloud to the Resistance*)
105 minutes
Photography: Saverio Diamanti, Gianni Canfarelli (35 mm, color)
Sound: Louis Hochet, Georges Vaglio
Actors: Olimpia Carlisi (Nephele, the Cloud), Gino Felici (Hippolocus), Ennio Lauricella (Tiresias), Mauro Monni (The Bastard), Carmelo Lacorte (Nuto)
Based on the books *Dialogues with Leucò* and *The Moon and the Bonfires* by Cesare Pavese

Published screenplay: *Filmkritik* 11 (1980)

1980–1981　*Zu früh, Zu spät/Trop tôt, Trop tard/Troppo presto,*
*Troppo tardi/Too Early, Too Late*
105 minutes
Photography: William Lubtchansky, Robert Alazraki (16 mm, Eastmancolor)
Sound: Louis Hochet
Voices: First part, letter sent by Friedrich Engels to Karl Kautsky: Danièle Huillet; second part, excerpt from *Luttes sociales en Egypte* by Mahmud Hussein: Gérard Samaan (German and Italian versions), Bhagat el Nadi (French and English versions)
Filmed on locations in France (including Tréogan, Motreff, Marbeuf, Harville, and outside Lyon and Rennes) in June 1980 and in Egypt in May 1981

1982　*En Râchâchant*
$7\frac{1}{2}$ minutes
Photography: Henri Alekan (35 mm, black & white)
Sound: Louis Hochet
Actors: Olivier Straub, Raymond Gérard, Nadette Thinus, Bernard Thinus
Based on the story "Ah Ernesto" by Marguerite Duras
Filmed on location in Paris in August 1982

1983　*Klassenverhältnisse (Class Relations)*
126 minutes
Photography: William Lubtchansky, Caroline Champetier (35 mm, black & white)
Sound: Louis Hochet, Georges Vaglio, Manfred Blank
Actors: Christian Heinisch, Reinald Schnell, Anna Schnell, Klaus Traube, Hermann Hartmann, Jean-François Quinque, Alfred Edel, Libgart Schwarz, Mario Adorf, Gérard Samaan, Manfred Blank, Andi Engel, Harun Farocki
Based on the novel fragment *Amerika* by Franz Kafka
Filmed on location in Hamburg, Bremen, New York, and Missouri in 1983

Published screenplay: *Klassenverhältnisse. Von Danièle Huillet und Jean-Marie Straub nach dem Amerika-Roman "Der Verschollene" von Franz Kafka*, ed. Wolfram Schütte (Frankfurt am Main: Fischer, 1984)

1986　*Der Tod des Empedokles oder: wenn dann der Erde Grün von neuem euch erglänzt (The Death of Empedocles)*
132 minutes
Photography: Renato Berta, Jean-Paul Toraille, Giovanni Canfarelli (35 mm, Eastmancolor)
Sound: Louis Hochet, Georges Vaglio, Alessandro Zanon

Actors: Andreas von Rauch, Vladimir Baratta, Martina Baratta, Ute Cremer, Howard Vernon, William Berger, Frederico Hecker, Peter Boom, Giorgio Baratta
Based on *The Death of Empedocles* by Friedrich Hölderlin (first version, 1798)
Filmed on location in Ragusa and on Mount Etna in 1986

1988  *Schwarze Sünde (Black Sin)*
40 minutes
Photography: William Lubtchansky, Christophe Pollock, Gianni Canfarelli (35 mm, Eastmancolor)
Sound: Louis Hochet, Sandro Zanon
Actors: Andreas von Rauch, Vladimir Baratta, Howard Vernon, Danièle Huillet
Based on *The Death of Empedocles* by Friedrich Hölderlin (third version, 1798)
Filmed on location on Mount Etna in 1988

Published screenplay: *Empédocle sur Etna* (Toulouse: Editions Ombres, 1990)

1989  *Cézanne*
51 minutes
Photography: Henri Alekan (35 mm, color)
Sound: Louis Hochet
Actors: Voices of Jean-Marie Straub, Danièle Huillet
Based on the dialogues of Cézanne and Joachim Gasquet; with excerpts from the films *The Death of Empedocles* and *Madame Bovary* (Jean Renoir, 1933)
Filmed on location in Paris, La Montagne Sainte-Victoire, London, Edinburgh, Basel, and Ascona in 1988

1991–1992  *Die Antigone des Sophokles nach der hölderlinschen Übertragung für die Bühne bearbeitet von Brecht 1948 (Suhrkamp Verlag)* (*Antigone*)
100 minutes
Photography: William Lubtchansky (35 mm, Eastmancolor)
Sound: Louis Hochet
Actors: Astrid Ofner, Werner Rehm, Ursula Ofner, Hans Diel, Kurt Radeke, Michael Maassen, Rainer Philippi, Libgart Schwarz
Based on Sophocles' *Antigone* (translated into German by Friedrich Hölderlin, 1800–1803) as adapted by Bertolt Brecht (1947–1951)
Filmed on location in Segesta (Sicily) in 1991–1992

Published screenplay: *Antigone. Sophocle. Hölderlin. Brecht. Huillet. Straub.* (Toulouse: Editions Ombres, 1992)

1994 *Lothringen!* (*Lorraine!*)
21 minutes
Photography: Christophe Pollock (35 mm, color)
Sound: Louis Hochet
With extracts from the novel *Colette Baudochè* by Maurice Barres

# Index

Acting, 16, 23–24, 56, 65, 68, 88, 89, 101, 115, 171, 200, 207–208, 210–211, 222–223
"Action," 105–106, 114, 126, 149, 223
Actors, 3, 48–50, 72, 92–93
Adorno, Theodor W., 4, 34, 140–141, 193, 233–248
Aesthetics, 21–23, 243–248; materialist, 33
*Antigone*, 3, 16–17, 20, 45, 46, 47, 215–232
Audience, 27, 85–86, 103–104, 113–115, 126, 136, 146–147, 151–152, 153–154, 203, 230, 233, 234–235, 239, 247; attitudes towards, 8, 38–39, 41–42, 102; implied, 63, 91–92
Avant-garde, 4, 31, 32, 245–247

Bach, J. S., 51–70; music in *The Bridegroom, the Comedienne, and the Pimp*, 86–88; music in *The Death of Empedocles*, 212; music in *History Lessons*, 137; music in *Machorka-Muff*, 75, 81–82; music in *Not Reconciled*, 113
Barthes, Roland, 55
Bazin, André, 16, 22, 32
Benjamin, Walter, 4, 8, 50, 133; and cinema, 165, 236; and translation, 199–214
*Black Sin,* 17, 19, 50, 179, 181, 183
Böll, Heinrich, 52–53, 71, 72, 73, 74, 85, 96; *Billiards at Half Past Nine,* 72, 95–100; "Bonn Diary," 74–82
Brecht, Bertolt, 101; *Antigone,* 215–232; and cinema, 236–238; and formalism, 33; "learning plays," 206, 207; and Nazism, 119, 123–124; and novelistic structure, 123; *St. Joan of the Stockyards,* 24–25, 101
Brechtianism, 4, 13, 24–26, 41, 42, 43, 67, 90, 118, 200–201, 211, 224, 245
Bresson, Robert, 16, 23, 84, 85
*The Bridegroom, the Comedienne, and the Pimp,* 13, 37, 38, 46, 71, 85–94
Bruckner, Ferdinand (*Pains of Youth*), 88

Camera movement, 58–59, 63–94, 83, 105, 108–109, 112–113, 134, 143, 149, 159, 223
Camera placement, 21, 79–81, 130, 149, 151, 197, 226–230; diagrams, 196, 227
Camera work, 86, 88, 89, 91–94, 106–107, 110–112, 127–128, 145–148, 152–153, 173–175, 188, 193–196; framing, 134, 150; meaning of, 93; zoom, 137. *See also* Shot composition
*Cézanne,* 18, 19
Chaplin, Charlie (*The Great Dictator*), 212–213
Characters, movement of, 91–93, 106–112
*Chronicle of Anna Magdalena Bach,* 37, 38, 42, 44, 51–70
Cinematography, 180–182
Classicism, 33, 182, 208–209, 211
*Class Relations,* 35, 112, 164–177
Culture industry, 8, 238, 241–242

Death, theme of, 66–68, 69, 106, 214
*The Death of Empedocles,* 30, 32, 48, 178–198, 199–202, 208–214, 226, 230–231

*301*

Dedications, with political intent, 54, 84
Distribution, 73–74
Documentary style, 43, 113–114, 156, 201
Documents, use of, 42–43, 51, 66, 83–84, 101, 113–114, 154, 157–159, 162–163

Early cinema, 4, 21–22, 23, 44–45, 48, 65, 86–87, 88, 91, 197, 225–226
Eastwood, Clint (*Unforgiven*), 225
Editing, 86–87, 103, 107, 131–133, 143, 180, 222–223
Eisenstein, Sergei, 259; *Alexander Nevsky*, 212–213
Emotion, 15–16, 23, 57, 61, 63–64, 66, 67, 69, 113, 114, 115, 207–208
*En Râchâchant*, 18–19
*Every Revolution Is a Throw of the Dice*, 18–19
Exile, 45, 230; of Bertolt Brecht, 123–124; of language, 206; of Arnold Schoenberg, 161; of Helene Weigel, 219, 220–221
Expressionism, 88, 210–212

Fassbinder, Rainer Werner, 87, 88–90, 233; as actor, 92–93; relation to Hollywood, 39, 47, 48; Straub/Huillet's influence on, 38, 89–90
Feminist theory, 26, 27
Film history, relation to, 38–39, 88, 89–90. *See also* Early cinema
*Filmkritik* (journal), 37
Film theory, 13; feminist, 13, 165–166, 173; in 1970s, 25–28, 118; semiotic, 55–57, 62
*filmwärts* (journal), 32
Financing, 36, 52, 53, 72–73, 165
Fortini, Franco, 18, 124–125, 160
*Fortini/Cani*, 18, 42, 160
French-language films, 17–20
*From the Cloud to the Resistance*, 18

German history, 32, 35, 39–40, 46, 50, 71–72, 162, 191, 221–222; Straub/Huillet's relation to, 95–96
German identity, 39–40, 46–47
German landscape, 50
German language, 3, 50, 199–201, 223
Germany: Straub/Huillet's depictions of, 35; Straub/Huillet's relation to, 40, 45, 86, 95–96; remilitarization of, 72, 74, 83
Gielen, Michael, 141, 142, 143, 150, 218
Godard, Jean-Luc, 4, 42, 63, 181, 183, 233
Griffith, D. W. (*A Corner in Wheat*), 225

Hauff, Reinhard (*Stammheim*), 32
Herzog, Werner, 37, 50
Historical reenactment, rejection of, 62–63

History: and myth, 18, 143–145, 187, 197, 205, 224–225, 245; Straub/Huillet's attitude towards, 126. *See also* German history
*History Lessons*, 18, 43, 117–138
Hitchcock, Alfred (*Foreign Correspondent*), 212–213
Hölderlin, Friedrich, 178–179, 182, 183; and the Left, 184–189. See also *Antigone*; *The Death of Empedocles*
Hollywood, 38–39, 47
Huillet, Danièle, 143–144; biography of, 14; in credits, 14; and feminism, 12–13; influence on Straub, 15, 44; nonrecognition of, 11–12, 15; as performer, 183; photographs of, 11, 146, 159, 177, 228, 230; role in collaboration, 12, 15, 87

*Introduction to Arnold Schoenberg's "Accompaniment to a Cinematographic Scene,"* 42, 87, 154–163
Italian-language films, 17–20

Kafka, Franz: *Amerika*, 164–177; "The Judgment," 165–166
Kluge, Alexander, 4, 37, 41, 42–44

Landscape, 176, 181, 182, 198, 212, 228–230
Lang, Fritz, 41, 183, 260 n. 48; *M*, 20, 83
Language. *See* German language; Translation
Location, 20, 50, 54–55, 86, 104, 110–111, 145–146, 152–153, 182
*Lothringen!*, 19

*Machorka-Muff*, 42, 46, 52, 65, 71–85
Mallarmè, Stèphane, 18–19, 24
Mannheim Film Festival, 85
Memory, 44, 62–63, 68–69, 76–79, 95, 205, 240
Metz, Christian, 55
Meynell, Esther, 51, 59, 66
Modernism, 14, 20, 140, 189–190, 192, 197; political, 25–28
Monuments, 46, 95, 101–102
*Moses and Aaron*, 15, 17, 84, 139–154, 182
Music: in *Antigone*, 218; Belà Bartók's, 101; and editing, 55, 86–88; in *Machorka-Muff*, 75, 81–82; and narrative structure, 115–116; in *Not Reconciled*, 101, 113; and rhythms of speech, 200, 201. *See also* Bach; Schoenberg
Musical performance, 55, 57, 60–61, 142–143
Myth. *See* History: and myth

Narration, 59–60, 82–83, 103–104, 120, 160–161, 167–169; voice-over, 59–60, 75, 103–104
Narrative, 118, 125–126, 165–171, 192, 246; Oedipal, 165, 175–176, 238–239
Narrative space, 102, 104–106, 133, 145, 167, 170
Nature, 154, 182–183, 190, 209, 212–214
Nazism, 35, 39, 80–82, 96, 103, 119, 185–186, 213, 221, 230
New German Cinema, 35–39, 71
New Munich Group, 38
Nostalgia, rejection of, 45, 48
*Not Reconciled,* 52, 95–96, 100–116

Oberhausen Festival, 35, 36, 38, 72, 74, 85
*Othon,* 17–18, 31, 182

Pavese, Cesare, 18
Photography, 16, 22
Point of view, 227–228, 243
Political modernism, 25–28, 32, 245–247
Politics, radical, and the 1960s, 4, 5–6, 8, 26, 29–30, 36, 47, 84–85, 124, 182–183, 184, 188–189, 234, 245, 247
Postmodernism, 17, 30
Psychoanalysis, rejection of, 16

Realism, 32, 184, 237
Reception, 5, 25, 29, 32, 35, 37, 51, 73, 85–86, 118, 164, 180–181, 201; by female critics, 15; by Leftists, 30–31, 74, 84; in United States, 7
Reitz, Edgar (*Heimat*), 44–46
Renoir, Jean, 20, 23, 24, 68
Resistance, 69, 98, 213, 221, 244
Romanticism, 209, 211

Schoenberg, Arnold: "Accompaniment to a Cinematographic Scene," 139–140, 154–163; *Moses and Aaron,* 15, 17, 139–154, 182; *Von Heute auf Morgen,* 14
Screenplays, 17

Semiotic film theory, 55–57, 62
Semiotics, rejection of, 16
Sex, 78–79
Shot composition, 57, 114–115, 146, 157–159, 194–196. *See also* Camera work
Silent cinema. *See* Early cinema
Sound, 16, 20, 22–24, 59, 87–88, 115–116, 127, 129, 157, 212, 213–214
Space, 56–59, 63–64, 91–92, 170–172, 226–227, 260 n. 48; treatment of, 20–23, 92, 147
Stage plays, in films, 88
Stockhausen, Karlheinz, 73
Straub, Jean-Marie: biography of, 9, 40, 52, 54; photographs of, 10, 146, 157, 177, 228, 230
Straub/Huillet: collaboration, 8, 11–16; film-making approach of, 15; influence of, on other filmmakers, 38, 90; as narrators, 160–161; residence in Germany, 51
Subtitles, 203–204
Syberberg, Hans Jürgen (*Our Hitler*), 44–46, 119

Time, 86–87, 89, 102–103, 114, 162; portrayal of, 77–78
*Too Early, Too Late,* 18, 19, 32, 182
Translation, 199–214

Utopian dimension, 27, 47, 156, 191, 204, 209–210, 211, 213, 230–232, 240–245

Versions, multiple, 16–17, 180
Violence, 92–93, 100–101, 111–112, 223–225

Wenders, Wim, 30, 38, 39, 47, 48, 233
"Western," 20, 72, 225
Women, in Straub/Huillet's films, 12–13

Young German Cinema, 35–36

Zimmerman, Berndt Alois, 218

| | |
|---:|:---|
| Designer: | U.C. Press Staff |
| Text: | 10/12 Times Roman |
| Display: | Gill Sans |
| Compositor/Printer/Binder: | Braun-Brumfield, Inc. |